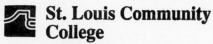

ARCHITECTURE AND THE AFTER-LIFE

The mausoleum at Castle Howard in Yorkshire, England, built by the 1st Earl of Carlisle in 1729–36 to the designs of Nicholas Hawksmoor (Angelo Hornak).

(*Preceding page*). Engraving of the Roman mausoleum near Naples known as 'Virgil's Tomb', made by John Pine to illustrate an edition of Horace published in 1733.

ARCHITECTURE
—— AND THE ——
AFTER-LIFE

Howard Colvin

YALE UNIVERSITY PRESS
NEW HAVEN AND LONDON
1991

Designed by Gillian Malpass
Set in Linotron Bembo by Excel Typesetters Company, Hong Kong
Printed in Hong Kong by Kwong Fat Offset Printing Company

Library of Congress Cataloging-in-Publication Data

Colvin, Howard Montagu.
   Architecture and the after-life/Howard Colvin.
      p.   cm.
   Includes bibliographical references and index.
   ISBN 0-300-05098-4
   1. Mausoleums. 2. Martyria. 3. Sepulchral monuments. 4. Church
architecture. I. Title.
NA6120.C65 1991
726′.8′094—dc20   91-6768
                                    CIP

SIBI SUISQUE

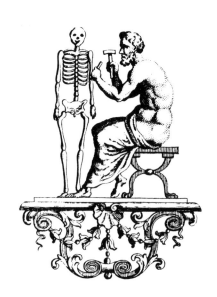

CONTENTS

PREFACE

MUCH OF WHAT WE ADMIRE TODAY in the art and architecture of the past owes its existence to motives, sentiments and beliefs that are alien and even repugnant to modern thinking. It was to honour and placate their capricious gods that the Greeks and Romans built the exquisite temples whose altars they regularly drenched with the blood of slaughtered animals. It was to worship a crucified Christian deity and to commemorate a host of other cruelly murdered men and women that the noblest cathedrals were built, and it was to display their pride and to defend their conquests that kings and barons created the castles of romance. Faced with the supreme crisis of death, man has in the past devised elaborate social and religious rituals and has spent enormous sums on sculptured tombs and on buildings to house them. The rituals may now seem bizarre or at best picturesque, the tombs speak a dead language of symbolism, and few of the buildings still fulfil the religious purposes for which they were originally built. Some of them are, nevertheless, among the most celebrated of historic monuments, the most popular of tourist attractions. For man has known few greater stimuli to architectural and artistic creativity than the attempt to transcend his own mortality. From Antiquity almost to the present day, many of the finest works of European architecture have been designed either to commemorate the dead in this world or to ensure their bodily or spiritual comfort in the next, and it is to mortal man as a patron of funerary architecture that the following pages are devoted.

Although much has been written on many aspects of this subject by archaeologists on the one hand and by art historians on the other, there has been no general study of funerary architecture in western Europe except James Stevens Curl's introductory book, *A Celebration of Death* (1980). In so far as architectural historians have dealt with tombs, mausolea and funerary chapels they have not unnaturally tended to treat them as subordinate to those developments in temple or church architecture that are their main concern. In books such as Dinsmoor's *Architecture of Ancient Greece* or Ward-Perkins's *Roman Imperial Architecture* the complicated history of the classical mausoleum is consequently fragmented into a few paragraphs in chapters devoted to other building types. Although death as a social and religious phenomenon from the Middle Ages onwards has been the subject of celebrated works by Ariès, Chaunu, Vovelle and other French historians, and although tombs have been studied as works of art by generations of art historians, chantries and family chapels have very largely fallen between these two academic stools, while the revival of the free-standing mausoleum in the seventeenth and eighteenth centuries has attracted much less attention than the establishment of the public cemetery in the nineteenth.

Rather than attempt to write a comprehensive history of funerary architecture in all its aspects, I have preferred to explore in each chapter one or two important themes. The result is a series of interconnected essays which, read in order, will provide the reader with a continuous but by no means exhaustive history of funerary architecture in western Europe.★ Many of these chapters are no more than a report to the educated reader on the present state of scholarly knowledge and opinion. In others I have tentatively offered some new ideas about such matters as the origin of chantries or the transition from family chapel to free-standing mausoleum.† In either case I hope that I may have drawn attention to some significant developments which others may investigate further.

If the text is selective, the Bibliography is somewhat wider in its scope, and in it the reader will find references to further buildings of importance (especially Roman mausolea) that are not mentioned in the body of the book.

Writing this book has been a prolonged trespass on other people's scholarly territory, and I am particularly grateful to those who, far from warning me off, have been kind enough to aid and abet me in my incursions into their specialist fields: in Prehistory, Stuart Piggott; in Antiquity, Jim Coulton and Nicholas Purcell; in Late Antiquity and the early Middle Ages, Martin Biddle, Donald Bullough and Bryan Ward-Perkins; in the later Middle Ages, Barbara Harvey; in the Renaissance, Rosalys Coope and Deborah Howard. Their critical perusal of my typescripts has saved me from many pitfalls, but they are, of course, in no way responsible for any inaccuracies or misconceptions of which, despite their guidance, I may have been guilty. To Angus Fowler I am grateful for much valuable information about funerary chapels and mausolea in Germany. But for the kindness of Professor Ove Hidemark and of Dr Göran Hoppe I would have seen few if any of the Swedish family chapels described in Chapter XIII.

Others to whom I am indebted for help in various ways include Dr Elizabeth Baigent, Mr Bruce Bailey, Mr Giles Barber, Mr John Bate, Dr John Blair, Mr Stephen Brindle, Mr Iain Brown, Dr Ian Campbell, Dr James Graham Campbell,

---

★ Geographically the scope of this book is confined to western Europe (with occasional references to eastern Europe) from the early Middle Ages onwards, but the earlier chapters necessarily deal with the whole of the Mediterranean world which fell within the boundaries of the Roman empire.

† In English the word 'mausoleum' normally means a substantial free-standing, roofed building designed to contain a tomb or burial, with an internal chamber large enough to stand up in, or at least having that appearance. In France and Italy, however, *mausolée* or *mausoleo* means any important funerary monument, whether inside a church or standing on its own. Thus, to an Englishman, Westminster Abbey is 'the mausoleum of kings', but to a Frenchman it is a large church full of royal mausolea. In the last resort it is impossible to draw a clear line between a tomb which is a work of sculpture and one which is a work of architecture, but in this book the word 'mausoleum' is reserved as far as possible for the latter.

M.J.-D. Candaux, Dr Maurice Craig, Mr M.R. Dudley, Professor A. Duncan, Mrs Susan Gold, Mr Michael Good, Professor Francis Haskell, Dr J.R.L. Highfield, Professor G.A. Holmes, Miss Jean Kennedy, Mr Michael Kissane, Miss Mary Markus, Mr M.C. Morgan, Mr Michael Olmert, Professor Alistair Rowan, Mr and Mrs D.F.O. Russell, Professor P.E. Russell, Dr Cinzia Sicca, Dr David Thomson, Sir Keith Thomas, Dr David Walker and Mr Adam White. Photographs were kindly provided (and in some cases specially taken for me) by Mrs Elisabeth Beaton, Dr Rosalys Coope, Mr John Crook, Mr J.A.K. Dean, Mr John Harris, Mr Angelo Hornak, Mr Edward Impey, Dr Michael Howard, Mlle Frédérique Lachaud, Mr Thomas Lloyd, Dr M. Meyer, Mr Peter Smith, Dr A.J. Taylor, and Messrs Sims, Reed, Fogg, Ltd. Mr Dean generously offered to make the drawing of the Downhill mausoleum reproduced as fig. 338. All but a few of the other plans and elevations were drawn to my specifications by Mr Edward Impey, from whose skill in interpreting my instructions they have greatly benefited.

The expenses of foreign travel in connection with this book were assisted by grants from the British Academy and the Swedish Institute. But without the generosity of the President and Fellows of St John's College, Oxford, in allowing me to retain, in retirement, a room in close proximity to the Bodleian and Ashmolean Libraries, it would hardly have been possible to write it at all.

I

MEGALITH AND TUMULUS

ARCHITECTURE IN WESTERN EUROPE begins with tombs. The earliest surviving structures that we can recognise as architecture were funerary monuments. They date from three to four thousand years before Christ, and they were the product of a primitive agricultural society which had not yet discovered the use of metal and made its tools of wood and bone and stone. This was the civilisation known to archaeologists as Neolithic, and it followed an even more primitive one in which men did not practise agriculture but depended on hunting and food-gathering for their sustenance. Despite their limited technological and economic resources, Neolithic men were great builders of monumental tombs. Indeed, no western European society has probably devoted more of its resources to tomb building than the Neolithic. Thousands of Neolithic tombs are still to be seen in Britain, Denmark, northern Germany, France, Spain, Portugal and various parts of the western Mediterranean (fig. 1). Known in England and Scotland as cairns and barrows, in Wales as cromlechs, in Denmark as *dysser*, in France and Spain as dolmens, in Portugal as *antas* and in Sardinia as *tombe di giganti*, they take many different forms but have one characteristic in common: they are all built of stone without mortar. The main structure is typically formed of huge pieces of stone set vertically in the earth and covered by horizontal slabs to form a roof. Drystone walling is often used too, either to fill gaps between the bigger stones, or in some cases to construct a false vault consisting of corbelled-out courses of flat stones, each overhanging the one below (fig. 2). The principal stones are often very large indeed, weighing 20, 30, 40 or even more tons, hence the term 'megalith' which they share with 'henge' monuments like Stonehenge, Avebury or Carnac in Brittany. Such tombs were generally covered with rubble or earth so as to form a prominent mound. This protective covering has sometimes been removed by man or eroded by nature, leaving the structural stones exposed to form a picturesque group. Such are the Pentre-ifan cromlech in Pembrokeshire (fig. 9), Kits Coty near Aylesford in Kent, the Dolmen de la Frébouchère in France (Vendée) or the Anta do Silval near Evora in Portugal. Megalithic tombs were often sited in conspicuous positions in the terrain and were clearly intended to impress by their size and often by their silhouette. The largest, such as New-grange in Ireland, might measure as much as 260 feet in diameter and 35 feet in height, and contain as much as 200,000 tons of material.

1. Map of western Europe showing the general distribution of Neolithic tombs built of stone (after Piggott). The recent discovery in Cambridgeshire, England, of a Neolithic tomb with a burial chamber and facade of timber shows that in regions where stone was not readily available, similar structures were sometimes built with less durable materials.

The variety of form exhibited in these structures is very considerable. The chambers can be rectangular, polygonal, circular, cruciform or tunnel-like, and the barrows or cairns that cover them can be round or oval, trapezoidal or elongated. The use of megalithic stones to build the walls of the chambers tended to produce roughly rectangular or polygonal shapes, while a space covered by a corbelled vault had to be more or less circular. Such a vault needed a heavy abutment of stone or earth to prevent it collapsing, and this in turn entailed a passage between the chamber and the open air (fig. 2). In the absence of a vault there could be direct access to the chamber, but an external forecourt often added architectural consequence to the entrance (figs. 6, 7). Although the basic forms of these tombs were fairly simple, investigation often reveals that the original structure has been altered or enlarged, sometimes by the addition of a second chamber, sometimes by the extension of the barrow to form a different shape (fig. 4). In fact, some megalithic tombs had an architectural history almost as complicated as that of a small medieval church.

Most megalithic tombs contain several chambers or compartments, and were clearly designed for the burial of more than one person. Some of them (notably in Orkney) were designed as ossuaries where the bones of the dead were deposited after the flesh had been removed by exposure or other means. Older burials were sometimes cleared out to make way for new ones, so that the limited space was

2

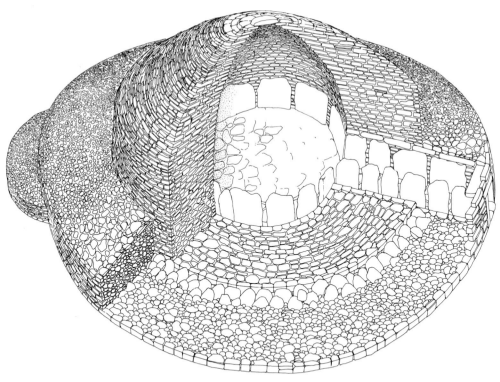

2. The megalithic tomb at Bazoges-en-Pareds (Vendée, France), known as the 'Ciste des Cous'. The central chamber has a diameter of 4.5 metres (after Joussaume).

not necessarily occupied in perpetuity by the original burials. But neither the dimensions of the chambers nor the quantity of human remains found within them suggests that they were intended to serve as general cemeteries for any given locality. The size of the Neolithic population of western Europe is of course unknown, but the amount of labour needed to construct one of these tombs can be calculated. Thus, to mine, transport and assemble the material for one of the largest Irish tombs it is necessary to envisage a force of 1,000 men working more or less full-time for at least eight years. This in turn implies a population (and consequently a death rate) quite out of proportion to the capacity provided. Although neighbouring communities may sometimes have co-operated in building megalithic tombs, it is fairly certain that most of these earliest mausolea were (like those of all subsequent ages) intended as the resting-places of an elite, and if so, they may well reflect not only that elite's ideas about the proper way to dispose of its dead, but also a desire to reinforce its power and prestige by the building of conspicuous monuments. Exactly how one of these structures would have been viewed by Neolithic man is, of course, a matter for speculation. It has been argued that, in the minds of their builders, some of them served a double purpose: the house of the dead may have helped to demarcate the territory of the living. Not only could they have stood as visual symbols of personal or tribal possession, but even in death the ancestors whose remains they contained could

3

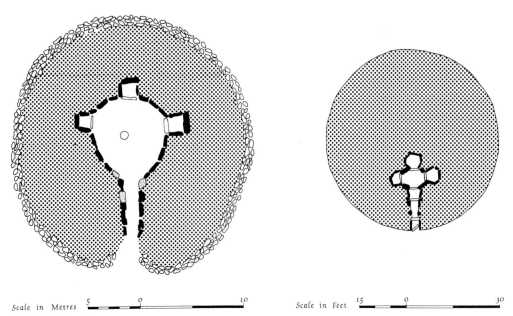

Scale in Metres 5   0   10   Scale in Feet 15   0   30

3. Megalithic tombs with radiating burial chambers at *left*, Fourknocks, Co. Meath, and *right*, Carrowkeel, Co. Sligo, Ireland. At Fourknocks the roof of the central chamber may have been supported by a post standing in the central post-hole.

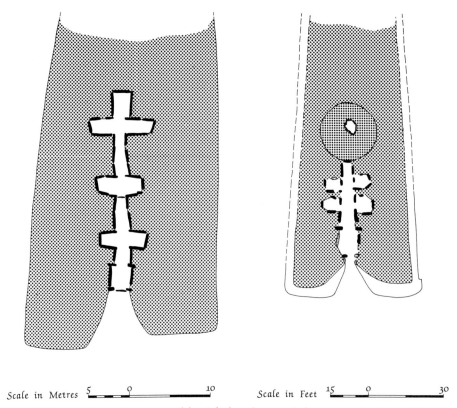

Scale in Metres 5   0   10   Scale in Feet 15   0   30

4. Megalithic tombs with transeptal burial chambers at *left*, Stoney Littleton, Somerset, and *right*, Notgrove, Gloucestershire, England. Notgrove began as a circular domed structure enclosing a single burial place. This was later enveloped in a large elongated cairn with an inturned entrance, leading to a tomb with ante-chamber, central passage and two pairs of transeptal chambers. At Stoney Littleton a similarly inturned entrance leads to three sets of transepts laid out with exceptional regularity.

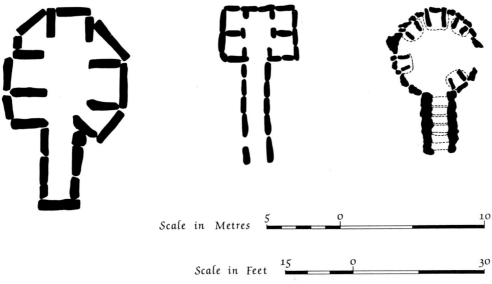

Scale in Metres 5 0 10

Scale in Feet 15 0 30

5. Megalithic tombs at *left*, Carnbane West, Co. Meath, Ireland, Marie-Groh, Brittany, and *right*, Mont-de-Ville, Jersey, showing varied plan-forms.

still guard over the territory they had helped to clear or conquer. So a megalith, whether family tomb or dynastic burial place, may have been in part an assertion of territorial proprietorship, a kind of monumental title-deed for all to see.

At first sight these rude stone monuments, however valuable as evidence of prehistoric society, seem scarcely to repay study as architecture, while the rites and burial practices with which they were associated were in all probability of a kind repugnant to modern susceptibilities. One is inclined to share Horace Walpole's reluctance 'to know how awkward and clumsy men have been in the dawn of the arts, or in their decay'. But on further investigation they turn out not to be quite so uncouth as they initially appear. Lacking adequate tools to cut and dress the stone, their builders could not produce squared ashlar or regular joints. But they could transport and manoeuvre huge blocks weighing up to a hundred tons and set them upright with a considerable degree of precision. That thousands of their constructions should have remained standing for four or five thousand years is sufficient testimony to their competence as builders. Moreover, when their materials allowed, they sometimes showed themselves capable of more elegant workmanship: in Malta the soft limestone was cut and shaped into forms prophetic of pilaster and cornice, while far away at Maes Howe in Orkney the neat lamination of the local sandstone was exploited to produce regular coursing and internal buttressing that was quite architectural in form (fig. 8). Elsewhere relatively smooth surfaces were formed by pounding and rubbing down, and individual stones were sometimes decorated with patterns built up out of a series of small pits made with a sharp point, perhaps of flint or quartz. Even if not laid out with the Pythagorean precision that some have professed to detect, the outlines of the enclosing mounds were carefully drawn and the entrance was

5

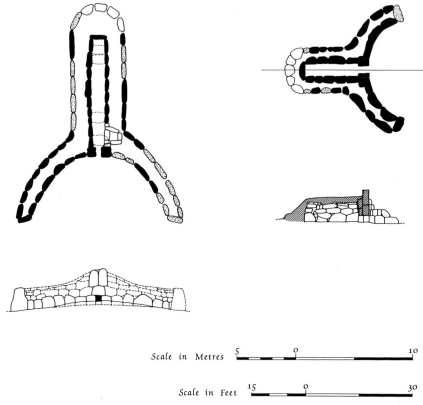

Scale in Metres 5 ____ 0 _____ 10

Scale in Feet 15 ____ 0 _____ 30

6. Megalithic tombs with curved stone facades in Sardinia. Tombe di Giganti at *left*, San Prigionas (plan and elevation) and *right*, Muraguarda (plan and section).

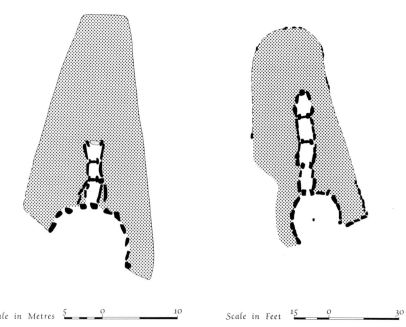

Scale in Metres 5 __ 0 __ 10   Scale in Feet 15 __ 0 __ 30

7. Megalithic tombs with curved forecourts at Goward, Co. Down, and Browndod, Co. Antrim, both in N. Ireland. At Browndod a stone stands upright in the centre of the forecourt.

frequently dignified by a row of large, upright stones which forms a rudimentary facade and serves to delimit a more or less formal forecourt. When at Newgrange we find that the entrance is so arranged that at the winter solstice the rising sun shines through a specially formed aperture, down the entrance passage and into the burial chamber at the heart of the mound, it is clear that we are looking at something more than just a burial place. The mausoleum must presumably have been the scene of some religious ritual connected with the solstice: it may have been a cult centre of the people who built it as well as the tomb of their rulers. The same is probably true of other tombs where no clue exists as to the nature of the ritual, though broken pots found outside megalithic burial places have suggested the ritual breaking of vessels after they had been used to pour libations, and at Bryn Celli Ddu in Anglesey a sacrificial ox had been buried in front of the entrance.

For the archaeologist, intent on using these tombs as evidence of a remote society, what matters is their classification into types that may be indicative of racial or cultural affinities. For the architectural historian, however, it is the remarkable diversity of plan within the recognised formulae that is striking. Lacking pattern-books or written prescriptions, their builders must have been left largely to their own devices in thinking out variations on the type that was traditional in their society – variations that are as likely to have been the response to changing social or religious needs as to any external influences. With nothing (one supposes) but sticks, stones, string and sand as drawing materials some of them envisaged shapes that would be quite sophisticated if realised in better and more tractable materials than the rocks and boulders provided by nature. With surprise, we recognise cruciform, radiating and transeptal plans of the sort that medieval masons were to exploit some four thousand years later (figs. 3, 4, 5). On the island of Jersey there was a circular tomb which might be a rudimentary sketch for the Roman Pantheon (fig. 5), and in Scotland, Ireland and Sardinia there are many Neolithic mausolea with facades based on a concave plan that was one day to form part of the repertoire of baroque architects like Bernini and Borromini (fig. 6). The Neolithic architect who, at Browndod in Northern Ireland, set an upright stone like an obelisk at the centre of his semi-circular forecourt (fig. 7), would surely have found much to admire in the Rome of Sixtus V. Whether the men who designed these tombs were (as some believe) priestly geometers or (as seems more likely) professional stone-setters, they deserve to be recognised as the first Europeans to think in architectural terms.

It was in Mycenean Greece that the megalithic tomb achieved its most sophisticated form. The similarity between a Neolithic corbelled tomb such as one at Ile Longue in Brittany and the so-called 'Treasury of Atreus' at Mycenae is obvious (fig. 10), so much so that it used to be thought that the Neolithic tombs of France, Britain and Iberia were derived from those of the eastern Mediterranean, and that the idea of building them was exported to the west by conquest, colonisation or trade. However, radiocarbon dating has now shown that some of the western tombs are two thousand years earlier than those of the Aegean, so the theory of diffusion from east to west has had to be abandoned. For many reasons

8. Maes Howe, Orkney, interior of a Neolithic tomb. The local sandstone splits into regular slabs in a manner that enabled the prehistoric builders to achieve perfectly coursed walling. The rectangular opening was the entrance to a side-chamber and was closed by the block of stone on the floor (Historic Buildings and Monuments, Scotland).

9. Pentre-ifan, Nevern, Dyfed, Wales, the chamber of a megalithic tomb denuded of its protective cairn (Dr A.J. Taylor).

the converse hypothesis that the influence was in the opposite direction, and that the prehistoric Greek tombs were more refined versions of those in Spain or Brittany, is equally out of the question, so the cultures that produced the megalithic mausolea are now seen to have developed independently in different places and at different periods. Although there may well have been some exchange of ideas between, say, the megalith builders of Brittany and those of Ireland, the eastern Mediterranean tombs represent a different architectural tradition.

The Mycenean tombs, like the 'passage graves' of Neolithic Europe, consist of a burial chamber covered by a mound and approached by means of a stone-lined passage. The circular chamber or *tholos* is, however, much more accurately laid out and is covered by a corbelled vault often beautifully built to a regular profile. The passage or *dromos* is walled but not roofed and provides a formal approach to the entrance or *stomion*. This is built of carefully dressed stone often with an architrave round the monumental doorway and sometimes with pilasters or half-columns on either side. Above the massive lintel there is the equivalent of a relieving arch of corbelled-out stones, forming a triangular tympanum which might contain sculptured or painted decoration (fig. 11). The whole structure shows how building in stone had been transformed by the new bronze metallurgy which provided saw and hammer with which to cut and dress the material to the required dimensions. Nevertheless, the building techniques available were still relatively primitive. No mortar was used (other than clay), nor was any centering

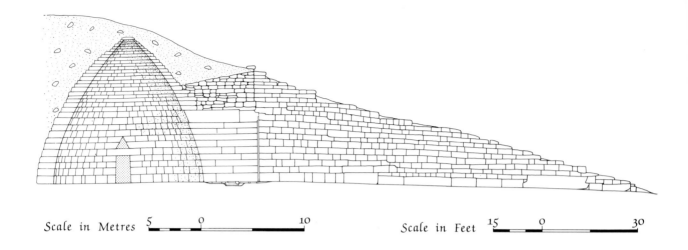

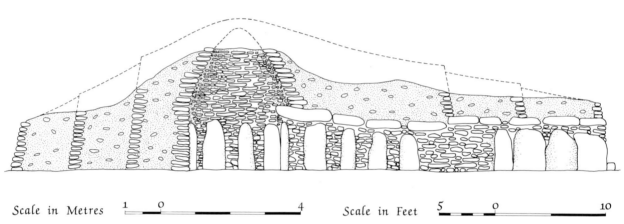

Scale in Metres 1 ___ 0 ___ 4   Scale in Feet 5 ___ 0 ___ 10

10. The 'Treasury of Atreus' at Mycenae, Greece (*top*) compared in section with a Neolithic tomb at Ile Longue in Brittany (*bottom*). Note that the former is much larger as well as built of superior masonry.

needed, the correct radius of each successive drystone course being determined by a string attached to a centrally placed pole. Expert opinion differs as to the architectural mechanics that ensured the stability of the structure. According to one theory each corbelled-out course was held in place by the simple force of gravity and needed no further support. A different view insists that the beehive form is unstable unless external pressure is applied in such a way that each ring of stone is wedged together like the voussoirs of an arch lying on its side. It is certainly the case that tombs of this sort were normally built in cuttings dug into slopes or hillsides where the surrounding soil would be securely held in place by the mass of rock on either side. The protective covering was raised high enough to form a visible tumulus marking the burial place, and the periphery of the tumulus was sometimes defined by a low retaining wall. The fact that the erosion of the tumulus has often resulted in the partial collapse of the *tholos* would suggest that the weight of soil played a part in ensuring the stability of the structure within.

Well over a hundred of such tombs have been identified on the Greek mainland

11. The entrance to the 'Treasury of Atreus', with its original decoration. Evidence for most of the latter exists in the British Museum, but the infill of the triangular panel is conjectural.

and its Aegean islands. They date from the fifteenth to the thirteenth centuries BC and were a product of the Mycenean civilisation that preceded that of classical Greece. The finest and best preserved of them are to be seen at Mycenae itself, the city of Agamemnon, the most powerful of the Greek kings in the Homeric epic of *The Iliad* and their leader in the Trojan war. Whether Agamemnon himself, his father Atreus, or his wife Clytemnestra, were buried in any of the tombs that traditionally bear or bore their names is another matter, but it is certain that these splendid sepulchres were the resting-places of the rulers of Mycenae, as those at Dendra were of the kings of Midea (the legendary seat of Perseus and Andromeda) or those at Pylos of the ruling family of which Nestor was the patriarch. For these were, even more than the Neolithic monuments, privileged tombs. The great domed space was reserved for only a few prestigious burials, burials that were accompanied by such riches of gold, silver, bronze, ivory and precious stones as clearly point to royal status. In any case, in the semi-tribal society of Mycenean Greece only a king could command the labour and expertise to construct a mausoleum like the 'Treasury of Atreus', whose lintel weighs over a hundred tons and whose entrance looks like a city gate.

Such mausolea must normally have been built during the ruler's lifetime and the *dromos* would remain open until after his death, when the entrance to the chamber was walled up, perhaps to keep the dead from walking abroad, and certainly to prevent the living from disturbing their remains. Then the *dromos* was filled in, completing the profile of the tumulus and concealing the buried facade from view. The tumulus, however, remained as a visible reminder that here was a royal tomb, to be respected so long as the dynasty lasted, but thereafter to be at the mercy of tomb-robbers and ultimately of archaeologists.

The *tholos* tombs span a period of some two centuries, and during that period Mycenean building techniques developed considerably. Some of the earliest examples in Messenia (south-west Greece) were built above ground and consequently lacked adequate abutment to sustain their vaults. There are remains of similar tombs in Minoan Crete and these may have been the prototypes of the earliest *tholoi* in Greece. But although the walls of the Cretan tombs lean inwards in a way that may suggest that they were designed to support the thrust of a dome, the upper part of the structure has invariably disappeared, and other forms of construction involving the use of timber were probably employed. In fact, all the evidence suggests that the fully developed *tholos* tomb was a Mycenean invention, and that some later tombs in Crete with corbelled roofs were built under Mycenean influence.

In southern Greece the monumental *tholos* tomb disappeared in the wake of the Mycenean civilisation of which it is archaeologically the most distinctive feature. But tombs of this sort were also favoured in Thessaly and continued to be built there far into the Iron Age, at dates between 1000 and 800 BC. Although the Thessalian tombs were not architecturally of the same quality as those at Mycenae, they show that the tradition of the *tholos* tomb was kept alive in northern Greece and help to explain how tombs of similar character dating from as late as the fourth century BC have been found in what is now southern Bulgaria and was

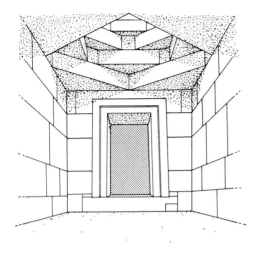
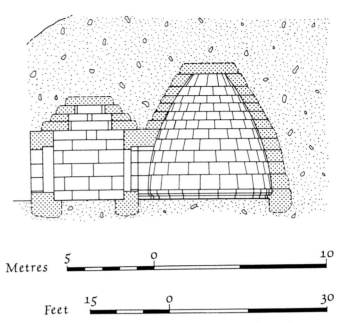

Metres 5   0   10

Feet 15   0   30

12. Kurt-Kale near Mezek, Bulgaria, a tomb of the fourth century BC, built in Mycenean style (after Filov).

then Thrace, and in the territory of the Scythians to the north of the Black Sea. The nomadic Scythians often buried their chieftains in tent-like wooden chambers lined with felt and covered with a large mound, but near Kerch in the Chersonese (now the Crimea) a group of prestigious stone-built tombs has been found which strongly resembles those of Mycenae, and must have been built under Greek influence and in all probability by Greek workmen. Here the entrance passage is roofed over and the masonry is rusticated in a manner often seen in ancient Greek walls. At Kurt-Kale near the village of Mezek in Bulgaria there is a similar tomb of even more sophisticated design, its walls of dressed ashlar cramped with iron and the roof of its vestibule formed of corbelled-out rectangles, each superimposed on the one below in such a way as to create a striking effect of diagonal recession, especially when seen by the flickering light of funeral torches (fig. 12).

Very few megalithic tombs are known from prehistoric Italy, but a notable example is preserved at Quinto Fiorentino in Tuscany, and another, from Casal Marittimo near Volterra, has been reconstructed in the grounds of the Archaeo-logical Museum in Florence. Both these tombs are dated to the seventh century BC and are attributed to the influence of Etruscans who may have had contacts with the Aegean. Their builders, presumably lacking confidence in their ability to construct a self-supporting corbelled vault, provided a massive central pillar. A central pillar, complete with base and capital, is also a feature of an even later tumulus in a cemetery at Tútugi in southern Spain (fig. 13). Here the flat roof was nearly ten feet across and a central support was essential to support the slabs of which it was made.

Meanwhile, in Greece itself few monumental tombs were built during the

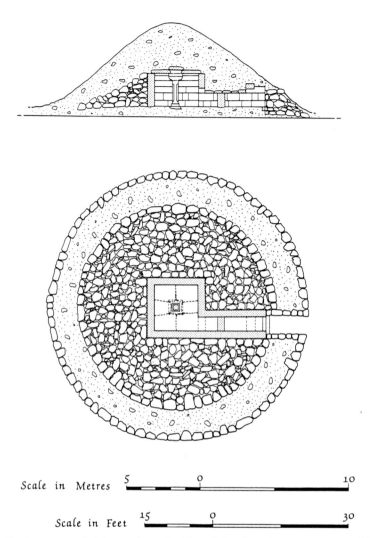

13. Tútugi, Spain, a megalithic tomb probably of the fourth century BC, with a central column supporting its flat roof (after Cabré and De Motos).

so-called 'Dark Age' that followed the decline and collapse of the Mycenean civilisation. Some of those already in existence were broken into and despoiled of their treasures. Burials took place under tumuli, in rock-cut chambers, in stone-lined cists, in terra-cotta sarcophagi, in jars and urns, and occasionally in stone-built structures resembling the *tholoi* of old. But few of these were of a size or character to qualify as architecture.

14

II

FROM TUMULUS TO MAUSOLEUM

IT WAS DURING THE FIRST MILLENNIUM BC that the monumental tomb underwent
the first great transformation in its long history. Architecturally speaking, a
prehistoric tomb, buried in its mound, has no exterior other than its entrance, and
even that might be hidden from view once the dead were in possession. However
large, such a tomb was essentially subterranean in character, whereas the mausoleum of the classical world was an autonomous structure standing above ground
and designed to be seen as such. The transformation was more than just an
architectural one. The prehistoric tomb was a capsule of primitive culture for the
dead man to take with him to the after-life. With the nomadic chieftain, horses,
servants, even wives, were all entombed to serve his needs on the eternal steppes.
The function of his tomb was to protect him and his entourage from disturbance
during his long sleep, rather than to remind the passing horseman of his name or
tribe. In Antiquity, however, the primary purpose of the funerary monument
was to address the living and to inform them of the rank and achievements of the
deceased: in other words, to preserve his memory as well as his physical remains.

The transformation was not a sudden one. When men bury their dead they tend
to follow established custom. Long after the first architectural monuments were
built, the tumulus continued to be a common form of tomb. Many even of the
wealthy and sophisticated rulers of Lydia and Pergamon chose to be buried under
tumuli, some of enormous size. That of King Alyattes of Lydia (d. 560 BC) was
some 400 yards in diameter and so large in circumference that the Great Pyramid
could have stood within its base. Its remains can still be seen at Bin Tepe some
miles to the north of the Lydian capital of Sardis in modern Anatolia. According
to Herodotus it was constructed by the co-operative labours of Alyattes' subjects.
There were inscriptions recording the amounts of work contributed by each class
of the populace, such as merchants, artificers and even prostitutes. At Pergamon
the largest of the tumuli presumed to cover the remains of the Attalid kings of
the third to second centuries BC has a circumference of 1,700 feet and rose a
hundred feet above the plain. Another great tumulus, some 130 feet high, was the
one thrown up in Bactria by Alexander the Great's army to commemorate his old
friend Demaratus, who died there in 327 BC. In Macedonia itself Alexander's
father, Philip II, lay buried beneath a tumulus, and although Alexander vowed to
make for him 'a monument to rival the greatest of the pyramids', he did not live

to carry out his intention. Elsewhere lesser men went on burying (or cremating) in accordance with their local customs, often reusing existing family sepulchres one generation after another. Nevertheless, amid the variety of funerary practice prevalent in the Ancient World during the first millennium BC, some significant trends can be distinguished. One was the spread of the *stele* or inscribed gravestone; a second was the emergence of the architectural monument; a third, the evolution of the tumulus itself into a stone structure capable of highly expressive architectural form.

The gravestone, like the tumulus, was a form of memorial too elementary to have any localised origin: indeed, some tumuli were provided with stone markers as well. But from the seventh century BC onwards *stelai* were in common use in Attica and were to be found in considerable numbers in the cemeteries of other Greek city states. In disposing of its dead a city state has very different requirements from a nomadic tribe or even from a settled agricultural community. Burial within the walls was obviously undesirable, and at Athens there is some evidence that by about 500 BC it was formally forbidden. At any rate, the great majority of Greek citizens were buried in cemeteries close to the roads leading out of their city. Even here space was apt to be limited, and by the sixth century BC the modest earthen mounds of the 'Archaic Period' (seventh to sixth centuries BC) had generally given way to upright gravestones or *stelai*. On these gravestones were carved the names of the dead, often accompanied by sculptured reliefs recalling their manner of life or the circumstances of their death. Here we have the beginning of the personal commemorative monument in a form in which it was (with local variations) to spread throughout the Hellenistic world. These *stelai* often have architectural frames with pedimented tops and sometimes take the form of free-standing Doric columns (fig. 14), but in general they belong to the history of sculpture rather than to that of architecture. Tombs of a more elaborate character were occasionally built by the state to commemorate those killed in battle, but in Athens and in some other Greek cities the development of a monumental funerary architecture was inhibited by legislation which limited the size and type of memorial, as well as the cost of the funeral rites. In Athens a law of 317/16 BC laid down that burials could be marked only by a small column, a simple slab, or a *labellum* (a vessel for libations).

But elsewhere in Greece, particularly in Macedonia, some elaborately architectural tombs were constructed in the late fourth and third centuries BC for powerful or wealthy persons. They took the form of rectangular buildings of stone consisting of an ante-room and a burial chamber with an entrance facade. Structurally, they are notable for their barrel-vaulted roofs, which are the earliest true vaults in Greek architecture. In the inner chamber the deceased were generally laid out on sleeping-benches *(klinai)*, as in a bedroom. The facades were often decorated with an order and were further embellished by painted figures or friezes. At Aegae (Vergina) the richly appointed tomb believed to be that of the great Philip II of Macedon, the conqueror of Athens and Thebes (d. 336 BC), had a simple facade of the Doric order. Another at Lefkadia affords an early example of superimposed orders, Doric and Ionic, separated by a painted frieze (fig. 15).

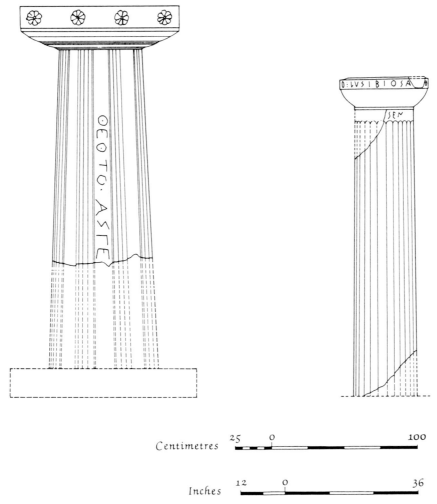

Centimetres 25 0 100

Inches 12 0 36

14. Ancient Greek funerary monuments in the form of small Doric columns. Vase paintings and written descriptions show that such columns might support urns, vases or legendary creatures such as sirens or sphinxes. The two examples shown here are *left*, from Vaste in the heel of Italy (*Taras* iii (1–2), 1983, tav. lxvi) and *right*, from the Akropolis in Athens (*Jahreshefte des Österreichischen Archäologischen Institutes* 31, 1937, Beiblatt, p. 30). The former dates from the sixth to fifth centuries BC, the latter from the seventh to sixth.

These facades were merely screens, having no structural relationship to what lay behind them, and thus established, as early as the fourth century BC, the fictive character that was to be a feature of tomb architecture throughout its history. Despite their careful detailing and painted decoration they were intended to be seen only for a brief period, for all the Macedonian tombs were buried deep beneath tumuli of earth. One of the functions of the facade was to conceal the end of the barrel vault (an awkward feature to which Greek architecture had yet to adjust itself), and the vault itself was an improved method of protecting the chamber from the weight of the superincumbent earth. So the buried architecture

17

of the Macedonian tombs was a new solution to an old problem. However, the idea of constructing a monumental facade only to hide it from view for ever must have seem perverse even to a people accustomed to burying the equivalent of the crown jewels with their rulers. Elsewhere the tumulus itself was to be given architectural form (see pp. 26–7), but in other parts of the Greek world the burial chamber was to shake itself free from its mantle of earth, and monumental tombs of unprecedented size and magnificence were soon to be constructed above ground as perpetual, if vulnerable, memorials of the great.

It was in Asia Minor that such tombs were to be erected both by the satraps of the Persian empire and by rulers of the Hellenistic states established in the wake of Alexander's conquests. In Athens itself two monuments are mentioned by Pausanias as bigger and more magnificent than any others. Significantly, they were both built by non-Athenians, one by a man from Rhodes and the other by Alexander the Great's Treasurer Harpalus to commemorate his mistress, a courtesan called Pythionice, who had died in the east and for whom he had already constructed a splendid tomb at Babylon. Unfortunately, little is known about the cenotaph at Athens except that it cost an enormous sum, was designed by an architect called Charicles and was dedicated to Pythionice as Aphrodite. This makes it clear that it must have been a monument of the kind known as a *heroön*. In ancient Greece a 'hero' was a dead man (or woman) who was given semi-divine status, to whom sacrifices were due and whose tomb consequently had something of the character of a temple. Heroic status might be accorded by a city state to one of its founders, to men killed in war or to a great statesman such as Lycurgus. But no formal act was needed to establish the cult of a hero, and in the course of time almost anyone could be given that status. Heroisation ultimately became little more than a euphemism for burial, and by the fourth century AD even a Christian citizen of Sardis could describe his modest tomb in the local cemetery as a *heroön*. In Athens in the fourth century BC, however, the heroisation of a woman of such dubious character as Pythionice caused something of a scandal, and the contrast between the splendour of her cenotaph and the simplicity of the tombs of some of the great men of the Athenian republic did not go unnoticed. In fact, when Harpalus fell from grace, someone in Alexander's entourage wrote a satire in which the ex-Treasurer was represented living miserably in exile in a mausoleum (called 'the harlot's temple') in atonement for his past misdeeds.

A more respectable case of heroisation is recorded from the island of Thera in the Cyclades. Here, in about 200 BC, a widow called Epikteta established a *heroön* in memory of her husband Phoenix and her two deceased sons. She wished to associate the cult of the dead with that of the Muses, so there were statues of the Muses as well as of Epikteta herself and of her husband and sons. To ensure the continued celebration of the cult Epikteta left money for an annual sacrifice to the Muses and 'to the heroes Phoenix and Epikteta and their sons'. The priesthood was to be hereditary in the male descendants of her surviving daughter, Epiteleia. The whole establishment was the ancient equivalent of a medieval chantry, and many similar funerary foundations were no doubt to be found in the Hellenistic world. Although the architectural form of Epikteta's *heroön* is not precisely

18

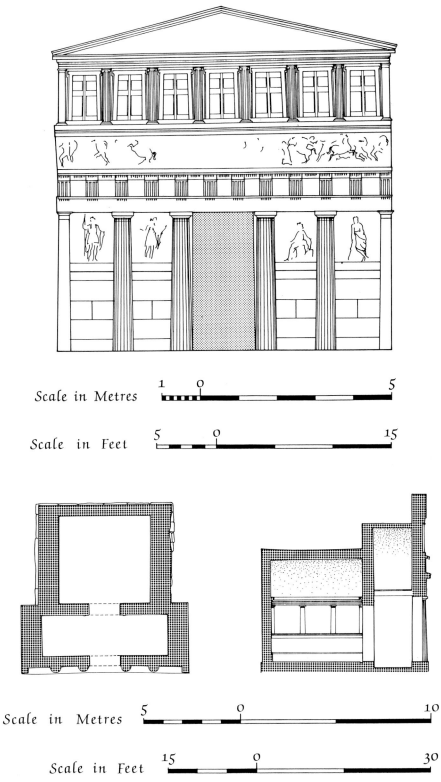

Scale in Metres   1   0   5

Scale in Feet   5   0   15

Scale in Metres   5   0   10

Scale in Feet   15   0   30

15. Lefkadia, Macedonia, Greece, plan, section and facade of a buried tomb of the fourth century BC, with superimposed Doric and Ionic orders (after Petsas).

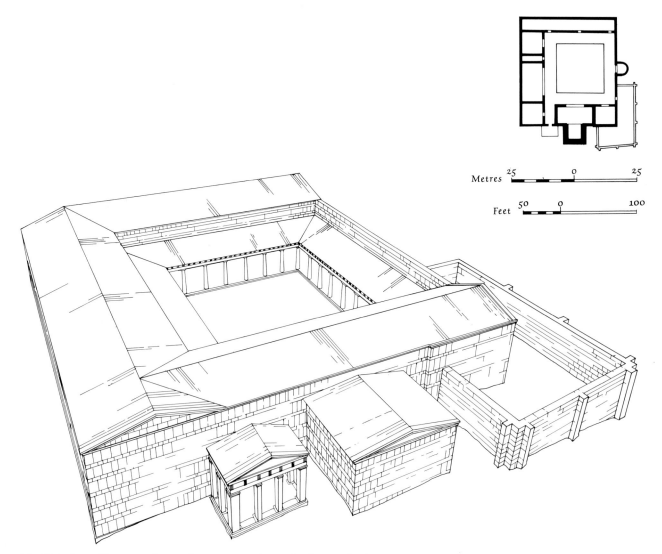

Metres 25   0   25

Feet 50   0   100

16. Calydon, Greece, plan and reconstruction of a *heroön* built in about 100 BC. The portico gives access to a colonnaded courtyard from which the windowless tomb-chamber projects (after Dyggve).

recorded, there was presumably a shrine or small temple-like building in front of which the sacrifices were to be performed. Indeed, the foundations of one such building, consisting of a *cella* and a portico, have been found on the island close to the church of the Evangelist. About a hundred years later a *heroön* built at Calydon on the Greek mainland to commemorate a man honoured as 'the new Hercules' took the form of a colonnaded courtyard with a projecting cult chamber beneath which was a vaulted crypt for the burials (fig. 16). The whole building closely resembled a *palaestra* or athletic centre, and here, as elsewhere, games of strength probably formed part of the commemorative rituals.

It was above all the idea of the *heroön* that was responsible for transforming the tomb into a major architectural monument such as the Mausoleum at Halicar-

17. Xanthos, Turkey, the 'Harpy Tomb', a Lycian tower-tomb (Edward Impey).

nassus. Once great men were accorded divine honours, then it followed that their tombs should be conceived in the likeness of the temples of the gods. The practice was still exceptional in the fifth century BC but spread throughout the Greek world in the fourth century. Architecturally speaking, it reached its fullest development not among the city states of the mainland, but in Asia Minor and the islands. Here it encountered native architectural traditions among the satrapies of the Persian empire that considerably altered its character. In Lycia, for instance, the most prestigious form of monument was neither a tumulus nor a temple, but a tower or pillar. About forty examples of these tower-tombs are known (fig. 17). What distinguishes them from other sepulchral monuments of their age is the position of the tomb-chamber, which is not in the ground or at the base of the

21

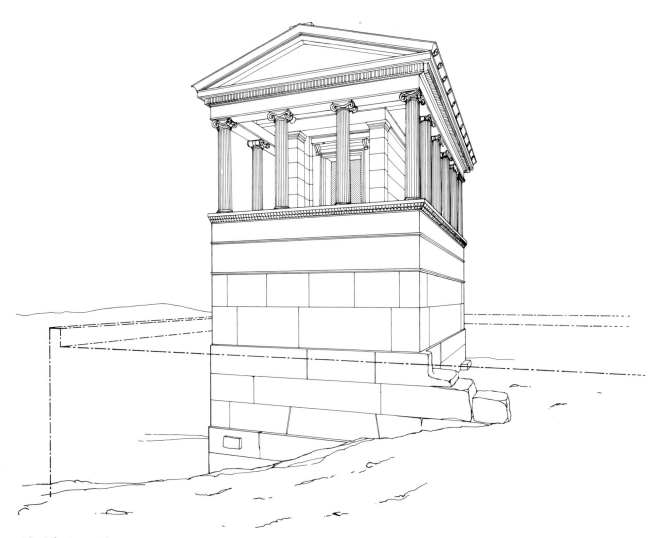

18. The Nereid Monument on the acropolis at Xanthos, Turkey (after Coupel and Demargne). The broken lines indicate the approximate level of the artificial terrace surrounding the monument, as proposed by Roux. The sculptural decorations are omitted. They included two friezes round the top of the podium and the statues of the 'Nereids' or *Aurai* (personifications of sea-breezes) which give the monument its modern name. Most of it is now in the British Museum.

monument, but at the top. In Lycia, as in Phrygia, the idea that the tomb was 'the house of the dead' was strong and might be expressed in simulated timber-framing or (in the case of a hill-side tomb) in the form of a symbolised doorway or house-front cut in the rock-face. Elsewhere in Anatolia, the tomb thought appropriate for a local ruler would often be a two-storeyed structure consisting of a massive podium supporting an architecturally more elaborate upper storey. The principal burial chamber was at the upper level, a lower chamber in the podium being reserved for slaves or relatives of lesser status. Either the podium or (occasionally) the upper storey might be stepped.

The design of these native tombs was affected by influences both from Persia

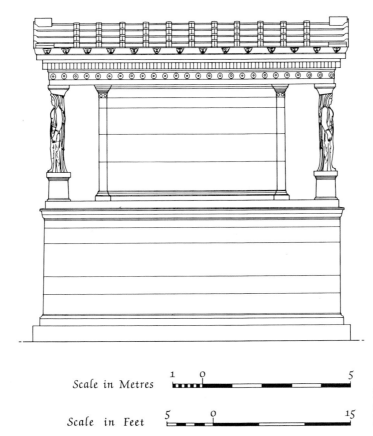

Scale in Metres

Scale in Feet

19. Limyra, Turkey, *heroön* with caryatid porticos (after Borchhardt).

and from Greece. The work of Greek sculptors, executed in Greek marble, can already be seen in the reliefs of the 'Harpy Tomb' from Xanthos in the British Museum. In other respects this is entirely Lycian in character, but in the great tomb of *c.*400 BC, known as the 'Nereid Monument', also from Xanthos and also in the British Museum, we can recognise something that at first sight looks like a standard Greek temple (fig. 18). However, it is perched up on a tall base with vertical sides so that there is no direct access to the portico or *cella* from the ground, as there is to a temple.★ It is possible (as has often been claimed) that in this respect the Nereid Monument reflects the tradition of the Lycian tower-tomb, but the rectangular base seems rather to derive from the substantial podia of the widely disseminated Anatolian tombs of the sixth to fifth centuries BC than from the slender shafts of the Lycian tower-tombs. Whatever the sources of the design, details of the architecture and construction show that the monument was built by Lycian rather than Greek craftsmen. The stonework was held together by elaborate joints of a kind derived from carpentry, and the doors to the *cella* were false ones made of stone with sliding panels in a manner characteristic of Lycia rather than of Attica. The marble sculpture, of course, is Greek and was held in

★ Whether or not there was a burial chamber within the podium is uncertain, but in any case, it would not have provided a means of access to the upper storey.

23

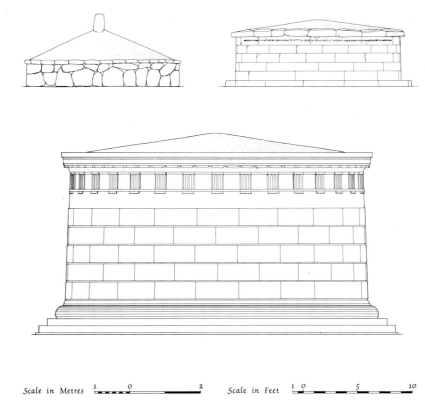

Scale in Metres 1 0 2   Scale in Feet 1 0 5 10

20. The tumulus develops into a stone monument. *Top left*, one of several tumuli with stone revetments in a cemetery of the sixth to fifth centuries BC at 'Larisa' in the Hermos valley in Ionian Turkey. *Top right*, the tomb of Menekrates at Corcyra in Corfu (*c*.600 BC). *Bottom*, a slightly later example with a Doric frieze and channelled masonry in the Kerameikos cemetery in Athens.

21. The Médracen, Algeria. This huge tomb was probably that of a native ruler of the second century BC (Deutsches Archäologisches Institut, Rome).

22. The so-called 'Tombeau de la Chrétienne', near Tipasa, Algeria, a tomb of similar character to the Médracen, but later in date (Deutsches Archäologisches Institut, Rome).

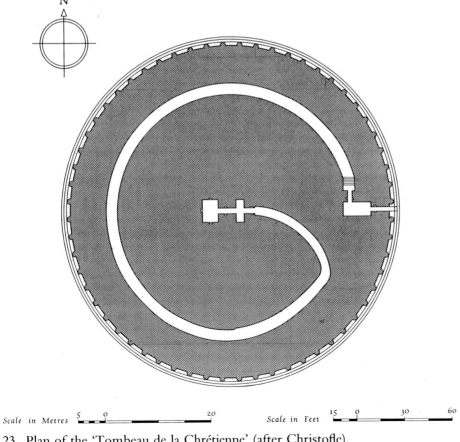

N

Scale in Metres 5 0 20   Scale in Feet 15 0 30 60

23. Plan of the 'Tombeau de la Chrétienne' (after Christofle).

place by cramps of Greek type, but the way it is arranged in two superimposed friezes is Lycian. Handsome though it is, the building as a whole is notably lacking in the fastidious elegance of contemporary Greek architecture.

In its fusion of Greek and Lycian architectural traditions the Nereid Monument was highly influential. Many imitations of its facade are to be seen in the rock-cut tombs of south-west Anatolia, and other monuments were built with temple-like structures raised up on high bases, notably one at Limyra (possibly the tomb of the fourth-century Lycian dynast Pericles), whose porticos were supported by caryatids imitated from the Erechtheum (fig. 19). A new formula had been established which was soon to be exploited in the most famous funerary monument of Antiquity – the Mausoleum of Halicarnassus.

Meanwhile, the tumulus was undergoing transformation. Not only were tomb-chambers becoming more and more sophisticated in architectural treatment, but the tumulus itself was taking on an architectural form which could be highly expressive. Already in the sixth century BC small monuments consisting of a mound of earth contained by a dressed-stone drum were being built in Greece. In Corfu the tomb of Menekrates (d. c.600) is a simple example of this type (fig. 20). A slightly later and more elaborate one from the Kerameikos cemetery at Athens combines a Doric frieze with mouldings of Ionic character (fig. 20). A similar development can perhaps be discerned in North Africa, culminating in two particularly spectacular mausolea, the Médracen, about fifteen kilometres north-west of Lambaesis in what is now Algeria, and the 'Tombeau de la Chrétienne' at Kbour-er-Roumia near Tipasa in ancient Mauretania. The Médracen, probably the tomb of a native king of the second century BC, stands in isolated grandeur far from any known ancient settlement, but at a place where caravan routes intersected. Despite the ravages of time and the depredations of tomb-robbers, the details of its design can still be clearly seen (fig. 21). The drum is surrounded by sixty unfluted Doric half-columns of a Greek type similar to those of the fifth-century temple at Segesta in Sicily, but the three false doors and the cornice moulding reflect Egyptian influence. The real entrance to the small central burial chamber is by means of a concealed opening in the stepped roof. The flat top may have been surmounted by a pyramidal finial, of which fragments have been found. The even larger 'Tombeau de la Chrétienne' (so-called because of the cross-like pattern formed by the stone panels of its false doors) follows the same formula. The number of half-columns is again sixty, but the order is Ionic and access to the burial chamber is by means of a circular passage remarkably similar to that of Hadrian's mausoleum in Rome (figs. 22–3). The dating is uncertain, but is probably not earlier than the first century AD.

If the antecedents of the Médracen and the 'Tombeau de la Chrétienne' are sought in North Africa, then they and other smaller but highly architectural tombs from places such as Cyrene and Ptolemais (fig. 24) must be seen as developments of the cairn or *bazina*,* which was a common form of funerary

---

* *Bazina* is a term originally used by the Berbers in eastern Algeria and Tunisia for any sort of mound, including a sepulchral one, and subsequently adopted by archaeologists working in North Africa for a tumulus with a stone revetment.

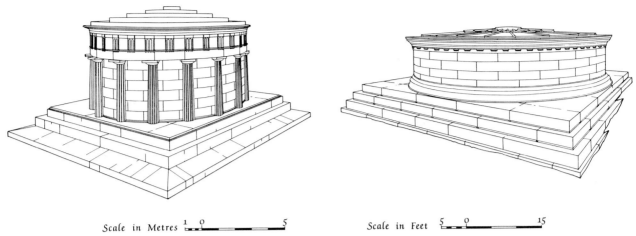

Scale in Metres 1 0 ———— 5   Scale in Feet 5 0 ———— 15

24. Circular tombs in North Africa. *Left*, from Ptolemais (third to second century BC). *Right*, from Cyrene (mid-fourth century BC), both in modern Libya (after Stucchi).

monument among the native peoples who occupied the North African coast before Greek and Phoenician settlement from the eighth century and Roman conquest in the second and first centuries BC (fig. 26). The dating of these *bazinas* is apt to be imprecise, but a typological evolution can in theory be traced from tumuli whose circular base is defined by a rough revetment of undressed stones to tumuli consisting of a ring of carefully cut and coursed masonry with an infilling of earth or rubble to cover the burial chamber (fig. 25). It would remain only to add first base and cornice mouldings and then columns or pilasters to transform the tumulus into an architectural monument. However, pre-Roman North Africa was neither an isolated nor a culturally homogeneous area, and the changing forms of funerary monument may have been due as much to outside influence as to autonomous development. In the case of the Médracen the Greek element points to Sicily rather than to the eastern part of the Hellenistic world as the likely source of architectural influence, but the possibility that both these great North African mausolea in some way reflect that of Alexander the Great at Alexandria cannot be excluded.

Although the stone-built tumulus was not unknown in Asia Minor (especially in Caria), it did not develop such elaborate architectural forms in the eastern Mediterranean, the inventive genius of the Hellenistic architects concentrating rather on that fusion of tomb and temple that has been described above. In Italy the Etruscans were great builders of stone-ringed tumuli in the seventh and later

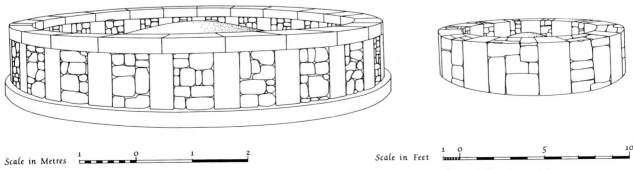

Scale in Metres 1 0 ———— 2   Scale in Feet 1 0 5 10

25. Stone-revetted tumuli from Cyrene in North Africa, fourth century BC or later (after Stucchi).

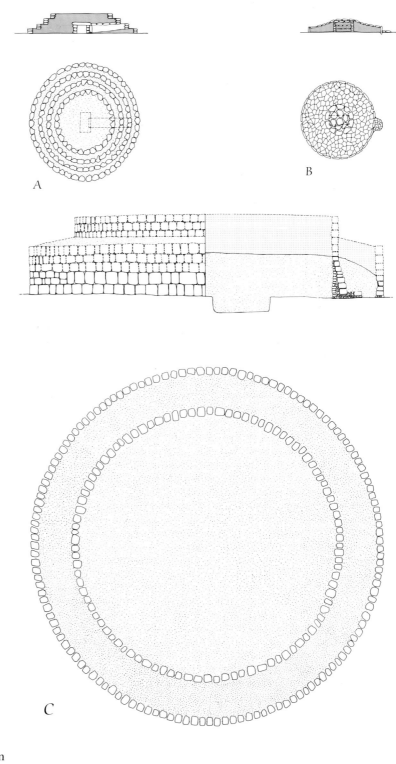

26. North African *bazinas*.
A. Djebel Mistiri, Algeria. B. Ain
el-Hamara, Algeria. C. Le Gour,
Morocco (after Camps).

Metres 5 0 10

Feet 15 0 30

centuries BC, but (although not immune to Hellenistic influence) never applied an order to their low circular retaining walls. It remained for the Roman nobility of the first century BC, headed by Augustus, to commission tombs comparable in size and grandeur to those of North Africa. However, with the notable exception of the mausoleum in Campania known as 'le Carceri Vecchie', these Roman mausolea are normally astylar,★ and so represent a different and probably quite independent architectural interpretation of the tumulus (see below, pp. 66– 70). But once again, the enigmatic form of the tomb of Alexander the Great may lie behind the imperial Roman as well as the two North African mausolea.

★ The mausoleum of Hadrian had pilasters clasping the angles of its square podium.

III

THE MAUSOLEUM OF HALICARNASSUS

THE MAUSOLEUM WAS A MONUMENT to an incestuous marriage. According to Ancient historians it was built by Artemisia, the devoted wife of Mausolus, ruler, under Persian suzerainty, of the rich satrapy of Caria in Asia Minor. Mausolus and Artemisia were not only husband and wife, they were also brother and sister. Marriages of this sort, though abhorrent to the Greeks, were not uncommon in Antiquity among the ruling families of the east and may have been motivated by a desire to keep the royal blood pure. Mausolus died in 353/2 BC, after a successful rule of twenty-four years, Artemisia two years later. Her grief for Mausolus is well attested, and there is no reason to doubt that the monument was largely her work. Modern historians have, however, pointed out that two years was far too short a time in which to build and decorate such a large and ornate building: if Artemisia began it, then it must have been completed by her successors Idrieus and Ada (another incestuous couple). Alternatively, it may have been begun by Mausolus himself and completed by his spouse in her widowhood. However much inspired by conjugal affection, the Mausoleum was at the same time a memorial to the power and wealth of the Carian dynasty at its height in the middle of the fourth century BC.

Although politically a province of the Persian empire, culturally Caria was a country open to Greek influence. Halicarnassus, its principal city, was largely rebuilt by Mausolus on Greek lines. The Mausoleum was its principal architectural monument, standing in a dominant position on rising ground above the harbour. According to the Roman architect Vitruvius, who in the first century BC may have visited Halicarnassus in person, it was built under the direction of two Greek architects named Satyros and Pytheus, who also wrote a treatise about it (now lost). Pytheus was almost certainly the architect of the temple of Athene Polias at Priene in neighbouring Ionia; Satyros may have been the Satyros of Paros who signed the base of a statue erected at Delphi in honour of the next two Carian rulers, Idrieus and Ada. Their team included at least four Greek sculptors of the first rank, Scopas, Bryaxis, Timotheos and Leochares, who, according to the Roman historian Pliny, were each given one side of the structure to decorate. Vitruvius and Pliny agree that it was their work especially that gave the Mausoleum its place among the seven Wonders of the World. Pliny goes on to provide some basic facts about its architecture, including dimensions that are probably corrupt. Disregarding these, what Pliny tells us is that the building was rectangular (but not square), that it was surrounded by a colonnade of thirty-six columns, and that above the colonnade there was a pyramidal superstructure receding in twenty-four steps to the summit. On the top there was a four-horse chariot of marble.

The building was adorned both with sculptural friezes and with free-standing figures. At least one of the friezes was probably set in the podium. The free-standing figures were arranged at five or six different levels, culminating in the chariot group at the top. By the nineteenth century all that remained were the foundations and a quantity of broken sculpture. Exactly how and when the Mausoleum was destroyed may never be established. It was solidly built on rock, and left to itself would probably have survived as a recognisable ruin to the present day. However, it could have been damaged by an earthquake (there was a particularly severe one in this part of Asia Minor in AD 1222), and stone-robbers and treasure-seekers may well have contributed to the disintegration of a structure already shattered by earth-tremors. It was certainly stone-robbing that destroyed what was left of the building at the end of the Middle Ages, for between 1494 and 1522 large quantities of stone were removed by the Knights of St John of Jerusalem to fortify their castle of Bodrum, while much of the marble was burned for lime. In the process the tomb-chamber below ground level was broken into and destroyed, though enough remained for its plan to be recovered by excavation in 1972. One of the knights described how in the course of the work of demolition they came upon a small opening leading down to a square room decorated with marble columns and sculptured reliefs. 'Having first admired these', he wrote, 'and entertained their fancy with the singularity of the sculpture, they proceeded to pull it to pieces and break it up like the rest'. In another compartment they found a sarcophagus with a marble lid, but they were obliged to withdraw for the night before having time to examine it, and when they returned the following day it had been despoiled and the earth all around was strewn with fragments of cloth of gold and roundels of the same metal.

Even as the Knights of St John were destroying what then remained of the Mausoleum, one of Europe's earliest architectural antiquaries was endeavouring to reconstruct it on paper. This was the Milanese painter and architect Cesare di Lorenzo Cesariano, whose edition of Vitruvius, published in Como in 1521, includes a wood engraving showing the Mausoleum in a form that makes little attempt to conform to Pliny's description (fig. 27). Cesariano claimed to have found authority for this in an 'ancient Greek manuscript', but like all his successors before the nineteenth century, he envisaged the Mausoleum in terms of the architectural conventions of his own day. So did Antonio da Sangallo the younger, who sketched out a solution with four temple-front porticos of which Palladio might have approved (fig. 28). In England Sir Christopher Wren, with the help of his pupil Nicholas Hawksmoor, proposed a neat reconstruction that was closer to Ancient Rome than it was to Ancient Greece (fig. 29); in Austria Fischer von Erlach piled up a complex fantasy of baroque forms culminating in a

31

Scale in Metres 10 0 30

Scale in Feet 25 0 100

27. The Mausoleum of Halicarnassus: as envisaged by Lorenzo Cesariano 1521 (*top left*), Fischer von Erlach, 1721 (*top right*), the comte de Caylus, 1753 (*bottom left*), and C.R. Cockerell, 1848 (*bottom right*).

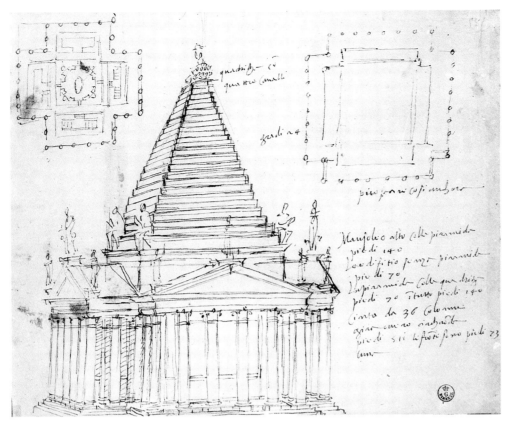

28. The Mausoleum of Halicarnassus as envisaged by Antonio da Sangallo (1484–1546) (Florence, Uffizi, Gab. Fotografico, Soprintendenza Beni Artistici e Storici di Firenze).

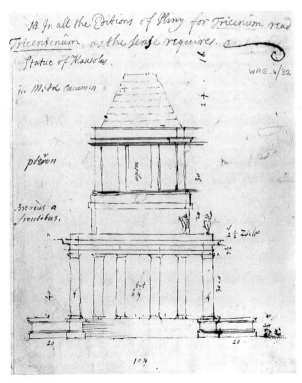

30 (*above*). The Mausoleum of Halicarnassus, reconstruction by Karl Friedrich Schinkel (1781–1841), drawn for a diorama in 1812 (after Breen's sketch of drawing destroyed in the Second World War).

29. The Mausoleum of Halicarnassus, attempted reconstruction drawn by Nicholas Hawksmoor under the direction of Sir Christopher Wren, *c.*1690 (British Architectural Library Drawings Collection).

huge obelisk-like pyramid (fig. 27); in France the connoisseur Comte de Caylus, aided by a young pupil of Jacques Soufflot called Petitot, did his best to solve the problem according to the chaster principles of a dawning neo-classicism (fig. 27); while in Germany Karl Friedrich Schinkel saw the Mausoleum as an exercise in the Sublime (fig. 30).

What invalidated all these reconstructions was Pliny's failure to specify the order to which the thirty-six columns belonged. Some favoured Doric as suitable for a victorious ruler, others Corinthian as appropriate to so splendid a monument. It was not until 1834 that the developing discipline of classical archaeology enabled the Italian Luigi Canina to declare that the order must have been Ionic 'because that was the regular order in use in Ionia and the other regions of Greek Asia including Halicarnassus'. The correctness of Canina's assertion was confirmed by the discovery on the site of fragments of Ionic capitals. Henceforth, any serious attempt at reconstruction would have to take into account not only Pliny's description but also the known conventions of the Ionic order as used in Asia Minor in the fourth century BC.

In 1846 precious evidence reached London in the form of thirteen slabs of sculptured frieze recovered from the walls of the castle at Bodrum which the British Ambassador to Constantinople, Sir Stratford Canning, had prevailed on the Sultan of Turkey to present to the British Museum. Then in 1856–8 the excavations conducted by C.T. Newton (later Keeper of Greek and Roman Antiquities at the British Museum) resulted in the recovery of further important fragments of sculpture and the laying bare of the foundations of the Mausoleum itself. Although Newton's archaeological technique left something to be desired, he established beyond doubt that the building was rectangular (as Pliny had in fact made clear) and not circular or octagonal, as some scholars maintained. The prolonged debate over the architectural form of the Mausoleum now resolved itself into the examination of two basic alternatives. Both started with a rectangular podium approximately 127 by 108 English feet, as measured by Newton, which might be equivalent to 120 by 100 Ancient Greek feet, so agreeing with the figure given by Pliny for the total circumference of the building, which is 440 feet. The divergence of opinion arose over the figure of 63 feet which Pliny says was the length of the two larger sides. This was difficult to reconcile either with Pliny's other figure of 440 feet or with an Ionic peristyle of as many as thirty-six columns. In 1848 the English architect C.R. Cockerell showed how these apparently conflicting figures might be reconciled by arranging the columns in a double row, thus reducing the upper part of the structure to smaller dimensions and standing it on a wider base corresponding to the excavated foundations. This 'smaller' plan was followed, with minor differences, by the English architects Edward Falkener (1851) and J.J. Stevenson (1896), but it was open to serious objections, not least on structural grounds, and did not have the support of Newton and his fellow excavator A.H. Smith, who had first-hand knowledge of the site and of the fragments recovered from it. The alternative is simply to ignore the awkward figure of 63 feet as a textual corruption in the surviving manuscripts of Pliny (which are certainly by no means free from error) and to reconstruct the

Metres 5   0   10   Feet   15   0   30

31. The Mausoleum of Halicarnassus, a conjectural reconstruction of the monument in accordance with modern scholarship. Only the major elements of the sculptural decoration are indicated.

Mausoleum with a single colonnade standing on a high base and surrounding a central mass supporting the pyramid above. According to this formula the thirty-six columns are distributed so that eleven appear on the long side and nine on the shorter side. The abundance of sculpture found on the site justifies the addition of plinths and offsets to support it, but the form of the inner structure supporting the pyramid remains almost entirely conjectural. This 'larger' solution, first propounded by Newton and Pullan in 1862, has been followed in essentials by Bernier (1877), Adler (1900), Six (1904), Dinsmoor (1908) and Krischen (1923), and now commands general agreement among scholars, including Waywell, who has meticulously studied the sculpture, and Jeppesen, who has re-excavated the foundations.

Although there is still scope for much scholarly discussion, it may reasonably be supposed that figure 31 represents with some degree of verisimilitude the spectacle that would have presented itself to a Hellenic traveller approaching Halicarnassus harbour under sail in Ancient times. From a distance it would have been the bulk of the building rising above the town that impressed him, and especially the pyramidal upper part which, separated from its podium by the deep shadow cast by the colonnade, seemed to a Roman poet 'to hang in mid-air'. As he went ashore it would have been the mass of sculpture that amazed him – some eighty-eight life-sized figures of warriors in combat at ground level; up to seventy-two heroic portraits on the middle step of the podium; further groups of warriors, huntsmen, etc. on the upper step; thirty-six colossal statues of Mausolus's ancestors stationed between the columns; fifty or more lions standing guard round the base of the pyramid; and on its apex the chariot, whose significance, much debated by modern scholars, would presumably have been immediately obvious to him. If he was a man of refined taste he might have felt rather like a modern connoisseur confronted with the Vittorio Emanuele Monument in Rome. But much of the sculpture was of the highest quality and fully justified the enrolment of the Mausoleum among the accepted Wonders of the World.

The Mausoleum was not only the largest and most pretentious funerary monument of its time, it also established a new architectural form for buildings of this kind. Its predecessor, the Nereid Monument, was a temple turned into a tomb: only its high base distinguished it externally from a conventional Greek temple, and only a fragment of a stone couch proves beyond doubt that its *cella* was a funeral chamber rather than the shrine of a god. In the Mausoleum the temple form has almost vanished. A vestige of it remains in the oblong (rather than perfectly square) plan, but the pediments have gone and the colonnade runs continuously round all four sides without any hint of an entrance behind it. Above all, the pyramid proclaims its purpose as a funerary monument. Whether the stepped pyramidal form derived from Egypt, from Mesopotamia, from the base of a tomb like that of Cyrus at Pasagardae or from the receding stages of funeral pyres, it was a form with strongly sepulchral associations. By fusing tall podium, temple columns and pyramidal roof into one, the designers of the Mausoleum had created a new architectural formula for the glorification of the dead.

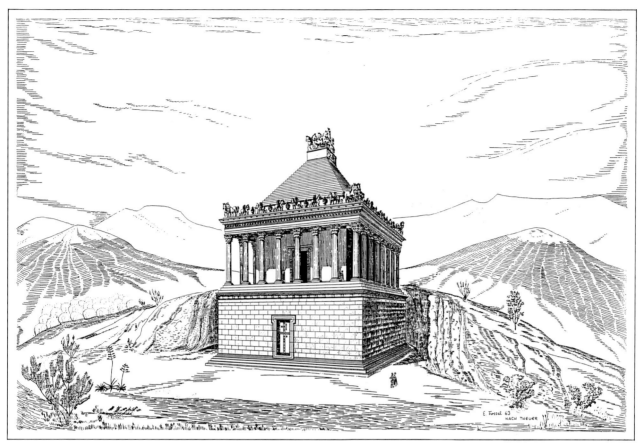

32. Belevi, near Ephesus, Turkey, reconstruction of mausoleum of the third century BC (from a drawing by Elisabeth Fossel-Peschl in Praschniker & Theuer, *Das Mausoleum von Belevi*, Österreisches Archäologisches Institut, Vienna, 1979).

Conspicuously sited close to the harbour of one of the most prosperous cities of Asia Minor, this most ornate and extrovert of funerary monuments was bound to be well known and widely imitated. Writing in the second century AD, the Greek topographer Pausanias says that the Mausoleum was 'of such a size and so marvellous in its construction that even the Romans have been utterly astounded by it and use the word "mausoleum" for their own grandiose tombs'. In fact the tomb of the Emperor Augustus himself was known as his 'mausoleum' when it was built at the end of the first century BC.

Although the verbal and architectural echoes of the tomb of Mausolus were to reverberate throughout the Ancient World, it is in Asia Minor that its influence can be most clearly traced. Here there are several monuments whose debt to the Mausoleum is obvious. One, at Belevi near Ephesus, incorporated a convenient rock out of which the tomb-chamber was hewn. Round this the marble podium was built, forming an exact square, and above it was a colonnade which was probably designed to support a stepped pyramid (fig. 32). The order, however, was not Ionic, but Corinthian, and round the top of the podium there was a plain

33. Mylasa, Turkey, mausoleum (**Edward Impey**).

Doric frieze. Though robbed in Antiquity, the barrel-vaulted tomb-chamber still contained a massive sarcophagus with a reclining male figure accompanied by that of a servant (both now in the Ephesus Museum at Selçuk). Architecturally, the most striking feature of the building is the combination of the Doric and Corinthian orders, of which this may be the earliest known example. The use of the Corinthian order is itself precocious, for on the Greek mainland it was still only in process of evolution in the middle of the fourth century BC. This has a bearing on the dating of the monument and hence on the identity of the occupant of the tomb. Several suggestions have been made, of which the most likely seems

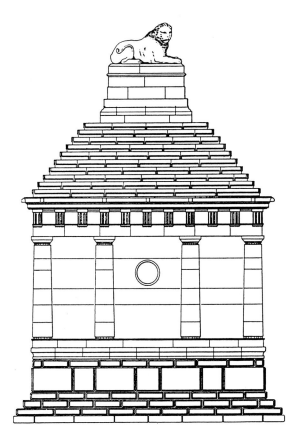

34. Cnidus, Turkey, the Lion Tomb, conjectural restoration (after Newton and Pullan). The structure was approximately forty feet square at the base.

to be the Seleucid monarch Antiochus II, who died at Ephesus in 246 BC. It may, however, have been begun – and left both unfinished and untenanted – by the Thracian king Lysimachus, whose rule over this part of Asia Minor was terminated by his death in battle in 281 BC, and may subsequently have been appropriated by or for Antiochus.

Whether or not Antiochus II was buried at Belevi, this large monument – nearly one hundred feet square – was clearly intended for a person of high rank. At Mylasa in Carian territory there still stands almost complete a much more modest memorial whose architectural dependence on the Mausoleum at Halicarnassus is nevertheless obvious (fig. 33). In a structure only twenty-nine feet high, the essential elements of the Mausoleum – podium, columns and pyramidal roof – are all present. The order is again Corinthian, but the date is uncertain and may be as late as the second century AD.

Another form of monument that stems from the Mausoleum is represented by the Lion Tomb at Cnidus which stood on a promontory not far from Halicarnassus (fig. 34). Here the difficulty of poising a heavy pyramidal roof on a fragile colonnade is avoided by the use of solid walls with engaged columns. The basement contained eleven small burial chambers radiating from a circular room. Other examples of the type represented by the Lion Tomb at Cnidus are recorded from Bargylia in Caria and from Amphipolis in Macedonia. Lions were a regular symbol for military valour, so, like the one set up over the general grave of the Thebans killed in battle against Philip of Macedon at Chaeronea in Boeotia in 338, some of these monuments may have been war memorials rather than princely tombs.

On the island of Cos the two-storeyed *heroön* known as the Charmyleion represents a rather different version of the type of Hellenistic monument of which the Mausoleum is the grandest example. It was probably founded by a certain Charmylos as a family tomb in the first half of the third century BC. In front was the altar, and on the ground floor were two rooms connected with the cult of 'the Twelve Gods and of the hero Charmylos'. In the basement there was a vaulted crypt with burial compartments on each side, and above, a stage with Ionic columns conjecturally restored by Schazmann as a sort of belvedere (fig. 35). A surviving inscription makes it clear that the building stood (like others of its kind) in a carefully tended garden, and in the summer those participating in the commemorative rituals could perhaps sit in this elevated loggia and enjoy the view.

The diffusion of monuments and other structures inspired in part by the Mausoleum probably owed much to the patronage of Greeks enriched by the overthrow of the Persian empire. Alexander and his army would have seen the Mausoleum with their own eyes when they besieged and captured Halicarnassus in 334, and a monument such as the one Harpalus erected to his mistress on the Sacred Way in Athens (above, p. 18) may well have had features derived from Halicarnassus. Had Alexander lived to build a monument to his closest friend and companion-in-arms Hephaestion it would doubtless have eclipsed the Mausoleum and have been the greatest funerary monument of all time. As it was, the pyre upon which the body of Hephaestion was cremated was a prodigious example of a form of funeral art of which there is inevitably little literary and still less archaeological record, though representations of several Roman pyres are preserved on commemorative medals. The task of designing it was given to an architect called Deinocrates of Rhodes. Deinocrates was a large man (according to Vitruvius he first attracted Alexander's attention by dressing up as Hercules, complete with lion's skin and club), and he had large ideas. A few years earlier he had offered to sculpt Mount Athos into a gigantic statue of Alexander holding a fortified city in one hand and in the other a bowl from which all the streams in the mountain would pour their united waters into the sea. Now at Babylon he was given unlimited resources to stage the most lavish funeral ever seen in east or west. The pyre was so large that a substantial section of the mud-brick walls of Babylon had to be demolished to make way for it. It stood on a foundation of trunks of palm trees. The first stage was decorated with the gilded prows of 240 quinqueremes (60 on each side), each bearing the figures of kneeling archers and armed men over six feet high. The second stage consisted of huge funeral candelabra above which eagles with outstretched wings (symbols of Macedonian conquest) gazed down on their prey in the form of serpents. The third stage had a frieze of hunting scenes, the fourth, a battle of centaurs, the fifth, a display of golden bulls and lions. At the sixth stage trophies of Macedonian and Persian

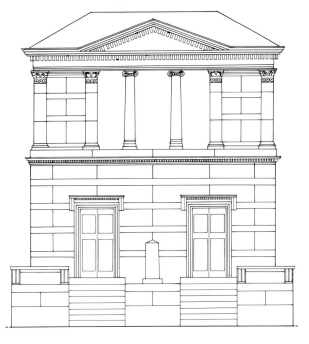

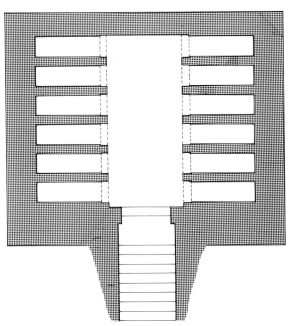

Scale in Metres 5 0 10

Scale in Feet 15 0 30

35. The Charmyleion
on the Greek island of
Cos, a *heroön* of the third
century BC: plan of the
burial chamber as
excavated by Schazmann
in 1933, with his
conjectural restoration of
the principal elevation
(after Schazmann).

arms symbolised the victory of the former and the defeat of the latter. At the top there were figures of sirens (birds with women's heads) with hollow bodies in which funeral choirs were concealed to sing a lament for the dead man. The whole construction, nearly 200 feet high, must have looked like a Babylonian ziggurat decked out in Hellenistic finery.

When Alexander himself died less than a year later (323 BC), his body was not cremated but embalmed, with the intention of taking it back to Macedonia for burial. A magnificent funeral car – a kind of mobile mausoleum – was constructed for the purpose. But possession of Alexander's body could be seen as a symbol of legitimacy for one of the kingdoms into which his empire was in process of being divided. The winner was Ptolemy Soter, the new Greek ruler of Egypt, who diverted the funeral procession to Memphis, where a tomb was constructed 'in the manner of the Macedonians'. Either Ptolemy or his successor Ptolemy II removed the body to the recently founded city of Alexandria, where a later Egyptian king, Ptolemy IV Philopator (222–204) built a mausoleum in which space was provided not only for Alexander's body, enclosed in a golden coffin, but also for those of himself and other members of his family. Of this mausoleum, known as the 'Sema' ('the Tomb'), nothing whatever survives: even its site is uncertain, and it may have been destroyed as early as the third century AD, when the suppression of a revolt entailed the devastation of part of the city. For the architectural form of this immensely prestigious tomb we are dependent on a few passing references in literature and on the dubious evidence of some small and highly conventionalised representations of Alexandria made to decorate pottery lamps. What both sources seem to indicate is that the mausoleum was circular in plan, and it is conjectured that it consisted of a drum surmounted by a domical superstructure, probably with the profile of a tumulus rather than a cupola. If so, Ptolemy IV may have intended to recall the tumuli of Alexander's native Macedonia rather than the Hellenistic mausolea of Asia Minor. Later Ptolemies, more conscious of their Egyptian heritage than of their Greek ancestry, had themselves buried under pyramids, but it may well have been with Alexander's tomb in mind that in about 28 BC the Emperor Augustus began to build his own mausoleum in Rome.

IV

THE MAUSOLEA OF THE ROMAN EMPERORS

IN THE YEAR 28 BC Caius Julius Caesar Octavianus, soon to be known as Augustus, was engaged in building a huge mausoleum in the Campus Martius at Rome. Although the Campus Martius was not then within the city boundary (where burial was forbidden) it was one of Rome's most important and prestigious public spaces. One or two famous men had been buried there in the past, but no ordinary citizen would have been allowed to build a mausoleum on its soil. Octavian was not an ordinary citizen. He was the victor of Actium, the conqueror of Egypt, the man who in the course of the last ten years had made himself the sole master of the Roman world. In 28 BC the reality of his power was not in doubt, but his consitutional position as the *princeps* of what was nominally a republic was still ill-defined. So building a mausoleum in the Campus Martius was more than just an assertion of privilege: it was an indication that Octavian intended to found a ruling dynasty. Most mausolea are tributes to past greatness; this one was a tangible expression of political ambition.

The mausoleum stood in the northern part of the Campus Martius between the River Tiber and the Via Flaminia (fig. 36). In his *Geography* Strabo describes it as a great circular mound raised on a lofty base of white stone, and thickly covered with evergreen trees or shrubs. On the top stood a bronze statue of the emperor. Within were the tombs of himself, his family and intimates. Nearby was the *ustrinum* or site for funeral pyres, surrounded by a marble wall and shaded by black poplars. On either side of the entrance bronze tablets bore the text of the *Res Gestae Divi Augusti*, the official record of Augustus's reign. In front, two Egyptian obelisks stood sentinel. ★ All that now remains of this most famous of all Roman tombs is the concrete core of its walls, stripped of their facing of travertine stone. Its destruction began in 410, when it was ransacked by the Goths. Much more damage was done during the Middle Ages, when it was converted into a castle by the Colonna family. By the end of the sixteenth century it had been reduced to a shell, within which a formal garden was laid out (fig. 37). Subsequent use as a bullring, a theatre and a concert hall continued its degradation.

★ One of these is now in front of the apse of the church of S. Maria Maggiore, the other in the Piazza del Quirinale.

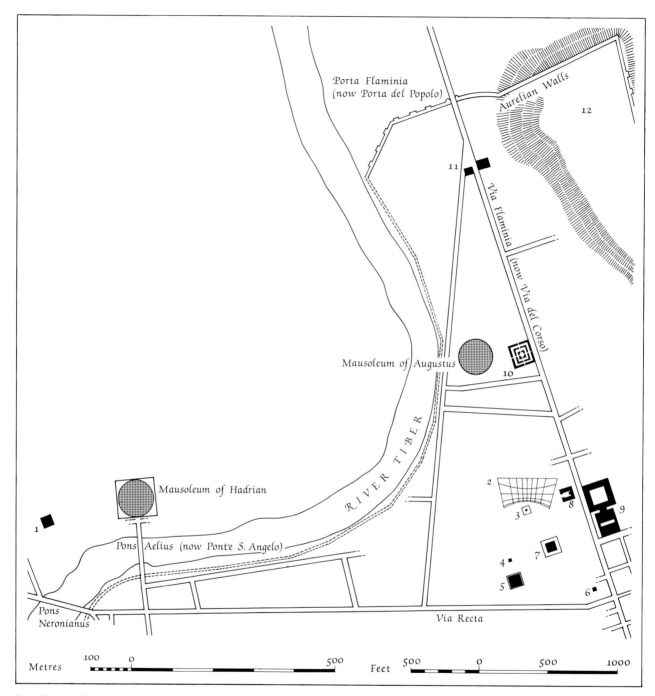

36. Rome, the neighbourhood of the Campus Martius, showing the mausolea of Augustus and Hadrian in their original setting. 1. Pyramidal mausoleum (the 'Meta Romuli'). 2. *Horologium*. 3. Obelisk. 4. Column of Antoninus Pius. 5. *Ustrinum* of Antoninus Pius. 6. Column of Marcus Aurelius. 7. *Ustrinum* of Marcus Aurelius. 8. *Ara Pacis*. 9. *Templum Solis*. 10. *Ustrinum* of Augustus. 11. Two mausolea. 12. The Pincian Hill (*Collis Hortulorum*).

37. The mausoleum of Augustus as a garden: engraving in E. Dupérac, *Vestigi dell'Anti-chità di Roma* (Rome 1639) (Ashmolean Museum, Oxford).

Finally, in 1936-8 the theatre was removed by the fascist government and the battered remains were consolidated as an archaeological monument.

The complex plan (fig. 38) was determined partly by the need to provide a burial chamber, partly by the engineering problems caused by the enormous weight of the piled-up earth and partly by the silhouette that it was desired to project. The emperor's tomb was in the middle, in a chamber hollowed out of a central pillar which rose to support his statue. Round it was a circular chamber containing three niches for urns or sarcophagi, and round that was a continuous corridor probably designed for ritual processions (see below, p. 71). The compartmentation of the remaining space was designed to take the weight of the earth filling in a manner also employed in fortifications. As Vitruvius explains, such fillings increase in bulk and weight by absorbing water in winter, when they are liable to burst their containing walls. To prevent this the mass of earth was subdivided by the radiating partitions and the outward pressure was taken by a series of horizontal arches bearing on the seventeen-foot external wall. The whole was an impressive display of Roman structural engineering, and the same principles were applied to the design of smaller mausolea of this kind, for instance, one at Canosa in Apulia and another associated with a Roman villa at West Mersea in Essex (fig. 39).

Unfortunately, it is the silhouette that is the most difficult feature of the mausoleum to reconstruct. Sketches made by the architect Peruzzi and others early in the sixteenth century record important details of the masonry, including a Doric frieze, portions of which came to light in 1939, but they do not make clear how high any of the walls rose. Attempts to reconstruct the external appearance of the mausoleum on paper have ranged from a giant tumulus to a series of concentric terraces (fig. 38). Although the basic concept behind the mausoleum is

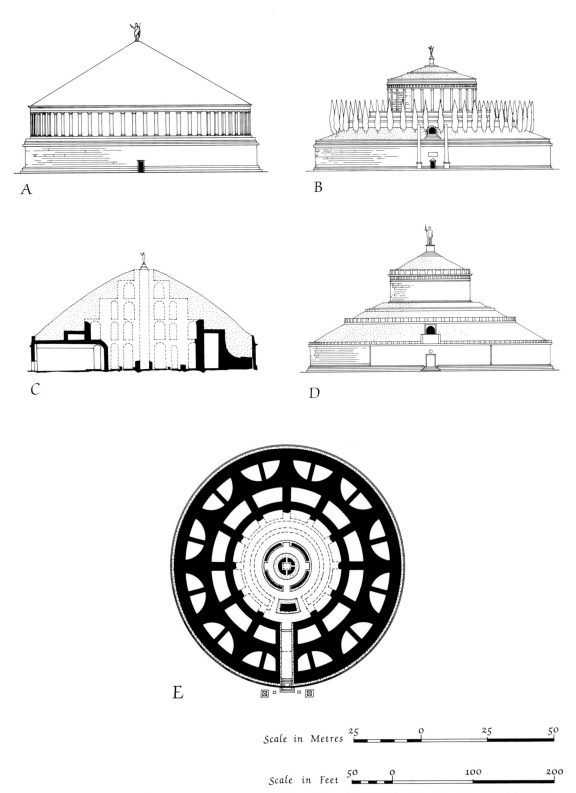

Scale in Metres 25 0 25 50

Scale in Feet 50 0 100 200

38. The mausoleum of Augustus. A as restored by E. Fiorilli (1927), B by G. Gatti (1934), D by H. von Hesberg (1988). C section according to Giglioli (1930). E plan based on the surviving remains.

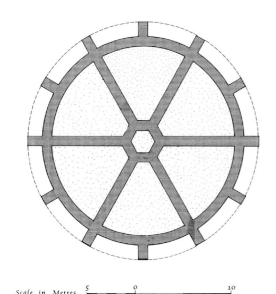

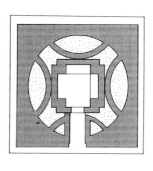

39. Plans of Roman mausolea at, *left*, West Mersea, Essex, England, and *right*, Canosa, South Italy, showing structural engineering comparable to that employed in the mausoleum of Augustus.

Scale in Metres 5 0 10

Scale in Feet 15 0 30

that of an earthen mound it seems unlikely that the elaborate substructure was not expressed externally in at least one inner ring of masonry, and for this reason the reconstructions of Gatti and von Hesberg are to be preferred to those of Fiorilli and Giglioli.

In choosing a tumulus for his tomb Augustus was reviving one of the most ancient and traditional forms of monument. It was under tumuli that the heroes of the Trojan war were buried. Tumuli marked the graves of many famous kings of the past in both Asia Minor and Europe. In Italy they were a common sight in the great Etruscan cemeteries to the north of Rome. But two particular tombs may have been in the mind of Augustus in 28 BC. One was in the Campus Martius itself. It covered the remains of L. Cornelius Sulla (d. 78 BC), whose brief rule as dictator in some ways presaged his own rise to absolute power in the Roman state. The other was the tomb of an even greater forerunner of Augustus, Alexander the Great, which the *princeps* had reverently inspected in person only two years previously. No other tomb is more likely to have been the model for his own. For if Augustus saw himself in Roman history as a new Romulus, in world history he saw himself as a new Alexander. Both Sulla's tomb and Alexander's have vanished almost without trace, either literary or archaeological, and it is only a conjecture – though a plausible one – that Sulla's tomb was in the form of a tumulus.★ But (as we have seen) there are some slight indications that

★ The fact that Lucan refers to Sulla's tomb as a *tumulus* in his *de Bello Civili* or *Pharsalia* is often supposed to prove that it was a tumulus in the sense in which that word is used in modern archaeological literature. The word *tumulus* occurs thirty-two times in Lucan's book, in most cases in contexts that make it clear that he simply means 'a tomb'. Once he uses it in reference to the pyramids of Egypt, and seven or eight times to describe the hasty burial of Pompey's ashes in a shallow grave by the shore, marked only by a stone. The form of Sulla's tomb is therefore an open question, but it is tempting to suppose that it was under an earthen mound that the ashes of that formidable dictator were buried.

Alexander's tomb may have been circular in plan and so possibly tumular in form.

The first burial in the mausoleum of Augustus was in 23 BC, when the ashes of his heir designate, Marcellus, were placed within it. In subsequent years it received the remains of other members of his family, as well as those of his great political ally, Agrippa. The ashes of the *princeps* himself were ultimately to be placed in the central chamber when his long reign ended in AD 14. Meanwhile, the symbolical role of the mausoleum as a dynastic monument had been greatly enhanced by bringing it into relationship with a gigantic sundial which was marked out to the south on the pavement of the Campus Martius. The gnomon of this sundial was an Egyptian obelisk one hundred feet high. It was one of two that Augustus had brought from Heliopolis in 10–9 BC. Re-erected in the Campus Martius on a base which proclaimed that 'Egypt had been brought under the sway of the Roman people' (*Aegvpto in potestatem populi Romani redacta*), it accurately marked the time for a city in which mechanical clocks were unknown. Not only did the spoils of Egypt tell the hours for the citizens of Rome, the *horologium* was so designed as to pay perpetual tribute to the memory of the emperor who had commissioned it. The obelisk was sited so that to the north it faced directly towards the mausoleum with its crowning statue of Augustus, and to the east towards the Ara Pacis, the altar erected to mark his victorious return from Spain and Gaul in 13 BC. The huge dial, inlaid with gilded bronze in the marble pavement, was carefully designed to commemorate the emperor's birthday, which happily coincided with the autumnal equinox on 23 September. From dawn to dusk on that day every year the tip of the shadow cast by the gnomon ran the length of the equinoctial line which stretched from east to west and pointed towards the Ara Pacis (fig. 36). Thus the whole complex of obelisk, sundial, altar and mausoleum formed a grandiose memorial to the reign of Augustus. Unluckily, the site of the *horologium* was susceptible to flooding and subsidence caused by the Tiber, and in the course of the first century AD the gnomon and its marble dial had more than once to be reset at a higher level. Today the obelisk is in Piazza Montecitorio, the Ara Pacis has been reconstructed in a new position to the west of the mausoleum, and the *horologium* (though located by excavation in the basement of no. 48 Via di Campo Marzio) is buried under several feet of accumulated soil and debris.

The mausoleum of Augustus continued to serve as the burial place of the Julio-Claudian dynasty up to the death of the Emperor Caligula in AD 41, and the ashes of the latter's successor Claudius were presumably placed there too when he was buried 'with all the honours that had been given to Augustus'. Nero's ignominious end deprived him of a state funeral, and his ashes ended up with those of his relations on the Pincian Hill. The Flavian emperors – Vespasian (d. 79), Titus (d. 81) and Domitian (d. 96) – had their own place of burial in the *templum gentis Flaviae* built by Domitian on the Quirinal Hill, which (if accurately represented on a contemporary coin) was a building of some pretensions and rectangular rather than circular in form. Nerva (d. 98) was buried in the mausoleum of Augustus, and was the last person to be interred there. The ashes of Trajan

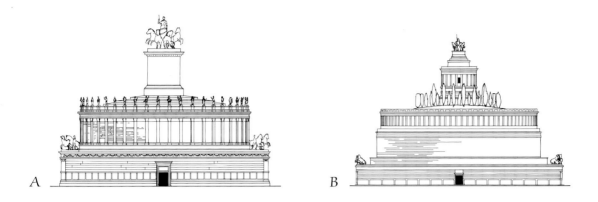

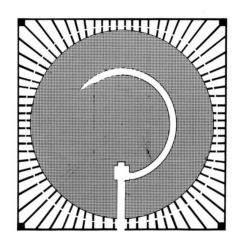

Scale in Metres |25 0 25 50| Scale in Feet |50 0 100 200|

40. The mausoleum of the Emperor Hadrian. A as restored by M. Borgatti (1931), B by S. Rowland Pierce (1925). C plan based on the surviving remains.

(d. 117) were deposited in a chamber in the base of his column in the Forum Trajani (see below, pp. 92–4).

In the late 120s Hadrian (d. 138) built a new imperial mausoleum on a site on the further bank of the Tiber. A stone bridge, the Pons Aelius, was constructed to link it to the Campus Martius. Hadrian's mausoleum, now the castle of S. Angelo, was similar in size and character to that of Augustus, but differed from it both in structure and in decorative detail. It consisted of a great circular drum rising out of a square podium and was surmounted by a large pedestal supporting a quadriga (fig. 40). The drum appears to have been plain (though in many reconstructions from the fifteenth century onwards it has been provided with pilasters), but the ten-metre high podium was faced with marble and had large pilasters at the corners and an entablature decorated with *bucrania* and garlands. The interior of the drum was a solid mass of rubble within which a spiral ramp formed an annular corridor and ultimately gave access to the central burial chamber, which was furnished with rectangular recesses for urns or sarcophagi.

Many features of the building have been destroyed in the course of its long history as a papal fortress, and the external form of the upper portions is largely conjectural. It is probable but by no means certain that there was provision for the planting of trees either on the podium or at the upper level, and the arrangement of the statuary is of course unknown. At ground level the whole was enclosed by bronze railings adorned with gilt bronze peacocks, two of which survive in the Cortile del Belvedere in the Vatican. Peacocks were the birds of Juno. From the second century onwards they were associated with the deification of empresses, as the eagle was with that of emperors. The peacocks that decorated Hadrian's mausoleum may therefore have symbolised the apotheosis of his wife, Sabina, who was deified when she predeceased him in AD 136 or 137. Hadrian's mausoleum subsequently became the established place of burial of members of the Antonine dynasty and its successors, including Marcus Aurelius (d. 180), Septimius Severus (d. 211) and Caracalla (d. 217). Severus died at York and his ashes were taken to Rome in an urn made of a 'purple stone' which may have been Derbyshire 'Bluejohn'.

When Hadrian built his mausoleum, the bridge that linked it to the Campus Martius was merely a convenience. But the building of the Aurelian walls in the third century converted the mausoleum into a bridge-head, and thereafter it had a dual role as part of the city's defences. As such, it played an important part in the siege of 537, and the historian Procopius gives a vivid picture of the Roman garrison breaking up the decorative statuary and hurling the pieces of marble down on the besieging Goths. By then bridge and mausoleum were already linked by a *porticus* or colonnade to the forecourt of St Peter's, and by the tenth century the mausoleum had been appropriated as a fortress by the pope.

Hadrian was the last emperor to build a mausoleum for well over a century. The failure of later emperors to follow his example was a symptom of the decline in the prestige of the imperial office which lasted until the reign of Diocletian (284–305). Provided he died in his bed or campaigning against an external enemy, an emperor could expect deification almost as a matter of course. He would be entitled to an elaborate funeral ceremony, during which an eagle would be released as a symbol of the ascent of the emperor's spirit to its home among the gods. But if he had the misfortune to be deposed or assassinated, then the elimination from the record known as *damnatio memoriae* would follow: there would be no state funeral, his statues would be smashed or defaced, his legislation annulled, and his name erased from public inscriptions. In the course of the third century far more emperors were damned than deified, so few built mausolea and fewer still came to occupy them. Diocletian reasserted imperial authority and successfully shared the burden of defence and administration with Maximian as co-emperor and Constantius and Galerius as subordinate caesars. After Diocletian and Maximian had both retired in 305, Constantius and Galerius succeeded them as co-emperors. Constantius died in 306, Galerius in 311, and in 312 Constantius' son Constantine defeated Maximian's son Maxentius and made himself sole

41. The mausoleum of the Emperor Diocletian at Split, Yugoslavia, now the cathedral. In this drawing the Christian accretions (campanile, chancel, pulpit, tombs, etc.) have been removed, and the destroyed portico and the roof of the peristyle have been restored. The form of the upper part of the portico is conjectural, as are the indications of decoration in the dome.

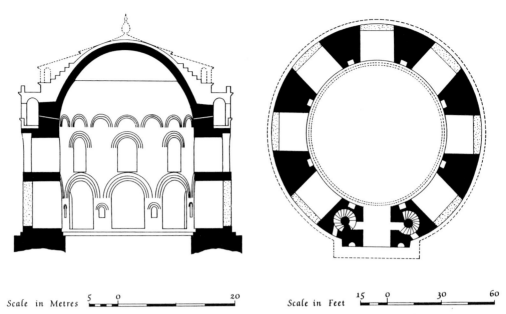

Scale in Metres 5 ___ 0 _____ 20   Scale in Feet 15 _ 0 ____ 30 ____ 60

42. The rotunda at Thessalonica (Greece), believed to have been intended as the mausoleum of the Emperor Galerius. The hatched portions have been altered in its subsequent
adaptation as a church (after Hébrard).

emperor. Of these six emperors or caesars, four are believed to have built
mausolea: Diocletian, Maxentius, Galerius and Constantine.★ Constantine, as a
Christian, belongs to a later chapter, but the mausolea of the other three have an
important place in Roman architectural history. Diocletian's was at Split in
Dalmatia, where he died in 311 or 312, Maxentius' on the Via Appia at Rome, and
Galerius' at Thessalonica in Macedonia.

These three tetrarchic mausolea were all associated with imperial residences.
Maxentius' mausoleum stood close to his villa off the Via Appia, Galerius built
his in formal architectural relationship with his palace at Thessalonica, and
Diocletian actually sited his within the protective enclosure of his palatial retirement villa at Split. Of Maxentius' mausoleum only the basement remains, but it
clearly implies a structure with a circular domed body and a pedimented portico
of the Pantheon type (fig. 43). His son Romulus was buried in it after his death
in 309 and his own remains would doubtless have lain there too but for his defeat
by Constantine in 312. Of similar character was the mausoleum on the Via Prae-
nestina near Rome, traditionally associated with the Gordian emperors who ruled

---

★ Constantius died at York in 306 and may have been buried at Trier, the chief city of northern
Gaul, his principal province. His tomb has not been identified, but the epitaph is recorded in
manuscript copies (published by Mommsen in *Hermes*, 28, 1893, p. 33). Maximian, after several ill-
advised attempts to resume his former status as one of the two *Augusti*, was made to commit suicide
by Constantine in 310, and *damnatio memoriae* followed. If he had built a mausoleum in his lifetime it
would probably have been either at Milan or on the estate in Campania or Lucania to which he
retired. His name is one that needs to be considered in connection with the mausoleum at Milan
whose plan is illustrated in fig. 100.

52

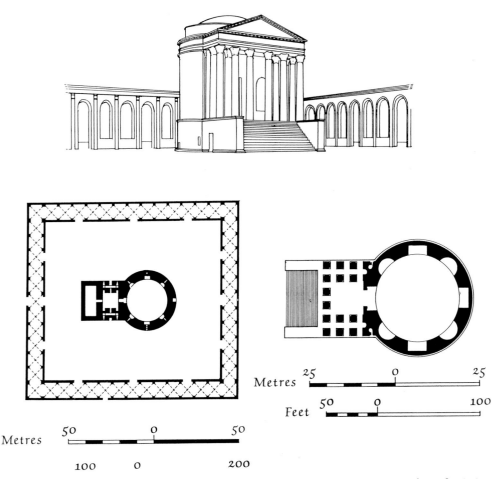

43. The mausoleum of the Emperor Maxentius on the Via Appia, Rome: plan of existing basement, conjectural plan of destroyed upper level and conjectural perspective showing alternative restorations of the arcaded quadrangle, with and without pilasters (after Frazer and Rasch).

238–44, but in fact dated by brick stamps to *c*.300. The mausolea of Diocletian and Galerius both survive as churches.★ The former is externally octagonal (with a matching peristyle), but inside there is a circular domed chamber with recesses (alternately round and rectangular) separated by large Corinthian columns of red Egyptian granite (fig. 41). The emperor's sarcophagus has disappeared, but must have stood at this level rather than in the unadorned crypt. Galerius' mausoleum provided seven large recesses for sarcophagi in the walls of a domed rotunda

★ While it is generally accepted that Diocletian's mausoleum was the building that has been the cathedral church of Split since the seventh century, the identification of the late Roman rotunda at Thessalonica as the intended mausoleum of Galerius is not regarded as certain by all scholars. In the event, Galerius died at Romuliana (Gamzigrad), a fortified palace in Serbia, where recent excavations have not yet satisfactorily established his actual place of burial (see N. Duval's review of these questions in *Bulletin Monumental* 144, 1986, pp. 354–61).

whose decoration was carried out in marble veneer (fig. 42). All three of these mausolea stood within formal enclosures which in the case of Maxentius' consisted of a large arcaded quadrangle whose remains have suggested a simplified architectural treatment of the sort associated in English neo-classical architecture with the name of Soane (fig. 43). At Split Diocletian's mausoleum stood in a rectangular precinct on one side of the arcaded area that leads like a street up to the apartments reserved for the residence of the ex-emperor. On the other side was a temple dedicated probably to Diocletian's tutelary deity Jupiter. Mausoleum and temple faced one another across the axial space in a formal relationship that was emphasised by the use of red granite shafts for the columns flanking the entrances to their respective precincts.

V

THE ROMANS AND THEIR MONUMENTS

IN THE ANCIENT WORLD funerary monuments were part of an outdoor display of architecture and sculpture that played an important role in public life. In the modern world the image of the great is projected partly photographically and partly through the medium of the written word. In Renaissance and Baroque Europe political power and political aspiration were projected above all through the arts: on facades, on walls and ceilings, in theatres and through public spectacles. In Antiquity they were projected in essentially the same manner, with the difference that the three-dimensional arts were more prominent as instruments of propaganda than the pictorial ones. The written word, of course, was by no means of negligible importance, but the public saw it mainly in the form of inscriptions in public places. Statues were immensely prestigious: there was no more gratifying indication of public esteem than to have a statue erected in one's honour in the forum; no greater mark of disgrace than to see it cast down or defaced. In this world of visual media the funerary monument had its place. In Rome the two great dynastic mausolea, of Augustus and Hadrian, were among the most prominent symbols of imperial authority, and it was outside the entrance to the former that the proud record of Augustus' reign was inscribed in bronze. For private citizens, too, the family tomb was a witness to their standing in society, a monument to the military valour or civic attainment of their ancestors. A concise *curriculum vitae* of many a leading Roman citizen was cut in stone or marble on his monument: indeed, much of our biographical knowledge of such men is derived from funerary inscriptions.

However important it might be as a symbol of social status and public standing, the basic purpose of a funerary monument was religious. Belief in an after-life was general throughout the Roman world. Some philosophers (especially of the Epicurean school) denied it, and some writers (notably Lucian) derided it, but many – perhaps most – believed in some form of continued existence, however shadowy. As pagans, unlike Christians, had no coherent body of doctrine to guide them, the notion of the after-life was subject to a great variety of interpretation. Some believed in a nether world that was literally underground and that constituted the kingdom of the dead, ruled over by Pluto and Proserpina. At various places there were gates to this subterranean realm which were opened on certain days to give the dead free access to the world they had once inhabited. One of these infernal adits was in the city of Rome itself. It was covered by a stone, the *lapis manalis*, which was ceremonially raised three times a year. Gradually this primitive but persistent conception of the after-life was superseded by the notion of a celestial heaven in which the human soul ended up as an immaterial essence living in eternal bliss in the company of the gods.

Between these two extremes there were many variations of belief and still more of custom in the face of death. All, however, were agreed that the after-life, whatever its character, began in the tomb. Burial, whether of the body or of the cremated ashes, was the indispensable prerequisite to its enjoyment. A corpse had to be committed to the earth with appropriate ceremonies in order to ensure the safe passage of the soul to the after-life, escorted by the *Manes*, or ancestral spirits of the family. If burial was denied, the ghost of the dead would roam the earth in perpetual distress, and might do untold harm to the living. Even if safely conducted to the nether world, it could still exercise an influence over the living that might just as likely be malevolent as benevolent. It was, therefore, imperative to treat the dead with due respect and, above all, to give them proper burial. If there was an element of affectionate solicitude in this, there was still more an element of fear. The dead were in communion with the mysterious forces that controlled the destinies of men★ and if not propitiated might turn them against their descendants. A tomb was, therefore, more than just an honourable receptacle for a corpse: it was the point of contact between quick and dead, the means of communication with spirits with whose welfare the living had every reason to concern themselves.

To ensure that welfare it was incumbent on the living to do more than just provide a tomb. Honour had to be done to the dead at regular intervals, and neglect of this sacred duty might have consequences as sinister as failure to provide proper burial. Just as the gods were propitiated by sacrifices, so the dead were solaced by the offering of food and drink. This might be done by leaving food on the tomb or by symbolically pouring liquid refreshment into the grave through a grating or down a tube. The dead were notoriously thirsty. 'Confined as I am within my monument', reads an epitaph at Narbonne, 'I drink with all the more pleasure because I am obliged to remain sleeping here for ever' (*C.I.L.*,† xii, 5102). But it became customary to hold a family banquet at the tomb in which the dead were supposed to participate with the living. Eating in the presence of one's departed ancestors was a ritual conducive to a sense of family identity in the living, and the ancestors themselves were believed to be cheered by the conviviality of their descendants. Indeed, the consolations of the funeral banquet were mutual. 'Come here safe and sound, all together for a happy feast', enjoins

---

★ Hence at Olympus in Lycia there were tombs where the heroised dead were invited to make oracular pronouncements for the benefit of their posterity. The consultant drew by lot a letter of the alphabet and found a corresponding response engraved in verse on the tomb. However deviously expressed, the advice given was generally in terms of 'Proceed' or 'Wait' (G. Bean, *Turkey's Southern Shore*, 1968, pp. 172–3).

† *Corpus Inscriptionum Latinarum.*

an epitaph from Rome (*C.I.L.*, vi, 26554). 'Live happy and pour out wine to our *Manes*', says another in Syria, engraved beneath a scene of libation, 'recollecting that one day you will join us' (*C.I.L.*, iii, 14165). For poor people these occasions must have been in the nature of a picnic or barbecue, but for the wealthier there were proper facilities for cooking and eating in comfort. The will of a prosperous citizen of Langres (Andematunum) in Gallia Belgica (now France) not only prescribes the principal features of his mausoleum (including a statue of himself and an altar of Luna marble), but provides that it shall be furnished with blankets, dining cushions, and articles of attire for use on such occasions (*C.I.L.*, xiii, 5708). An inventory made in AD 6 of the contents of a mausoleum shared by some Roman freedmen lists as furnishings of the dining area one stone and three other tables, a cistern with taps, a fountain in the form of a bronze lily, three chairs and three benches (*L'Année Epigraphique*, 1986, p. 13). These family banquets were held (like an Irish wake) immediately after the funeral and subsequently on the anniversary of the death and on certain other dates such as the *Parentalia* or family festival in February, or the *Rosalia*, or feast of roses, in May, when monuments were often decorated with flowers. On these occasions the silence of the tomb was broken by the chatter of friends and relations wearing their best clothes and eating and drinking with a freedom that sometimes ended in drunken abandon.

The Romans believed that it had been the custom of their ancestors to bury their dead in the precincts of their town houses. In Rome and elsewhere intra-mural burial was eventually prohibited by law, and although exceptions might be made in favour of great men like the Emperor Trajan (below, p. 94), or of a notable benefactor such as Celsus Polemaeanus, whose sarcophagus was laid in a vault beneath the library with which he adorned the city of Ephesus, the normal practice was to bury outside the walls along the lines of the main roads. When one approached a Roman city one of the first things one noticed was the tombs of its citizens. Along the old Via Appia on the outskirts of Rome, or at Pompeii, or outside the ruins of some Hellenistic city such as Hierapolis in modern Turkey, the visitor today can still see the remains of innumerable tombs on either side of the road. They were placed there because the Romans did not want to segregate their dead in walled cemeteries: they wanted their tombs to be seen. The injunction *Siste Viator* . . . ('Stop Traveller . . . ') in order to read the *elogium* that followed was a standard way of beginning an epitaph. In modern Rome the ruins of these tombs are mostly shapeless masses of brickwork stripped of their ornamental facing and standing forlornly in fields and backyards, but originally many of them were the focal points of carefully tended gardens. The citizen of Andematunum already mentioned provided in his will for the pay of three gardeners and their apprentices to maintain the orchard that he had planted round his tomb. At Briord in the south of France a vineyard was attached to the mausoleum of Marcus Rufius Catullus, formerly chief officer of the guild of Rhone boatmen (*C.I.L.*, xiii, 2494), and a funerary garden containing trees, vines and roses is recorded at Nemausus (Nîmes) (*C.I.L.*, xii, 3637). In Rome the plan of one such garden has been preserved, inscribed on marble as a legal record of the property (fig. 44). In such a setting a funeral banquet would be an elegant *al fresco*

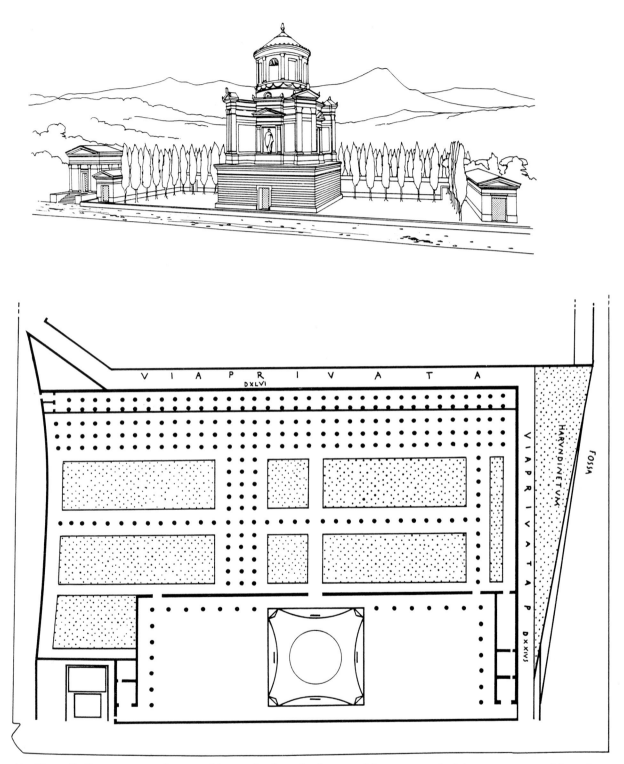

44. Plan of a Roman mausoleum and its garden inscribed on marble as a record of the property, and found in a cemetery on the Via Labicana near Rome. *Top*, a conjectural view of the building in its setting (after Huelsen).

45. A *columbarium* or communal mausoleum with tiers of niches for busts and urns. This one, found on the outskirts of Rome in 1840, was reserved for freedmen and relatives of the imperial family (photograph of 1868–9 in J.H. Parker Collection, Department of the History of Art, Oxford University).

meal, and often the garden produced fruit and vegetables for consumption by the owners as well as for sale. Tomb architecture, in fact, had come by the first century BC to be seen as a contribution to the suburban environment.

The tombs in question were, of course, those of the more prosperous citizens. For the poor there were public cemeteries where their remains were summarily disposed of without any memorials. In Republican times there had been some notorious burial pits on the Esquiline Hill in Rome. These were abolished in the time of Augustus as a public nuisance, and their place was taken by suburban crematoria popularly known as 'the kitchens' (*culinae*). It was to avoid this fate (the equivalent of a 'pauper's grave' in Victorian England) that wealthy Romans provided the communal mausolea known as *columbaria* for their slaves and that independent men of modest means joined burial clubs which maintained similar *columbaria* for the benefit of their members (fig. 45). The wealthiest of all often

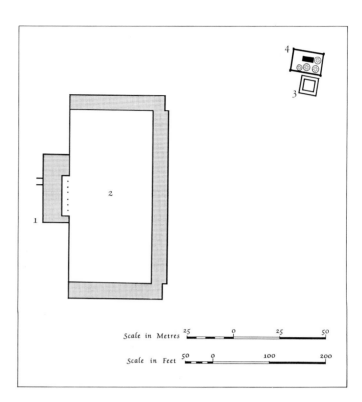

46. A Roman villa with its private burial place: Newel, near Trier in Germany (after Wightman). 1. House. 2. Farmyard. 3. Temple. 4. Burial enclosure containing four tumuli and a monument.

Scale in Metres 25 0 25 50

Scale in Feet 50 0 100 200

built their mausolea on their country estates. A good example from the neighbourhood of Trier in Gallia Belgica is illustrated in figure 46. Here the burial enclosure contained four tumuli as well as a monument whose base survives. Close by was a small rectangular temple. In England the tumuli at Bartlow, south-east of Cambridge, probably formed part of a private cemetery belonging to a neighbouring villa, while at the Lullingstone villa in Kent the burials were actually made within the *cella* of a rectangular temple similar to the German one. Mausolea such as these sometimes marked the boundaries of their owners' property and are mentioned in the Roman land surveyors' manuals as features to look out for. The *piles* of southern France, tower-like structures almost certainly funerary in character and often standing in rural isolation, would have made excellent landmarks, and one of them, at Aumagne near Saintes in Aquitaine, continued to mark the limits of three counties in medieval times.

In the history of Roman Italy the monumental tomb begins to emerge in the late Republican period – that is, in the course of the two centuries before the birth of Christ. In the seventh century BC the inhabitants of the Latin cities were still burying their dead with rich grave-goods. The abandonment of these ancient customs in the sixth century seems to have been due as much to the influence of the Greek laws against excessive funeral display as to any change in religious belief, though it was consistent with the idea that the dead were disembodied spirits living in Hades rather than prisoners of the tomb with physical needs indistinguishable from those of the living. What was formally prohibited in the

'Laws of the Twelve Tables' (a codification of *c.*450 BC) was modern extravagance rather than ancient superstition. Nothing made of gold might be deposited in a tomb (though an exception was made for gold dentures), the number of musicians hired for the funeral lament was limited to ten, and the wood for the funeral pyre might not be smoothed. These restraints, in keeping with the stern character of the founding fathers of the Republic, proved difficult to enforce. Grave-goods were on the way out, but funeral pomp and family pride were not easily curbed. By the end of the Republic the Via Appia outside Rome was lined with the tombs of the new aristocracy, while inside the city itself memorials were sometimes built at public expense in honour of specially deserving citizens who were buried else-where. Such honorary memorials often took the form of an altar (the essential feature of a Hellenistic *heroön*), and this may have set the fashion for monuments in the form of altars, such as that of L. Cornelius Scipio Barbatus, consul in 298 BC, now in the Vatican Museum (fig. 47).

By the end of the first century AD a Roman citizen (and from AD 212 every free inhabitant of the empire enjoyed that status) had a great variety of tombs to choose from. From one end of the Mediterranean to the other the range of funerary monuments was immense. Indeed, funerary architecture has probably

47. The altar-tomb of L.Cornelius Scipio Barbatus, consul in 298 BC., from an engraving published soon after the excavation of the Scipio family tomb on the Via Appia in Rome in 1780–2. In the course of the next century this altar-tomb with its Doric frieze was to be the model for monuments in nearly all the major cemeteries of western Europe and North America (cf. fig. 357).

48. The monument of the Julii at Glanum (Saint-Rémy) in Provence. An inscription shows that this exceptionally well-preserved monument was erected, probably in about 30/20 BC, to the memory of their progenitors by three members of a family whose name, the Julii, indicates that they owed their Roman citizenship to Julius Caesar. The two toga'd statues standing within the ring of columns very likely represent their father and grandfather. There is no burial chamber and the monument was probably designed as much to emphasise the standing of a ruling family in the civic society of Glanum as to commemorate the dead (Archives photographiques, Paris, S.P.A.D.E.M.).

49. The monument of the Secundinii at Igel near Trier in Germany, probably of the early third century AD. The Secundinii were in the cloth trade, and cloth-making scenes can be seen among the reliefs with which the surface of the monument is covered (from Dragendorff & Krüger, *Das Grabmal von Igel*, Trier 1924).

50. Rock-cut tombs at Caunus, Lycia (Turkey), probably of the fourth century BC, but of a type that continued to be both reused and imitated well into Roman times. The one on the right is unfinished (Edward Impey).

never been more varied and more innovative that it was in the Roman empire during the first three centuries AD. In practice, of course, choice was limited by personal experience and by the availability of architectural expertise. There were no illustrations of famous buildings to refer to, and only a minority of proconsuls, soldiers, imperial officials and merchants had seen with their own eyes such outstanding exemplars as the Mausoleum of Halicarnassus or the tombs of the Pharaohs. Designs could be drawn on parchment or papyrus, or on boards, or even on walls, and the established conventions of classical architecture no doubt helped to facilitate its dissemination. One of the advantages of the system of interrelated proportions described by Vitruvius was precisely that it made it possible to design a Doric order (for instance) simply by following the written precepts in his book. But Vitruvius gives no directions for building mausolea, and there was nothing academic about the design of Roman funerary monuments. Many of them must have been produced by masons and sculptors working without professional architectural supervision. A workshop or itinerant team of this sort has been identified in southern Gaul, and to it have been attributed well-known monuments at Lugdunum (Lyon) and Glanum (Saint-Rémy), in which a profusion of sculptural decoration, combined with a certain clumsiness in architectural design, suggests the hand of the mason rather than that of the architect

64

51. The tomb of Amyntas at Telmessos, Lycia (Turkey), a rock-cut tomb of the fourth century BC (Edward Impey).

(fig. 48). The elaborately decorated monuments found in the Rhineland (fig. 49) are likely to have been the products of a similar workshop. Elsewhere native traditions persisted at a popular level. By the time of Augustus (30 BC – AD 14) the empire extended from Asia Minor to Spain and from North Africa to Britain. Each of the many societies of which it was composed had its own tradition of funerary monument: earthen mounds in north-east Gaul and Britain; rock-cut chambers with pedimented facades in Asia Minor (fig. 50); underground tombs (*hypogea*) in Syria; stone cairns in North Africa (fig. 26); anthropomorphic gravestones in Iberia. But, in general, the more ambitious funerary monuments of the Roman empire represent an architectural common market that knew no geographical limits and in which invention had free play. Moreover, there was a constant interchange of design between mausolea and buildings of other sorts: temples, trophies, altars, shrines. Even a column and a library could fulfil a double function as at once a public monument and a tomb.

It is this variety and fluidity of form that is the great attraction of these monuments, and that at the same time makes it so difficult to impose on them any meaningful classification, let alone any typological development of the sort that establishes an intelligible stylistic progression or a convincing chronological sequence. It is fairly easy to distinguish the mausolea that derive from, or

65

52. Cerveteri (Caere), Lazio, Italy, an Etruscan tumulus of the seventh to sixth centuries BC. Note the stone revetment (Alinari).

approximate to such readily recognisable prototypes as temples, columns or altars. Much more resistant to classification are those that are made up of combinations of primary geometrical forms – cubes, cylinders, pyramids and the like – with or without the addition of columns, pilasters or other classical ornaments. In addition, there are the sarcophagi with miniaturised architectural decoration.

We begin with the cylindrical mausoleum, because typologically it must be related to the prehistoric tumulus. The latter consisted of a circular mound of earth or rubble whose base was often defined by a kerb, made at first of irregularly shaped stones, but later of properly dressed and coursed masonry. A good example from one of the Etruscan cemeteries of the seventh to sixth centuries BC is illustrated in figure 52. In the first century BC this type of mausoleum was often adopted by the Roman aristocracy. The largest and most prestigious of all was the one built for himself by Octavian, the future Emperor Augustus (see above, p. 43). To whatever source the mausoleum of Augustus should be traced, there can be no doubt that it set the fashion for others.* A

---

* Even when the identity of the person for whom one of these mausolea was built is known, the date of its erection is usually uncertain, as it may have been built either before or after his death. So far no mausoleum of the cylindrical type in Italy has been proved to be earlier than that of Augustus, and most of them are certainly later. See R. Ross Holloway in *American Journal of Archaeology*, 2nd ser., 70 (1966), pp. 171–3.

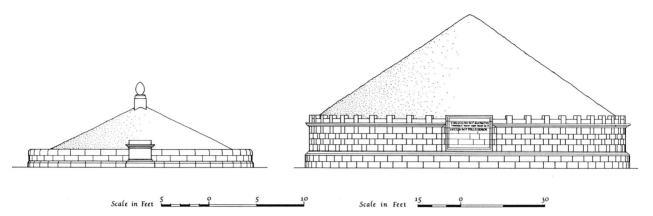

53. Roman tombs in the form of tumuli with masonry revetments: *left*, at Bill in Luxemburg, early third century AD (after Heyart); *right*, the monument of M. Lucilius Paetus outside the Porta Salaria in Rome, late first century BC (after Pietrangeli, 1941, and Nota, 1984).

contemporary example is the tomb of M. Lucilius Paetus outside the Porta Salaria in Rome (fig. 53). Here the ring of stone, though built of beautifully laid masonry, is still only four courses high above the plinth, clearly indicating its typological relationship to the kerb of the prehistoric tumulus. The inscription is carved on a moulded tablet. We recognise the same type (though some two hundred years later in date) in a tomb at Bill in modern Luxembourg, where an altar (containing the ashes of the person commemorated) takes the place of the tablet (fig. 53).

The next stage in the development of this type of tomb is illustrated by the mausoleum of L. Munatius Plancus, a dexterous politician of the Augustan era who held the consulship in 42 BC. It stands high above the town of Gaeta in Campania, where he was a major landowner. The stone ring has now grown into a tall drum, topped by a Doric frieze (fig. 54). Q. Lollius Urbicus, who governed Britain under Antoninus Pius and subsequently reached the pinnacle of a senator's career as Prefect of the City of Rome, built a similar mausoleum for himself and his family near Constantine in his native Numidia (fig. 56). At Falerii (Civita Castellana) and probably also at Vicovaro, east of Tivoli, mausolea of this type stood on a low rectangular plinth (fig. 57). In the well-known mausoleum of Caecilia Metella on the Via Appia outside Rome, the plinth has been heightened into a rectangular substructure (fig. 58). Caecilia Metella was the daughter of one of the great Roman aristocratic families. Her father, Q. Metellus Creticus, had been consul, as had her grandfather and great-grandfather in their day. She married (in about 63 BC) Marcus Crassus, the eldest son of another consul, and in 30 BC their son Marcus Crassus junior was consul in his turn. Although it is Caecilia alone who is honoured in the inscription, the trophies in the frieze must allude to the military exploits either of her husband, who commanded a legion in Gaul under Julius Caesar, or of her son, whose campaigns in the Balkans in 29 and 28 BC earned him a triumph. The lower part of a similar tomb at Ponte Lucano near Tivoli was decorated, at least on the side open to view, with blind arcading on which were carved the funerary inscriptions of M. Plautius Silvanus and his

54. Gaeta, Italy, the mausoleum of L. Munatius Plancus, a Roman magnate of the first century BC, from an eighteenth-century water-colour in the Ashby Collection, Vatican Library, Rome.

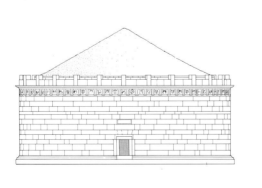

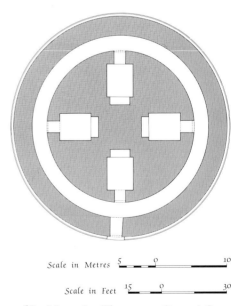

Scale in Metres

Scale in Feet

55. Plan and restored elevation of the mausoleum of L. Munatius Plancus at Gaeta (after Fellmann).

56. The mausoleum of Q. Lollius Urbicus, governor of Britain and Prefect of the City of Rome, near Constantine in Algeria (from Gsell, *Les monuments antiques de l'Algérie*, 1901).

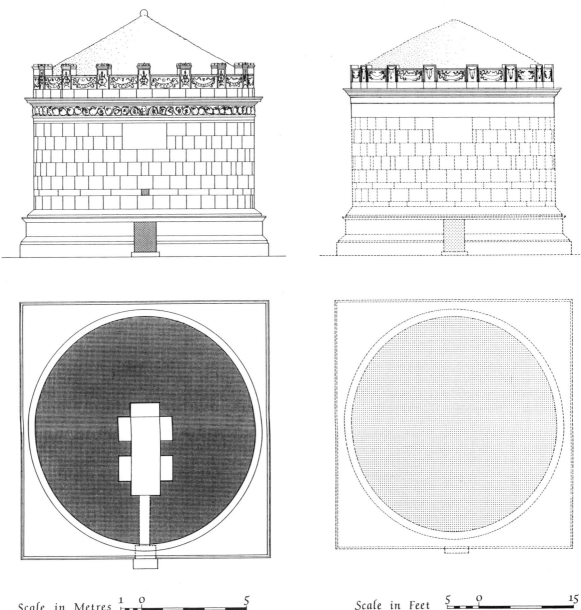

Scale in Metres 1 0 5

Scale in Feet 5 0 15

57. Cylindrical Roman mausolea from, *left* Falerii (Civita Castellana) and *right*, Vicovaro, near Tivoli, Italy, the latter restored from the evidence of the upper portions now in the Vatican Museum, Rome (after Götze and Daltrop respectively).

58. Rome, the mausoleum of Caecilia Metella, a great Roman lady of the first century BC, and her family (Fototeca Unione, Rome). The battlements are medieval.

family. Plautius Silvanus was co-consul with Augustus in 2 BC, and his rise to power was attributable to his mother's friendship with the emperor's wife Livia.

The grandest of all the mausolea of this type was the one built by the Emperor Hadrian, still, as the castle of S. Angelo, one of the landmarks of Rome (fig. 40). Its transformation into a fortification in the sixteenth century, has, however, somewhat altered its character, and the best-preserved example of a cylindrical mausoleum with a rectangular substructure is the one close to the harbour at Attaleia (now Antalya) in Turkey (fig. 59). The twelve fasces carved on either side of the entrance indicate that a man of high rank was buried here, possibly M. Calpurnius Rufus, who attained consular status as governor of Lycia and Pamphylia in the reign of Claudius. Here then we have a coherent group of mausolea associated with the highest ranks of Roman society under Augustus and his immediate successors. These great impenetrable drums of masonry expressed the patrician pride of an aristocracy that had won the Roman empire far more eloquently than the Hellenistic finery of some marble mausoleum.

59. Antalya, Turkey, a large and well-preserved cylindrical mausoleum probably of the first century AD.

A feature of several of these cylindrical mausolea was a circular passage surrounding the burial chamber or chambers (fig. 55). This was probably to enable those participating in the funeral to walk in procession round the tomb immediately after the deposition of the corpse or ashes, a ceremony inherited from a remote past. There is evidence of ritual dancing round tumuli in the Bronze Age, and in *The Iliad* Achilles and his Myrmidons rode three times round the body of Patroclus at his burial. When Alexander the Great visited Troy he and his suite ran naked round the tomb of Achilles before placing a wreath on the funerary stele. The original purpose of these rituals seems to have been to confine the spirit of the dead within a magic circle, but by the time the Roman mausolea were built the ceremony was an archaic funeral custom whose significance may no longer have been fully understood.

Another elementary geometrical form that was much favoured as a component of Roman funerary architecture was the pyramid. Its inherent durability and its striking and distinctive shape have recommended it for monumental use from the time of the pharaohs to the present day. For the Romans (at least from the first century AD) anything Egyptian was fashionable, and their capital was full of obelisks, statues of Isis and the like, some exported from Egypt, many manufactured in Italy by immigrant Egyptian craftsmen. Literal imitations of Egyptian pyramids were, however, rare: indeed, only two are recorded, both in Rome. One, long known as the 'meta Romuli', stood between the mausoleum of

71

60. Rome, the pyramidal mausoleum of Caius Cestius, erected in the first century BC.

61. Pyramidal tombs of the thirteenth and twelfth centuries BC at Deir-el-Medineh in Egypt (restoration drawing by B. Bruyère from the *Encyclopédie Universelle*).

Hadrian and the Vatican (fig. 36:1) and was destroyed by papal building operations early in the sixteenth century. The other, known as the 'meta Remi', still stands close to the Porta Ostiensis on one side of what is now the Protestant cemetery (fig. 60). An inscription records that it was built under the will of Caius Cestius, a praetor and tribune of the plebs of the first century BC, and that his executors completed it within a year. Both these pyramids were relatively small (that of Caius Cestius is about one hundred feet high) and were more sharply pointed than those of the pharaohs. The kings of Meroë in the Sudan had been building comparable pyramids since the fourth century BC, but it is doubtful whether these were known to Roman architects or their clients, and it is probable that the reason for the sharper profile was the same in both cases – namely, the desire to make a small pyramid look as large as possible.

It was as the crowning feature of a rectangular or circular building that the pyramid was widely employed in Roman funerary architecture. Here a distinction must be made between the stepped pyramid and the smooth-sided one. The former was, as we have seen, a prominent feature of the Mausoleum at Halicarnassus, and so became part of the vocabulary of Hellenistic architecture. That it could be used to cap quite small tombs in Magna Graecia is shown by Apulian vase paintings of the fourth century BC, and by the survival of a grave-marker from Syracuse with its top carved in this form. In North Africa, on the other hand, it rises like a gigantic stepped tumulus over the huge circular tombs of the native kings (figs. 21, 22). Although both these areas (as well as Halicarnassus itself) came ultimately under Roman rule, the stepped pyramid was rarely used by Roman architects and did not long persist in Asia Minor. Mausolea capped with smooth-sided pyramids were, however, to be seen from Syria to Spain and from Mauretania to the Rhine valley, and in some areas were still being built as Christian tombs in the fourth and fifth centuries AD. Like the Pyramid of Cestius they may have had a direct Egyptian ancestry, for rectangular tombs surmounted by small pyramids were fashionable in Egypt in the thirteenth and twelfth centuries BC, under the XIXth and XXth dynasties of pharaohs (fig. 61). However, the influence of a precedent so remote both in time and in space may be doubted, and so simple an architectural idea as a pyramidal top to a rectangular tomb must surely have occurred spontaneously to architects as sophisticated as those of imperial Rome.

The simplest form of pyramidally roofed tomb is seen in figure 62, a more elaborate version in figure 295. Sometimes the pyramid was elongated into something more like an obelisk (fig. 63). With the addition of columns or pilasters such attenuated monuments invited the inventive Roman or Hellenistic architect to essay compositions of superimposed stages as complex in form and as picturesque in profile as some of the steeples designed by Sir Christopher Wren for London's churches in the seventeenth century AD (fig. 64). Conical and polygonal as well as four-sided pyramids are recorded, and the profile of the pyramid could be concave, as in the well-known mausoleum near Jerusalem known as the 'Tomb of Absalom' (fig. 65). An eccentric variation on the pyramid theme is represented by the monument on the Via Appia near Albano called the 'Tomba

73

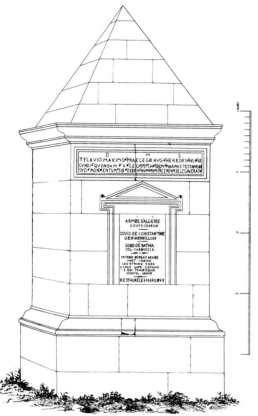

62. Roman funerary monuments with pyramidal roofs: *left*, at Lambaesis, *right*, at Akbou near Bougie, both in Algeria. The former bears two inscriptions, one commemorating T. Flavius Maximus, a Roman officer of the second century AD, the other its repair by the French army in 1849. The tomb at Akbou dates from the third century AD (after Renier and Gsell, respectively).

degli Orazi e Curiazi' (fig. 66). It consists of five cones standing on a rectangular base. This seems to have been a first- or second-century attempt to recreate the tomb of the sixth-century BC Etruscan king Lars Porsenna, which was described by Pliny as being surmounted by five pyramids, 'four in the angles and one in the middle'. At Petra, in what ultimately became the Roman province of Arabia, the remarkable rock-cut tombs include one of the first century AD which is surmounted by four pyramids or obelisks represented in profile.

A third basic form was an open ring or rectangle of columns. This might either stand on a plinth at ground level as a self-sufficient structure or be incorporated into a vertical composition terminating usually in a dome or a pyramid. The circular form went back to Greek shrines or temples such as the well-known ones (all probably of the fourth century BC) at Delphi, Epidaurus and Olympia, while the Monument of Lysicrates at Athens (commemorating a choral victory in the theatre in 334 BC) provided a precedent for its use as a decorative feature on a small scale. As for the rectangular form, it began its career in funerary architecture as one of the most striking features of the Mausoleum of Halicarnassus. In Hellenistic architecture these two columnar arrangements became interchangeable, some mausolea having a square peristyle over a square base (fig. 64), others, a round one (fig. 48). In either case, the substitution of pilasters for columns or half-columns provided the architect with a further permutation of forms. Arcading as

63. Obelisk monument at Msellat in the Wadi Merdum in Tripolitania (from De Mathuisieulx, *Nouvelles Archives des Missions Scientifiques*, xii, 1904, pl. xix).

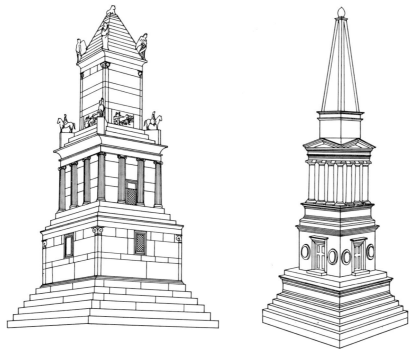

64. Mausolea of native North African rulers, built under Hellenistic influence in the second century BC: *left*, at Dougga (Thugga) in Tunisia, as re-erected in 1908–9, and *right*, a partially conjectural restoration of the mausoleum at el-Khroub near Constantine (after Bonnelli and Stucchi).

65. The 'Tomb of Absalom' in the Kedron Valley near Jerusalem. The lower part is carved from the rock, the upper stages only being built of masonry. The date is uncertain but perhaps early first century AD (Dr M. Meyer).

Sepolcro antichissimo in Albano detto uolgarmente de Curaty

66. The 'Tomba degli Orazi e Curiazi' near Albano, Italy (from Bartoli's *Gli Antichi Sepolchri*, Rome 1697).

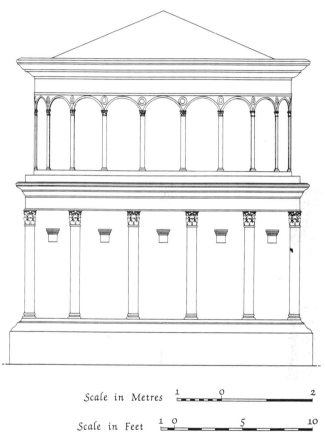

Scale in Metres

Scale in Feet

67. Destroyed Roman mausoleum at Pietrabbondante, Molise, Italy, as restored from fragments by von Sydow: probably late first century BC.

68. Late Roman mausoleum at Dana in Syria consisting of four Ionic columns supporting a canopy (from De Vogüé, *Syrie Centrale*, 1865–77).

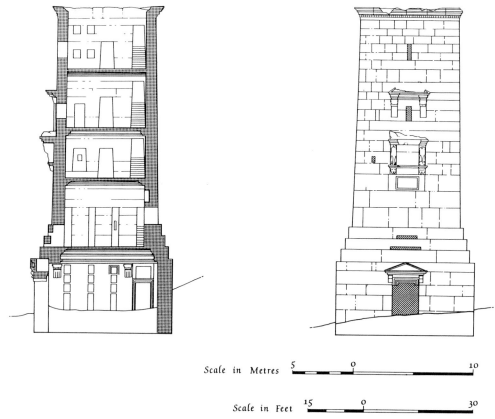

Scale in Metres

Scale in Feet

69. Palmyra, a tower-tomb (The Tower of Iamlikhō), dated AD 83 on the framed panel beneath the external niche which probably contained bas-reliefs representing the founder and his family. The five chambers contained spaces for more than 200 burials (after De Vogüé, *Syrie Centrale*, 1865–77).

an alternative to simple columns or pilasters is not often found in surviving examples of Roman funerary architecture, but one stage of the monument of the Julii at Glanum (Saint-Rémy in Provence) consists of four arched openings (fig. 48), while the upper part of a destroyed mausoleum at Pietrabbondante in Italy has been restored with a continuous blind arcade (fig. 67). When reduced to its simplest form as four columns or four arches standing at ground level and supporting a canopy (fig. 68), this type of monument closely resembles an indoor baldacchino of the kind that sheltered some pagan shrines and later many Christian ones.

Although the monuments discussed above have often been classified as 'towers', they were not towers in the normal sense of the word. The term is best reserved for the true tower-tomb that was a speciality of Palmyra (fig. 69). For two centuries the desert state of Palmyra flourished as an *entrepôt* and buffer between the two great empires of Rome and Parthia, before succumbing to the former in AD 274. Although the Palmyrenes built funerary monuments of other kinds, the tower was the most favoured form, and probably the earliest. Four, five or even six storeys high, these towers were filled with *loculi* or burial compartments, to

78

which internal stone staircases gave access. As many as 200 *loculi* were fitted into some of the large towers. The awkwardness involved in carrying corpses up narrow staircases and the fact that the Palmyrenes also built *hypogea* and temple-tombs suggest that the tower form had some special religious significance. In Palmyra's principal temple, dedicated to the solar god Bel, there were staircases to give access to the roof for ritual purposes, and it is possible that the staircases of the tower-tombs had a similar function. Unfortunately, the uppermost part of the structure is invariably too much ruined to enable any conclusion to be reached. Every tower appears originally to have been inscribed and dated precisely to day, month and year, probably for astrological reasons. The surviving inscriptions indicate that the type was established by the first century BC, and that it continued to find favour during the two succeeding centuries. As the product of a Semitic people, half oriental, half Hellenistic in culture and living on the margin of the Roman world, the Palmyrene tower-tomb had no counterpart in the western provinces of the empire and remains outside the mainstream of funerary architecture described above. The rustic *piles* of southern France are, however, tower-like in form, and a few very simple tower-tombs, dating from before the Roman conquest, have been found in Cyrenaica.

The combinations of architectural form so far discussed were more or less peculiar to funerary monuments, though also employed in designing the very similar 'trophies' or victory monuments, well-known examples of which can be seen at Adamklissi in Romania and at La Turbie in the French Alps. Other types of Roman funerary monuments, however, derive from obvious prototypes in public or religious architecture, such as temples, columns and altars.

In view of the semi-religious character of the Hellenistic *heroön*, part tomb and part temple, it is not surprising that many Roman funerary monuments took the form of temples. When Cicero wanted 'the finest memorial that Greek and Latin genius can supply' to commemorate his daughter Tullia, he made it clear that what he envisaged was a shrine or temple (*fanum*) rather than just a tomb (*sepulcrum*), so that deification (*apotheosis*) would follow. The exact form of the structure that his architect Cluatius designed is not known, but it must have had some of the attributes of a temple. It could have been a simple one-cell affair, like the one that survives at Fabara (near Saragossa) in Spain, or it might have had a projecting portico like a tomb whose foundations have been excavated in the Giambertoni cemetery at Agrigento in Sicily. In the highly finished brick mausoleum on the Via Appia at Rome formerly believed to be that of the wealthy and well-born Annia Regilla, wife of Herodes Atticus,★ a portico was apparently dispensed with, as it was probably in the similar mausoleum on the Via Nomentana known as the 'Sedia del Diavolo'; but in both buildings the temple form is implied by the raised podium and the Corinthian pilasters (fig. 70). A

★ Although the nineteenth-century identification of this mausoleum as that of Annia Regilla is no longer accepted, since she is known to have been buried in Athens, the neighbouring temple, later converted into a church under the name of S. Urbano alla Caffarella, may have been built as a sort of *heroön* in her memory by her husband (see P. Gros in *Mélanges de l'Académie française de Rome* 81, 1969).

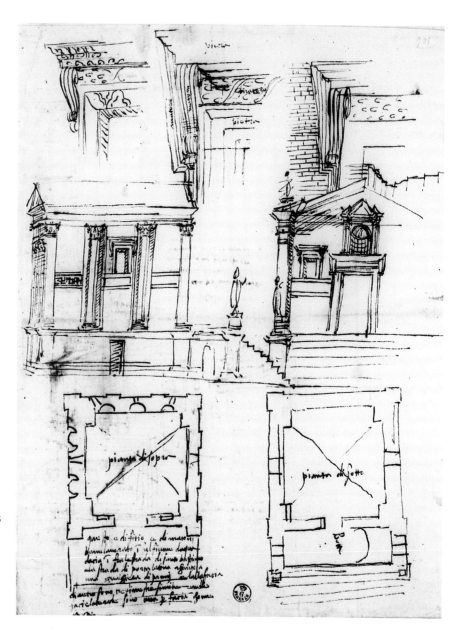

70. Mausoleum on the Via Appia, Rome, formerly known as 'the tomb of Annia Regilla', as recorded by Antonio da Sangallo in a drawing in the Uffizi, Florence (Gab. Fotografico, Soprintendenza Beni Artistici e Storici di Firenze).

mausoleum consisting of a full-size temple with an impressive portico and an order of half-columns all round the exterior is to be seen in ruins close to the shore at Side in Pamphylia (fig. 71). Like the mausoleum of the Emperor Maxentius at Rome (fig. 43), it stands in an arcaded enclosure of which the outer walls survive. The builder of this sumptuous mausoleum has not been identified, but the date is likely to be late in the second century AD. Remains of another imposing temple mausoleum of similar date exist at Patara in Lycia. Careful but partly conjectural drawings made for the Society of Dilettanti in the nineteenth century show a hexastyle portico at the entrance to a vaulted chamber containing the principal

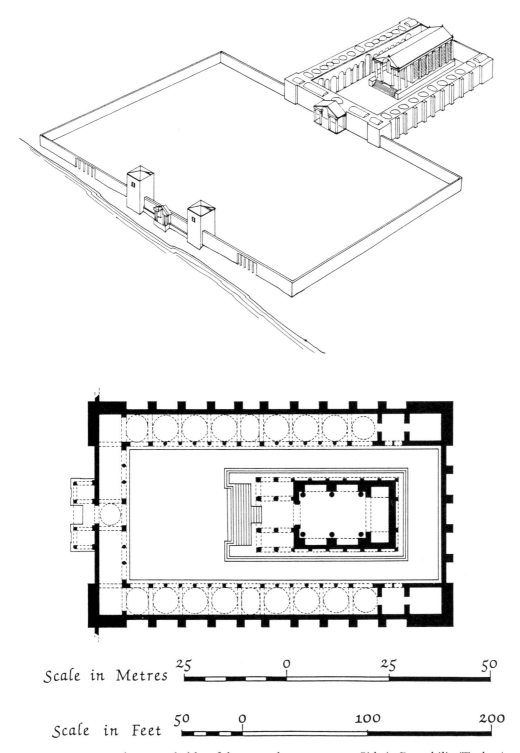

71. Roman mausoleum probably of the second century AD at Side in Pamphilia (Turkey). Substantial ruins of this temple-like mausoleum and of its arcaded courtyard remain by the sea-shore at Side (after Mansel).

72. Portico of Roman mausoleum at Patara in Lycia (Turkey), as recorded in a drawing made by F.O. Bedford for the Society of Dilettanti in 1811–13. Evidence remained for most of the principal features but the Corinthian capitals are conjectural (British Architectural Library Drawings Collection).

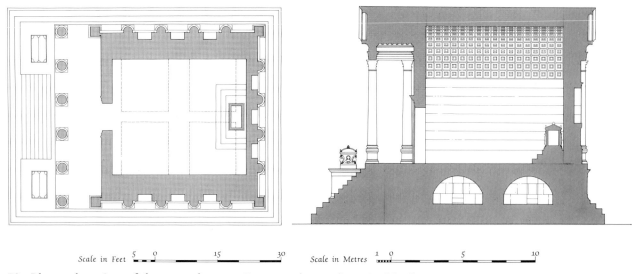

Scale in Feet   5 0   15   30   Scale in Metres 1 0   5   10

73. Plan and section of the mausoleum at Patara, redrawn from Bedford's survey.

74. Termessos, Pisidia (Turkey), mausoleum of T. Cl. Agrippina, first half of the second century AD (from Heberdey & Wilberg in *Jahreshefte des Österreichischen Archäologischen Institutes* 3, 1900).

tomb and two further sarcophagi standing in front of the portico (figs. 72–3). In a smaller mausoleum from another site in Asia Minor, the rocky cemetery of Termessos in Pisidia, the chamber has been eliminated, and the sarcophagi stand on an open platform within the peristyle of a miniature Ionic temple (fig. 74).

The type of temple represented by the Pantheon in Rome – a circular domed structure with a portico – was the inspiration of several important domed mausolea associated with the Tetrarchy and discussed above (figs. 41–3). This was one of a number of centrally planned forms that was favoured in the third century for mausolea, small temples, garden pavilions, the entrance vestibules of public baths, and other prestigious buildings. The variety of complex geometrical plans available to a rich client was remarkable, and if sixteenth-century antiquarian draughtsmen such as Pirro Ligorio, Antonio da Sangallo the younger and G.B. Montano could be trusted, the outskirts of Rome and other Italian cities were full of mausolea offering elegant and ingenious variations on the central plan (fig. 76). Unfortunately, these pioneer classical archaeologists of the Renaissance rarely distinguished between what they actually saw and what they imagined by way of restoration. The greatest caution is needed in interpreting the fantasies of Montano or the erudite speculations of Ligorio. When the plan of such a mausoleum is reconstructed on the evidence of surviving remains, it usually resolves itself into a version of one or two relatively simple forms, such as the circular domed space with alternate round and rectangular recesses, or the cruciform plan seen in figure 39 (*right*). The octagon is found at Pola and Cyrrhus, the trefoil at Sardis (fig. 77).

It was a feature of these domed mausolea that they were intended to be seen from within as well as from without. Although sometimes elegantly decorated (fig. 75), the interior spaces of most earlier mausolea were relatively small, and the architectural effect was concentrated in the exterior. The great development in vaulting that was demonstrated in the Roman baths no doubt encouraged this revolution in the design of mausolea: indeed, the mausoleum of Galerius (fig. 42)

75. Decorated interior of a Roman mausoleum of the second century AD: that of L. Valerius Felix, which formerly stood outside the Porta S. Pancrazio at Rome and was recorded by P. Santi Bartoli in 1690. Note the recesses for urns indicated in the thickness of the side walls (British Architectural Library Drawings Collection, Bartoli album, f. 2).

Sepolcro antico nella Via Appia vicino ad Albano.

76. An engraving of 'an ancient tomb on the Via Appia near Albano' from G.B. Montano's *Scielta di varii tempietti antichi* (Rome 1624), showing a typical architectural fantasy in which the surviving remains cannot be distinguished from the author's imaginary reconstruction.

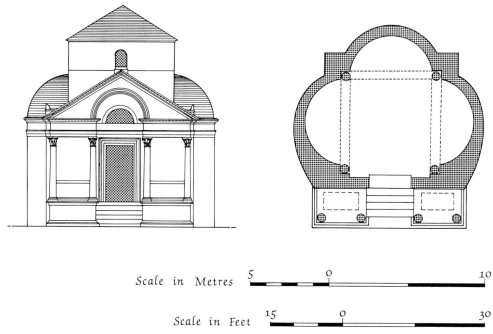

Scale in Metres

Scale in Feet

77. Trefoil-shaped mausoleum excavated at Sardis in Lydia (Turkey). The elevation is conjectural (after Butler).

has been described as 'a free-standing version of the caldarium of the Baths of Caracalla'.

Only the very rich could afford to build a mausoleum in the form of a real temple, complete with portico and *cella*. Often the monument was telescoped (fig. 78) or was just a portico with a false doorway and nothing behind it – a symbolical temple nevertheless (fig. 79). Others contented themselves with the semblance of an altar. This was very often elevated on a podium containing the burial chamber. A notable example is the tomb at Pompeii of a young magistrate, C. Vestorius Priscus. Coiled snakes carved in stone keep guard over the altar in a manner that recalls a passage in Virgil's *Aeneid* (v, 84), and the elaborate painted decoration on the podium and encircling wall includes a picture of Vestorius Priscus as a presiding judge in court. In other tombs a large sarcophagus might take the place of the altar. The so-called 'Tomb of Nero' at Rome romanticised by Piranesi belongs to this class (figs. 80–1).

Another architectural feature that was exploited for sepulchral purposes was the exedra, or recess, usually curved, but sometimes rectilinear. Exedras had many uses, from the ceremonial apse to the garden seat. At Pompeii large stone seats in the form of curved exedras were a form of memorial much favoured by the municipal oligarchy. They would presumably have provided a convenient setting for a funeral banquet. The name of the deceased could be inscribed on the back (fig. 82) or on a small column. A much grander form of exedra is represented at Pompeii by the tomb of the priestess Eumachia outside the Nocera gate, and at Athens by the well-known monument erected in AD 115 to the memory of Gaius

78. Termessos, Pisidia (Turkey), mausoleum of M. Aurelia Ge, late second century AD (from Heberdey & Wilberg in *Jahreshefte des Österreichischen Archäologischen Institutes* 3, 1900).

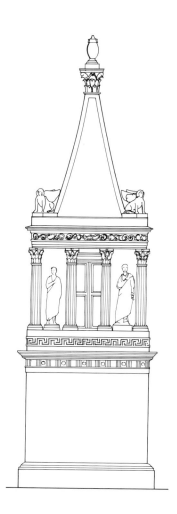

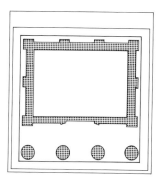

79. Sarsina, Emilia Romagna, Italy, the mausoleum of Asfionius Rufus (probably late first century BC), consisting of a portico with a false door behind raised up on a pedestal with a pyramidal roof-feature (after Finamore). A similar mausoleum, that of Lucius Poblicius, can be seen reconstructed in the Römisch-Germanisches Museum at Cologne.

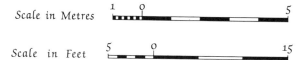

Scale in Metres   1   0   5

Scale in Feet   5   0   15

80. The 'Tomb of Nero' as represented in an engraving by G.B. Piranesi (1720–78).

81 (*left*). The sarcophagus-tomb near Rome known as the 'Tomb of Nero', but actually of Publius Vibius Marianus, governor of Sardinia in the third century AD (photograph of *c*.1870 in J.H. Parker Collection, Department of the History of Art, Oxford University).

82. Pompeii, an exedra tomb with the name of the person commemorated (a priestess of the age of Augustus named Mammia) inscribed on the back of the curved seat.

83. Pompeii, another kind of exedra tomb, with an aedicule to shelter those sitting in the semi-circular recess beside the road outside the Herculaneum Gate (from F. Mazois, *Les Ruines de Pompei*, Paris 1824–38).

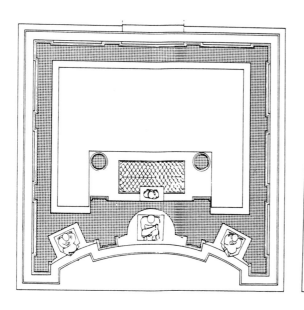

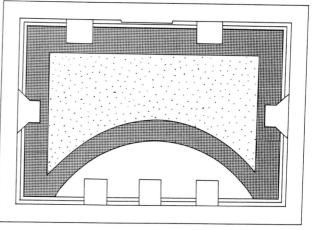

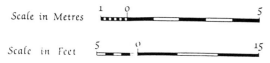

Scale in Metres

Scale in Feet

84. The Monument of Philopappos at Athens, erected in AD 115 to commemorate an exiled prince of Commagene in Asia Minor, restored plan and elevation (after Kleiner).

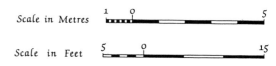

Scale in Metres

Scale in Feet

85. Base of a ruined Roman monument known as 'La Sarrasinière' at Andance in France, with features inviting comparison with the Philopappos Monument (after Burnard).

86. 'La Conocchia', a Roman mausoleum on the Via Appia at S. Maria Capua Vetere near Naples. It has lost nearly all its architectural detail, but the surviving matrix of masonry indicates a sophisticated design of interpenetrating forms.

Julius Antiochus Philopappos, an exiled prince of Commagene in Asia Minor who was a great benefactor to that city. Both the siting of the latter monument on a hill and the incorporation of seated figures of Philopappos's ancestors may have been deliberately reminiscent of the Commagene royal necropolis at Nemrud Dağ, but the concave facade, the narrative reliefs and the hint in the superstructure of the tripartite form of a triumphal arch all derive from Roman architectural traditions (fig. 84). At Rome there was a comparable monument on the Via Appia

91

to a military commander of the first century BC, possibly Publius Ventidius, who won a notable victory over the Parthians in 39 BC, and the remains of another exist at Andance on the west bank of the Rhone between Valence and Vienne (fig. 85).

Both these monuments were intended to be seen from the front only. For a piece of street architecture like the one on the Via Appia this was natural enough. But the Philopappos monument stands all on its own on Mouseion Hill with its curved front beamed on the Parthenon like a radar dish. Much more successfully three-dimensional are two Campanian mausolea. In one, at Pozzuoli, a heptagonal domed superstructure stands over and contrasts with a curved recess. The other, known as 'La Conocchia' (the distaff), stands close to the Via Appia at S. Maria Capua Vetere (fig. 86). Its date is disputed, the archaeological favouring one as early as the first century BC because of the use of *opus incertum* (a kind of random rubble) for much of its masonry, the art-historical preferring one as late as the second or even the third century AD because of its 'baroque tendencies'. Like so many baroque designs, its architectural form is capable of being read in more than one way. Is it basically a tower with four columnar extrusions, is it four exedrae conjoined, or is it a plastic *tetrakionion* or group of four columns? It hardly matters, for the masterly interplay of forms makes it one of the most sophisticated and aesthetically satisfying of Roman mausolea.

Another outstanding design of equal distinction is illustrated in figure 87. It is a reconstruction based on the remains of a monument excavated at a necropolis near Siga in modern Algeria. Siga was the capital of the Maesaesylii, a Numidian people who were ultimately conquered by Rome in the middle of the first century BC. If this monument commemorates one of their princes, it must be of earlier date, and may, like the better-known but architecturally less distinguished monument at Dougga (fig. 64), have been the work of a native Numidian architect exposed to Hellenistic influence. At Siga the basic form is that of a tripod. Three concave faces are conjoined and surmounted by a three-sided pyramid to form a composition worthy of a Borromini or a Vittone. Other monuments derived from the tripod plan, varying in date from the second century BC to the second century AD, are recorded from pre-Roman Sabratha in Tripolitania, from Aquileja, Bolsena and Cosa in Italy, and from Miletus in Asia Minor.

A further architectural feature that offered itself for adaptation as a memorial to the dead was the free-standing column. Small inscribed Doric columns, sometimes surmounted by urns, formed part of the repertoire of Greek funerary architecture (fig. 14). Larger ones, usually supporting statues, stood in public places to commemorate victories or victorious individuals. Notable examples of these were Diocletian's Column ('Pompey's Pillar') at Alexandria, and those of Trajan, Antoninus Pius and Marcus Aurelius at Rome. Of these, only that of Trajan served also as the repository of the ashes of the emperor whose victories it commemorated. It is clear that even if the column may originally have been conceived without either burial chamber in the base or staircase to the top, both were incorporated in the structure as it was built in Trajan's lifetime.

87. Mausoleum probably of the second century BC from a Numidian royal cemetery excavated at Siga in Algeria: porcelain model by Hugh Colvin following archaeological reconstruction by Rakob.

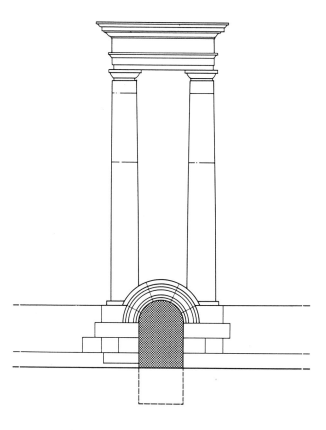

88. Columnar monument at Quatura (Khatoura) in Syria to the memory of Æmilius Reginus, a young Roman staff-officer who died in AD 195 (after Garcia Bellida & Menendez Pidal).

Scale in Metres

Scale in Feet

Hadrian must therefore have been fulfilling his predecessor's wishes when in AD 117, in a funeral ceremony that was also a posthumous triumph, he placed the golden urn containing the latter's ashes in the chamber. Not only was the use of a column in this way unusual, it stood within the *pomerium* or sacred area within which no burials were normally permitted. But the rule was easily waived in favour of the man who had died in the hour of victory against the Parthians, who in his lifetime had already been hailed by the senate as *pater patriae* and *optimus princeps*, and who in death was a symbol of the Roman empire in its finest hour.

In the third century BC a new version of the column monument appeared in the form of two columns sharing a plinth and joined at the top by an architrave. A number of these, all of the Ionic order, were set up at Delphi, and in later centuries bi-columnar monuments were to be found throughout the Roman empire. Not all of them are funerary: at Brindisi a pair of giant Corinthian columns on the quayside marked the end of the Via Appia and the point of embarkation for Greece and Asia Minor. Several dated examples from Syria were

Metres 1 0   5   10   Feet 5 0   15   30

89. A large columnar Roman monument of which the lower part survives as the belfry of a church at Zalamea de la Serena in Spain (after Garcia Bellida & Menendez Pidal). *Right*, restored elevation.

recorded in the nineteenth century by the pioneer French archaeologist De Vogüé: one, in memory of a young soldier and member of the governor's staff called Æmilius Reginus, stands astride the entrance to his tomb. The order, appropriately, is Doric (fig. 88). The only bi-columnar monument at present known from western Europe is an unusually large one that survives picturesquely as the belfry of a church at Zalamea de la Serena in the province of Badajoz in Spain (fig. 89). Although commercial links could account for the presence in Spain of a monument whose known parallels are all in the eastern Mediterranean, there may have been other examples in the west that have fallen victim to earthquake or stone-robbing.

Cylinder, pyramid, temple, tripod, exedra, column . . . How did the builder of a funerary monument choose between these alternatives? Like Pompey, who ordered plans and drawings to be made of a theatre he admired at Mytilene in order to build one like it at Rome, he might take as a model an existing monument that he liked, possibly (if he were a travelled man) in some distant city of Greece or Asia Minor.★ More often, no doubt, his social standing would suggest a type appropriate to his station in life: for a great Augustan aristocrat a huge cylindrical tomb, at once imitative of the emperor's own mausoleum and reminiscent of those tumuli in which the heroes of the past were everywhere buried; for a landed proprietor of equestrian rank a large monument of two or more stages, culminating in a columned feature which might display family statues; for a magistrate of Pompeii a semi-circular stone bench, nicely carved with his name and dignity; for a professional secretary or administrator in the imperial civil service in Rome a substantial brick structure with a modest facade and an attractively painted and stuccoed interior; for a tradesman or craftsman a simple pedimented brick box standing in a row with many others in a cemetery such as that at Isola Sacra near Ostia.

In many cases the stylistic initiative would come from the architect or mason. No client would have prescribed anything as sophisticated as 'La Conocchia' or as carefully worked out in its geometry as the 'Doğu' mausoleum at Side in Pamphylia (fig. 90). Occasionally, a very rich man would insist on a pretentious display that broke away from the normal conventions of his class. Outside the Porta Maggiore at Rome there still stands the egregious monument of M. Vergilius Eurysaces, a great baking-contractor of the late first century BC (fig. 91). The body of the tomb is made up of large stone cylinders representing stylised grain measures or storage vessels, some stacked vertically, others horizontally. Round the top there is a frieze showing the successive stages of breadmaking. On three sides large letters proclaim that 'This is the monument of Marcus Vergilius Eurysaces the contract baker' (EST HOC MONIMENTUM MARCEI VERGILEI EURYSACIS PISTORIS REDEMPTORIS). In 1848 the tomb of the Haterii, a family of building-contractors, was discovered on the Via Labicana. What remains of it is now in the Vatican Museum. One relief shows the tomb itself, a portico'd temple in form, covered with busts, swags, putti and ornamental reliefs, and to one side a great wooden crane, complete with ropes, pulleys and the tread-wheel that provided its motive power (fig. 92). The Haterii were responsible for erecting some of the great public buildings of imperial Rome in the time of Domitian (AD 81–96), and another relief shows some of the structures for which they were the contractors,

---

★ An actual instance is recorded in the *Digest of Justinian* (xxxv, 2.27). A man provided in his will that his heirs should erect a monument like that of Publius Septimius Demetrius in the Via Salaria at Rome; if they failed, they would be liable to a substantial fine. When no monument bearing precisely that name could be found, the heirs sought the guidance of a court of law, which laid down that they must identify the monument the testator had in mind, or else erect a monument 'appropriate to the wealth and standing' of the deceased.

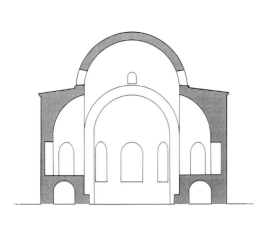

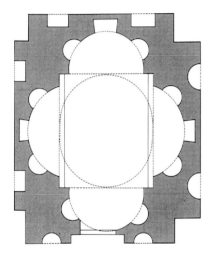

Scale in Metres

Scale in Feet

90. Side, Pamphilia (Turkey), the Doğu mausoleum (after Mansel).

91. Rome, the pretentious monument of M. Vergilius Eurysaces, a wealthy baker of the late first century BC. The cylindrical forms represent grain measures or storage vessels used in Eurysaces' trade, and breadmaking is represented in the sculptured frieze (nineteenth-century photograph in J.H. Parker Collection, Department of the History of Art, Oxford University).

including the Colosseum, a Corinthian temple (probably that of Jupiter Stator) and two triumphal arches. The tomb itself appears never to have been completed in the form shown in the relief, possibly for financial reasons, but equally likely because the assassination of Domitian supervened, and the Haterii thought it inexpedient to advertise their connection with the works of that tyrannical and detested emperor.

As self-made men, both probably ex-slaves, M. Vergilius Eurysaces and Q. Haterius Tychicus had their literary counterpart in the vulgarly rich merchant satirised by Petronius as Trimalchio. In maudlin mood he enumerates the features

97

92. Relief showing a mausoleum and a building-contractor's crane, from the tomb of the Haterii in the Vatican Museum, Rome.

he wants incorporated in his monument: a statue of himself accompanied by his little dog, another of his wife with a dove, a broken urn with a boy weeping on it, and in the middle a sundial, a standard symbol of the transitoriness of human life which appealed to Trimalchio because anyone looking at the time would read his name, 'whether he likes it or not'. The sources of his wealth were to be indicated by representations of ships in full sail and of big wine jars sealed with gypsum. The whole was to stand on a plot 100 feet wide and 200 feet deep, planted with fruit and vines, and there was to be a caretaker to look after it. Its execution was to be entrusted not to an architect, but to a monumental mason who belonged to the same association of freedmen as Trimalchio himself.

As far as it can be envisaged, Trimalchio's tomb, however tasteless, would have been fairly conventional. But in the museum at Trier in Germany there is a monument to a Moselle wine merchant, found in the neighbouring town of Neumagen (Noviomagus), that rivals that of the Roman baker. Essentially an altar-tomb, it incorporates stone models of two wine ships, complete with their

93. Monument to a Roman wine merchant found at Neumagen, Germany, and now in the museum at Trier. The tomb is surmounted by a stone model of Moselle river-boats laden with casks of wine (Landesmuseum, Trier).

crews and piled high with casks of wine (fig. 93). Between them is a pyramid of enormous amphorae. Even Petronius can hardly have imagined such a literal interpretation of Trimalchio's desire to have ships and wine jars included in the decoration of his tomb.

In the present state of knowledge about Roman funerary architecture the number of equations that can be made between social status and architectural form is very limited. Although thousands of monumental inscriptions survive, many of them are fragments detached from their settings on tombs long since destroyed, and even when the cost of the monument is recorded (as it sometimes is), as well as the name and status of the person commemorated, the architectural result of the outlay is all too often no longer extant. Nor can the style or handiwork of individual architects or sculptors often be identified. Typological analysis can suggest influences and outline developments in very general terms, but it cannot go far in arranging these protean structures in historically or architecturally meaningful sequences; nor is it probable that it ever will, for architects, workmen and their patrons went back and forth across the Mediterranean carrying visual images with them and weaving a complex web of architectural forms which is unlikely ever to be satisfactorily unravelled. Occasionally a single thread can be traced: such, for instance, as that which seems to lead from Syria, by way of northern Italy, to the Rhineland, where a group of monuments is found with ornamentation of a kind more characteristic of the orient than of

94. *Stele* or tombstone of a British woman called Regina whose husband was a man from Palmyra called Barates. They were living at the fort of Arbeia at the east end of Hadrian's wall in the second half of the second century AD. The architectural frame takes a baroque form that is characteristically Palmyrene (South Shields Museum, Tyne & Wear Museums Service).

Gallia Belgica (fig. 49). Here the original customers were probably Roman legionaries, some of whom may have served in Rome's Asian provinces, but only someone trained in the complex geometry of Syrian architectural decoration could actually have designed the monuments at Igel or Neumagen.

Another thread, so tenuous as probably to represent a single craftsman, links Palmyra and the fort of Arbeia at the east end of Hadrian's Wall in modern County Durham. An architectural stele (now in the museum at South Shields) bears the name of Regina, a British freedwoman married to one Barates of Palmyra and living at Arbeia in the second half of the second century AD (fig. 94). The pedimented niche with the arch rising up into it is characteristically Syrian or Palymrene, and a second stele (to a Mauretanian freedman called Victor), showing figures reclining in Palmyrene fashion, makes it clear that there must have been at least one mason from Palymra at this remote fort whose cosmopolitan garrison included a contingent of Euphrates boatmen. Elsewhere there must have been many architect-sculptors like those Cossutii whose Latin signature, inscribed in Greek on half-a-dozen of their surviving works (none of them, as it happens, a funerary monument) shows us how Hellenised Romans as well as Romanised Hellenes placed Greek refinement and Greek invention at the disposal of Roman patrons.

VI

FROM MAUSOLEUM TO
MARTYRIUM

THE CHANGE FROM A PAGAN to a Christian empire was a long-drawn-out process. In the first and second centuries AD Christianity was only one of several new cults of oriental origin, but a particularly disturbing one because of its uncompromising refusal to make even token sacrifices to an emperor whose divinity it could not accept. In the third century it was a religious phenomenon to be reckoned with; in the fourth, a major divisive force. By 400 the emperors themselves were wholly committed to the new faith. By 500 pagans were a dwindling minority; by 600, an almost extinct species except on the fringes of an empire that had lost not only its ancient gods but its political and geographical unity as well.

The religious regime of the Roman empire had been among the most undoctrinaire the world has ever known. Christianity on the other hand was an exclusive religion that neither recognised any other faith, nor permitted any local or personal deviation from a single body of doctrine that was intended to be of universal validity. Some minor variations of observance were, of course, inevitable, but any serious divergence in theological belief was liable to be denounced as heresy. So far as death and the after-life were concerned, Christianity introduced a new and radical idea: that of salvation. To the pagan, the after-life was at best a shadowy affair, a postscript to the real life on earth. But for the Christian, life on earth was merely the prelude to an after-life infinitely richer and (for those who deserved it) more rewarding than anything human life could offer. What is more, Christians believed in the resurrection of the body – something that had no place in pagan eschatology. Death for Christians meant the temporary separation of body and soul, ultimately to be reunited at the Last Judgement. What happened to the soul in the meantime was a matter for theological debate, but on one point all were agreed: martyrs were privileged to go straight to Heaven, there to await the Second Coming and the General Resurrection.

These beliefs affected funeral custom. If the body was to be reanimated at the Resurrection then it must be wrong deliberately to destroy it by fire. So the practice of cremation, prevalent throughout the Ancient World, but never universally adopted, was finally abandoned. Only in the barbarian north was the funeral pyre still to be seen, and even there it tended to flicker out long before it was finally extinguished by Christian missionaries. In other respects, however,

95. Pyramidal mausoleum of the fifth century AD at Il–Bârah in Syria. One of several mausolea of this form built by Syrian Christians (Butler Archive, Department of Art & Archaeology, Princeton University).

Christian burial did not differ markedly from pagan. Christians continued to inter their dead in the suburbs, at first alongside their pagan fellow citizens, later in separate cemeteries. The pagan commemoration feast continued as the *refrigerium* or memorial banquet, and was sometimes attended with the same unseemly conduct. For those who could afford them the masons turned out the same stone or marble sarcophagi with suitably varied iconography, while mausolea continued to be commissioned by those of greater wealth and standing.

Architecturally, a Christian mausoleum is often indistinguishable from a pagan one. Only a Chi-Rho monogram or some other carved or painted symbol shows that it was built for a Christian rather than for a pagan burial. In Syria Christians continued to build massive mausolea with pyramidal roofs that differ only in detail from those of two centuries earlier (fig. 95). There and in North Africa such established forms of funerary architecture as the miniature temple or the vaulted stone box with symmetrical recesses inside persisted into the fifth and sixth centuries. At Tipasa in Mauretania there was even a large circular Christian mausoleum whose exterior, decorated with half-columns, obviously recalled that of the nearby pagan monument now misleadingly known as the 'Tombeau de la Chrétienne' (fig. 22), though it was in every other respect quite different, for the interior was an unroofed space, with a ring of tomb recesses round the perimeter (fig. 96). The influence of the 'Tombeau de la Chrétienne' is also apparent in

102

another Mauretanian mausoleum, at Blad Guitoun (near the modern Ménerville), of uncertain date, but built some time between the fourth and sixth centuries and decorated with Christian symbols. Although the plan is octagonal, the small central chamber, the circular corridor, the engaged Ionic order, the false door-ways, and other features, all recall the pagan monument (fig. 97).

Elsewhere Christian mausolea were often built in the form of circular or octagonal structures such as had long been in use for funerary purposes. The Christian emperors themselves favoured the same great vaulted rotundas as their pagan predecessors. Christians might worship a new god and adopt a new code of morals, but they had not renounced the Roman culture in which they had been brought up, and if they needed to assert their faith in their funerary monuments, they did so by commissioning appropriate painting and sculpture rather than by any sudden change in architectural form. Indeed, they treated their martyrs much as their ancestors had treated the heroes of old, by enshrining them in a mausoleum and establishing a cult in their honour. There was, however, an important difference between the cult of a hero and the worship of a martyred saint. The pagan hero was honoured by sacrifices, but his mortal remains were kept decently out of sight. It was, of course, understandable that Christians

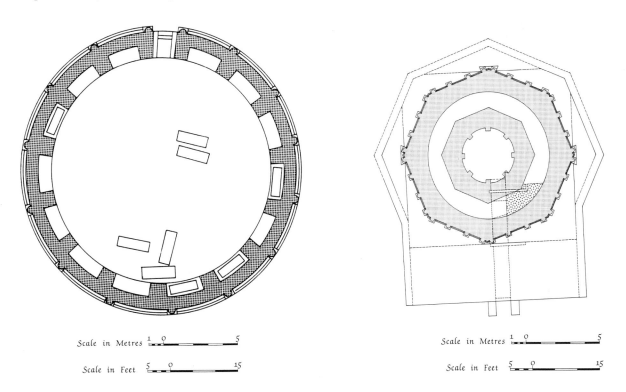

Scale in Metres   1   0   5

Scale in Feet   5   0   15

Scale in Metres   1   0   5

Scale in Feet   5   0   15

96 (*above left*). Christian mausoleum of the fourth century AD in the West Cemetery at Tipasa, Mauretania (Algeria). The exterior of this circular unroofed burial enclosure recalled the great pagan mausolea illustrated in figures 21–2. Only the lower parts of the structure survive (after Gsell).

97 (*above right*). Blad Guitoun, Mauretania (near Menérville, Algeria), plan of a Christian mausoleum of the fourth to sixth centuries following established pagan precedents. The entrance passage is shown in broken lines (after Gsell).

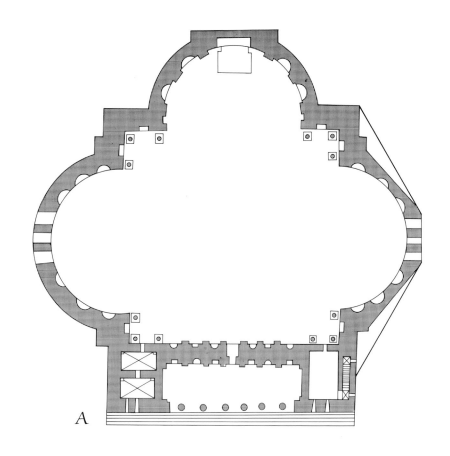

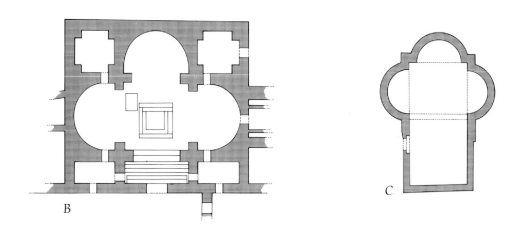

98. The trefoil plan in Roman and Early Christian funerary architecture. A. A pagan mausoleum or *columbarium* on the Via Cassia near Rome recorded by Pirro Ligorio in the sixteenth century (after Bodleian Library, MS. Canonici Ital. 138, f. 9). B. *Martyrium* attached to Early Christian church at Tébessa, Algeria (after Duval & Cintas). C. Early Christian chapel from the Catacomb of St Callistus, Rome (after Zovatto).

should wish to give proper burial to the tortured or mutilated bodies of their co-religionists, but their desire for access to their place of burial, even for physical contact with their relics, was something new. To a non-Christian it was repellent, for dead bodies (however prestigious) were a source of pollution. For the Christian, however, they were a source of spiritual power, a point of contact with a saintly protector. For ordinary sinful mortals needed the support of a heavenly patron as surely as they needed that of an earthly one. The martyr's privilege of direct access to God gave him that status and encouraged the belief that his intercession would be effective. Although his spirit was in Heaven, his body was still on earth, and constituted a means of access to his influence, even (in emergencies) a source of miraculous intervention. To possess the body of a saint was to have a monopoly of his good offices in this world and the next; to possess even a fragment of his mortal remains was to acquire a share in his spiritual capital. In theory, Christians worshipped only one God (triune though he might be), but in practice, martyred saints provided a substitute for the innumerable local divinities of Antiquity. Most Christian communities in the Mediterranean world had their martyr and his or her cult was a focus of devotion that sometimes supplemented, sometimes rivalled and sometimes almost superseded that of Christ himself.

The tomb of a martyr was, therefore, nearly always a point of religious growth and as such the nucleus of an architectural complex whose development often continued for well over a thousand years. Many of the most famous edifices of Christendom had as their ultimate *raison d'être* a Christian *martyrium*, and that *martyrium* was essentially a mausoleum containing the revered body of a martyred saint. Other great churches developed round places in Palestine associated with the life and death of Christ and the Virgin Mary, and in Syria the columns upon which the stylite saints spent their lives like living statues sometimes became the focal points of major Christian cults. It was, however, to a *martyrium* that hundreds of important early Christian churches owed their existence, and in the present century their rediscovery has been one of the main achievements of Christian archaeology.

Very few surviving *martyria* can be dated to the period before the year 313, when three centuries of sporadic persecution were finally brought to an end by the Emperor Constantine. It was only when the threat of persecution was lifted that Christians could openly do homage to those who had perished for their faith. Many of the *martyria* they built took forms already well established in Roman funerary architecture – octagons, rotundas, exedras and the like. These were, of course, part of the common stock of late Roman architecture, and it is not always possible to distinguish between plans that were in general use and plans that had a specifically funerary ancestry. The trefoil or 'triconque' is a case in point. In Roman architecture it was often used for buildings both secular and religious – nymphaea, baths, dining rooms and shrines, and from the fourth century onwards it was a favourite form both for *martyria* and for private Christian mausolea (fig. 98). Only a few pagan Roman mausolea of this shape are, however, known, the principal example being from Sardis in Asia Minor (fig. 77). Given the

105

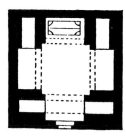

99. The 'cross-in-square' plan: a mausoleum at Hâss in Syria dated by Butler to the sixth century AD, with restored section. This type of late Roman domed mausoleum was influential in the design of Christian *martyria* and also probably in that of some Islamic tombs.

practice of holding funeral meals in *martyria*, the example of the secular *triclinium* affords as likely a model as that of the pagan mausoleum.

Another form of Christian *martyrium* that certainly had abundant pagan precedent was the 'inscribed cross', or cross-in-square, in which the entrance and three arched recesses for sarcophagi (known to archaeologists as *arcosolia*) formed symmetrical extensions of the central space (fig. 99). No symbolical significance probably attached to this neat and elegant arrangement, but when the cruciform plan is given external expression, then Christian symbolism may be suspected. Writing in about 380 from his native city in Cappadocia, Gregory of Nyssa describes a *martyrium* there whose arms were, he says, in the shape of the Cross (Migne, *Patrologia Graeca*, xlvi, 1095). Equally well rooted in the pagan past was the circular or octagonal mausoleum, but this form was also much favoured for the baptisteries which, in an age of mass conversion, were important features of Christian architecture, so much so that in some instances it is impossible to say which was the building's original purpose.

The architectural equation of baptistery and mausoleum is not so strange as it sounds, for baptism provided the passport to the Eternal Life which followed death and burial. As an early fifth-century bishop put it, a baptistery was a place where a man 'dies to things earthly and is born to things eternal'. This was clearly in the mind of the wealthy Christian politician Flavius Rufinus when (in about 394) he built himself a private *martyrium*-cum-mausoleum at Chalcedon on the shores of the Bosporus and had himself baptised on the day of its dedication. So baptism and burial were linked symbolically in a way that made it quite appropriate for a common architectural form to serve for both. The key building here is

106

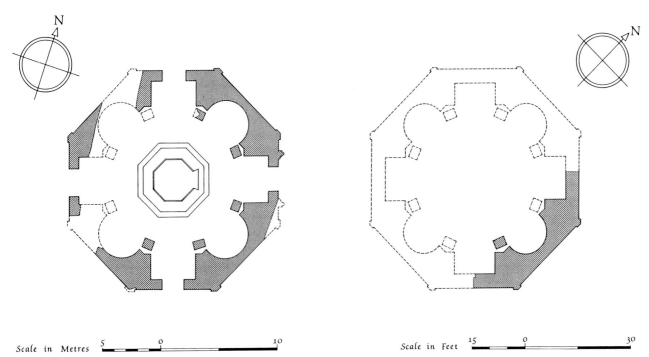

Scale in Metres 5 0 10   Scale in Feet 15 0 30

100. Baptistery and mausoleum. *Right*, plan of fourth-century mausoleum partially excavated at S. Vittore, Milan. *Left*, fourth-century baptistery built by St Ambrose at S. Tecla, Milan, as excavated in 1943. The position of the entrance to the former is not known (after Roberti).

the baptistery built by St Ambrose (d. 397) close to his cathedral church of St Tecla in Milan. This was demonstrably copied from an important mausoleum that had recently been constructed outside the same city, whose form and dimensions it followed exactly (fig. 100). The symbolic association between baptism and burial, baptistery and tomb, is alluded to in the inscription, attributed to St Ambrose himself, in which the octagonal shape is given further Christian significance by reference to the 'eighth day' on which Christ was resurrected.★ There was no more prestigious church in northern Italy than that of St Ambrose, and its influence ensured that the octagonal form of the late Roman mausoleum was transferred to a whole constellation of baptisteries in Lombardy and beyond.

An octagon is also the basic form of the building illustrated in figure 101, whose compulsive geometry is more easily intelligible than the function of the resulting spaces. This is the *martyrium* at Hierapolis in Phrygia, dating probably from the early fifth century and associated with the name of St Philip (probably the 'Evangelist' of that name rather than the Apostle). The focus of the cult was presumably in the central domed space, and the small rectangular chambers that define the outer square may have provided accommodation for pilgrims and others.

★ So called because the Resurrection took place on the day after the Sabbath, which is the seventh day of the week.

107

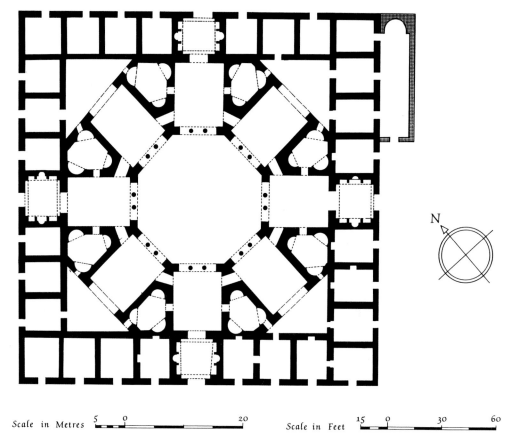

Scale in Metres 5 0   20   Scale in Feet 15 0   30   60

101. *Martyrium* at Hierapolis in Phrygia (Turkey), built probably in the early fifth century
(after Verzone). The plan is of a type that derives from the 'Golden House' of Nero in
Rome (mid-first century AD).

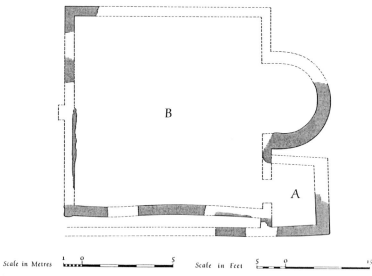

Scale in Metres 1 0   5   Scale in Feet 5 0   15

102. *Memoria* and church of La Madeleine excavated at Geneva. The rectangular *memoria*
(A) was built in the fifth century, the slightly later church (B) being the first of five to
occupy the site (after Bonnet).

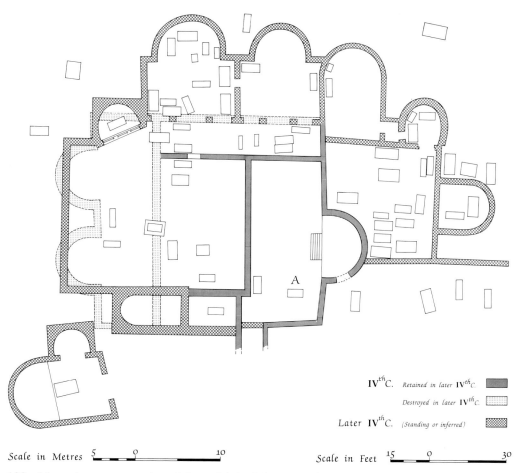

IVthC.	Retained in later IVthC.	▨
	Destroyed in later IVthC.	☐
Later IVthC.	(Standing or inferred)	▨

Scale in Metres 5 ⸻ 0 ⸻ 10   Scale in Feet 15 ⸻ 0 ⸻ 30

103. *Martyrium* excavated at Manastirini, Salona, Dalmatia (Yugoslavia). This Early Christian church grew up round a martyr's tomb (A) in what was originally an unroofed burial enclosure. The plan shows the accumulation of apsidal burial chapels by the early fifth century, when the whole building was demolished to make way for a larger church on the site (after Egger, *Forschungen in Salona*, 2, 1926).

North of the Alps *martyria* and *memoriae*★ tended to be architecturally less sophisticated: they were generally simple rectangular structures just large enough to allow commemorative ceremonies to be held in the immediate vicinity of the tomb. One recently excavated at Geneva may serve to illustrate the type (fig. 102). But whatever their form, the prestige of the martyrs or relics that they enshrined tended to attract other burials. In death the faithful crowded round the bodies of the martyrs in order to gain the protection of their sanctity. Burial *ad sanctos* became the aspiration of every fervent Christian, and partly to facilitate the cult of the martyr or holy man, partly to accommodate these extra interments,

★ A *martyrium* was, by definition, the tomb of a martyr, an *apostoleion* that of an Apostle. *Memoria* was a less precise word which could embrace any kind of funerary monument, including *martyria*, but which often indicated a less prestigious shrine for relics, or even a private burial place.

what had begun as small centres of devotion sometimes grew into huge churches. An early example of an expanding *martyrium* is shown in figure 103.

Meanwhile, at Rome the emperor himself was giving his mind to the architectural implications of Christianity. Temples did not convert easily into churches: besides, pagan worship was not to be officially outlawed for many years, and many temples remained in use for the time being. So a new monumental architecture was needed to serve the new religion, and Constantine set in motion an extensive programme of church-building. The result was a series of great basilicas, aisled halls with timber roofs, clerestory lighting and apsidal ends, which were to serve as a pattern for Christian church-building for over a thousand years. The origin of the Christian basilica is a problem that need not concern us here. The word 'basilica' could be used by contemporaries for buildings of widely different shapes and purposes, not excluding the funerary, but in the great audience halls of the imperial palaces it took a form that may well have provided the inspiration for Constantine's churches. Some of these (notably the Lateran basilica) were inside the city, but most of them were outside. For their function was to serve the rites of the dead as much as those of the living. For regular masses, people resorted to the churches within the walls. Although on occasion the new basilicas without the walls might be used for the same purpose, they were designed primarily for funerary occasions, in particular for the lavish funeral feasts that filled their interiors with guests and with the poor who were fed as an act of charity. In Rome they were usually sited over the catacombs★ in which the Christian population had been buried for the last two centuries, and in each case the basilica was associated with the adjacent tomb of a martyr, which provided the dedication to St Agnes, St Lawrence, St Marcellinus or St Sebastian. At St Peter's the shrine of the Apostle was accommodated within the church, where, sheltered by a baldacchino of twisted columns, it formed an object of veneration for pilgrims. On the festivals of their patronal martyrs these vast, simple, wooden-roofed buildings were thronged with devotees from far and near and with the sick and destitute seeking relief. Throughout the fourth and most of the fifth century they continued to serve as the foci for Christian burial. Their floors were literally paved with tombstones, while mausolea attached themselves like limpets to their walls (fig. 104).

The example set by Constantine at Rome was followed by other Christian leaders throughout the empire. Every city of any consequence had both its cathedral church and baptistery, usually within the walls, and its funerary church without, often incorporating a *martyrium* and serving as a focus for the tombs of the Christian community. Having different functions, these two centres of religious attraction – the *ecclesia maior* or *senior* within the walls, and the basilica

★Underground cemeteries excavated in the soft tufa stone. Most of them are cramped and labyrinthine, but a few (notably one discovered in the 1950s under the Via Latina) are in effect underground mausolea designed for architectural effect and beautifully decorated with frescoes, by no means always wholly Christian in inspiration. They form a study in themselves, for which see J. Stevenson, *The Catacombs* (1978) and J. Guyon, *Le cimetière aux deux lauriers* (Ecole française de Rome, 1987).

without – were not necessarily in competition. Many bishops were themselves buried in the suburban church, and the presence of their tombs sometimes gave additional prestige to a basilica whose resident saint was only of minor repute. Thus at Reims the memory of the Roman martyr Agricola, whose relics were installed in a cemetery church founded in the fourth century by a general called Jovinus, was eventually superseded by that of a more recent martyr, the fifth-century bishop Nicasius. In the same way, at Auxerre it was the formidable St Germanus (he who came to Britain in 429 to combat a heresy and ended by routing a barbarian army) whose burial place in his private estate on the outskirts of the city eventually took precedence over the neighbouring cemetery where his predecessors were buried. For centuries the churches of Saint-Nicaise at Reims and Saint-Germain at Auxerre bore witness to the posthumous prestige of these two famous figures from the heroic age of the Gallic church, while at Tours the great pilgrimage church of Saint-Martin (destroyed in 1790) had its origin in similar circumstances.

No one could well deny the right of a bishop to be buried close to the local saint, especially if that saint was one of his predecessors in office. But it was the hope of every early Christian to be buried, not just in consecrated ground, but in the same church or cemetery as a saint or martyr. Even the vast cemetery churches could not hold them all. Death may be the great leveller and Christian thought may deprecate the attempt to perpetuate rank and status in the grave, but in practice the mortal remains of the great continued to be given special architectural treatment. The most striking instances of this were the great mausolea built for himself and members of his family by the first Christian emperor, Constantine (d. 337).

When he entered Rome as a victor in 312, Constantine may have intended to make the city the Christian centre of a Christian empire. However, it soon became clear that the senatorial aristocracy was resistant to the new faith, and this must have been one of the considerations that in 330 led him to move his capital to a new site – Constantinople – where there was much less need to compromise with the pagan past. At Rome much of his church-building was outside the walls, and it was as an annexe to the suburban cemetery church of SS. Marcellinus and Petrus that he built the circular domed mausoleum that he probably intended for himself and his family (fig. 105). In the event, his mother Helena was its only occupant, and when her son died in 337 he was buried in Constantinople. Whether it was he or his son Constantius who built the family mausoleum attached the church of the Holy Apostles in that city is uncertain. There is an early, but far from clear description of it in the Life of Constantine attributed to Eusebius. According to this, church and mausoleum were combined in a single building in which the imperial sarcophagus not only stood next to the altar, but was surrounded by twelve *stelai* (monuments of uncertain form) commemorating the twelve Apostles. If correctly described, this unprecedented arrangement may be seen as an attempt to cope with an unprecedented situation: the Christian burial of a Roman emperor who, but for his conversion, would himself have ranked as a divinity. The intention was evidently to place the emperor's sarcophagus in the

111

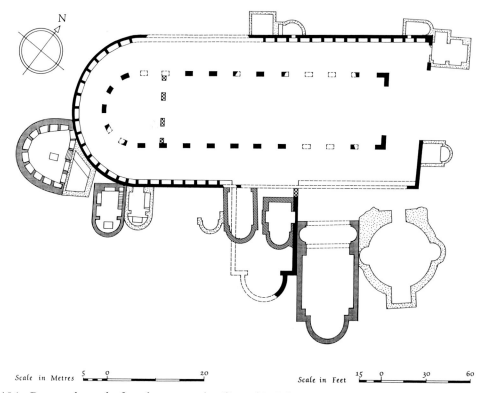

Scale in Metres

Scale in Feet

104. Rome, the early fourth–century basilica of S. Sebastiano, as excavated (after Tolotti). The hatching of the subsidiary chapels is designed to distinguish them from one another and not to identify periods of construction.

place of honour, even perhaps to imply that, as the man responsible for converting the empire, he ranked as a thirteenth Apostle. However the text is interpreted (and its authenticity is not unquestioned), either the writer was mistaken or the arrangement he described had been superseded by the end of the fourth century. For by then the imperial sarcophagus was housed in a mausoleum adjoining the church. It was a circular domed mausoleum★ of the traditional imperial form and appears to have stood in much the same relationship to the church of the Apostles as the one Constantine had built in Rome did to the basilica of SS. Marcellinus and Petrus. It remained in use as the principal burial place of the East Roman emperors up to the time of Justinian, who, finding it full, built a new mausoleum of cruciform shape for himself and his successors. Both, together with the church, were destroyed by the Turks after their conquest of the city in the fifteenth century.

★A reference in a description written in about 1200 to 'columned angles' may, however, suggest a polygonal interior with columns at the angles. The exterior was certainly circular. For an ingenious interpretation of Eusebius's description which places busts of the twelve Apostles in roundels above columns standing between the recesses in the polygonal interior of a circular mausoleum, see the article by Nordenfalk cited in the bibliography.

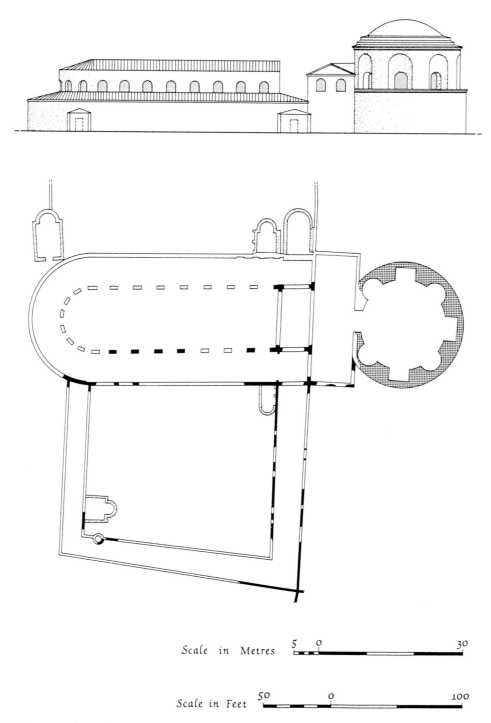

Scale in Metres 5 0 30

Scale in Feet 50 0 100

105. Rome, the early fourth-century basilica of SS. Marcellinus and Petrus, with the imperial mausoleum in which St Helena, the mother of the Emperor Constantine, was buried after her death in *c*.330. The site has not been fully excavated, and more subsidiary chapels probably flanked the main church (after Deichmann, 1957 and Guyon et al., 1981).

106. The interior of the mausoleum of Constantine's daughters Constantia and Helena, now S. Costanza, Rome. The principal features of the decoration of the central space are shown as recorded before their destruction in 1620. The two recesses to right and left may have been designed to contain the sarcophagi of the two sisters.

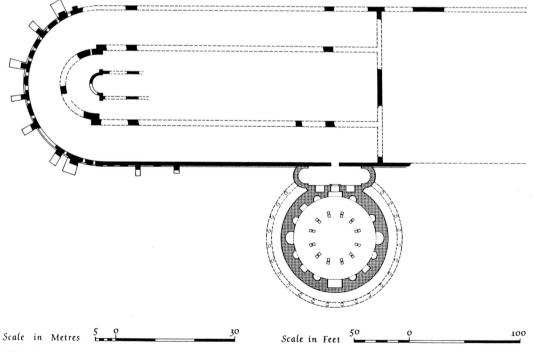

Scale in Metres   5   0   30   Scale in Feet   50   0   100

107. Rome, the ruins of the early fourth-century basilica of S. Agnese, with, on its south side, the surviving imperial mausoleum in which Constantine's daughters Constantia and Helena were buried, now known as S. Costanza (after Deichmann, 1957).

Meanwhile, in Rome the series of domed imperial mausolea was continued. One, now known as S. Costanza, was attached to the basilica of St Agnes on the Via Nomentana. Unlike the mausoleum of Helena, it stood on one side of its parent basilica instead of at the end (fig. 107). In this respect it resembled many other mausolea that clung to the sides of cemetery churches in Rome and elsewhere. In plan, however, it was unusual in having both an external colonnade (of which only the circular basement wall survives) and an inner ring of paired columns supporting the dome. These columns are topped by reused Composite capitals, and they define a well-lit central space surrounded by an annular aisle or corridor (fig. 106). The building resembles several early baptisteries, including that of the Lateran as remodelled in the fifth century, and a passage in the early sixth-century *Liber Pontificalis* (a collection of biographies of the early popes, with details of their works) suggests that it was built by Constantine as a baptistery at the request of his daughter Constantia or Constantina. According to other early sources, however, it was built as a mausoleum, and both Constantia, who died in 354, and her sister Helena, who died in 360, were certainly buried in it. The walls are hollowed into recesses, two of the largest of which, facing one another in the east and west walls, may have been designed to contain the sarcophagi of the two sisters rather than the rectangular one opposite the entrance in which there formerly stood the magnificent porphyry sarcophagus that is displayed in the Vatican Museum as that of Constantia. The surviving mosaic decoration of the aisle (considerably but tactfully restored in 1836–43) consists largely of exquisite formal patterns quite innocent of religious significance, while that of the cupola, unhappily destroyed in the seventeenth century, exhibited Christian subjects of a kind that did not speak unequivocally either of baptism or of burial. It is probable that the building was designed as a mausoleum and that if it was ever used as a baptistery, that must have been at a later date (probably in the early sixth century). For many centuries it certainly served as a mausoleum, and today it ranks with Diocletian's mausoleum at Split as an outstanding example of its kind which can be experienced in three dimensions and not just as a plan in an archaeological report.

Among the many mausolea that surrounded the basilica of St Peter in Rome, the two largest were circular rotundas of the same type as that of St Helena. They stood side by side immediately to the south of the basilica, one attached to the end of the great western transept, the other close by (fig. 108). The former, later known as S. Petronilla, was destroyed in 1514–19 to clear the site for the baroque St Peter's; the latter, called S. Andrea, or S. Maria della Febbre, from a thaumaturgic image it contained, survived until the eighteenth century, when it made way for a new sacristy. S. Maria della Febbre is dated to the early third century by brick stamps found when part of its foundations were excavated in 1957–8. Its site had once formed part of the Circus of Gaius, of which the obelisk that stood beside it (and which now stands in front of St Peter's) was a feature, and as the circus (though by then disused) would still have been imperial property in the third century, the mausoleum was presumably built by a member of the imperial family. Early in the sixth century, however, it was appropriated as a chapel by

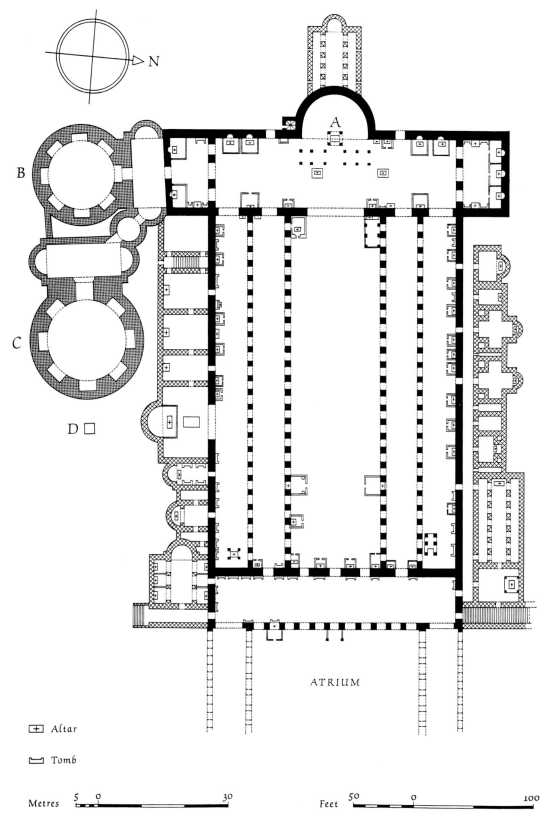

N

B

C

D □

A

ATRIUM

⊞ Altar

⊏⊐ Tomb

Metres 5 0   30   Feet 50   0   100

108. Old St Peter's, Rome, based on the engraved plan published by Alfarano in 1590. The basilica of Constantine (begun *c*.333) is shown in solid black. The two imperial mausolea (stippled) are as recorded in a sixteenth-century MS in the Uffizi, Florence. Other mausolea and chapels are hatched. A. Shrine of St Peter. B. Imperial Mausoleum (later S. Petronilla). C. Imperial Mausoleum (later S. Maria della Febbre). D. Obelisk.

109. Old St Peter's, Rome. The former mausoleum (S. Maria della Febbre) as painted by Pieter Sanredam in 1629 after a sixteenth-century drawing by Martin van Heemskerck. The obelisk (fig. 108, D) is seen in the foreground, and part of the mass of the new St Peter's rises in the background (National Gallery of Art, Washington, D.C.).

Pope Symmachus. The other mausoleum was in the fifth century the burial place of the Emperor Honorius (d. 423) and his family. In 757 the body of S. Petronilla (a supposed daughter of St Peter) was transferred to it from the catacombs on the Via Ardeatina, and it enjoyed some celebrity as her place of burial. It was placed under the patronage of the Frankish kings (then the allies and protectors of the papacy), and various persons of French origin were subsequently interred in it, including Agnes of Poitou, the wife of the Emperor Henry III (d. 1077). Late in the fifteenth century it was repaired at the expense of King Louis XI of France (1461–83), and it was as one of its ornaments that Michelangelo's Pietà was commissioned by a French cardinal who was buried in the chapel in 1499.

The architectural history of these two mausolea and their relationship both to one another and to St Peter's is complicated and controversial. At first sight the way in which S. Petronilla obstructed the entrance to S. Maria della Febbre might suggest that the former was later in date than the latter. However, there is a strong case for thinking that, like S. Maria, S. Petronilla was already standing before the building of St Peter's in the fourth century, for the south wall of the south transept of the basilica was built at an angle to accommodate itself to the vestibule of the mausoleum. Futhermore, it has been argued that in the form in which they existed in the sixteenth century (when the only reasonably reliable plan was made) the upper parts of both mausolea had been rebuilt to correspond to the level of the floor of the basilica, some nine metres above that of the imperial circus. If so, it would be possible to see their relationship to the basilica of St Peter

117

110. Milan, S. Aquilino, the exterior of the mausoleum, showing the gallery.

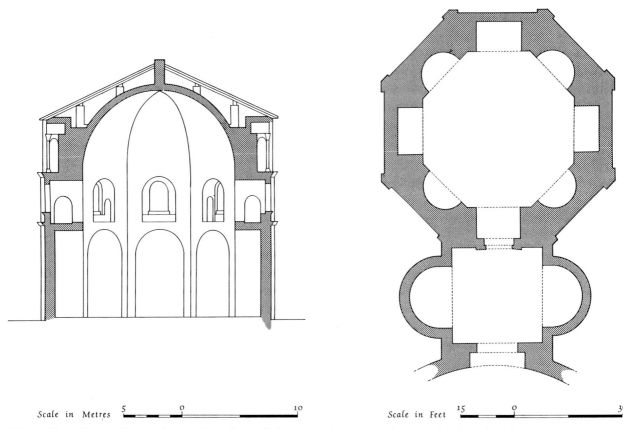

Scale in Metres   5   0   10   Scale in Feet   15   0   30

111. Milan, S. Aquilino, plan and section of the mausoleum attached to the late fourth-century church of S. Lorenzo (after de Angelis d'Ossat, *Arte Lombarda* 14 (1), 1969).

as similar to the relationship of the other Constantinian mausolea to the basilicas to which they were attached, and the way in which the vestibules of the two buildings interconnect could have been due to the desire to link them both to the church rather than to any awkwardness in their original siting. For whose burial the rebuilt mausolea were intended remains obscure. Constantine's sister Anastasia is one possible candidate. The first recorded occupant of S. Maria della Febbre was the Emperor Honorius's first wife, Maria, who died before 408, when he married her sister Thermantia. Honorius himself was buried there in 423, to be followed perhaps by his sister Galla Placidia, who died in Rome in 450, and certainly by the latter's infant son Theodosius and her surviving son, the Emperor Valentinian III (d. 455).

Meanwhile, Milan (Mediolanum), the principal town in northern Italy, had become a favourite imperial residence and almost a rival to Rome as the capital of the western part of the empire. It was here that in 305 the Emperor Maximian announced his retirement, and it is very likely that he was the builder of the octagonal mausoleum already mentioned (fig. 100), although the circumstances of his death in 310 (by enforced suicide at Marseilles after a futile attempt to resume power) make it doubtful whether his body was ever interred in it. A similar octagonal structure (known since the fifteenth century as S. Aquilino) is attached to the south side of the huge late fourth-century church of S. Lorenzo which stood close to the imperial palace in Milan. This has all the architectural characteristics of a mausoleum, and the fifteenth-century architect Giuliano da Sangallo noted that the interior was 'all covered with porphyry', a material reserved for imperial use. As the mausoleum appears to be contemporary with the church, it may have been built by one of the fourth-century emperors such as Gratian (367–83) or Theodosius I (379–95). Excavation has revealed foundations that indicate that it was begun as an octagon directly attached to the parent church but was completed with an intervening vestibule of a sort often associated with major late Roman mausolea (fig. 111). Externally an arcaded gallery runs round the top of the walls (fig. 110).

All these late imperial mausolea were in the direct line of descent from those of the Tetrarchy, themselves characteristic examples of late Roman architecture. Those that survive were built of brick with domes of the same material, and it is reasonable to suppose that those that have been destroyed were of similar construction. The last great Roman mausoleum is, however, idiosyncratic in both design and construction. This is the tomb, at Ravenna, of the Ostrogothic king Theodoric, who commissioned it before his death in 526. It was built of stone, not of brick, and it stands on its own, unrelated to any church or saintly shrine. It is a two-storey structure, made of large and carefully dressed blocks of Istrian stone, joggled and interlocked to give the maximum strength (fig. 112). The upper storey, containing the circular burial chamber, stands on a wider decagonal base with a deep arched recess on each face. It is surmounted by an enormous capstone hewn out of a solid piece of stone and furnished with projecting lugs which bear on their vertical faces the names of the four Evangelists and of eight of the Apostles. Despite the holes with which they are pierced, it is doubtful

119

whether these lugs can have been of any use in manoeuvering the capstone into position, and their purpose (whether practical or symbolical) remains unexplained. The lower chamber is cruciform and surviving slots and mortices suggest that it was fitted up as a chapel, probably within a century of Theodoric's death. At first-floor level the exterior is decorated with shallow vertical recesses topped by puzzling indications of features either destroyed or projected but never executed. These have generally been interpreted as indicating an external gallery of the sort that was incorporated in the design of some late Roman mausolea and can still be seen at Milan (S. Aquilino). An alternative interpretation would see them as evidence of a scheme of decoration blocked out for carving but left incomplete. The top of the drum is defined by a boldly projecting frieze carved with a motif of Germanic character and of Sassanian rather than classical derivation. To find men capable of this massive work of masonry Theodoric is likely to have looked to the east rather than to the west, but the monolithic dome is without parallel in Byzantine architecture, and suggests that he may have mistrusted the expertise that within a few years of his death was to enable Justinian to build the brick dome of S. Sophia in Constantinople. While the survival of the building for over fourteen hundred years is his justification, its cumbrous mass and inelegant detailing betray the taste of a barbarian ruler striving unsuccessfully after Roman grandeur.

Up to the sixth century the classical mausoleum had had an unbroken history stretching back to the time of Augustus. In Constantinople and Rome the emperors of east and west lay in their sarcophagi beneath domed rotundas of characteristic Roman construction, while at Ravenna the mausoleum of Theodoric showed that in death, as in life, he was determined to be seen as a Roman ruler. All over the empire prominent tombs of various forms marked the places of burial of Roman citizens, both pagan and Christian. Not only was that tradition soon to end, together with many other features of Roman civilisation, but the destruction of existing monuments had already begun.

Tombs were protected by Roman law, and so long as imperial authority lasted, no monument could theoretically be damaged or destroyed with impunity. In practice, however, it was difficult to protect funerary monuments against either casual vandalism or deliberate destruction. Many an inscription includes an imprecation against alienation or misuse of what might, in different hands, be a potentially valuable piece of property. The passage of a few generations could easily turn a carefully tended tomb enclosure into a derelict plot, and even the sanctity of the grave might be set aside when it stood in the way of public works. At Rome in the third century a number of tombs were dismantled or demolished to make way for the Aurelian wall and its gateways, while many early Christian churches, including the basilica of St Peter, overlay older interments. In fifth-century Ostia some old tombstones underwent the ultimate degradation of being reused as seats in a municipal lavatory. The wholesale destruction of the memorials of the dead was, however, a sign of Rome's declining power in the face of barbarian invasion. At Saintes (Mediolanum Santonum) many monuments, including some great drum-like mausolea of the early imperial period, were pulled

112. Ravenna, the mausoleum of King Theodoric, early sixth-century (Deutsches Archäologisches Institut, Rome).

down to build fortifications in the second quarter of the fourth century, and both here and at Neumagen (Noviomagus) in Gallia Belgica it is from the ruins of the fourth-century walls that the dismembered fragments of numerous tombs have been recovered. At Igel (fig. 49) it was only the absurd belief that the statues of the Secundinii represented the Christian emperor Constantine and his mother St Helena that saved a now celebrated monument from destruction, and some similarly beneficent misapprehension may perhaps account for the survival of that of the Julii at Saint-Rémy (Glanum) in Provence. Well might the fourth-century author Ausonius muse over a mutilated epitaph and ask rhetorically, 'Are we surprised that men perish when monuments themselves decay? For death comes even to stones and the names they bear.'

Here and there a mausoleum was given a new lease of life as a church. At Split the mausoleum of Diocletian became the cathedral; at Thessalonica the great rotunda built for his burial by that arch-enemy of Christianity, Galerius, was put to Christian uses as the church of St George. In Spain a large fourth-century mausoleum at Las Vegas de Pueblanueva (Toledo) served first the Christians and then the Muslims as a place of worship, while on the remote Aegean island of Sikinos the tiny church at Episkopi preserves much of the fabric of a third-century *heroön*. Even in the lost province of Britain at least one abandoned mausoleum (at Stone-by-Faversham in Kent) was utilised as part of an early Anglo-Saxon church. But in many places, Rome included, not only were pagan tombs without the walls abandoned as towns drew in on their defences, but even the Christian cemetery churches themselves were sometimes left to decay. In the course of the fifth and sixth centuries Rome was repeatedly besieged by Vandals, Goths and Lombards, at whose hands both churches and cemeteries suffered spasmodic destruction. In the late sixth and seventh centuries some of the damage was made good by the popes, and new (though smaller) basilicas were built at the tomb of St Lawrence on the Via Tiburtina and at that of St Agnes on the Via Nomentana. But after the Lombard invasion of 756 the relics of many martyrs were transferred to the safety of churches within the Aurelian walls. In 609 twenty-eight waggon-loads of bones were taken to the Pantheon, newly consecrated as the church of St Mary of the Martyrs, while Pope Paschal I (817–24) is said to have had the bodies of over two thousand martyrs reinterred at S. Prassede. At Rome the long tradition of suburban burial had finally been broken: elsewhere it sometimes continued, but the period between the fifth and the eighth centuries saw the final extinction of those funerary practices that Christian Europe had inherited from its pagan past.

VII

CHRISTIAN BURIAL
AND MEDIEVAL CHURCH
ARCHITECTURE

ONE CASUALTY OF THE PAINFUL TRANSITION from Antiquity to the Middle Ages
was the artistic representation of the individual. In Antiquity personal identity
had been freely expressed in literature and art, and nowhere more so than in the
strongly characterised portraits of Roman citizens on their funerary monuments.
But from the fourth century onwards portraiture is rarely attempted, and the
human figure begins to lose the dignity with which it had been endowed by the
Hellenistic sculptors. In funerary art this tendency was accentuated by the Christian emphasis on humility and the transitory nature of human life: the Church, in
fact, set its face against some of the established conventions of Roman art, preferring the ideal to the particular, the symbolical to the representational, creating
a climate of opinion in which a pretentious tomb was condemned as a sign of
worldly pride, a portrait bust as something almost idolatrous. To a popular
preacher such as St John Chrysostom any funerary luxury was a form of vanity,
and bare earth was all that a true believer needed. While an early and devout
Christian might acquiesce in a simple and unadorned tomb, a later one whose
conversion was dictated by conformity rather than by conviction might be less
disposed to forego a handsome monument or sarcophagus of the kind to which
his family had been accustomed. In any case, neither could accept that the place
of his burial was of no importance. If the pagan tomb was designed to keep alive
a man's memory on earth, the purpose of the Christian one was to secure him a
place in the queue for Heaven on the Day of Judgement. For this the prayers of
the faithful and, above all, proximity to the body or the relics of a saint were
important. For a time (as we have seen) the funerary architecture of the past was
adapted to the new priorities. Private mausolea continued to be built by the
powerful and wealthy, but instead of proudly challenging the passer-by, they
clustered round the magnetic body of the holy man. It was exceptional for them
to stand in any formal relationship to the parent church: when this occurs it is
likely that a single patron was responsible for both church and mausoleum (fig.
113). But such patrons were rare, and in the last resort proximity mattered more
than public display: a simple tomb within the walls of a church and close to the

123

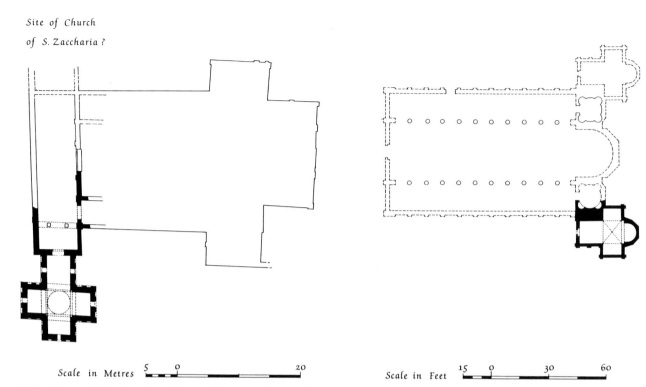

Site of Church
of S. Zaccharia ?

Scale in Metres   5   0   20

Scale in Feet   15   0   30   60

113. Early Christian churches with mausolea or funerary chapels as planned features. At Ravenna (*left*, after Cortesi), the building known as the mausoleum of Galla Placidia originally formed part of an ecclesiastical complex consisting of a large church (S. Croce) with colonnaded porticos at the sides and at the west end a narthex which was flanked by two smaller cruciform buildings. The one on the north is believed to have been the church of S. Zaccaria, while that on the south, which alone survives, was reputedly designed as a mausoleum for Galla Placidia, the builder of S. Croce and the virtual ruler of the Western Empire from 425 to 450. However, it appears to have been built not as an imperial mausoleum but as a *martyrium* dedicated to St Lawrence, and although it did attract burials, Galla Placidia herself was probably buried with other members of her family in Rome when she died there in 450. The main church, already much reduced in size, was further curtailed at the west end in 1602, but its original plan has been partly recovered by excavation in recent years. At Pola, Yugoslavia (*right*, after Morassi), two cruciform chapels flanked the east end of the church of S. Maria del Canneto built by Archbishop Maximian of Ravenna in the middle of the sixth century. One of them is known to have contained the sarcophagus of a bishop, and as they were inaccessible from the interior of the church they were probably designed as funerary chapels. The church was destroyed in the seventeenth century, but the south-east chapel survives.

source of spiritual power might be more efficacious than a grand one outside. So mausolea went out of fashion. A ruler like Theodoric who was anxious to emphasise his Romanity might still build one in the early sixth century, but already in 457 the former western emperor Avitus had been buried at Brioude in Auvergne, 'at the feet' of his chosen saint, St Julian. Soon, in a Europe harassed and impoverished by the barbarian invasions, a reused Antique sarcophagus would be the height of funerary luxury, and many were buried without either visible monument or (in an increasingly illiterate world) epitaph to identify them.

Within those churches that could boast of a saintly body or relic the competition for a place of burial was intense. Repeated efforts were made to control it, but with only limited success. It was generally accepted that the higher clergy had

124

the right of burial in churches, and that especially worthy priests or laity might sometimes enjoy the same privilege. At Ravenna the founder of S. Vitale had an inscription graven on its bronze doors to the effect that only bishops were to be buried there, and in 813 the Council of Mainz reiterated that 'no dead body was to be buried within a church, except those of bishops and abbots, or worthy priests, or faithful laity'. 'Faithful laity' naturally included kings, and from Clovis onwards all the Frankish kings were buried in churches. There were doubtless many others who, like a sub-deacon buried at Trier, were deemed to have 'deserved to rest among the saints' (*qui meruit sanctorum sociari sepulcris*). Thus in Syria a fifth-century architect was buried in one of the churches that he had designed, while at Arles a British layman called Tolosanus was privileged to be interred in the basilica of Saint-Genès which was the chosen place of burial of the bishops of that city. From the seventh century onwards the proliferation of burials within churches was repeatedly forbidden by church councils and later by Carolingian royal edicts. Theodulf, Bishop of Orléans in the early ninth century, was particularly worried by the problem. Churches designed for the service of God were, he said, being used as cemeteries. An exception might be made for a priest or for someone of specially virtuous life, but bodies improperly buried in the past must be reinterred below the pavement, so that no sign of them was visible. If the burials were so numerous as to make this impossible, then the altar must be removed to a new church, leaving the old one to serve purely as a cemetery.

In 658 the Council of Nantes, confirming earlier decisions, forbade burial within a church, but permitted it in an *atrium* or *porticus* or outside (*in atrio aut in porticu aut extra ecclesiam*). This was reiterated at the Council of Aachen in 809. A *porticus* was an external chamber or chapel. It differed from a private mausoleum in that it was either an original feature of a church or at least an addition planned in proper architectural relationship to the existing fabric. Often there were matching *porticus* symmetrically placed to north and south like transepts or aisles. Unlike a transept or an aisle, however, a *porticus* was not designed as an extension of the interior space but as a separate compartment which communicated with the main body of the church by means of a doorway or low archway. The plan of the seventh-century church of SS. Peter and Paul at Canterbury (fig. 114) offers an excellent example of such *porticus*, in the northern of which were buried the archbishops of Canterbury from Augustine (d. 604/9) to Deusdedit (d. 664), with Theodore (d. 690) and Berhtwald (d. 731) close by in the nave, while in the southern lay Ethelbert (d. 616), the first English king to become a Christian, and his wife Bertha. Similar *porticus* were a feature of other early Anglo-Saxon churches such as Reculver (Kent) and Bradwell (Essex), and examples are recorded on the continent from the fourth to the seventh centuries (e.g., Andernos, near Arcachon, the ancient *civitas Boiorum*, Teurnia in Carinthia or Notre-Dame sous le Bourg at Saint-Maurice d'Agaune in Switzerland). In England the *porticus* was invariably enclosed, but in Antiquity the word had meant a covered space with a wall on one side and a colonnade on the other. It was undoubtedly in this form that the *porticus* had first been used as a burial place attached to a Christian church. An example from Lyon is illustrated in figure 114. Here the two colonnaded

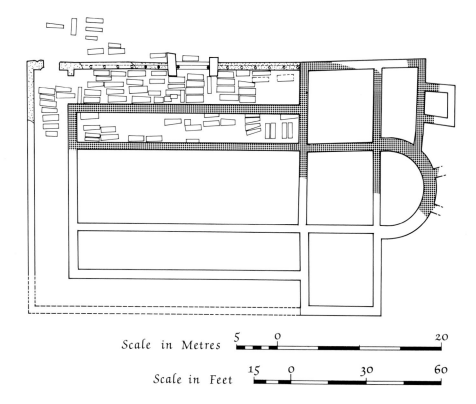

Scale in Metres   5   0   20

Scale in Feet   15   0   30   60

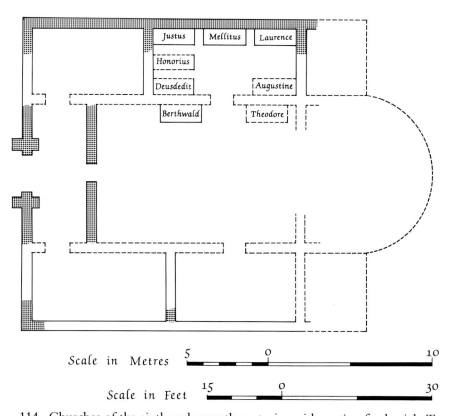

Scale in Metres   5   0   10

Scale in Feet   15   0   30

114. Churches of the sixth and seventh centuries with *porticus* for burial. *Top*, Lyon, France, St Laurent, showing burials in the northern *porticus* (the southern has not been excavated) (after Bonnet, 1977). *Bottom*, SS. Peter and Paul, Canterbury, showing the tombs of the early archbishops in the northern *porticus* (after Taylor).

porticus appears to have been added soon after the church was first built late in the sixth century. By the end of the seventh they were already full of tombs, which had invaded the north aisle of the church itself, though the nave and chancel were kept free of burials.

The *atrium*, in which burial was also authorised by the Council of Nantes, was originally an arcaded courtyard at the west end of a church.★ Like the simpler vestibule or narthex, it was a favourite place of burial. In Rome, for instance, the *atrium* of the church of S. Maria Antiqua in the Forum was found to be entirely filled with graves when it was excavated in 1900, and the narthexes of S. Lorenzo in Lucina and S. Clemente were both used for burials in the early Middle Ages. To be buried outside the west door of a church could be a deliberate act of humility. The epitaph of an archdeacon called Sabinus, buried at the Roman church of S. Lorenzo fuori le Mura in about 400, declares that he had chosen to lie there as the porter, refusing to 'mingle with the tombs of the pious' inside, 'for what is closest to the merits of the saints is a perfect life'. In 858 Pope Benedict III had himself buried outside the doors of St Peter's because he considered himself 'unworthy of joining the saints' within. According to his tenth-century biographer, it was in the same spirit that in 862 St Swithin insisted 'as a man of no account' (*quasi vilis homo*) on being buried outside the doorway of the nave of the Old Minster at Winchester instead of in the church or in the monks' cemetery. But sanctity prevailed over humility, and when in 971 Swithin's body was translated to a place of honour within the church, a memorial building was erected on the site of his former grave which became the nucleus of a massive western extension of the nave. By the tenth century many other churches in northern Europe had developed similar western complexes, often twin-towered, whose liturgical functions (connected at least in some cases with the celebration of the Resurrection) were not deemed incompatible with their continued use as places of burial. Indeed, any association of the *Westwerk* with Resurrection and Redemption could well have attracted burials. It was in a western compartment of the church of San Juan de Pravia in northern Spain that members of the family of its founder, King Silo (774–783), were buried, and the royal burial chamber at Oviedo was at the west end of the church of the Virgin founded by King Alfonso the Chaste of the Asturias in about 800. In the eleventh century these examples were followed in the siting of the royal 'pantheons' of the kings of Castile at León and of Aragon at San Juan de la Peña.

It was, however, the east end that was ultimately to prevail as the favoured situation for a prestigious place of burial. Although churches are usually built on an east-west axis, there was nothing in Christian doctrine that gave preference to the east end as the liturgical focus, and in many Late Antique and early medieval churches important altars were placed elsewhere. Nevertheless, by the twelfth century it was at the east end that the major altar was to be found in most cathedral, monastic and parish churches, and it was in the vicinity of that altar that

★ By the eleventh century, and probably earlier, the word had come to mean an open churchyard.

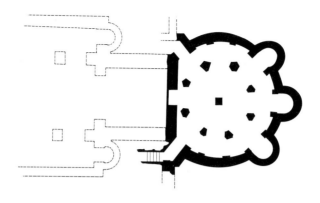

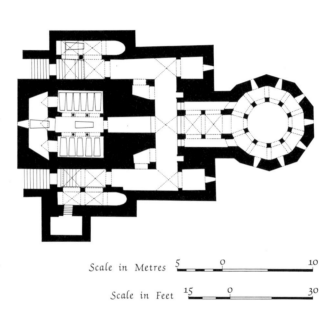

115. Churches with polygonal eastern crypts designed for the veneration of a tomb or of saintly relics. *Bottom*, Saint-Germain at Auxerre in France, ninth century (after Louis). *Top*, Saint-Pierre, Louvain, Belgium, probably eleventh century (after Mertens). At Auxerre the rotunda contained the tomb of St Maxime, a disciple of St Germain, whose coffin is seen with those of later bishops in the western part of the crypt.

Scale in Metres 5 — 0 — 10

Scale in Feet 15 — 0 — 30

the shrine of the patron saint was usually sited, either in a crypt beneath it or in an architecturally defined space beyond it. The eventual triumph of the east end has yet to be fully explained in either architectural or liturgical terms, but it is certain that ritual was as important a determinant of architectural form in early medieval Europe as it was (for instance) in Victorian Britain. So the new emphasis on the east end has to be accounted for in terms of new relics (sometimes from the Holy Land), new forms of devotion (e.g., to the Virgin Mary), new processional services which required new circulatory routes.

The architectural response varied from church to church, but a persistent feature is a circular or polygonal eastern chapel, often two-storeyed, with the tomb of the patron saint in the vaulted lower chamber or crypt. Well-known examples are Saint-Germain d'Auxerre (mid-ninth century), Flavigny abbey church (ninth and eleventh centuries), Saint-Pierre-le-Vif at Sens (probably early eleventh century), Saint-Aignan at Orléans (c.1028 onwards) and Saint-Pierre at

Louvain (probably eleventh century) (fig. 115). The series is continued into the twelfth century by the eastern octagon over the shrine of St Olaf in Nidaros cathedral in Norway, planned in the 1180s but not completed until early in the thirteenth century. Forty years ago André Grabar claimed that an unbroken architectural tradition linked these eastern rotundas with the circular or polygonal *martyria* of Late Antiquity, themselves derived from the mausolea of imperial Rome. Striking evidence of this continuity seemed to be afforded by such churches as Saint-Pierre at Geneva, where a rotunda discovered by piecemeal excavation beneath the east end was believed to be the mausoleum of the sixth-century king Sigismund of Burgundy. Now more thorough investigation has shown that this feature was really a Romanesque structure of the eleventh century. Between the Late Antique mausoleum and the Carolingian or Romanesque rotunda there is, in fact, a gap that archaeology has tended to widen rather than to narrow, and although in some instances those who designed or commissioned the latter may conceivably have had Late Antique mausolea in mind, the Roman Pantheon (known since its consecration in 609 as 'S. Maria Rotonda'), the Holy Sepulchre at Jerusalem and the polygonal Tomb of the Virgin nearby are other likely prototypes.

The polarity between east and west that is apparent in the plans of many major churches of the ninth and tenth centuries may not be unconnected with another characteristic feature of early medieval church architecture, the consolidation into a single structure of what had earlier been several buildings grouped round or placed in line with the shrine or *martyrium* which was their *raison d'être*. Only gradually were these complexes integrated into a single major church containing both shrine and sufficient altars for the needs of the community that served it. St Augustine's abbey at Canterbury is a striking example of this process, whereby three separate churches were superseded in the eleventh century by a single Romanesque building, in which the relics of St Augustine and his successors were revered in chapels arranged in a *chevet* beyond the high altar (fig. 116). Here one of the original churches was SS. Peter and Paul, with its two funerary *porticus* (fig. 114), and elsewhere the sequence sometimes began with a mausoleum. Thus the remarkable seventh-century church at Grenoble whose plan has recently been established by excavation was built between what appear to have been two early Christian mausolea standing in a road-side cemetery on the outskirts of the Gallo-Roman city (fig. 117).

In Mercian England a similar process can be observed at Repton in Derbyshire and at St Oswald's priory in Gloucester (fig. 118). At Repton the chancel of the parish church of St Wystan stands over an Anglo-Saxon crypt whose architectural history has been elucidated by Mr and Mrs Martin Biddle and Dr H.M. Taylor. The presence of a drain suggests that in its original form (perhaps in the middle of the eighth century) this crypt may have served as a baptistery connected with an adjoining church. But as the baptism of adults gave way to that of infants, so fonts took the place of baptisteries, and at Repton as elsewhere the redundant baptistery would have offered itself for use as a mausoleum. In its original form the building was half sunk into the earth, with an external plinth at ground level

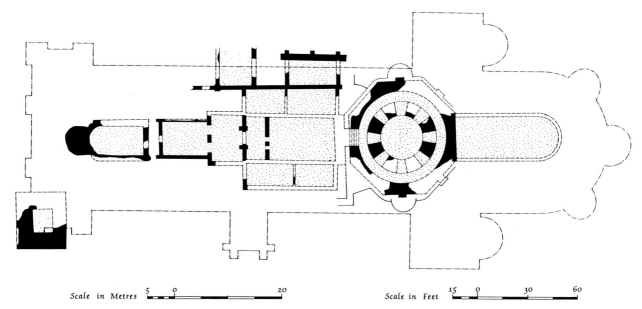

Scale in Metres   5   0   20   Scale in Feet   15   0   30   60

116. St Augustine's abbey, Canterbury, England, showing the complex of Anglo-Saxon churches superseded in the eleventh century by the Norman Romanesque church indicated in outline. The pre-Conquest churches are, from east to west, St Mary, Abbot Wulfric's rotunda of *c*.1050, SS. Peter and Paul (cf. fig. 114), a western church of unknown dedication and (at its west end) the foundations of an eleventh-century stair-turret (after Peers, Clapham and Taylor).

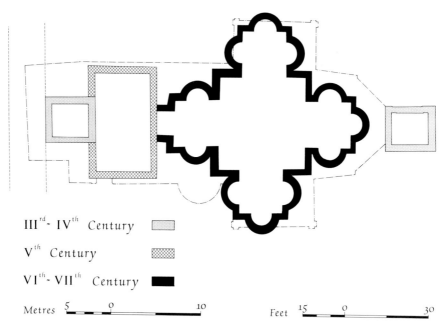

IIIrd- IVth Century   ▨

Vth Century   ▨

VIth- VIIth Century   ■

Metres   5   0   10   Feet   15   0   30

117. Grenoble, France, Saint-Laurent, a seventh-century funerary church built between two earlier roadside mausolea, one of which had been enlarged in the fifth century. The broken line shows the existing church, within whose walls the foundations of the earlier structures have been excavated (after Colardelle, 1986).

and arched openings in all four walls. Before 873–4, when Repton was occupied by a Viking army, the interior had been transformed by the insertion of a stone vault of nine small compartments carried on four monolithic twisted columns and eight corresponding pilasters (fig. 119). Probably soon afterwards the chancel of the adjoining church was extended over the building , which now became a crypt of a familiar type, with two passages for the circulation of visitors to a shrine. It was at Repton that King Æthelbald of Mercia had been buried in 757, and it was 'in the mausoleum' (*in mausoleo*) of his grandfather Wiglaf (d. 839/40) that St Wystan was buried after his murder in a family feud in 849. Wystan was soon recognised as a saint, and as spiral columns had a well-established association with sanctity that went back to the shrine of St Peter at Rome, their presence at Repton can probably be associated with the veneration of this Mercian saint in the family mausoleum. After the disappearance of Mercia as a separate kingdom, Wystan's relics were transferred to Evesham, and there is now no visible trace above ground of any Saxon burials within the crypt, though many have been found by excavation in the adjoining churchyard. At Gloucester another rectangular mausoleum stood immediately to the east of the ninth-century church, with which by the eleventh century it had been linked (fig. 118). Like the Repton mausoleum, it may have been both shrine and royal burial place, the saint in this case being St Oswald and the rulers, Æthelred, earldorman of Mercia (d. 911) and his wife Ætheflaed, daughter of King Alfred (d. 918). At Gloucester, as at Repton, the tombs themselves have long been destroyed, but at Jouarre in France (Seine-et-Marne) the vaulted burial crypt of a seventh-century aristocratic nunnery, formerly attached to the east end of a demolished church, still contains the decorated sarcophagi of a bishop and of several abbesses.

While kings and bishops and heads of religious houses were honourably buried in churches or their annexes, ordinary people were laid to rest in churchyards. By the eighth and ninth centuries the suburban cemeteries of Late Antiquity had often been abandoned,* and even when they remained in use (usually because the tomb of a saint ensured their continued popularity) the ancient prohibition of intra-mural burial was increasingly forgotten. In shrunken cities space was not a difficulty, and the dead as well as the living needed the security of their walls. As late as 563 the old rule was recalled by a council of Spanish bishops, but already in the mid-sixth century burials were taking place in the cathedral church at Cologne, and in 542 a bishop of Arles was buried in a church that was almost certainly within the walls of that city. Eventually most of the major urban churches would stand in the middle of a graveyard. Many such graveyards remain in the British Isles, and although on the Continent they have usually been paved over, a record of medieval burials sometimes survives in the form of inscriptions carved on the external walls of the churches (e.g., S. Nicola, Bari, and the Duomo at

---

* A notable exception is the suburban cemetery known as the Aliscamps at Arles, which remained in use throughout the Middle Ages and is mentioned by Dante in the *Inferno* (ix, 112–15). At Bordeaux the canons of the collegiate church of Saint-Seurin controlled the cemetery to the north-west of the walled city and did their best to prevent any burials within the walls, even in the cathedral church of Saint-André.

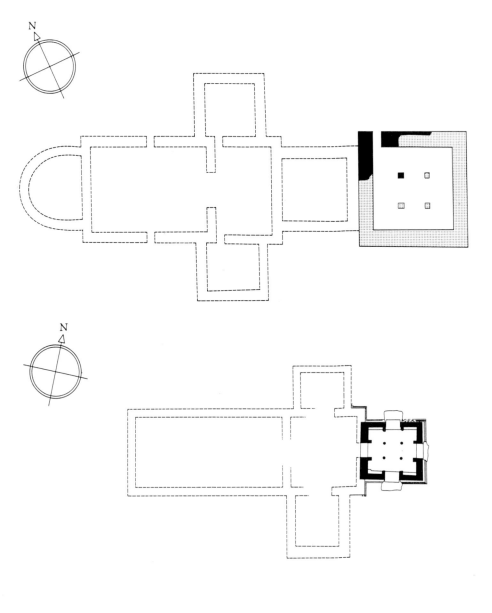

Scale in Metres 5 ___ 0 ___ 10   Scale in Feet 15 ___ 0 ___ 30

118. Anglo-Saxon mausolea at, *bottom*, St Wystan's Church, Repton, Derbyshire (after Biddle), and *top*, St Oswald's Priory, Gloucester (after Heighway and Bryan), with the outlines of the churches to which they were eventually linked architecturally.

Pisa). In the country the subdivision of dioceses into smaller units and the building, sometimes by ecclesiastical authority, often by territorial proprietors, of a parish church or its equivalent in every substantial community normally meant the establishment of a new rural churchyard cemetery (unless, as was sometimes the case, the cemetery was there before the church).

In northern countries which were not converted to Christianity until the seventh, eighth or even later centuries, pagan cemeteries were still in full use in the countryside. Most of them were eventually abandoned in favour of new

132

Christian graveyards, but cases of continuity are not unknown, though the change-over from pagan to Christian practice is rarely so dramatically illustrated as it is at Jelling in Denmark, where a medieval church standing midway between two great tumuli is accompanied by a runic inscription recording the conversion of the Danes to Christianity by King Harald (d. *c.*985). The church was orginally a timber structure, probably of the tenth century, and in the middle of its floor was the tomb of a royal personage of the same period. The archaeological evidence suggests that this personage was not King Harald himself, but his pagan father Gorm, originally interred in one of the tumuli, and reburied in the church by his newly converted son. In England the existence, close to the former churchyard at Taplow in Buckinghamshire, of a large tumulus containing a richly furnished grave of the seventh century, may indicate another case of pagan burial in one generation being followed by Christian burial in the next.

119. Repton, Derbyshire, the mausoleum-crypt with the twisted columns inserted in the ninth century, probably in connection with the burial there of St Wystan (d. 849) (John Crook).

Although by the eleventh century most rural cemeteries were associated with a parish church, some, for historical or topographical reasons, were situated at a distance from the village. If a church already existed on the site, it might be reduced to the status of a chapel dependent on the new parish church; if not, a chapel might be built for the performance of funeral services. Traces of what may have been timber-built funerary chapels have been found by excavation in one or two Merovingian cemeteries in France, but few if any existing chapels can be dated before the eleventh century. In France and Spain Romanesque chapels of this sort include some centrally planned buildings of exceptional interest (fig. 120).

The most prestigious of all centrally planned religious buildings was, of course, the Holy Sepulchre at Jerusalem. All over Europe there were churches that were built in imitation of this much visited and highly venerated prototype. Many of them were themselves dedicated to 'St Sepulchre', and sometimes a contemporary source states explicitly that the church at Jerusalem was the model. The church of the Anastasis (i.e., the Resurrection), to give it its formal title, has a long and complicated history. But from the fourth century onwards its most striking feature was the domed rotunda built over the tomb in which Jesus was buried after his Crucifixion, a rotunda whose architectural affinities were with late imperial mausolea such as S. Costanza in Rome. Begun by the Emperor Constantine, but not completed until after his death, and destroyed by the Muslims in 1009, it was reconstructed in the eleventh century in a Byzantine Romanesque style. But in plan it remained essentially unchanged, with an inner ring of piers and columns supporting the dome, an encircling ambulatory and an outer wall from which there projected three apses. Few of the medieval derivatives of the Holy Sepulchre follow the design of the original at all closely. Lack of accurate plans and differences in building traditions would have made that difficult in any case. But medieval churchmen were not concerned about archaeological accuracy in a building any more than they were with portraiture in a picture. What they wanted was something that recalled the original rather than an exact reproduction. So some of these churches are circular, some polygonal. Very few of them attempt to reproduce the alternating rhythm of piers and columns found in the original, and only one or two (notably the twelfth-century church of Lanleff near Caen in Normandy) have the three apsidal projections (fig. 121). Nevertheless, their general resemblance to their distant prototype is obvious.

In England the best-known churches of this type are those associated with the military orders dedicated to the defence of the Holy Places recaptured by the Crusaders in 1099: the Templars and Hospitallers, for whom the church of the Holy Sepulchre had a special significance. The Templars' chief church in London (dedicated in 1185) was of this form, and so were those of four of their subordinate houses, at Dover, at Garway in Herefordshire and at Aslackby and Temple Bruer in Lincolnshire. The Hospitallers built similar churches at Clerkenwell and at Little Maplestead in Essex, while at Cambridge a round church was constructed by a third but short-lived Order of the Holy Sepulchre. Thus in England at least eight round churches can be associated with the military orders. However, both

120. Torres del Rio, Navarre, Spain, the octagonal funerary church of the Holy Sepulchre, built late in the twelfth century to serve a now vanished cemetery.

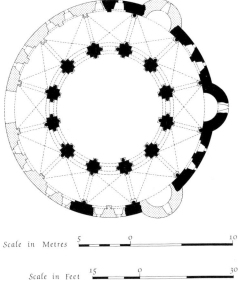

Scale in Metres 5 0 10

Scale in Feet 15 0 30

121. Llanlef, Normandy, plan of the ruined twelfth-century church built in imitation of the church of the Holy Sepulchre at Jerusalem. The hatched portions have been destroyed (after Rhein).

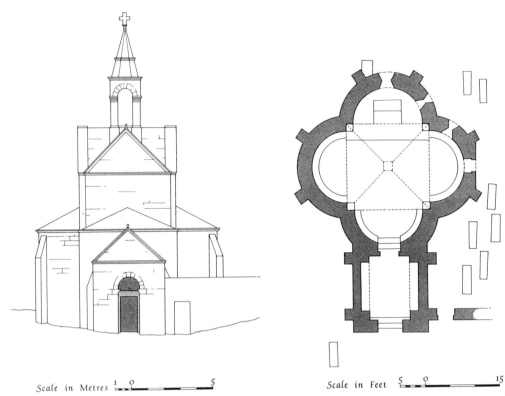

Scale in Metres 1 0   5   Scale in Feet 5 0   15

122. The early twelfth-century chapel of Saint-Croix in the cemetery of the abbey of Montmajour, southern France (after Viollet-le-Duc, *Dictionnaire de l'architecture française* 1858–68, 2, pp. 445–6).

the Templars and the Hospitallers had many other churches for which the circular plan was not adopted, and neither in England nor on the Continent was it in any way exclusive to them. Many palace chapels were of this shape, and so were a number of cemetery chapels. A type of church that was intended to recall the Resurrection of Christ was particularly suitable for cemeteries, for there it held out to the believer the hope of his own future resurrection. In a cemetery chapel the form of the original in Jerusalem would necessarily be scaled down, often to a simple circular or octagonal building, without any internal arcade or ambulatory, but the symbolic significance of the plan remained the same. When a trefoil or quadrilobed plan is adopted (fig. 122), all connection with the Holy Sepulchre has been lost, but the tradition of symmetrical, centrally planned mausolea that goes back to Antiquity and that lies behind the Holy Sepulchre itself has once more reasserted itself.

VIII

THE REVIVAL OF THE ARCHITECTURAL TOMB

By the tenth century the tomb had long disappeared from most parts of western Europe as a form of architectural or sculptural art. Only the bodies of the saints were still sometimes enclosed in masonry structures that were monumental in character, rather than in portable shrines. The church itself had become a mausoleum, with the tomb of the saint as its focal point, surrounded by the bodies of the faithful. Kings and other great personages lay either beneath the floor (like the Frankish kings at Saint-Denis) or in crypt-like appendages (like the kings of the Asturias at Oviedo). Rarely was the tomb of an individual, secular or ecclesiastical, marked by anything more elaborate than a crudely carved sarcophagus made of stone or plaster.

By the twelfth century the funerary monument had begun to reappear, not only as a work of art, but also as the reminder, for the benefit of posterity, of an individual's life on earth, and not merely as a receptacle for his mortal remains awaiting the Day of Judgement. The year of death (an historical event) is given more frequently, rather than just the day of the month (all that was needed for Christian commemoration). Even the old Roman formula, *Siste Viator*, bidding the passer-by stop and read the epitaph, is occasionally seen once more (e.g., at Brive in France). These were manifestations of that revival of humane values in thought, literature and art that is associated with the twelfth century. Some of these monuments commemorated kings, notably those porphyry sarcophagi that Roger II of Sicily (d. 1154) had set up in the cathedral at Cefalù 'as a perpetual record of my death' (*ad decessus mei signum perpetuum*) and to ensure that 'the famous memory of my name' (*insignem memoriam mei nominis*) should not be forgotten. But most of them were erected by the clergy themselves. As leaders of a Church then at the height of its power and prestige, popes, cardinals, bishops and abbots felt a desire to inform posterity of their names and achievements that would have horrified St Augustine or St Ambrose. For the spiritual there was still ample scope for pious anonymity in cloister or hermitage. But anonymity no longer appealed to the heads of a papal monarchy that saw itself as the equal of emperors, or to the bishops and abbots who controlled the religious life of Europe as it had never been controlled before. For popes in the twelfth century a porphyry sarcophagus was one way of claiming parity with emperors, and Pope

Innocent II (d. 1143) actually appropriated for his own tomb the sarcophagus in which the Emperor Hadrian had been buried in his mausoleum, now itself converted into the papal castle of S. Angelo. But freshly quarried porphyry had long been unobtainable from Egypt (its only source). The choice lay between finding an old porphyry sarcophagus for reuse or having a new one cut out of a large Antique column of the same material. So this ancient symbol of authority had a limited currency. Meanwhile a new one was emerging in the form of the effigy, a type of memorial that, if it did not yet attempt to portray the features of pope or prelate, could and did indicate their official status by a careful representation of clerical costume. By the thirteenth century effigies had become so firmly established as symbols of dynastic or episcopal continuity that the lack of them in the past was sometimes felt to be an iconographical gap which had to be remedied. Hence in England the manufacture of effigies purporting to be of Saxon bishops at Wells cathedral and of Norman and Angevin ones at Hereford, and in France the commissioning, by King Louis IX, of sixteen royal effigies to represent the Carolingian and early Capetian kings buried at Saint-Denis.

It was sculpture rather than architecture that responded first to the new desire for personal commemoration. With the notable exception of the cathedral at Speyer, designed by its founder, the Emperor Conrad II (d. 1039), to be a symbol of royal power and the mausoleum of the Franconian dynasty, nearly all the churches built by western European rulers of the eleventh and twelfth centuries for their own burial were monastic. The monastic orders had their own liturgical requirements, expressed in characteristic plans, to which even royal founders had to conform. Thus the use of monastic churches as dynastic burial places did not usually result in any notable modification of their plan. Churches like the two Benedictine abbeys at Caen in Normandy, intended by William the Conqueror for the burial of himself and his queen, or the one (of the Augustinian order) at Cefalù built by King Roger II of Sicily, might be among the largest and grandest of their type, but their plans were not significantly altered to accommodate the monuments of their founders. In Spain the Cistercian nunnery of Las Huelgas near Burgos was built as the burial place of the house of Castile, but the layout of its church corresponds closely to the standard pattern of its order, and there is no architectural provision for the sarcophagi of the royal family, which clutter the floor of the choir and aisles. Here, as at Caen, the place of honour was in front of the high altar, and in death the pride of royalty was subordinated to Christian humility. Even at Saint-Denis, which had been the most favoured place of burial for the kings of France since the eighth century, the only architectural features of a specifically funerary character were one or two recesses in the walls and a small apsidal projection at the west end added by Charlemagne to protect the tomb of his father. The tombs of all the other Merovingian, Carolingian and Capetian kings were scattered about the church until in the thirteenth century most of them were neatly rearranged under the crossing, probably at the behest of King Louis IX. Torn between their continental and their insular territories, the Norman and Angevin kings of England took much longer to establish a regular place of burial. Indeed, it was not until after the loss of Normandy and most of the Angevin lands

138

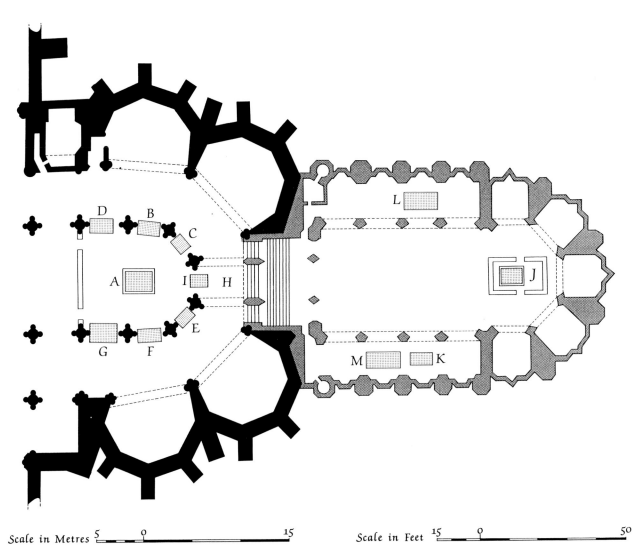

123. Westminster Abbey; the east end and Henry VII's Chapel, showing the royal tombs. A. Shrine of St Edward the Confessor. B. King Henry III (d. 1272). C. Queen Eleanor of Castile (d. 1290). D. King Edward I (d. 1307). E. Queen Philippa (d. 1369). F. King Edward III (d. 1377). G. King Richard II (d. 1399). H. Henry V's Chapel. I. King Henry V (d. 1422). J. King Henry VII (d. 1509) and Queen Elizabeth of York. K. Lady Margaret Beaufort, Countess of Richmond and Derby (d. 1509). L. Queen Elizabeth I (d. 1603). M. Mary, Queen of Scots (d. 1587).

that Henry III began what became a dynastic church at Westminster, but here again there was no special architectural provision for the royal tombs, which occupied the spaces between the columns defining the area at the east end reserved for the shrine of Edward the Confessor (fig. 123). Only at Faversham abbey in Kent, founded by King Stephen in 1148, was there an eastern prolongation of the choir six bays long which appears to have been designed specifically to accommodate the tombs of the founder and his queen. The abbey was totally destroyed in the sixteenth century, but excavations in 1965 revealed the outlines of the plan

139

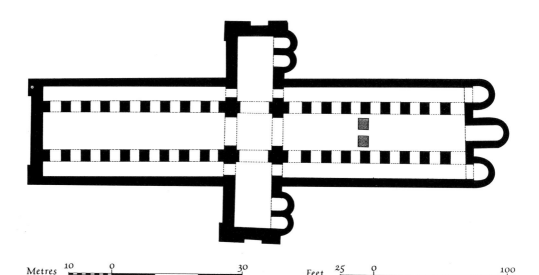

Metres 10 0   30   Feet 25 0   100

124. Faversham abbey, Kent, England, the foundations of the destroyed Norman church, showing the two rectangular pits believed to have been the graves of the founder King Stephen (d. 1154) and Queen Matilda (d. 1152) (after Philp).

and identified two large rectangular pits which were probably the royal graves (fig. 124).

So, despite their size and grandeur, these royal burial churches of the twelfth and thirteenth centuries did not offer a new architectural model for the Christian burial of princes and other great men. As for the idea of reviving the Antique mausoleum in its Christian form, that seems to have occurred to two men only, one in southern Italy, the other in remote and recently converted Sweden. At Canosa in Apulia the mausoleum of the Norman Bohemund, Prince of Antioch (d. 1111), stands on the south side of the cathedral church (fig. 125). Bohemund was a native of Apulia who, although a benefactor to his family's abbey of Venosa, had founded no monastery of his own. The ruins of mausolea of the first and second centuries are still visible on the outskirts of the town, and Bohemund may well have seen others in Syria and the Holy Land, but with its hemispherical dome★ his mausoleum seems to belong to the same architectural world as the half Romanesque, half Islamic churches of Norman Sicily. The way it is attached to the side of the cathedral might suggest that in this respect Bohemund or his executors may have had in mind some of the early Christian mausolea that clung to the external walls of old St Peter's in Rome (fig. 108). At Vreta in Sweden a Romanesque funerary chapel whose internal form, with domed roof and four symmetrical niches, is even more suggestive of Antique mausolea, occupies a similar position on the south side of an early twelfth-century church, to which it was added before the middle of the same century (fig. 126). Vreta was a royal church associated with the early Swedish kings, and it is possible that the chapel

★The existing dome is, however, a modern reconstruction, based apparently on reliable evidence.

125. Canosa, southern Italy, the mausoleum of Bohemund, Prince of Antioch (d. 1111) on the south side of the cathedral (Alinari).

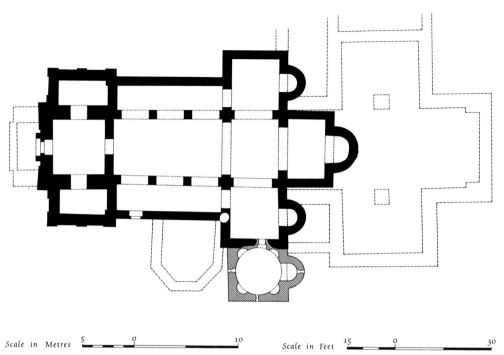

Scale in Metres 5 _____ 0 _____ 10   Scale in Feet 15 _____ 0 _____ 30

126. Vreta, Sweden, showing the Romanesque funerary chapel added to the south side of the early twelfth-century church. The latter is shown in its original form, before the later extensions indicated in broken line (after *Sveriges Kyrkor: Östergötland*, 2, 1935).

was the burial place of King Inge the Younger, who died at Vreta in about 1120/30. What contacts, religious, commercial or diplomatic, were responsible for this unlikely reminiscence of Roman Antiquity in a country that had never known Roman authority is a matter for speculation. No other European prince would be buried in such a manner until the sixteenth century. By that time the endowment of private masses had created a new form of Christian burial place, the chantry chapel, out of which the mausoleum was eventually to re-emerge. Meanwhile, the tomb itself was to have an independent development that took a strongly architectural form.

The history of the architectural tomb begins with the arched recess known to the learned as the *arcosolium*, to the French as the *enfeu* and to the English as the tomb-recess. Thousands of early Christians were buried in such recesses in the Roman catacombs, nearly always with some painted decoration on the wall enclosed by the arch. These recesses were carved out of the soft tufa rock into which the catacombs were tunnelled. When the catacombs went out of use in the sixth century, it was natural to construct similar recesses in the walls of churches above ground. No early examples appear to survive in Rome, but the tomb of Pope Gregory III (d. 741) in old St Peter's was of this form, with a mosaic decoration on the wall, and other examples of the eighth and ninth centuries are recorded. North of the Alps evidence of such tomb-recesses has been found in early churches excavated at Einigen on the Thunersee in Switzerland and at Saint-

127. Poitiers, France, Saint-Hilaire, external tomb-recess of the early twelfth century, with inscription commemorating one Constantine.

128. Trier cathedral, Germany, internal tomb-recess of the papal legate Ivo (d. 1142) (Bildarchiv Foto Marburg).

Julien-en-Genevois in Haute Savoie (France), and when the place of burial of the Merovingian king Dagobert (d. 639) at Saint-Denis is described as 'under an arch on the right-hand side' (*sub arcu in latere dextro*), or that of Charlemagne (d. 814) at Aachen, as being beneath 'a gilded arch' (*arcusque supra tumulum deauratus*), it is likely that a wall-recess is meant. From the late eleventh century onwards tombs of this sort reappear in various parts of Europe: in southern Italy, notably in the dynastic burial church of the Norman house of Hauteville at Venosa; in France at Poitiers, on the exterior of the church of Saint-Hilaire, with an inscription commemorating a certain Constantine (possibly a cleric of that name mentioned in 1104) (fig. 127); at Fontevrault (1123) and at Angoulême (1125); in Germany at Trier (tomb of the papal legate Ivo, who died there in 1142) (fig. 128); and in Rome at S. Maria in Cosmedin and SS. Cosmas and Damian (fig. 129). What is remarkable about the Roman tombs is not only the emphasis given to the architectural framework, which stands forward of the wall and begins to supersede the painted recess as the significant feature, but the self-conscious classicism that they share with a notable twelfth-century tomb in the narthex of S. Lorenzo fuori le Mura (fig. 130). They are architectural evidence of that new fascination with Ancient Rome which is also apparent in twelfth-century literature, and which encouraged men like the papal chamberlain Alfanus to think of being buried in a tomb complete with pediment, Corinthian columns, and classically inspired inscription.

129. Rome, S. Maria in Cosmedin, tomb of the papal chamberlain Alfanus, *c.*1123.

130. Rome, S. Lorenzo fuori le Mura, twelfth-century tomb of classical form.

This type of canopied tomb was to provide the basic formula from which in the thirteenth century a range of funerary monuments was to be developed by Arnolfo di Cambio and other Italian sculptors, mainly for popes, cardinals and other great ecclesiastics. All these, like their prototypes, were designed to stand against a wall and to be seen frontally. In its Gothic form the type consists of a trefoiled arch beneath a gabled baldaquin or canopy supported by a pair of columns. Within, on a tomb-chest or sarcophagus, lies a recumbent effigy that is often tilted to make it fully visible (fig. 131). On the wall beneath the canopy there are appropriate paintings or sculptured reliefs. Well-known tombs of this type survive in Rome (S. Maria sopra Minerva, S. Maria Maggiore, etc.), and at Anagni, Arezzo, Cortona, Perugia, Viterbo and elsewhere. They were fashionable in the late thirteenth and early fourteenth centuries and were not without influence in both France and England. In Italy they are often very tall, but the tallest of all was the towering tomb of Cardinal Jean de la Grange (d. 1402), once in the church of Saint-Martial at Avignon, which occupied the whole height of one bay of the chancel (fig. 132). Over seventeen metres high, it consisted of five registers of sculpture, stacked as if on shelves between the effigy of the cardinal at the bottom and the pinnacled canopy at the top.

Outside Italy the wall-recess, as a setting for a tomb-slab or effigy, was to be widely adopted, especially in northern Spain where it is often found in cloisters (e.g., at Roncesvalles, fig. 133) and in England, where single recesses, usually in inside, but occasionally in outside, walls, are a common feature of thirteenth- and fourteenth-century churches. Notable examples, their arches emphasised by

131 (*above left*). Viterbo, Italy, S. Francesco, tomb of Pope Adrian V (d. 1276) (Alinari).

132 (*above right*). Avignon, France, Saint-Martial, seventeenth-century drawing of destroyed monument of Cardinal Jean de la Grange (d. 1402) (Vatican Library, MS. Barberini Lat. 4426, f. 25).

striking geometrical forms, can be seen in the church at Winchelsea in Sussex and in Bristol cathedral (fig. 134). In France, the tombs of the counts of Provence, formerly in the Hospitallers' church at Aix-en-Provence, show the *enfeu* at its most architectural (fig. 135). In the north, however, vaulting-shafts and arcading often left less wall-space free for tombs than in Italian city churches, and larger piers and compound columns encouraged the siting of the more prestigious tombs beneath the arches of the nave or round the east end. Here they formed

133. Roncesvalles, Spain, Gothic tomb-recesses in the cloister.

134 (*above left*). Bristol cathedral, early fourteenth-century tomb-recess of a lord of Berkeley in the south choir aisle (from a drawing by Gordon Home).

135 (*above right*). Aix-en-Provence, France, Saint-Jean-de-Malte, tomb of Alfonso II, Count of Provence (d. 1209), erected *c.*1250, destroyed 1794 (from A.L. Millin, *Voyage dans le Midi de la France*, 1807, Atlas, pl. xli).

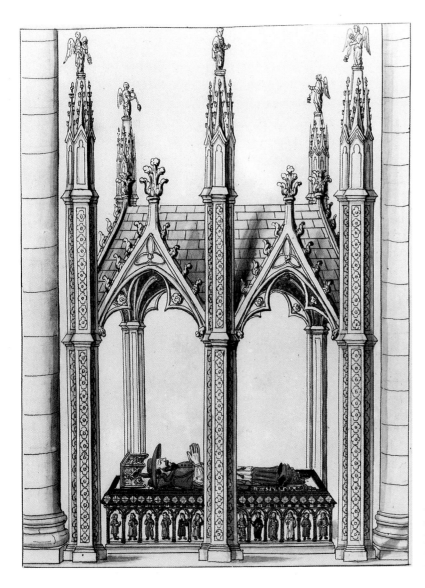

136. Beauvais, France, abbey church of Saint-Lucien, destroyed tomb of Cardinal Jean Cholet (d. 1292) (Bodleian Library, Oxford, MS. Gough Drawings Gaignières 9, f. 14).

autonomous structures, evidently derived from the canopied wall-tomb, but intended to be seen from either side. One of the grandest was that of the immensely wealthy Cardinal Jean Cholet (d. 1292), in the Benedictine abbey church of Saint-Lucien at Beauvais (fig. 136), while in the Cistercian church at Longpont near Soissons, the heraldic symbols of the powerful lords of Coucy extended from their tombs to the columns between which they were placed (fig. 137). In England the inventive genius of the early fourteenth-century masons turned the free-standing tomb into a three-dimensional fantasy of miniature buttresses, pinnacles and vaulted canopies such as can be seen rising above King Edward II's tomb at Gloucester (fig. 138), Hugh le Despenser's at Tewkesbury (c.1350) or that of one of the great ladies of the Percy family at Beverley (c.1340). The supreme example of this type of funerary fantasy is the tomb at Avignon of

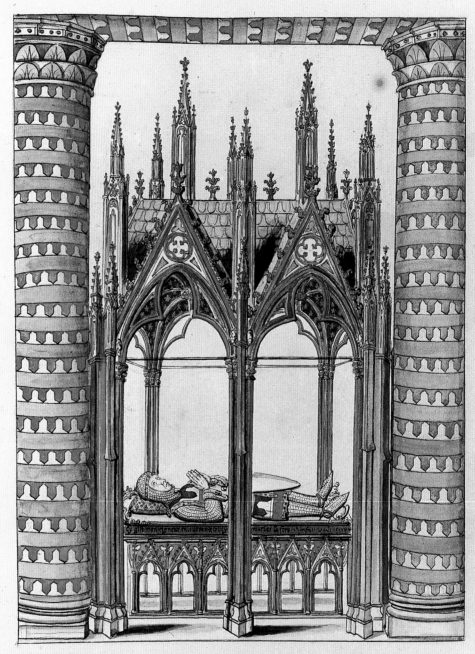

TOMBEAU *de pierre, peint entre deux piliers a gauche du grand Autel de l'Eglise de l'Abbaye de Longpont.*

137. Longpont abbey church near Soissons, France, destroyed tomb of Enguerrand IV de Coucy (d. 1312), flanked by columns entirely covered with the painted arms of the Coucy family (Bodleian Library, Oxford, MS. Gough Drawings Gaignières 13, f. 91).

138. Gloucester cathedral, England, canopy of the tomb of King Edward II (d. 1327) (Barry Capper).

Pope John XXII (d. 1334), in whose making an English mason then working at the papal court was probably concerned (fig. 139). The Italian sculptor Bonino da Campione achieved equally spectacular effects in one of the outdoor monuments of the Scaliger lords of Verona, while at Bologna the great Italian jurists of the late thirteenth and early fourteenth centuries were buried in sarcophagi under canopies whose simple pyramidal form with antefixes at the corners indicate clearly their desire to be as Roman in their monuments as in their law (fig. 140).

Whether pyramidal or Gothic in form, the canopy was an indication of status that these tombs shared with thrones and altars. Whatever misgivings there may at first have been over the use of this symbol of sanctity and authority to dignify private tombs, they were soon overcome. Just as, despite all the resolutions of church councils and monastic general chapters, burial inside churches continued to be widely practised, so canopies soon lost their mystique and became part of the established repertoire of funerary architecture for layman and ecclesiastic alike.

As burial in churches had for so long been tolerated rather than encouraged, it is not surprising that in the twelfth century, when monumental tombs first began to come back into fashion, little or no architectural provision should have been made for their placement. This was still generally the case in the thirteenth century. The south transept of York Minster was built largely at the expense of Archbishop Walter de Grey (d. 1255), but his canopied tomb (probably the earliest of its kind to survive intact in England) is an independent structure standing in the middle of the eastern aisle. However, in Spain cloisters with integral tomb-recesses were

Tomb of Pope John.
Avignon. 1880

Half Plan below.   Half Plan above.

139. Avignon, France, Notre-Dame des Doms, tomb of Pope John XXII
(d. 1334) (from A. Dunn, *Notes and Sketches of an Architect*, Newcastle 1886).

140. Bologna, Italy, churchyard of S. Francesco, tombs of thirteenth-century lawyers with pyramidal canopies over their sarcophagi. In the foreground is the tomb of the famous jurist Accursius (d. 1263).

built from the late twelfth century onwards, notably at Burgos (*c.*1270–80), and in the cathedral church of León (built from 1255 onwards) the tomb of a thirteenth-century bishop has been skilfully incorporated into the design of the transept. In England four elegantly designed tomb-recesses (two on each side) are an original feature of the Lady Chapel of Exeter cathedral, a work of *c.* 1260–70, while at Hereford cathedral the rebuilding of the choir aisles in about 1300 included the provision of eight uniform recesses for the series of bishops' effigies already mentioned. The tendency, from the late thirteenth century onwards, to integrate the tomb into its architectural setting was closely connected with a new development in its history. This was the chantry or family chapel, in which the dead were to make what was perhaps their most important contribution to the living architecture of the world they had left.

IX

CHANTRIES AND FUNERARY CHURCHES IN MEDIEVAL EUROPE

ALTHOUGH TO A CHRISTIAN DEATH is the gateway to eternal life, for most medieval Christians the distant prospect of Heaven was clouded by uncertainty. How would the balance tip between good and evil when they came to render their account at the Day of Judgement? Who would claim their souls – an angel or a devil? An adverse balance – and who could be sure that his record was favourable? – could be rectified by the prayers of those still on earth and by good works carried out posthumously in the name of the deceased. Hence the great apparatus of intercession that grew up to ensure the salvation of the souls of countless sinful men and women. Of that apparatus the monasteries were the first trustees. Every monastery had its founder. Some were founded by saints who needed no earthly advocacy; but most were founded by some great feudatory whose burial, normally before the high altar, was the signal for an elaborate sequence of vigils, masses (celebrated by those monks who were in priest's orders), recitations of psalms (by those who were not) and the distribution of food to the poor – a work of charity that itself engendered more prayers for the dead from the grateful recipients. Every year, on the anniversary of his death, some or all of the funerary ritual would be re-enacted. In this way the founder of a monastery set in motion an annual cycle of intercession which in theory would cease only on the Day of Judgement. Every monk of the house was entitled to commemoration, at least by the recitation of his name in chapter on the anniversary of his death, and laity and others might obtain participation in the prayers of the community by an appropriate benefaction. A calendar, or obituary register, was maintained, in which the names of all those entitled to commemoration were entered on the appropriate day. As the years went by the number of anniversaries naturally multiplied, but it was enormously increased by agreements between monastic communities for mutual commemoration, and one of the attractions of such great confederations as the Order of Cluny was precisely the interchange of names for commemorative purposes. The result was that by the twelfth century some of the registers of names contained thousands of entries, ranging from kings and bishops to ordinary monks and laity. Not only did this mean an annually increasing burden of commemoration on virtually every day throughout the year (the major feasts excepted), it entailed giving away a prodigious quantity of food. By the middle of the twelfth century the great abbey of Cluny itself was overwhelmed by its cumulative obligations to the dead and was obliged not only to abandon the attempt to commemorate every monk and benefactor individually, but also drastically to cut down its distribution of food to the poor. For, as its abbot, Peter the Venerable, put it, there was a real danger that 'the dead would drive out the living'. The Cistercians, anxious as ever to avoid the mistakes of their Cluniac brethren, were always more restrictive in the spiritual services that they provided for the dead, but even for them the burden of commemoration eventually proved too heavy. In 1225 the general chapter of the order decided that henceforth only one annual mass would be celebrated for the soul of any one person, and in the 1270s it abrogated all individual anniversaries and replaced them by twelve general commemorations.

The failure of the monastic orders to guarantee perpetual intercession was bad enough. But the admission by the Cistercians of their inability to maintain individual commemorations in perpetuity coincided with an important theological development: the official recognition that Purgatory was part of Christian doctrine. The notion of a probationary or purgatorial state, in which souls were suspended midway between Heaven and Hell, can be traced almost to the beginnings of Christian thought, but it was not until the thirteenth century that its implications were fully investigated by theologians, and it was only in 1274 that Purgatory figured in the formal pronouncements of a Church Council. Just how sins were expiated in Purgatory was a matter to which some of the best intellects of the thirteenth century devoted themselves. Their ingenious reasonings about such matters as the nature of purgatorial fire (which inflicted pain without consuming) need not concern us here, nor did they greatly matter to medieval laymen. What did matter to every Christian was that Purgatory was now a posthumous ordeal to which his soul would be subject, but one that (as the Church assured its members) could be mitigated by the routine of prayer offered by others on his behalf, and by the vicarious practice of good works set in motion by his will. To that extent the formalisation of Purgatory offered a reasonable hope of ultimate salvation to all. But on the other hand the layman was now well and truly caught in the toils of a triumphant Church. As the years went by even the most devoted Christian was conscious that (confession and absolution notwithstanding) his purgatorial indebtedness must be mounting, and the best remedy (if he had the means at his disposal) was to employ a priest to reduce it by saying masses after his death. The prayers of one's friends and relations could help, but a priest was a more efficacious agent of salvation because only a priest could say mass, and in terms of purgatorial accountancy masses were worth more than mere prayers.

Contractual arrangements for spiritual services go back at least to the tenth century. For the most part these early agreements between benefactor and monastery were merely for anniversary commemoration. In 918, however, King Charles the Simple of France established a body of canons who were to pray night and day for himself and his wife in a chapel in the royal palace at Compiègne, and in 1100 King Alfonso VI of Castile provided in his will for the establishment of two similar chantries (to use the English term) at Burgos. Both in France and in England foundations for daily masses in cathedral or other non-monastic churches begin to be recorded from the end of the twelfth century onwards, but it was only in the latter part of the thirteenth century that chantries became a widespread form of religious foundation, and there can be no doubt that their popularity was, in part at least, both a reaction to the breakdown of the monastic system of commemoration and a response to the new emphasis on the importance of intercession created by the doctrine of Purgatory.

A chantry (French, 'chapellenie'; Italian and Spanish, 'cappellaria'; German, 'Altarpfründe') was essentially an endowment for the performance of masses and other works of charity for the benefit of the souls of specified persons. It might be established in perpetuity, or only for a term of years, and it might imply anything from a single priest saying masses at some existing altar in a parish church to a collegiate foundation with a specially built church and residential quarters. Thousands of such chantries were set up all over western Europe during the thirteenth, fourteenth and fifteenth centuries, not only by kings and other great men, both lay and ecclesiastical, but also by the rural gentry and the urban bourgeoisie. Although the buildings connected with these foundations form a characteristic feature of late medieval church architecture, they have been little studied as a class except in England, and their history remains largely to be written.

Physically the essentials of a chantry were an altar and usually an associated place of burial. The altar might be accommodated almost anywhere in a church or cloister, and neither it nor the tomb necessarily required any structural alteration to the fabric. Many chantries have consequently come and gone without leaving any trace of their existence. In the medieval cathedral of Geneva over a hundred 'chappellenies' shared twenty-three altars. The only architectural provision for these altars was four transeptal chapels dating from the twelfth century and one large chapel containing the tomb of Cardinal de Brogny (d. 1426), which had been added by him to the south side of the nave in 1405–6. All the other altars stood against the side walls or the choir screen, and nothing now remains of them (fig. 141). A visitor to York before the Reformation would have found thirty or forty altars within the great volume of the minster church, most of which were used wholly or partially by chantry priests. Today only two or three survive because chapels (of which that founded by Archbishop Zouche is the most prominent) were specially built to contain them. These were well-endowed permanent chantries. For lesser ones a screen of wood or iron would suffice, and even this might be superfluous when (as was often the case) two or more chantry priests took turns to use the same altar.

When architectural provision was made for permanent chantries it naturally varied in accordance with time and circumstance, not to mention the personality of the founder. But three basic types can be distinguished: those that were built as part of a planned architectural programme controlled by the church authorities; those that were added to existing churches on private initiative; and those that took the form of a new and autonomous church or chapel.

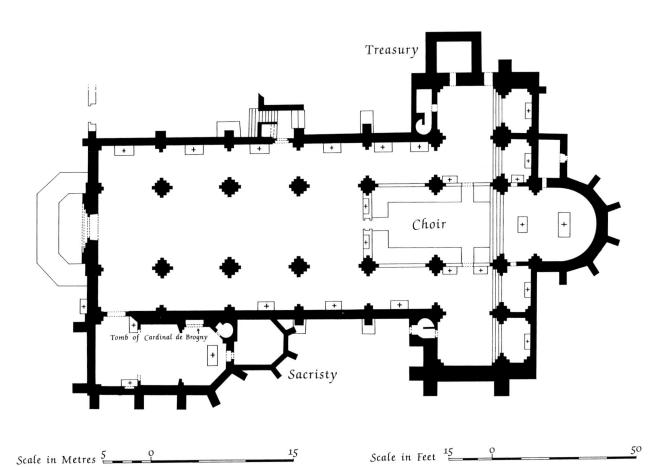

Treasury

Choir

Tomb of Cardinal de Brogny

Sacristy

Scale in Metres 5   0   15   Scale in Feet 15   0   50

141. Geneva, Switzerland, the medieval cathedral, showing the altars (after Blondel, *Genava* 24, 1946).

As examples of the first we may take the cathedral church of Notre-Dame in Paris and the Franciscan and Dominican churches in Florence: S. Croce and S. Maria Novella. As built from 1164 onwards Notre-Dame was a tall Gothic church supported by an imposing array of flying buttresses. There was an ambulatory and there were double aisles, but there were no chapels. In the course of the thirteenth century and the early years of the fourteenth the spaces between the buttresses were gradually filled up by a series of thirty-five identically designed chapels, each lit by a traceried window surmounted by a crocketted gable (figs. 142, 144). The result is so regular and harmonious that few realise that these chapels were not only not part of the original design, but were built at different times over a period of fifty or sixty years.★ Their purpose was to provide altars for the numerous 'chappellenies' founded by wealthy people of every station in

★ In the nave the process of insertion of the chapels is clearly demonstrated by straight joints externally and by dislocations in the masonry internally. In the *chevet* it is concealed externally because the faces of the buttresses were remodelled to match the architecture of the chapels, but inside the bases of the thirteenth-century responds are easily distinguishable from those of the twelfth century against which they abut.

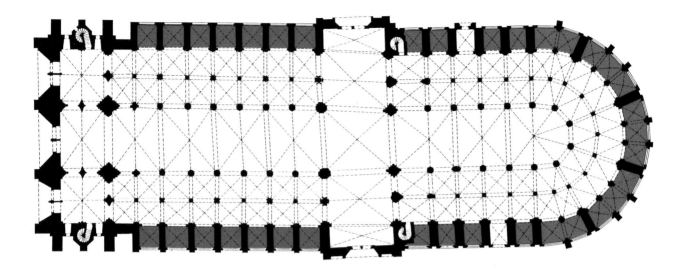

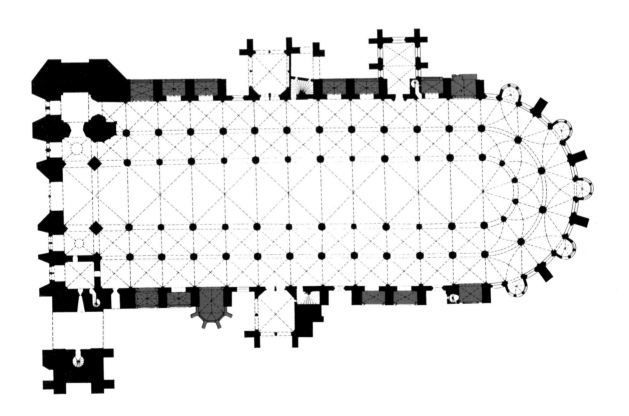

Scale in Metres 10 0 30   Scale in Feet 25 0 100

142. *Top*, the cathedral of Notre-Dame, Paris, showing in red the chapels added *c.*1255–1323. *Bottom*, Bourges cathedral, France, showing in red chapels added in the late fourteenth and fifteenth centuries.

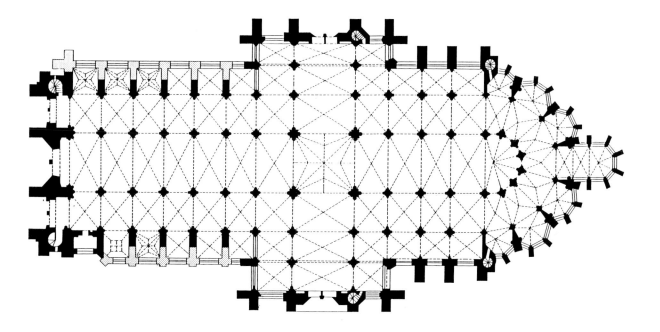

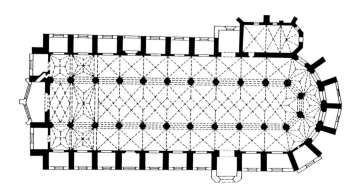

143. *Top*, Amiens cathedral, France, showing (stippled) chapels added on either side of the nave between *c.*1290 and 1375. *Bottom*, the church at Nysa in Poland, showing chapels added in the fifteenth century.

144. Paris, the cathedral of Notre-Dame, the east end showing some of the chapels inserted between the buttresses during the late thirteenth and early fourteenth centuries (Arch. Phot. Paris, S.P.A.D.E.M.)

life, from a king to a goldsmith. Directly or indirectly it was the beneficiaries of the intercessory masses who paid for the building of the chapels, either in their lifetime or through their will, but it is clear that the chapter of the cathedral kept control of the building programme and ensured that each chapel conformed strictly to a master plan drawn up by their architect. In this way the cathedral responded to the demand for personal intercession in a manner that preserved and indeed enhanced its architectural unity. At Amiens, too, additional chapels were skilfully incorporated into the design of the nave in a manner as deceptively regular as in the *chevet* at Paris (fig. 143). At Bourges, however, complete uniformity of design was not maintained when the spaces between the buttresses were filled in by local magnates from 1404 onwards (fig. 142), and at Nysa in Poland the process was never completed. Here the gaps in the ring of chapels added in the fifteenth century stand out in the plan like missing teeth (fig. 143).

In Florence the popularity of the privately endowed intercessory mass coincided with the advent of the mendicant orders of friars. Both the Dominicans and the Franciscans depended entirely on charity for their building funds, and in return for financial assistance they accommodated the desire of the laity for family chapels. For the friars themselves a spacious nave for preaching was the first priority and the provision of chapels at the east end was largely a response to the demands of the laity. In the Dominican church of S. Maria Novella (*c.*1246–1300)

158

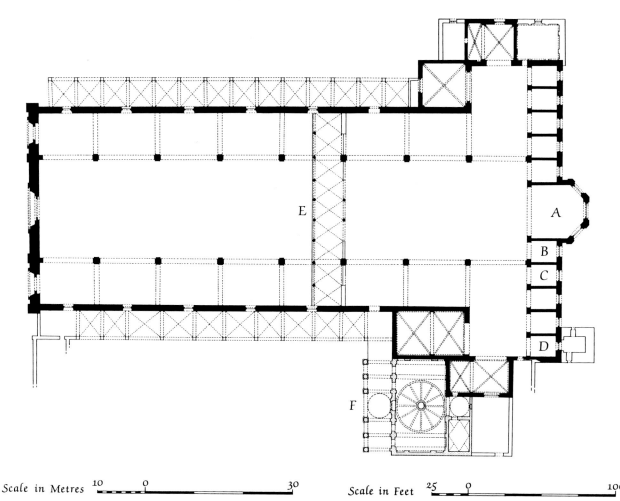

Scale in Metres 10 ⋅⋅⋅ 0 —— 30   Scale in Feet 25 ⋅⋅⋅ 0 —— 100

145. Florence, S. Croce in the fifteenth century. A. Cappella Maggiore (under patronage of the Alberti family). B. Bardi chapel. C. Peruzzi chapel. D. Velluti chapel. E. The screen or tramezzo, removed in the sixteenth century. F. The chapter-house or Pazzi chapel, built *c.*1430 onwards.

there were five structural chapels, besides several altars set up against screens; in the Franciscan S. Croce (begun 1295) there were ten of the former and a number of the latter (fig. 145). In both churches the chapels were an integral part of the design, and work on them often began before any donor came forward. But most of them were eventually adopted as a family chapel by a wealthy Florentine donor, who was able to pass on his rights to his heirs. The donor was expected to furnish and equip the chapel as well as to pay for its structure, and the outlay might be considerable: in 1363 it cost Andrea di Strozzi 500 gold florins to become the patron of a chapel in the Austin friars' church of S. Spirito. Some similar arrangement probably explains the enormous transept or 'north nave', containing ten identical chapels, that was added to the Franciscan church in Oxford in the course of the fourteenth century (fig. 146), while in the Dominican church at Toulouse several of the chapels forming a *chevet* built in the late thirteenth century

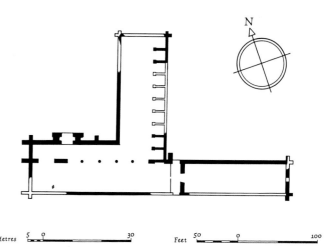

146. Oxford, the Franciscan church, plan as established by excavation (after Hassall).

Metres 5 0 30   Feet 50 0 100

are still distinguished by the painted coats of arms of the patrician families who adopted them.

Despite the popularity of the mendicant churches as places of burial in the thirteenth and fourteenth centuries, many people were still buried in their parish church or churchyard: indeed, in some places the right of the friars to offer burial was hotly contested by parish priests who saw in it a threat to that part of their livelihood that was represented by burial fees and payments for commemorative masses. Moreover, by the fifteenth century the friars had lost some of their appeal: as professional mendicants they had overstrained the charitable goodwill of many of the townspeople among whom they lived. The result was a return to the parish church as the most favoured place of burial. There is documentary evidence of this in the expressed wishes of many testators, and architectural evidence in the form of private chapels added to parish churches in the fifteenth and early sixteenth centuries. Sometimes these chapels conformed to a uniform design, as for instance in the Parisian churches of Saint-Séverin and Saint-Germain-l'Auxerrois (fig. 147), but often they were unashamedly individualistic expressions of family pride and private wealth which the clergy of a late medieval town or country church might have neither the wish nor the will to resist. The result was a series of more or less piecemeal additions to the existing fabric. The large town church of Notre-Dame la Grande in Poitiers may serve as an example (fig. 148). The Romanesque building with its three apses remained largely unaltered until the fifteenth century, when a series of private chapels began to be added both at the east end and on the north side, spoiling the symmetry of the plan but adding fresh architectural incidents to both interior and exterior. The first recorded was built by Colas Méhé, 'bourgeois', in 1420, the year of the Treaty of Troyes which ended hostilities between France and England. It was on the north side of the church and may have been a predecessor of the six chapels that eventually protruded from the nave. The next was the rectangular chapel added to the north side of the *chevet* by Jean de Torsay, lord of Lezay and seneschal of Poitou, who provided for its erection in his will dated August 1421. The founder of the similar chapel (since demolished) on the south side is not

160

147. Paris, Saint-Séverin, showing chapels added at the east end between 1489 and 1495.

recorded, but in 1475 Yvon de Fou, seneschal of Poitou and councillor of Charles VII and Louis XI, had leave to demolish the southern of the three Romanesque apses in order to build the lofty two-bay chapel which contained the tomb of himself and his wife.★ In 1514 a smaller chapel was squeezed in on the other side immediately to the west of the surviving apse for the benefit of François Fumé, mayor of Poitiers, and by 1531 a total of six rectangular chapels had been built along the north side of the nave, each raising its gable a little above the level of its neighbour's (fig. 149).

England was, however, the land where the architecturally nonconforming chantry chapel was most prevalent. With their low vaults, few English cathedrals had the massive projecting buttresses that in France provided ready-made spaces for chapels. With the exception of Chichester,† no English cathedral chapter appears ever to have initiated a planned sequence of chapels like those at Paris, and the square east ends of English churches did not in any case lend themselves to a continuous array of chapels on the model of Notre-Dame. However, the chapels added in the fourteenth century to the choir of Laon cathedral show that a square-ended presbytery could be adapted to provide a uniform series of chapels, and a

★ The sixteenth-century sculpture of the Entombment of Christ which now occupies the tomb-recess in this chapel was brought from the abbey of La Trinité at the time of its demolition in 1802.
† Here four chapels of uniform design were added to north and south of the nave in the course of the thirteenth century. As each chapel occupied two bays, they differed in architectural character, and perhaps also in function, from the single-bay chapels that were standard in France.

161

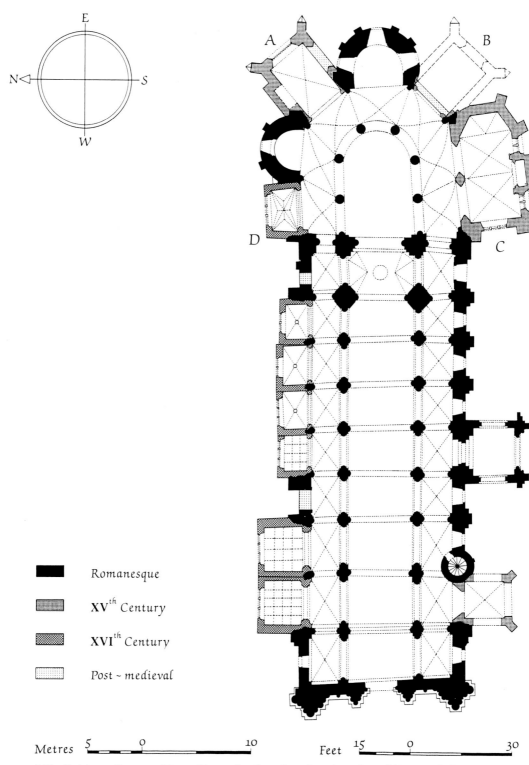

E

N ◁——————— S

W

Romanesque

XVth Century

XVIth Century

Post-medieval

Metres 5   0   10   Feet 15   0   30

148. Poitiers, France, Notre-Dame la Grande, showing the addition of chapels in the fifteenth and sixteenth centuries. A. Torsay chapel. B. demolished chapel. C. Fou chapel. D. Fumé chapel.

149. Poitiers, Notre-Dame la Grande, the sixteenth-century chapels on the north side of the nave.

150 (*below*). Scarborough church, Yorkshire, showing the three uniform chapels added to the south side of the nave, probably in 1380. The window tracery has been restored.

few individual chantry chapels were indeed built between the lateral buttresses of such English cathedrals as Exeter and Lincoln. At Scarborough the parish church offers the altogether exceptional sight of three identical chantry chapels added to the south side of the nave in the late fourteenth century, probably in 1380, when the vicar and two burgesses simultaneously took out licences to found chantries in the church (fig. 150). But only at King's College chapel in Cambridge was

North MORETON

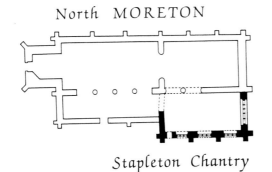

Stapleton Chantry

WIXFORD

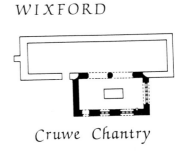

Cruwe Chantry

HEADCORN

BASING

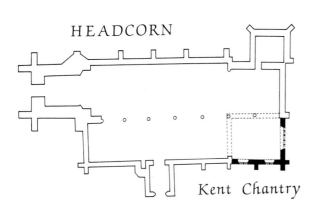

Kent Chantry

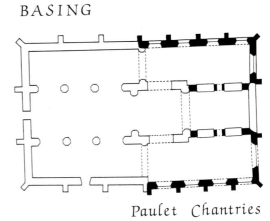

Paulet Chantries

TIVERTON

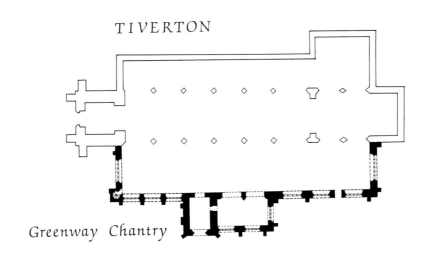

Greenway Chantry

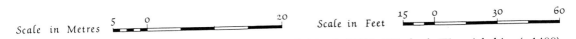

Scale in Metres   5   0   20   Scale in Feet   15   0   30   60

151. English chantry chapels at North Moreton, Berkshire (*c.*1300), Wixford, Warwickshire (*c.*1400), Headcorn, Kent (1466), Basing, Hampshire (early sixteenth-century), and Tiverton, Devon (1517). At Tiverton the founder of the chantry rebuilt the south aisle at the same time.

152 (*above*). North Moreton church,
Berkshire, the Stapleton chantry chapel,
c.1300 (cf. fig. 151).

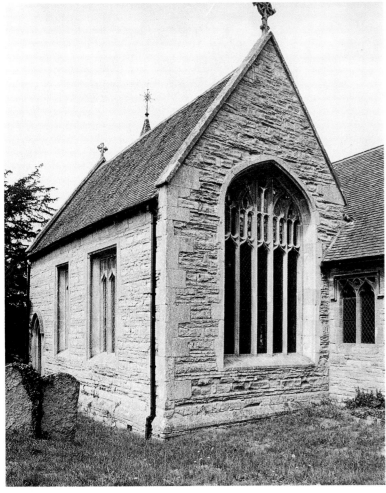

153. Wixford, Warwickshire, the Cruwe
chantry chapel, *c*.1400 (cf. fig. 151).

154 (*above*). Bromham church, Wiltshire, the Baynton chantry chapel founded by William Beauchamp, Lord St. Amand (d. 1457).

155. Tiverton church, Devon, the Greenway chantry chapel founded by John Greenway, a wool merchant, in 1517 (cf. fig. 151).

156. North Leigh church, Oxfordshire, interior of the Wilcote chapel founded by Elizabeth Wilcote (d. 1442) as a family chantry (Thomas Photos). For the exterior see fig. 232.

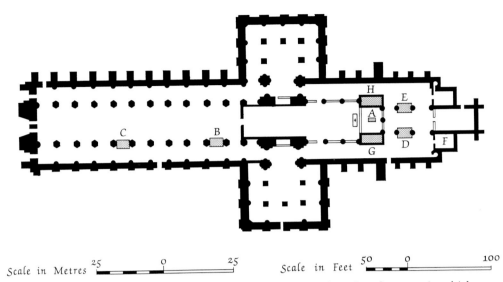

157. Winchester cathedral: plan showing the chantry chapels of successive bishops. A. The shrine of St Swithin. B. Bishop Edington (d. 1366). C. Bishop Wykeham (d. 1404). D. Bishop Beaufort (d. 1447). E. Bishop Waynflete (d. 1486). F. Bishop Langton (d. 1501). G. Bishop Fox (d. 1528). H. Bishop Gardiner (d. 1555).

provision made from the first for a series of identical 'closets' (as they are called in a contemporary document), occupying the spaces between the buttresses on either side, some of which were eventually used as chantry chapels. In English parish churches chantry chapels often formed eastern extensions of the transepts or aisles (fig. 151). Many English chantry chapels were, however, accommodated by appropriating space within the walls of existing churches. Often a complete bay would be screened off for the purpose. At Durham the powerful family of the Nevilles was allowed to appropriate two whole bays on the south side of the nave for their chantry, and in some great town churches the aisles were largely devoted to the chantry chapels founded by wealthy individuals or maintained by local guilds. Alternatively, an aedicule of stone or timber (or occasionally of iron) containing the tomb and a small altar would be set up between the piers of nave or choir. Of this arrangement Winchester cathedral is a striking example. Here not a single chapel disturbs the external uniformity of the great church, but within it, the chantry chapels of successive bishops—Edington (d. 1366), Wykeham (d. 1404), Beaufort (d. 1447), Waynflete (d. 1486), Langton (d. 1501), Fox (d. 1528) and Gardiner (d. 1555) – occupy the most eligible spaces in nave and presbytery (fig. 157).

The chantry chapel as an independent structure within a church appears to have been peculiar to England. The miniature Gothic building is almost invariably 'Perpendicular' in style, with rectilinear panelling, unglazed traceried windows and elaborately pinnacled or crested upper parts (fig. 158). Within, the rectangular space is or was shared by the tomb and an altar with a carved or painted reredos. The ceiling above is often vaulted in stone, and some of the earliest fan vaults in the country are to be found in chantry chapels in the abbey church of

158. Winchester cathedral, the chantry chapels of Bishops Beaufort (*right*) and Fox (*left*) (J.R.H. Weaver).

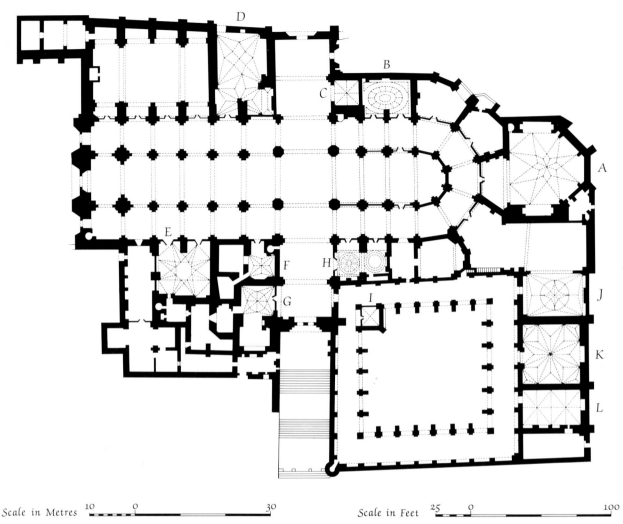

159. Burgos cathedral, Spain, showing the funerary chapels, with the names of their founders. A. Capilla del Condestable (the Constable of Castile, c.1486–94). B. Capilla de la Natividad (Doña Ana de Espinosa, 1560). C. Capilla de San Nicolas (Villahoz family, late thirteenth century). D. Capilla de la Concepción (Bishop Luis de Acuña, 1477–88). E. Capilla de la Consolación (Don Gonzalez de Lerma, 1519). F. Capilla de San Juan de Sahagun (Rojas family, fourteeth century). G. Capilla de la Visitación (Bishop Alonso de Cartagena, c.1440–50). H. Capilla de San Enrique (Archbishop Enrique Peralta, 1670–4). I. Chapel of Don Francisco de Mena, canon and protonotary, 1545. J. Capilla de San Juan Bautista (Bishop Juan Cabeza de Vaca, early fifteenth century). K. Chapter-house (non-funerary, 1316–54). L. Capilla de Corpus Christi (Don Garcia Fernandez de Castellanos, 1375).

Tewkesbury. Although nearly always deprived of their religious imagery, many of these exquisite buildings fortunately survived the dissolution (in 1545–7) of the chantries that they housed and remain as England's distinctive contribution to medieval funerary architecture.

Still within the category of chapels attached to existing buildings were a few highly prestigious foundations of exceptional magnificence. The two that will be mentioned here are among the best-known buildings of their kind in Europe: the

170

160. Burgos cathedral, exterior of the Capilla del Condestable.

161 (*below*). Burgos cathedral, the vault of the Capilla del Condestable.

Capilla del Condestable at the east end of Burgos cathedral and King Henry VII's Chapel at Westminster. The chapel at Burgos was built by Don Pedro Fernández de Velasco, first Constable of Castile, and his wife, Mencía de Mendoza. Their marriage had united two of the wealthiest and most aristocratic families of Spain, and the chapel was to be their joint memorial. The establishment provided for ten priests and two acolytes. Work began in the 1480s and was still in progress when the constable died in 1492, to be followed eight years later by his wife. The glazing was not completed until about 1520, and the effigies were not in place until 1532. Externally the octagonal chapel rivals the central tower of the cathedral (completed a few years later) in a *flamboyant* elaboration which clothes but does not conceal its form (fig. 160). Internally the geometry of the design is not so clearly expressed. At ground level it is a rectangle with a three-sided east end; at vault level, an octagon (fig. 159). The vault itself, pierced to form a traceried star (fig. 161), is a tour-de-force, but lower down there is a visual conflict between the great cusped arches and the slender vaulting shafts that is to the latter's disadvantage, and the scale is (at least to modern eyes) disturbed by the huge heraldic shields carved on the walls. On the floor the exquisitely carved marble effigies of the founder and his wife lie on a jasper sarcophagus whose squat form (influenced probably by that of Pope Sixtus IV in St Peter's, Rome) denies them the focal importance that was their due.

Both in its octagonal shape and in its decorative enrichment the Capilla del Condestable was a notable example of the *flamboyant* style of Gothic architecture which in the course of the fifteenth century became fashionable in most parts of continental Europe north of the Alps. Flanders and Germany were centres from which it spread south and west, and the chapel at Burgos was designed by a mason from Cologne, Master Simon. The earliest example of the *flamboyant* style in Spain was another funerary chapel – that in Toledo cathedral built for Don Alvaro de Luna by Master Hanequin of Brussels in the 1430s, and at Burgos there was already a smaller chapel designed by another German master, Hans (Juan) of Cologne, for Bishop Alonso de Cartagena in about 1440 (fig. 159). Although the latter chapel is rectangular in plan, it has a vault whose pattern looks forward to that of the Capilla del Condestable, itself to be much imitated in sixteenth-century Spanish architecture, for instance in the funerary chapel of Don Gonzalez de Lerma on the south side of Burgos cathedral (1519 onwards) (fig. 159), and in the octagonally vaulted sanctuaries of such late Gothic churches as La Vid at Burgos and Santo Tomás at Arnedo (Logroño).

In England, Henry VII's Chapel at Westminster (fig. 162) was probably the largest and certainly the most expensive structure ever built primarily for funerary purposes. Contemporary moralists emphasised the heavy burden of sin incurred by princes, and it behoved a king who had won his throne in battle and kept it by the devious expedients of statecraft to make ample provision for the safety of his soul. Henry's will shows that to ease its passage through the ordeal of purgatory the royal testator took every precaution that wealth could purchase, or authority prescribe. Immediately after his death ten thousand masses were to be said for the remission of his sins and the good of his soul: subsequently its

162. King Henry VII's Chapel, Westminster (Royal Commission on the Historical Monuments of England, National Monuments Record).

continued progress to salvation was to be ensured by the permanent suffrages of three monks of Westminster, who were to act as chantry priests, and by the solemn celebration of anniversaries in a long list of cathedral, conventual and university churches. Prayers, however, were not enough. They must be supplemented by works of 'charity and mercy'. Already in his lifetime Henry had founded the Hospital of the Savoy and an almshouse at Westminster. Now in his will he enjoined his executors to establish two further hospitals at Coventry and York, to complete the unfinished chapel of King's College, Cambridge, to contribute 500 marks to the completion of the nave of Westminster Abbey, and to give £500 to every house of Friars Observant. Above all, they were to complete the chapel that he had begun to build at the east end of the abbey church of Westminster in 1502/3.

The accounts for building Henry VII's Chapel are lost, but it was undoubtedly the work of a group of royal master masons well-known for their work at Windsor and elsewhere. In style it belongs to the same phase of highly ornate late Gothic as the Capilla del Condestable and shares with it some characteristic architectural features, including polygonal buttresses and cusped arches. In its vaulting and fenestration, however, it follows the conventions of the English Perpendicular tradition rather than those of the *flamboyant* style prevalent on the Continent. It appears to have been structurally complete at the time of the king's death in 1509, and the carving, glazing and other decoration were probably finished by 1512. The total cost is not recorded, but the available evidence suggests that it was not less than £20,000.

Had Henry VII carried out his original intention, the focal point of the chapel would have been the shrine of a canonised Henry VI. The normal place for a saint's shrine was behind the altar, while a founder's tomb usually stood in front of it. In the event, Henry VI's body remained at Windsor, and Henry VII's executors decided to place his tomb behind the altar, in the area reserved for the shrine. The tomb itself, made by the Florentine sculptor Pietro Torrigiano, was one of the first complete examples of Renaissance art to be seen in England. The chapel ceased to function as a chantry in 1547, but continued to serve as a place of royal burial throughout the sixteenth, seventeenth and early eighteenth centuries (fig. 123).

It was only a small step from a great chapel of this sort, often, as at Burgos, with its own establishment of priests, to one that was independent of any parent foundation. In large cathedral churches, such as Chartres or York, the chantry priests were sometimes organised into colleges, with residential accommodation in the vicinity, and a collegiate chantry with its own church was an alternative that offered itself to the wealthy founder. In England the great ducal houses of York and Lancaster each had its burial place in a collegiate church, with an establishment of priests or secular canons to maintain the service of intercession, the one at Fotheringhay in Northamptonshire, the other at Leicester. Of the 'exceding fair college chirch' seen by the Tudor antiquary John Leland at Leicester in the reign of Henry VIII, with its array of Lancastrian tombs round the high altar, nothing now remains; but at Fotheringhay the nave and west tower survive, though the 'faire cloister' and the choir were demolished in the sixteenth century, together with the tombs of the founder, Edward, 2nd Duke of York (who fell at Agincourt in 1415), his nephew Richard, 3rd Duke (d. 1460), and the latter's wife, Cecily, Duchess of York and mother of King Edward IV. In France King Louis XI (d. 1483) chose to be buried in a similar establishment at Cléry near Orléans, of which he was the patron and in large part the builder. His original monument was destroyed by Huguenots in the sixteenth century, but a seventeenth-century replacement stands in the late Gothic church whose restrained elegance is uncompromised by any superfluous detail. On the south side the personal chapel built in 1465 by one of the heroes of the Hundred Years' War, Jean Dunois, bastard of Orléans and lord of Cléry, is enlivened by the compulsive rhythm of a vault whose alternating pattern was much favoured by fifteenth-century masons.

Dukes and princes might set up new collegiate churches to guard their mortal remains, but for a lesser feudal lord such grand foundations were out of the question. A more economical expedient was to arrange for the college to be established in an existing parish church already in the founder's patronage. Architecturally, the principal requirement was a large chancel in which up to a dozen priests could perform their offices and say their masses, together with residential buildings in which they could live a life that, although corporate, was much less rigorously disciplined than that of monks. In accordance with long-established custom, the tombs of the founder and his family were usually placed in the chancel in front of the principal altar. Collegiate chantries of this sort were characteristic of the fourteenth and fifteenth centuries and were particularly common in England and Scotland. Well-known examples, with the names of their founders, are Bunbury, Cheshire (Sir Hugh Calveley, 1387), Cobham, Kent (John de Cobham, 1362), Corstorphin, Midlothian (Sir John Forrester, 1429), Cotterstock, Northants. (John Giffard, canon of York, 1338–9), Greystoke, Cumberland (Ralph, Lord Greystoke, 1382), Pleshey, Essex (Thomas, Duke of Gloucester, 1394), Roslin, Midlothian (Sir William Sinclair, c.1521), Tattershall, Lincs. (Ralph, Lord Cromwell, 1439), Tong, Shropshire (Elizabeth de Pembridge, 1410) and Tormarton, Gloucestershire (Sir John de la Rivière, 1344). Although continuing to function as parish churches, most of them were enlarged or rebuilt in a manner that reflected their status as aristocratic burial places, and at Bunbury, Cobham, Tormarton and Tong (figs. 163–4) the tomb of the founder remains to demonstrate the funerary purpose of the foundation. Architecturally, the most remarkable is the unfinished church at Roslin, where an attempt was made, by masons trained in the Scottish tradition, to rival the exhibitionist splendours of the Continental *flamboyant* style.

A variant form of the collegiate chantry was the academic foundation in a university. Here the good works provided for by the foundation took the form of promoting learning and scholarship in men who were almost invariably destined for holy orders, and who were bound to pray for the soul of their founder in a chapel that was often by far the largest and most decorative building in the college. When Henry Chichele, Archbishop of Canterbury, founded All Souls College, Oxford, in 1438, the fellows were required by their statutes to pray for

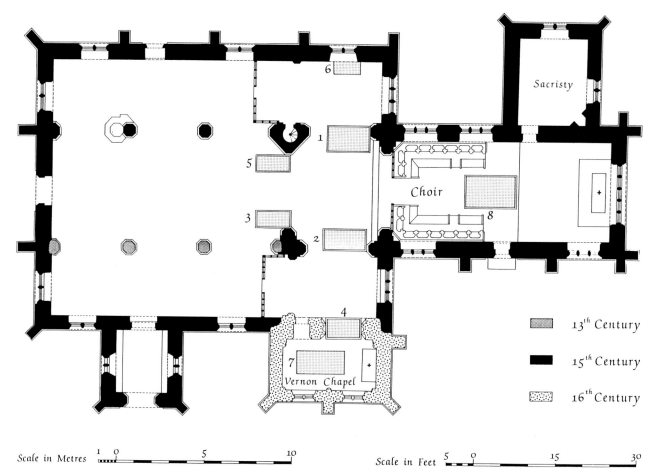

Sacristy

Choir

8

Vernon Chapel

7

4

1

5

3

2

6

Scale in Metres 1 0 5 10

Scale in Feet 5 0 15 30

163. The parish church of Tong in Shropshire, rebuilt and converted into a collegiate chantry by the widow of Sir Fulk de Pembridge in 1410, and thereafter the burial place of successive lords of Tong. The Vernon chantry on the south side was founded by Sir Henry Vernon (d. 1515). 1. Sir Fulk de Pembridge (d. 1409) and his wife Isabel, the foundress. 2. Sir Richard Vernon (d. 1451). 3. Sir William Vernon (d. 1467). 4. Sir Henry Vernon (d. 1515). 5. Sir Richard Vernon (d. 1517). 6. Sir Humphrey Vernon (d. 1542). 7. Arthur Vernon, M.A., rector of Whitchurch (d. 1517), brass on floor and bust in niche. 8. Sir Thomas Stanley (d. 1576), showing approximate original position of tomb now in south aisle.

the souls of King Henry V, of his brother the Duke of Clarence and of all those who, like the duke, had lost their lives fighting in France. The college's function as a place of intercession for the dead was emphasised by its dedication to 'All Souls' and by a relief over the main gateway showing Christ the Saviour with souls in Purgatory at his feet. College chapels did not necessarily enjoy the right of burial, but at All Souls the medieval cloister (destroyed in the eighteenth century) was intended to serve as a cemetery, and at Winchester College the two-storeyed chantry chapel of John Fromond, William of Wykeham's steward, was built over his grave in the middle of the cloister, its upper floor being intended to serve as a library.

Despite the popularity of the collegiate church as a form of intercessory

176

164. Tong church, Shropshire, exterior and interior of the chantry chapel founded by Sir Henry Vernon (d. 1515). His effigy is on the right. In a niche is the bust of Arthur Vernon, M.A. (d. 1517), shown in the attitude of preaching.

foundation, many kings and princes of the later Middle Ages continued as a matter of course to be buried among their ancestors in the churches of Benedictine, Cistercian or Augustinian abbeys such as Westminster, Saint-Denis, Holyrood, Las Huelgas or Poblet. There, a national saint or relic was often the focus of a sequence of tombs that emphasised the antiquity and legitimacy of the ruling family. Even when a new dynasty came to the fore, or an old one rose in status and power, similar considerations might lead to the choice of an ancient foundation as its place of burial.

But for those who wanted to entrust the welfare of their souls to a new monastic foundation, rather than to an existing one, the Order of Chartreux was by the late fourteenth century the only one whose reputation was still entirely untarnished. So the Carthusian monks were to count among their benefactors the kings of Aragon, Castile, England, France, Hungary and Scotland, the dukes of Bavaria, Brittany, Burgundy, Calabria and Milan, as well as many popes and bishops. One of their most munificent patrons was Philip the Bold, Duke of Burgundy. It was in 1378 that Philip, already Duke of Burgundy and in due course to inherit (through his wife) the rich counties of Flanders and Artois, decided that the time had come to make arrangements for a place of burial that would be both efficacious in terms of the after-life and commensurate with his status as one of Europe's greatest princes. Thus was established the Carthusian priory of Champmol, near Dijon, in which the salvation of the duke's soul was to be assured by the prayers of the most ascetic of all religious orders, while his worldly fame was to be perpetuated by one of the finest displays of sculpture in fourteenth-century Europe.

In plan, Champmol conformed to the normal specification for a Carthusian monastery, with a series of cells (one for each monk) arranged round a large cloister, and a modest church for those services that this introspective order held in common (fig. 165). In some Carthusian foundations private benefactors secured for themselves the prayers of an individual monk by paying for the construction of his cell, but here at Champmol all twenty-four were built at the duke's expense. Externally the church was unremarkable, but at the entrance the visitor was confronted with a striking reminder that this was a ducal foundation. On either side were kneeling figures, realistically carved, of the duke and duchess being presented to the Virgin Mary by their patron saints, St John the Baptist and St Catherine. The arrangement recalled the figures of donors on a Flemish altarpiece: the sculptor, Claus Sluter, was, in fact, from the Low Countries. Within, a screen separated the short nave from the monks' choir, in the middle of which stood the exquisitely carved tombs of the founder and his son John the Fearless, now in the Musée des Beaux-Arts at Dijon. Here the elaborate stalls, the glazed floor tiles, the coloured bosses of the vault, the great carved and painted altarpiece, the bronze plaque in the sanctuary with kneeling figures of the founder and his duchess, and the ducal portraits on panels and in stained glass, transformed the austere house of prayer into one of the most sumptuous of medieval funerary chapels. On the north side a newel staircase gave access to an upper pew or oratory, made comfortable with fireplace and panelling, from which the reigning duke could look down into the choir and see mass celebrated at the high altar. Although the building itself had been erected under the direction of a French mason, Drouet de Dammartin, the tombs and all the rich decoration of the interior were the work of artists and craftsmen whom the duke had summoned from his Flemish territories to work for him in Burgundy.

The patronage of the rich and influential Duke of Burgundy did much to popularise the *flamboyant* style in the courts of western Europe. Only insular England and an Italy never entirely forgetful of its classical past remained resistant to the frenetic elaboration of late Gothic geometry. One outstanding monument of Flemish Burgundian Gothic is, however, to be seen to the south of the Alps, and it is a funerary chapel. It forms the east end of the church of S. Giovanni at Saluzzo in Piedmont. The marquisate of Saluzzo was a vassal state of the duchy of Savoy, whose principal territories were in what is now south-west France, and its rulers were cosmopolitan figures who were frequently in France and who must have been familiar with Franco-Burgundian culture. The chapel at S. Giovanni represents the belated fulfilment of a project initiated by Marquis Tommaso III (d. 1416), who had intended to build it on a different site. As realised by his successors in the last years of the fifteenth century, the chapel has striking affinities with Burgundian Gothic in general, and perhaps with Champmol in particular in the planning of the east end with two low vestries projecting diagonally from the canted apse (fig. 165). Canopied recesses on either side, decorated with Gothic carving of exceptional virtuosity (fig. 166), provided prestigious settings for tombs, but only one of them is now occupied – by a Renaissance monument to Marquis Ludovico II (d. 1504), which may have been intended to stand in the middle of the chapel and which certainly fits awkwardly into the Gothic recess.

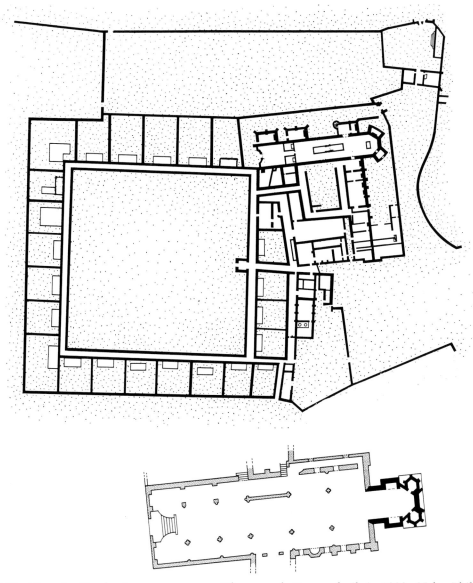

165. *Top*, the Carthusian monastery at Champmol, France, built in 1383–95 by Philip, Duke of Burgundy (d. 1404), as a place of burial for himself and his wife. The building was destroyed in the French Revolution, and this plan is derived from an eighteenth-century survey in the Archives Municipales, Dijon (after David). The ducal tombs stood in the enclosure in the middle of the church, with the monks' choir-stalls on either side. The central quadrangle was the monks' cemetery. *Bottom*, the church of S. Giovanni at Saluzzo in Piedmont, N. Italy, with the late fifteeth-century funerary chapel of the marquesses of Saluzzo at the east end. Note the similar arrangement of the vestries in the two churches. No scale is available for either plan.

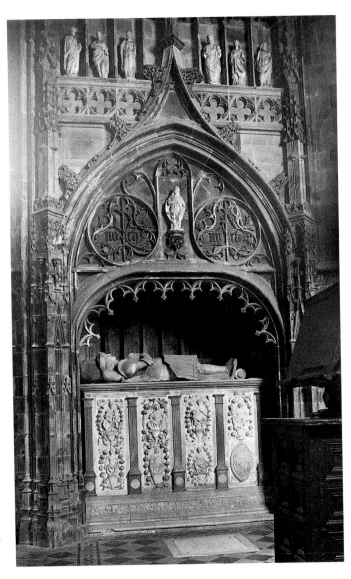

166. Saluzzo, N. Italy, S. Giovanni, tomb-recess in the fifteeth-century funerary chapel of the marquesses of Saluzzo. The tomb is that of Marquis Ludovico II (d. 1504).

Better known than this outlier of the Gothic north are three major monastic churches built as princely burial places: the Dominican foundation at Batalha in Portugal, the chartreuse of Miraflores near Burgos in Spain, and the Augustinian church of Brou at Bourg-en-Bresse in what is now France. Batalha is the Portuguese for 'Battle', and the monastery of Our Lady of Victory was founded by King John I (d. 1433), near the site of the Battle of Aljubarrota (1385) which had vindicated his claim to the throne of Portugal against that of Juan of Castile. He intended it to be not only a memorial of his victory, but also a place of burial for himself and his successors. King John's will of 1426 reveals the curious fact that he had started to build the monastery before deciding to which order of religious to offer it. The eventual choice of Dominican friars was (the will states) due to their special devotion to the Virgin Mary, to whom the monastery had

180

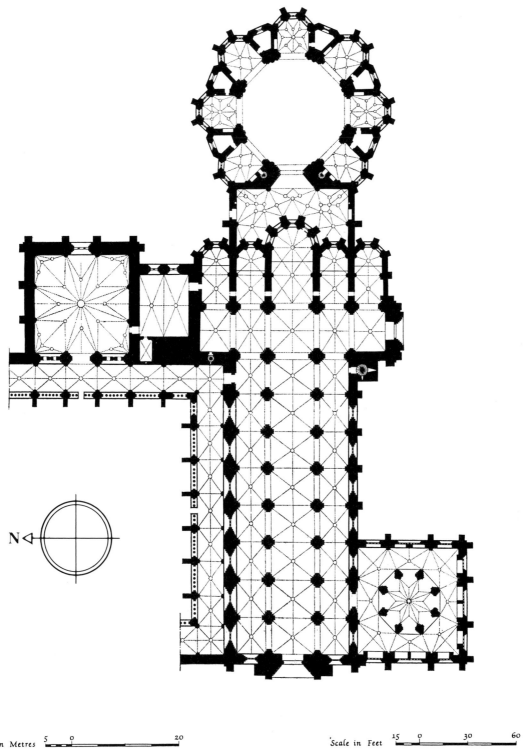

Scale in Metres 5 0 20   Scale in Feet 15 0 30 60

N ◁

167. Plan of the monastic church of Batalha in Portugal, built by King John I to commemorate the Battle of Aljubarrota (1385). The royal burial chapel projects from the south side of the nave.

168 (*following page*). Batalha, interior of the royal burial chapel built by King John I (d. 1433) (Portuguese National Tourist Office).

already been dedicated because the battle took place on the eve of the feast of her Assumption. For an order that normally operated from urban bases, the rural site must have been as much of a novelty as the great church, whose long nave and narrow aisles would have been more suitable for Benedictine monks or Augustinian canons than for the Order of Preachers (fig. 167). At least the eastern part of the church must have been complete by 1415, when the queen (Philippa, daughter of John of Gaunt, Duke of Lancaster) was buried before the high altar. However, John I subsequently built a separate burial chapel onto the south side of the nave at its west end (fig. 168). This building is as exceptional in its design as in its siting. It consists of a vaulted octagon standing on open arches within a square and was originally surmounted by a spire (destroyed in the earthquake of 1755). The octagon was reserved for the tomb of the founder and his queen (whose body was removed there from the choir), while handsomely decorated recesses were provided in the outer walls as burial places for their younger sons. In renouncing the founder's privilege of burial before the high altar, King John was determined that no one else should enjoy it, and laid down in his will that no one 'of whatever rank or condition' might be buried there. His eldest son and successor, Duarte (Edward), accordingly decided to build a new chapel for his own burial beyond the east end of the church, but died in 1438, leaving it incomplete. Work on this huge octagonal chapel was continued by King Manoel I (1495–1521), but it remains unfinished, a spectacular monument of that combination of intricate late Gothic and early Renaissance detail so characteristic of the Iberian peninsula (fig. 169).

The chartreuse of Miraflores near Burgos was founded in 1442 by King Juan II of Castile and was the work (1452–88) of Hans of Cologne and his son Simon, the latter of whom was later to build the Capilla del Condestable. Like Champmol, Miraflores conforms to the standard Carthusian layout, with a large cloister and a church of modest size, but, as at Champmol, Carthusian simplicity has been compromised by princely patronage. The church's function as a royal place of burial is proclaimed externally by the corona of pinnacled buttresses which surround and emphasise the east end. Within this results in a fan-like display of cusped vaulting ribs which converge on a boss carved with the arms of Castile. Immediately below is the royal tomb whose star-shaped form (essentially a 'rotated square' of a type much used in medieval architectural design) answers to the vaulting and brilliantly relates it to its polygonal setting. This tomb is the masterpiece of the Spanish sculptor Gil de Siloé, who was also responsible for the monument to the Infante Alfonso (d. 1468) on the north side of the sanctuary. Both date from 1489 to 1493. The kneeling figure of the young prince stands in a canopied Gothic recess surrounded by a virtuoso display of exquisitely carved detail.

The church of Augustinian friars or hermits at Brou was built by Margaret of Austria, daughter of the Emperor Maximilian and widow of Philibert II, Duke of Savoy (d. 1504), as a burial place for her husband, herself and her mother-in-law, Margaret de Bourbon. Brou (later annexed by France) then belonged to the dukes of Savoy and formed part of Margaret's dower. An unfulfilled vow by her

169 (*preceding page*). Batalha, the interior of the octagonal burial chapel at the east end of the church, begun by King Duarte (d. 1438) and continued by King Manoel (d. 1521), but never completed (Portuguese National Tourist Office).

mother-in-law to found a monastery there was the starting-point of the project. Margaret, who from 1507 to 1515 was regent of the Netherlands and guardian of her young nephew, the Emperor Charles V, had ample resources at her disposal, and was determined to build an impressive dynastic monument. To a court poet she was another Artemisia, builder of the Mausoleum itself. After negotiations with several distinguished artists and sculptors, including the Italian Pietro Torrigiano and the French Michel Colombe, she eventually employed as master mason Loys van Boghem or Bodeghem from Flanders and as designer of the tombs a Brussels artist called Jan van Roome.★

The church, built under van Boghem's direction between 1512 and 1532, is cruciform in plan, with aisles, transepts, an apsidal east end and flanking chapels (fig. 170). The relative width of the nave in proportion to its height shows that this is a church whose architectural affinities are to be sought not in France but in the Low Countries, notably in Antwerp cathedral. Compared with that of Miraflores or Henry VII's Chapel, the vaulting is conventional, but the pretentious west front has features of an almost mannerist character, including traceried windows cut in half and a gable of deliberately ambiguous form (fig. 171). The monuments within have often been described and illustrated. Almost perfectly preserved, they are among the best examples of late Gothic sculpture in Europe. The duke and duchess have separate tombs – his in the place of honour in front of the high altar, hers on the north side answering to that of Margaret de Bourbon on the south. While the latter is a conventional – if highly sophisticated – tomb-recess of a familiar type, that of the duchess is a canopied aedicule of a type common in England, but less so on the Continent (fig. 172). At Brou it stands between the main sanctuary and a side chapel which was the duchess's own chantry. The use of a canopied tomb open on both sides must therefore have been intended to relate the duchess's monument to that of her husband on one side and to her personal chapel on the other. Attached to her chapel there is a two-storey oratory or private pew from which she could see mass celebrated without herself being seen. As at Champmol it was furnished with a fireplace. The duchess permitted two of her entourage to found personal chapels. The abbé de Montecuto, her almoner and confessor, paid for one on the east side of the south transept; Laurent de Gorrevod, governor of Brou, endowed the corresponding chapel on the north side. Nothing now remains of their tombs. The bronze effigy of Gorrevod is known to have been melted down to make cannon in 1793, but kneeling figures of himself and his wife, with his arms and his motto *Pour James*,† remain in the stained glass windows. Eight smaller chapels flank the nave, four on each side. Private chapels were established in some of these, but the duchess would not allow their proprietors' arms to be inserted in the windows. The building luckily escaped serious damage in the French Revolution, but the profile of the roof was altered in the seventeenth century, and the tower (somewhat

★ The marble effigies were the work of a sculptor from Worms called Conrad Meyt and his brother Thomas, with various assistants, some of whom were Italian.

† *Pour Jamais*, 'For ever'.

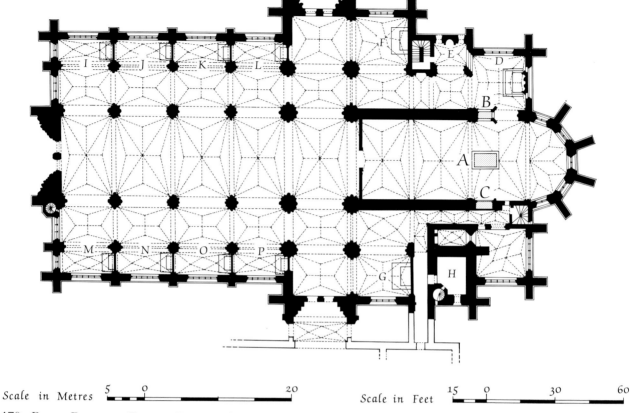

Scale in Metres 5 0 20   Scale in Feet 15 0 30 60

170. Brou, Bourg-en-Bresse, France, plan of the funerary church built by Margaret of Austria, 1512–32. A. Tomb of Philibert II, Duke of Savoy (d. 1504). B. Tomb of Margaret of Austria, Duchess of Savoy (d. 1530). C. Tomb of Margaret de Bourbon (d. 1483). D. Chantry chapel of Margaret of Austria. E. Oratory of Margaret of Austria. F. Chantry chapel of Laurent de Gorrevod. G. Chantry chapel of the abbé de Montecuto. H. Tower. I – P. Chantry chapels.

awkwardly placed to the south of the choir) has lost the stone crown with which it was originally surmounted.

The funerary churches and chapels described in this chapter are some of the surviving relics of the system of intercession for the dead to which medieval Europe devoted so much of its capital, both spiritual and temporal. In the early Middle Ages commemoration of the dead had been almost entirely in the hands of communities of monks whose penitential lives made them seem the ideal agents of salvation. Even in the later Middle Ages they continued to play an important part in the service of intercession. But the task of universal commemoration proved to be beyond their resources. In any case, changes in the social and religious geography of Europe were gradually but inexorably turning them into an anachronism. By the end of the twelfth century there had been substantial urban growth, accompanied by much church-building, while in the countryside virtually every rural community now had its own parish church. In the fourteenth and fifteenth centuries it was the parish church that in northern Europe at least formed the focus of devotion and attracted many of the chantry foundations. In Italy and the south of France, however, these were often attached to the conventual churches of one of the mendicant orders which continued to attract the loyalty and devotion of the urban bourgeoisie in cities like Arles and Toulouse, Venice and Florence.

But if prayers for the souls of the dead were the primary and ostensible purpose of these foundations, the perpetuation of the founder's memory on earth by architectural and sculptural display was a secondary and often almost equally compelling one. Few were as frank as Niccolò Acciaiuoli, Grand Seneschal of the kingdom of Naples, who wrote in 1356 that his purpose in founding a Carthusian house in Florence was to keep alive the memory of his name. 'For all other worldly goods that God has given me will go to my posterity . . . The monastery alone with all its ornaments will be mine for all time, and will make my name flourish and endure in the city.' But in hundreds of churches and chapels the

171. Brou, the church from the north-west (J. Feuillie, C.N.M.H.S., S.P.A.D.E.M.)

172. Brou, tomb of Margaret of Austria (Arch. Phot. Paris, S.P.A.D.E.M.)

carved and painted symbols of worldly rank and status made the same point. Today the voice of the chantry priest may be silent, but the chapel itself not infrequently survives as a Gothic mausoleum in which the history of a family can be traced by its heraldry in stone and glass. Not always, for in Protestant countries the Reformation led to the suppression of such foundations and often to the destruction of their buildings. In countries affected by the French Revolution it was the tombs themselves, with their symbols of aristocratic authority, that were the objects of attack. Only in Italy and Spain have these memorials of medieval piety been generally spared the alternative vandalism of religious intolerance and political hatred, and even in Italy there are few medieval tombs that remain undisturbed in their original settings. Enough, however, survives to enable us to see the funerary church or chapel as the architectural expression, both of that preoccupation with the after-life which was so marked a feature of late medieval society, and of that desire for posthumous fame which, long deprecated by the Church, was in the next century to be the dominant theme of funerary art throughout western Europe.

X

THE FAMILY CHAPEL IN RENAISSANCE ITALY

THE WAY IN WHICH the chantry chapel was at once a spiritual investment, a religious commitment and an expression of family pride is nowhere more apparent than in Renaissance Italy. Here, as elsewhere in Europe, the history of the *cappellania* went back to the late thirteenth century. The right of the laity to burial within the walls of Dominican and Franciscan churches was recognised by papal bulls in 1227 and 1250 respectively. In the churches of the Franciscan order at Assisi and Florence chapels can still be seen whose foundation can be traced to the last years of the thirteenth century. Complete with tomb, altar and mural painting, these chapels stand at the beginning of a tradition that was to enrich the churches of Italy with innumerable works of painting, sculpture and architecture. But for the family funerary chapel, in fact, many of the best-known works of such painters as Giotto or Masaccio, or of sculptors like Rossellino or Jacopo della Quercia, would never have been commissioned. One of the first of such chapels was attached to the south transept of the lower church of St Francis at Assisi. It was founded by Cardinal Napoleone Orsini to contain the tomb of his brother Giangaetano Orsini who had died in 1294. Though the tomb itself followed a Roman exemplar (the monument of Pope Boniface VIII in old St Peter's), its formal relationship to the architecture of the three-sided chapel and the complementary frescoes and stained glass (including the Orsini arms) created an artistic entity of a new type. Nothing is known of the financial arrangements between Cardinal Orsini and the Franciscans, but in Florence Donato Peruzzi, a member of a great banking family, left 200 *libbre* in his will for the construction of a family chapel in S. Croce, 'if the friars minor of Florence enlarge or rebuild their church within ten years of the testator's death'. He was still alive when in 1295 the first stone was laid of the great new Franciscan church of which the Peruzzi chapel formed a part. It was one of ten architecturally identical chapels which were adopted by other leading Florentine families such as the Bardi and the Velluti, and only its surviving wall-paintings by Giotto and the destroyed memorials of the Peruzzi family would have distinguished it from its neighbours (fig. 145).

For a Florentine family a chapel such as this was more than just a place of burial. In a society where several hundred rich and intensely competitive families lived in narrow streets within the confines of a walled city, the need to express their corporate identity was strong. At an earlier period first the defensive tower, then the loggia (used as a place of assembly) had been the architectural symbols of family solidarity. In the fourteenth and fifteenth centuries that role was increasingly taken over by the palace and the family chapel. On both palace and chapel the heraldic shield adopted from the feudal nobility proclaimed the aspirations of this urban elite who – although often possessed of some land – owed their wealth to commerce and banking rather than to agricultural lordship. In the chapels the heraldry might be displayed both internally and externally and sometimes even on the vestments provided for the officiating priests. The family tombs themselves were the visible evidence of a good pedigree, and descendants willingly accepted the obligation to maintain the masses that their forbears had instituted.

Secular patronage – or rather sponsorship – was not confined to private family chapels. It could extend to the chancel, or *cappella maggiore*, itself, to the chapterhouse, or the sacristy, or down the scale to altarpieces, fonts and holy waterstoups. Sponsorship of the chancel or sacristy or chapter-house would normally carry with it the right to be buried there. Thus in Florence the chancel of S. Croce was the burial place of the Alberti family, while the sacristy of S. Trinità still contains the tomb of Nofri Strozzi (d. 1418), who provided for its building in his will. In the chapter-house at S. Croce the heraldic insignia of the Pazzi family recall the fact that it was adopted by them and rebuilt to the designs of Brunelleschi from *c.*1430 onwards, and but for the execution of the leading members of the family and the forfeiture of their property after their insurrection in 1478, there would doubtless have been further evidence of the family's patronage in the form of funerary monuments and inscriptions. In Piedmont, however, Galeazzo Cavassa, vicar-general of the marquisate of Saluzzo (d. 1483), still reposes in the exquisite tomb set up in the chapter-house of the Dominican church there by his son Francesco early in the sixteenth century.

Not every family chapel was intended for burial, some being founded purely as chantries where masses would be sung for the soul of an individual who was buried in the churchyard or elsewhere. Nor did a prominent urban family necessarily choose to patronise the church nearest to its place of residence. In Florence, as in other Italian cities, it was the churches of mendicant or reformed orders that were the most favoured, and in these were concentrated the chapels of the leading patrician families: Bardi, Cavalcanti, Falconieri, Tornabuoni or Strozzi. The personal, social or religious considerations that led a family to select a particular church for its patronage are not easily disentangled. But family and business contacts could be as important as religious ones, and once the Medici had associated themselves with S. Lorenzo, political discrimination would doubtless direct their major rivals elsewhere – the Pazzi to S. Croce, the Strozzi to S. Trinità and S. Maria Novella. Whatever the immediate reason for its foundation, every such chapel tended to become a symbol of that family pride and solidarity that was so strongly marked a characteristic of the urban oligarchies of Renaissance Italy. From Niccolò Acciaiuoli (d. 1365), wanting his burial to be 'fine and rich and honourable for me and our successors', to Giovanni Tornabuoni (d. 1497), having his chapel in S. Maria Novella painted by Ghirlandaio 'to the exaltation of his house and family' (*in exaltationem sue domus ac familie*), the new spirit is manifest. No longer are grand tombs and chapels reserved for prelates and princes: the laity have at last come into their own and reclaimed the right to be 'pompous in the grave' that their early Christian ancestors had renounced a thousand years earlier.

The concession of burial rights and the permission to stamp a chapel with one's family arms – even, at S. Maria Novella, boldly to write one's name across a church's facade – was one symptom of a new phase in the relationship between the secular and religious spheres. To a reforming bishop of the twelfth or thirteenth century it would have looked alarmingly like the old proprietary church in a new and insidious guise. It certainly marked a fresh defeat for the Church in its long battle against intra-mural burial. But the arrangement was in many ways mutually beneficial. In return for regular intercession in the form of masses, the unendowed friars received substantial help towards their building programmes and funds with which to maintain their services. Their churches were embellished with altarpieces and devotional paintings by some of the best artists in Italy. Their relations with their patrons were often excellent. In some churches it was the custom for the head of the family to entertain the officiating priests to dinner on patronal feast days.

In these circumstances it is often difficult to determine whether the initiative for church-building came from the clergy or from the laity. Given the lay demand for chapels, monks or friars could commit themselves to a building programme with some confidence that sponsors would be forthcoming from wealthy citizens who lacked a chapel of their own. Prudent clerical builders normally operated with the assistance of a lay committee which helped to raise money and was well placed to judge the market for chapels. Nevertheless, there was sometimes difficulty in getting enough sponsors. At Bologna the new Franciscan church started in about 1240 boasted a *chevet* of chapels in the French manner, but of the nine chapels planned, only six were completed thirty years later. In 1371 a programme of rebuilding was well under way at the Vallombrosan abbey church of S. Trinità in Florence. Ten new chapels were envisaged, and all or most of them had been taken up by local families. But the chancel remained without a sponsor. The abbot appealed to the city authorities to finance it: if no help was forthcoming within six months he would give the patronage to anyone willing to pay for the structure. Eventually the Gianfigliazzi (a branch of whom already owned one of the new chapels in the nave) appear to have come to the rescue. In the 1430s the prior and canons of S. Lorenzo experienced even greater difficulty in finding enough patrons to replace the Romanesque nave of their church by a new one. The rebuilding of the east end had already been undertaken by a consortium of eight families, each of whom made itself responsible for one chapel, and one of whose heads, Giovanni di Bicci de' Medici, made architectural history by commissioning Brunelleschi to design in addition a sacristy adjoining his own chapel (fig. 173). But there was insufficient demand for chapels in the nave until in 1442 Giovanni's son Cosimo de' Medici undertook to complete it at his own expense on condition that no coats of arms or similar devices should be placed

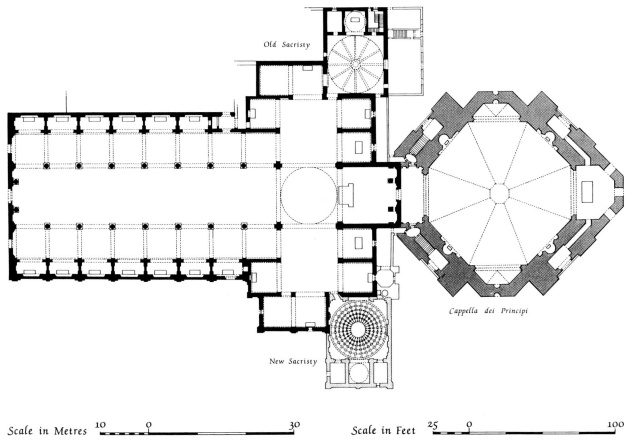

Scale in Metres   10   0   30   Scale in Feet   25 0   100

173. Florence, plan of the church of S. Lorenzo.

either there or in the chancel without his permission, and that no layman might be buried there without his leave. Ultimately nave chapels were built, many of them by friends or connections of the Medici, but the tombs of the families in question were all kept out of sight in the crypt. When Cosimo himself died in 1464 he was buried in the place of honour before the high altar, but with only an inscription in the pavement to mark the site of his tomb, which took the unusual form of a structural pier supporting the vaulting in the crypt below. The burial vault is within the pier, whose four faces are sheathed with marble to form a monument. Thus Cosimo, principal builder of the church in his lifetime, still helps to sustain it after his death.

In both these Florentine churches the chapels were an integral part of the structure and building could not proceed without them. At the Cistercian church of Cestello (now S. Maria Maddalena de' Pazzi), however, a more modest scheme for the addition of chapels to the sides of an existing nave permitted a more flexible programme of works. Formerly a nunnery, Cestello had become a house of Cistercian monks only in 1442, and it represented a local attempt to reverse the decline of a once famous order. It was, therefore, a congregation of some repute

193

that in 1488 indicated its readiness to allow chapels to be built on either side of the nave of its church, and in the course of the next ten years enough patrons came forward to implement the plan. The order of construction is shown in figure 174. Although the individual chapels are almost identical (differing only in the detail of the capitals and the decoration of the arches), the choice of site and the date of construction no doubt reflected the personal preferences and circumstances of the sponsors. Most of these were members of established Florentine families who had burial rights elsewhere, but they evidently attached importance to the commemorative masses that the Cistercians would celebrate for them, and their carved and painted arms showed that, here as elsewhere, the possession of a chapel was an assertion of privilege and status as well as a religious investment.

Once established, the vested interest of a family in a chapel was difficult to extinguish, and could be an obstacle to future architectural improvement. Early in the 1440s the rebuilding of the Dominican Observant church of S. Marco in Florence at the expense of Cosimo de' Medici was obstructed by the resistance of the patrons of family chapels who refused to surrender their rights. A few years later an ambitious plan (by Michelozzo) to provide the Servite friars of SS. Annunziata with a new circular choir ran into difficulties because it involved the building of additional family chapels to finance the project, and this conflicted with the claims of the Falconieri family to monopolise the right of burial in the church. In the end a compromise was imposed by the Archbishop of Florence, and Ludovico Gonzaga, Marquis of Mantua, was persuaded to become the patron of the new choir on the understanding that some money owed to him by the Signoria of Florence would be used to finance the building. Luckily his own family tombs were in Mantua, and he had no intention of claiming burial rights in SS. Annunziata.

The family chapel was, therefore, not merely an important feature of Renaissance church architecture, but a source of finance without which the great boom in church construction in fifteenth-century Italy would not have been possible. Moreover, from the sixteenth century onwards, it was the feature that most clearly distinguished a Catholic church from a Protestant one. But even in Florence, the history of the private chapel has been investigated in depth in only a few of its churches, and elsewhere, though much has been written about its painted and sculptural decoration, its changing architectural form has been little studied. What follows is an attempt to discern some of the outlines of a neglected aspect of Italian architectural history.

Chevets with radiating chapels on the French model were not common in medieval Italy, though they were a feature of the Franciscan church at Bologna (begun *c.*1240) (fig. 175) and of the thirteenth-century church of S. Antonio in Padua. The plan generally favoured by the mendicant orders was a simpler one derived from the Cistercians: it consisted of a row of rectangular chapels projecting from the east side of a spacious transept. Variations of this plan were used for most of the great Franciscan and Dominican churches that were built in the North Italian cities in the thirteenth and fourteenth centuries and that particularly attracted the patronage of their leading citizens. Such were S. Croce (Franciscan)

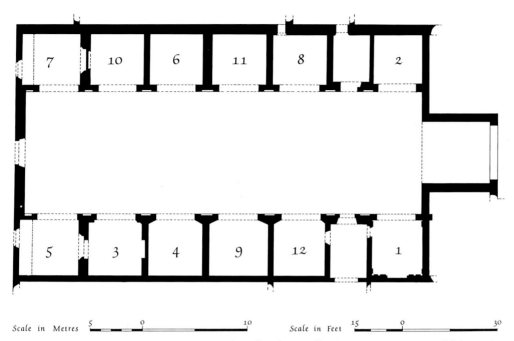

| 7 | 10 | 6 | 11 | 8 | 2 |

| 5 | 3 | 4 | 9 | 12 | 1 |

Scale in Metres 5 —— 0 ———— 10   Scale in Feet 15 —— 0 ———— 30

174. Florence, plan of the Cistercian church of Cestello (now S. Maria Maddalena de'
Pazzi), showing the order in which family chapels were added on either side of the nave
between 1488 and 1500 (after Luchs).

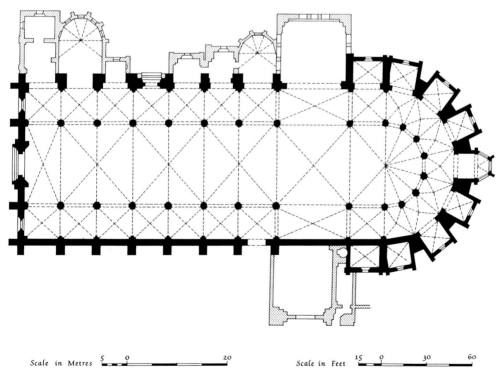

Scale in Metres 5 0 ———— 20   Scale in Feet 15 0 —— 30 —— 60

175. Bologna, plan of the Franciscan church, showing the *chevet* of radiating chapels built
in the thirteenth century and family chapels added later on the north side of the nave.

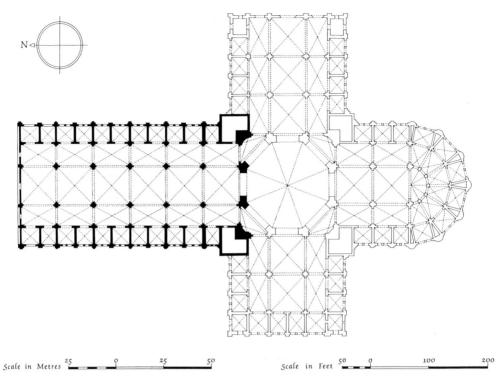

Scale in Metres   Scale in Feet

176. Bologna, S. Petronio, plan based on the wooden model showing the original scheme for a cruciform church with fifty-four chapels. The portion actually built from *c*.1390 onwards is shown in black (after A. Gatti, *La Fabbrica di S. Petronio*, Bologna 1889).

and S. Maria Novella (Dominican) in Florence, the Franciscan churches in Brescia, Lodi and Pavia, the Dominican ones in Venice and Siena. At Lodi and Pavia these eastern chapels were subsequent but early additions to the original thirteenth-century structure, and by the early years of the fourteenth century further chapels were beginning to be added to the sides of naves in response to the lay demand for commemorative masses. At Bologna new lateral chapels were built on the north side of the nave to supplement the eastern ones. In Florence the earliest examples are the first three chapels on the south side of S. Trinità, which were built onto the old Romanesque church in about 1300 and which formed the model for the general rebuilding of the church later in the fourteenth century.

By the late fourteenth century the provision of chapels had become a standard feature of church planning. In the great scheme of *c*.1390 for S. Petronio at Bologna no fewer than fifty-four identical chapels were envisaged in a monotonous procession round the cruciform church, and of these, twenty-two were actually built (fig. 176). In Milan and Pavia, where building in the Gothic style persisted well into the fifteenth century, architects of the local Solari family experimented with a semi-octagonal plan which not only gave the side chapel a more interesting shape, but also enabled its altar to be more effectively lit by two diagonally placed windows (fig. 177).

Meanwhile in Florence the first architects of the Renaissance were grappling

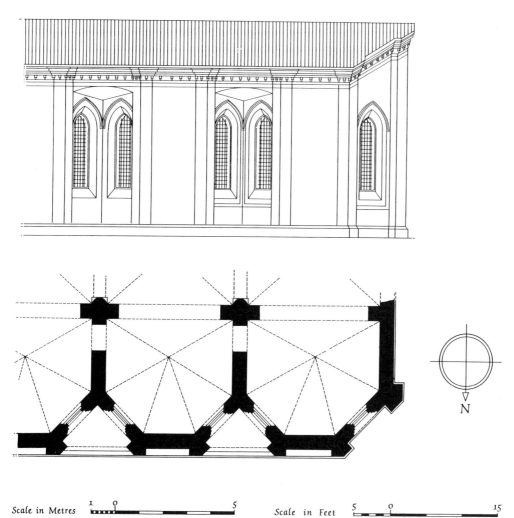

Scale in Metres |¦¦¦¦|‎ ‎ ‎ 5   Scale in Feet 5 ‎ 0 ‎ 15

177. Milan, S. Pietro in Gessate, late fifteenth-century lateral chapels with diagonally placed windows (after Patetta, 1987).

with the chapel as a component of a classical church. To anyone concerned – as most Renaissance architects were – with order and unity in design, chapels presented an awkward problem. They were part of an untidy religious ambience which was inimical to the new architectural ideals of men like Alberti and Brunelleschi. In the two great mendicant churches the original provision of chapels had proved inadequate, and private altars and enclosures stood against the walls or under the rood-screen which separated the friars' choir from the nave. Each formed a separate religious and artistic focus within a large and tolerant architectural space, and the art of the painter tended to predominate over that of the architect. This did not accord with Alberti's ideas about the proper role of decoration in churches, and Brunelleschi's aim as a pioneer classical architect was not only to reintroduce the discipline of an order but also to subordinate painting and sculpture to an overall architectural concept. At S. Lorenzo he made each

197

178. Florence, S. Lorenzo, showing chapels in the nave.

chapel into a rectangular recess whose arch reads as part of a continuous arcade (fig. 178). At S. Spirito the autonomy of the individual chapel was still further restricted by reducing it to a shallow apsidal recess flanked by half-columns which registered visually as supports for the vaulting of the aisles rather than as frames for the vestigial chapels (fig. 179). Externally the effect of a vertically corrugated wall was somewhat awkward, especially where adjoining chapels were squashed together in the angles between nave and transept, but this was later mitigated by encasing them in a continuous flat surface. In both churches there were coats of arms to identify the sponsoring families. At S. Lorenzo these were unobtrusively

198

179. Florence, S. Spirito, showing chapels in the nave. Note the oval shields of family arms over each window.

placed in the vaults of the respective chapels, but at S. Spirito they were clearly affixed to the walls, where they can still be seen today (fig. 180).★

Both the formulae offered by Brunelleschi had their imitators and proved to be capable of adaptation to the architectural circumstances of an aisleless church. The rectangular recess was used, for instance, at S. Francesco (alias S. Salvatore) al

★ In the nave of S. Spirito all the chapels have been refurnished at various dates, but several of the eastern chapels retain their original altars and altarpieces, often with heraldry corresponding to that on the shields affixed to the wall above.

180. Florence, S. Spirito, coats of arms on the exterior of the nave marking the patronage of individual chapels by Florentine families.

Monte, Florence (Il Cronaca, *c*.1490–1504) and at S. Maurizio (Monastero Maggiore), Milan (Giovanni Dolcebuono, 1503–19); the apsidal one at the church of the Carmine in Padua (after 1496) and at S. Pietro in Montorio in Rome (*c*.1480–1500).

There was, however, a certain monotony in the repetition of a single unit, especially in an aisleless church, and this was recognised by Alberti, who in his treatise on architecture (written *c*.1450, but not published until 1486) laid down two rules for the designing of chapels. One was to prefer an uneven to an even number, and the other was to use the round and rectangular forms alternately. Although Alberti did not mention it, such alternation in the shape of niches or recesses was a common feature of late Roman architecture, and it was in Rome, where Ancient examples were still extant, that Alberti's second precept was followed in the church of S. Marco, built in 1466–8 to the designs of an unknown architect. Thirty years later the same scheme was used in the nave of the cathedral of Turin. Meanwhile, in S. Andrea at Mantua (1472–94), Alberti himself had devised a much more sophisticated formula for the lateral chapels, in which large coffered arches alternated with broad piers (figs. 181–2). With pilasters applied to the piers and circular openings between them, the chapels were given something of the monumentality of the triumphal arch to which Alberti's design alluded. Variations on this powerful formula were to be used by Bramante and his successors in the new basilica of St Peter's, by Vignola in the Gesù, the Jesuit church in Rome (begun in 1568), and by Palladio in the church of the Redentore in Venice (1577 onwards).

From the sixteenth century onwards the resourcefulness of succeeding generations of architects in handling the subordinate chapel is one of the delights of
church architecture in the Catholic countries of Europe. The tendency was
increasingly towards the greater integration of chapels into the overall design of
the church, until in the great baroque churches of the seventeenth and eighteenth
centuries the private chapel has been brought into strict subordination to the
design of the interior space as a whole. In order to make them satellites of the high
altar, all the lesser altars are often turned to face east, or canted against piers, so as
to contribute to a perspective carefully contrived to enhance the drama of the
mass. These developments were due partly to changing architectural ideals, but
also to changes in the Church's own attitude to the conduct of worship, which
came to a head in the legislation associated with the Council of Trent (1534–63).
No longer would the celebration of the mass be a priestly mystery to be
conducted in the privacy of screened enclosures. Now it would be performed in
the sight of all, and the body of the church had to be designed to enable a
congregation to see and hear what was going on in the sanctuary. In older
churches visual obstructions like rood-screens and choir-stalls were swept away,
and with them went much of the accumulated paraphernalia of medieval piety,
including many private chapels and their enclosures. In Florence between 1565
and 1577 the interiors of S. Croce and S. Maria Novella were rearranged under
the direction of Giorgio Vasari so that each family chapel had a uniformly
pedimented altarpiece, and in S. Croce even the subject of the painting was
prescribed by the authority of Duke Cosimo. Exactly how these changes were
implemented in other Italian cities and in other Catholic countries remains to be
investigated, but similar pressures were undoubtedly brought to bear, either
directly by the Church or indirectly by Catholic rulers, in such a way as
drastically to restrict the role of the private patron and to prepare for the
overriding authority of the baroque architect.

But if patronage was sufficiently powerful it was not to be denied. A cardinal or
a duke could not be expected to accept the same constraints as a mere merchant or
gentleman. Paradoxically, moreover, the same striving for spatial unity that
subordinated the family chapel to some overall architectural concept could in
favourable circumstances encourage the building of self-contained, nonconforming chapels. It had been the ambition of every Renaissance architect to design a
centralised church based on some perfect geometrical figure – circle, polygon,
square or Greek cross. From Filarete to Frank Lloyd Wright, from Palladio to
Pugin, architects have been adept at giving theoretical plausibility to their
favourite fancies, and the literature of Renaissance architecture is full of classical
erudition on the one hand and of proportional systems on the other. In a circular
or polygonal or Greek-cross-shaped church the antiquarian were taught to
recognise the revival of a beautiful Antique form, while the philosophical were
encouraged to see the harmonic structure of the universe realised symbolically in
stone. Some clergy were no doubt susceptible to both types of persuasion. But for
others (notably St Carlo Borromeo, the influential Archbishop of Milan) Antique
forms were tainted with paganism and centralised churches were liturgically

181. Mantua, S. Andrea, interior of the nave designed by Alberti, showing the subordination of the lateral chapels to an architectural formula based on the triumphal arch.

inconvenient. When Cardinal Francesco Gonzaga saw the square plan of Alberti's S. Sebastiano at Mantua he declared that he did not know whether the outcome would be a church, a mosque or a synagogue. What was both inappropriate and inconvenient in a large church might, however, be perfectly acceptable in a funerary or family chapel. Many such chapels were already square or rectangular in plan and invited transformation into miniature centralised churches in which monuments could conveniently be placed in symmetrical recesses on either side of the altar. Moreover, in a constricted situation where there was often only one outside wall, a dome offered itself as an ideal source of light. As for pagan associations, those who used the Latin language to compose elegant epitaphs could hardly demur if tomb and chapel shared the same classical aspirations. For a church to take the form of a temple might well be open to objection on religious

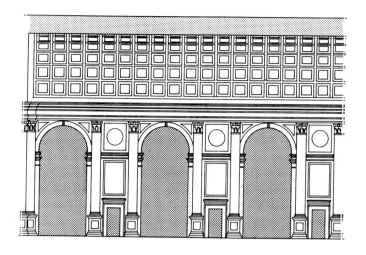

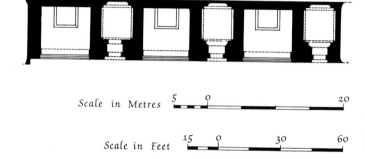

Scale in Metres

Scale in Feet

182. Mantua, S. Andrea, plan and elevation of the nave chapels.

grounds, but Christians had, after all, been using Ancient sarcophagi for their own tombs for centuries.

The first major family chapels of the Renaissance were dual-purpose buildings in Florence designed by Brunelleschi: the Old Sacristy at S. Lorenzo (1421–8), which was paid for by Giovanni di Bicci de' Medici (d. 1429) and contains his tomb, and the chapter-house at S. Croce (begun *c.*1430), which was to have been the Pazzi family chapel and still goes by that name (figs. 145, 173). Brunelleschi's lucid and elegant essays in classical geometry inspired several derivative versions, some of which were designed specifically as tomb-chapels. One of these was the Portinari chapel attached to the church of S. Eustorgio at Milan in 1462, another was the Tolosa chapel in the Monteoliveto church at Naples (*c.*1492–5). A third was the Medici mausoleum at S. Lorenzo designed by Michelangelo in 1520 and known as the 'New Sacristy' (fig. 183). The first was built at the expense of Pigello Portinari, the manager of the Medici bank in Milan, in order to house a marble shrine of St Peter Martyr made by Giovanni di Balduccio in 1338. It was therefore a sort of Renaissance *martyrium*,⋆ in which Portinari himself was buried when he died in 1468. The identity of the architect is not known, though the

⋆ Another example of this kind is the octagonal church of S. Flaviano at Giulianova in the Abruzzi, founded in 1470 by Count Giulio Antonio Acquaviva to house the body of a local martyr.

183. Florence, S. Lorenzo, interior of the 'New Sacristy' or Medici chapel, begun by Michelangelo in 1520, from a water-colour drawing by Gabriel Carelli (1821–1900) (British Architectural Library, Drawings Collection).

name of Michelozzo has often been put forward. The interior closely resembles its Florentine model, but the exterior is decorated with four ornamental turrets in the local Lombard tradition. Although almost identical in plan to the 'Old Sacristy', the 'New Sacristy' at S. Lorenzo is both a grander and a much more sophisticated building in which Michelangelo treated architecture almost as sculpture and used the classical vocabulary with that new and masterful freedom that art historians have called 'mannerism'. The chapel was intended to commemorate four members of the Medici family, Lorenzo the Magnificent (d. 1492), his brother Giuliano (d. 1478), and two younger men, one, Giuliano, Duke of Nemours (d. 1516), a son of Lorenzo, the other Lorenzo, Duke of Urbino (d. 1519), his grandson. The original intention was to construct a free-standing monument incorporating the tombs of all four, but the space available would hardly have permitted it to be seen properly, and eventually it was decided to place the tombs against the walls. Only those of the two dukes were executed. Each occupies one side wall, which is elaborately modelled to form part of it. The apparatus of tabernacles, aedicules, pilasters and swags is deployed in a manner that transforms Brunelleschi's bland Old Sacristy into an intensely emotive funerary chamber. Although Ammannati and Vasari were both to design some excellent monuments in the Michelangelesque style, and Michelangelo himself was to design the Sforza chapel in S. Maria Maggiore in Rome (1564–5), no other funerary chapel of the Renaissance is more expressive of its purpose than the New Sacristy.

Brunelleschi's chapels represent a clear break with the past, not only in the matter of style, but also in their freedom from the narrative paintings that cover the walls of most medieval Italian chapels. The architect is in full control, and any painted or terra-cotta decoration is strictly subordinated to the overall design. A different approach is seen in the chapel of the Cardinal of Portugal in the church of S. Miniato in Florence. Here the structure is a framework for an exquisite ensemble of carved, painted and moulded decoration in which architecture is no longer paramount. The Cardinal of Portugal was a prince of the royal house of Portugal who died in Florence in 1459 at the age of twenty-five. Chaste, pious, indeed deeply spiritual, Jaime of Portugal was an exception among Renaissance cardinals. His austerities were legendary, and he had long been attracted by the reformed order of Olivetan monks in whose church he asked to be buried. He left directions for the building of a chapel in which daily masses were to be said for his soul. To whom his executors entrusted the design of the chapel is not clear: the architect Manetti was involved, but the symmetrical plan with matching recesses was so obviously intended for the display of the funerary sculpture of Antonio Rossellino that Manetti's role may well have been subsidiary. The magnificent inlaid marble floor, the roundels by della Robbia in the ceiling, the altarpiece by Pollaiuolo and the religious paintings by Baldovinetti combine to make this an outstanding example of a Renaissance funerary chapel (figs. 184–5). A few years later Rossellino was asked by Antonio Piccolomini, Duke of Amalfi, to repeat the performance in a chapel in the Olivetan church at Naples erected to the memory of his wife Maria of Aragon, the illegitimate daughter of Ferdinand, King of Naples. In Venice the Martini chapel of 1471–6 at S. Giobbe is another artistic export from Florence that reflects the style of the Cardinal of Portugal's chapel. Yet another is the funerary chapel which Cardinal Tamás Bakócz built at his cathedral church of Esztergom in Hungary from 1506 onwards. Probably designed by the sculptor-architect Andrea Ferrucci of Fiesole, its plan reflects that of the chapel at S. Miniato, while its interior, carried out in a local red marble, is a sumptuous edition of the Brunelleschian formula.

Almost every Italian architect of any consequence designed at least one funerary chapel. Here it will be possible to discuss only a few important examples which, together with those already mentioned, illustrate the variety of form and style to which the family chapel lent itself. The Chigi chapel in S. Maria del Popolo, Rome, was built by Agostino Chigi, a rich banker and patron of the arts for whom Peruzzi designed the Farnesina, the first suburban villa of the Renaissance. About thirteen years before his death in 1520 he acquired a chapel in S. Maria del Popolo from its former owners, the Mellini family, and in c.1513–16 rebuilt it to the designs of Raphael. What is notable here is the monumental treatment of the interior, whose articulation by blind arches and pilasters suggests the central space of a cruciform church with three of the four sides filled up. There are no

184. Florence, S. Miniato, the chapel of the Cardinal of Portugal, 1461–6 (Index/L. Perugi).

185. Florence, S. Miniato, the tomb of the Cardinal of Portugal by Antonio Rossellino (Scala).

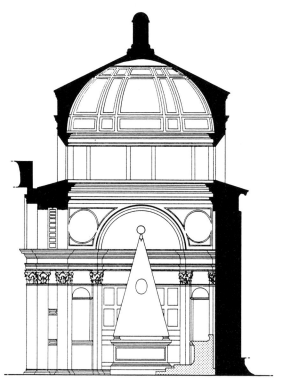

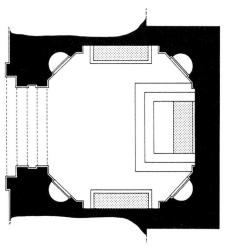

Scale in Metres 1 0   5

Scale in Feet 5 0   15

186. Rome, S. Maria del Popolo, the Chigi chapel built to the designs of Raphael *c*.1513–16 (after Rossi, *Disegni di Vari Altari e Cappelle*, Rome 1713).

187. Naples, S. Giovanni a Carbonara, interior of the Caracciolo di Vico Chapel, *c.*1515 (Alinari).

effigies, and instead Raphael used for the first time the motif of a pyramid or pyramidal obelisk★ set against the wall and bearing on its surface a portrait medallion of the person commemorated (fig. 186).[†] It was a perfect formula for a monument in the Antique taste and was to be widely imitated all over Europe. Nor was there any difficulty in giving Christian significance to pre-Christian forms: the pyramid was understood to symbolise 'Immortality', just as elsewhere the triumphal arch might indicate 'Triumph over Death'. Above, in the dome, God presides over a Platonic Heaven into which the occupants of the tombs are one day to be received. The whole is an ensemble of beautiful and evocative forms whose accomplishment is emphasised by comparison with the ponderous Caracciolo di Vico chapel of *c.*1515 in the church of S. Giovanni a Carbonara in Naples (fig. 187). Here a triumphal arch formula is applied to a

★ It is, in fact, a hybrid form, with the proportions of a pyramid, but standing on feet like an obelisk. In a contemporary document cited by Shearer (see Bibliography), this feature is described alternatively as *piramide* or as *colonna*, 'the latter being a common term for obelisk'.

[†] The existing medallions, like the statues of Daniel and Habakkuk, were added by Bernini in or soon after 1655.

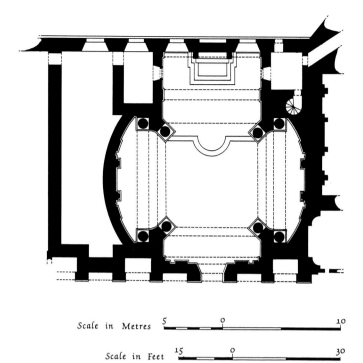

188. Rome, S. Maria
Maggiore, plan of the Sforza
chapel on the (liturgical)
north side of the nave built to
the designs of Michelangelo
1564–5 (after Letarouilly,
Edifices de Rome Moderne,
1840–57).

Scale in Metres

Scale in Feet

circular plan by an unknown architect anxious to give to the interior of his chapel
something of the solemn grandeur that a Roman mausoleum exhibited in its
exterior.

For the Renaissance architect the funerary chapel had been an ideal opportunity
to achieve the classical symmetry and perfection that were the aesthetic ideals of
the time. Mannerism varied the motifs rather than the overall conception, but the
drama and 'movement' of the baroque were less easy to express within the
confines of a small chapel. One way to transcend these limitations was to enlarge
a limited area visually by subdividing it into interpenetrating spaces; another was
to have recourse to illusionism; a third was to open the chapel up and relate it to
the church as a whole; a fourth was to accept the confines of the space and
organise within it a concentrated display of baroque effects.

Michelangelo showed how to achieve the first at the Sforza chapel in S. Maria
Maggiore in Rome (1564–5). Two segmental extrusions create a cross-axis and at
the same time provide convenient sites for monuments (fig. 188). Several
Roman architects, including Bernini and Carlo Fontana, played with this idea,
but its most successful realisation was the Schönborn chapel which Balthasar
Neumann designed at Würzburg cathedral in 1719–24.

Illusionism was the choice of the architect Antonio Gherardi (1644–1702) when
in about 1680 he was invited to rebuild the decayed chapel of the Avila family in
the church of S. Maria in Trastevere in Rome. As such a chapel could be viewed
from one point only, it offered the perfect opportunity for a carefully planned
perspective effect of a kind that appealed particularly to baroque architects.
Looking into the chapel, the spectator sees before him an altar set apparently in a

CAPPELLA IN SANTA MARIA IN TRASTEVERE DELLI SIG.^{RI} AVILA
Archit.ᵗᵉ di Antonio Gherardi.

Scala di Palmi uenti

189. Rome, S. Maria in Trastevere, the Avila chapel as rebuilt to the designs of A. Gherardi c.1680 (from Rossi, *Disegni di Vari Altari e Cappelle*, Rome 1713).

deep colonnaded recess which also contains a sarcophagus. On either side the urnlike tombs of the Avila family are displayed in aedicules of complex curvature, while overhead the lantern above the dome is supported by airborne angels. Light falls dramatically on altar, lantern and sarcophagus. Space has been artifically created in every dimension by the application of those principles of perspective that Gherardi, a painter as well as an architect, well understood. No photograph can do justice to this virtuoso performance but its mechanism can be seen in figure 189.

At almost the same time (1675–83) two members of the family of St Andrea Corsini, a medieval bishop of Fiesole whose eyes were perpetually averted from women (*mulierum perpetuo vitavit aspectum*, his epitaph assures us), decided to build in the church of S. Maria del Carmine in Florence a sumptuous chapel which would both glorify the pious misogynist and provide a place of burial for themselves. The site was at one end of the transept and occupied its full width, so there was no need for the architect, Pier Francesco Silvani, to have recourse to special perspective effects. The chapel reads as a domed crossing, three of whose arches are filled with baroque sculpture by Foggini commemorating the saint and the builders of the chapel, Bartolomeo and Neri Corsini, while the fourth is open to the church. As the chapel can be seen from the other end of the transept, its entrance was a matter of architectural importance, and this was treated as a two-storeyed composition with the arch itself framed by an upper order supporting a pediment (fig. 190). This formula went back to Antiquity, and forms the facade of one of the exedra tombs at Pompeii (fig. 83). It had been assimilated into Italian Renaissance architecture in the fifteenth century, for instance in the Piccolomini altar in Siena cathedral (by Andrea Bregno, *c.*1480), and although it had some-times been used to frame other, less grandiose, family chapels in the past (e.g., the sixteenth-century Valier chapel in the church of the Madonna dell'Orto in Venice), it is unlikely that for Silvani it had any special sepulchral associations. To an English reader the two-storeyed archway of the Corsini chapel is of special interest as a possible source from which James Gibbs may have derived the chancel arch of the church of St Mary-le-Strand in London.

The fourth example of a baroque chapel is the Cappella del Crocifisso in the cathedral of Monreale in Sicily, built by Archbishop Roano in 1687–92 (fig. 191). This hexagonal chapel is hidden behind a doorway on the north side of the Romanesque cathedral and astonishes the visitor with a profusion of coloured marbles cut, carved, bent, twisted and polished not only into the form of every component of classical architecture, but also in the semblance of drapery, mar-quetry and painting. This display of a peculiarly southern-Italian form of baroque craftsmanship (to be seen also in Naples and on the floor slabs in the two cathedral churches in Malta★) may distract attention from the medieval wooden crucifix in whose honour the chapel was built, but as it was designed as his place of burial by

★Two minor examples of this kind of marble work can be seen in England. One is the monument to Sir Thomas Dereham (d. 1722) in West Dereham church in Norfolk, which must have been made in Italy; the other, the tombs designed by William Burges for the Magniac family at Sharnbrook church in Bedfordshire in 1870.

190. Florence, S. Maria del Carmine, the chapel of S. Andrea Corsini, 1675–83 (Alinari).

191. Monreale cathedral, Sicily, the Cappella del Crocifisso, 1687–92. The effigy of the founder, Archbishop Roano, who built the chapel as his place of burial, is in the recess to the left of the altar, kneeling in adoration of the medieval statue of the crucified Christ, displayed as part of a Tree of Jesse (Scala).

an archbishop, planned by a Capuchin friar, and completed under the direction of a Jesuit, the Cappella del Crocifisso must represent what clerical taste in seventeenth-century Sicily thought appropriate for its dual purpose.

The family chapel did not play the same role in the history of neo-classical architecture as it had done in that of the Renaissance, partly because, in the age of the Enlightenment, the whole system of intercessory masses was brought into question, and partly because it was the free-standing mausoleum rather than the chapel attached to a church that appealed most to neo-classical taste. In Italy one of the last of the major family chapels was the Corsini chapel in the church of St

214

192. Rome, St John Lateran, the Corsini chapel, 1732–6 (Alinari).

John Lateran in Rome.★ It was built in 1732–6 by Lorenzo Corsini, Pope Clement XII, to contain his own tomb and those of other members of his family, and was designed by Alessandro Galilei (1691–1737). Although the papacy suffered serious reverses during his reign, Clement's personal resources enabled him to build an exceptionally splendid chapel and to provide an endowment for four priests to serve it in perpetuity. It was, therefore, the eighteenth-century equivalent of one of the major chantry foundations of the fifteenth and sixteenth centuries. Architecturally, it forms an instructive contrast to the Corsini chapel in Florence (fig. 192). The plan is essentially the same, but the effect intended is very different: a clearly defined space instead of one formed of blocked-up arches. Moreover, despite the richness of the decoration, a new restraint is apparent: here are no broken pediments, nor other baroque deviations from Vitruvian rule. A lucid architectural order prevails: coffered niche answers to coffered niche, radiating floor plan to radiating segments of the dome. The sculpture is still baroque in style, but restrained in expression. There are 'no excited gestures, no violent outpourings of emotion' (Enggass). In short, neo-classicism is in the air, and once more (but perhaps for the last time) a funerary chapel is in the forefront of taste.

★ The Torlonia chapel of 1830–50 in the same church was perhaps the last of all.

XI

TRIUMPHAL TOMBS AND THE
COUNTER-REFORMATION

THROUGHOUT ITS HISTORY THE FUNERARY MONUMENT has tended to borrow architectural forms, either from its own day or from some period in the past that could lend prestige to the present. In the twelfth century the columns and pediments of classical antiquity were sometimes adopted as symbols of authority by clergy conscious of their new power and status as leaders of a universal church. In the late fifteenth and early sixteenth centuries it was the triumphal arch that the designers of Italian tombs often made the basis of monuments to commemorate great men such as popes, cardinals or Venetian doges (fig. 193). Such tombs were closely related to the temporary arches that were erected in the capital cities of Renaissance Europe for the state entries of emperors, kings and other ruling princes. Indeed, they were sometimes designed by the same persons. In 1527 the Italian sculptors working in Westminster on an elaborate Renaissance tomb for Cardinal Wolsey interrupted their labours to construct two triumphal arches 'a l'anticha' for a temporary banqueting pavilion at the royal palace of Greenwich. The Flemish artist and engraver Jerome Cock, who was one of those responsible for designing the 'joyful entry' of Prince Philip into Antwerp in 1549, actually published in 1565 a design for his own monument in the form of a triumphal arch. Both tombs and temporary arches were full of imagery intended to arouse suitable sentiments – of piety and respect in the one case, and of loyalty and enthusiasm in the other. The pageant arches were ephemeral constructions of wood and canvas, while the tombs were facades standing against a wall, usually with the effigy of the person commemorated occupying the central archway. Occasionally monuments of the triumphal-arch type were so sited that the arch actually functioned as the entrance to a church or chapel. Several examples can be seen in Venice. The one illustrated here (fig. 194) commemorates Benedetto Pesaro, who died in 1503 fighting against the Turks. It frames the entrance to the sacristy of the Frari church which was also the Pesaro family chapel, and the image of the triumphal arch is reinforced by the use of real columns instead of mere pilasters.

Many of these Renaissance tombs were very large and ostentatious, and their imagery was apt to emphasise worldly status and achievement at the expense of Christian values. Their message was no longer the old medieval one of the

193. Rome, S. Maria del Popolo, monument to Cardinal Jeromo Basso, one of a pair made by the sculptor Andrea Sansovino in 1506 (from Letarouilly, *Edifices de Rome Moderne*, 1840–57).

194. Tomb of Benedetto Pesaro (d. 1503) in the Frari church, Venice (Osvaldo Böhm, Venice).

Triumph of Death over all mankind of whatever estate, but rather the Triumph (in privileged cases) of Fame over Death. Benedetto Pesaro's tomb is a good example: he is shown as a victorious general, flanked by nude figures of the pagan gods Mars and Neptune. Inscriptions and reliefs recording his naval campaigns are prominent features of the monument, and the only Christian images are a small Madonna and Child in the tympanum and inconspicuous roundels of the saints, Benedict and Jerome, after whom the general and his son were named. The design of this tomb scarcely left room for a standard feature of Renaissance funerary monuments: the sarcophagus, which in a wall-monument would be placed beneath the central arch, often with an effigy of the deceased recumbent on the lid. Here it is represented by the marble chest upon which Pesaro's statue stands. The unashamedly secular character of tombs such as this was paralleled by funeral ceremonies in which heraldic banners and pagan imagery vied with Christian symbols to do honour to the illustrious dead. Even the 'cappella ardente' – a cage of burning candles surrounding the coffin, whose history went back to the Middle Ages, had by the late sixteenth century not only become a glittering classical baldaquin with some of the attributes of a canopy of state, but in the case of a sovereign prince was sometimes seen as a symbolic re-enactment of the funeral pyre of a Roman emperor.

By the end of the sixteenth century attitudes were changing under the influence of a Counter-Reformation that aimed not only to combat Protestantism but also to repudiate much of the intellectual and artistic freedom that the Renaissance had engendered. Nudity in statuary or painting was frowned on, and so was the invasion of church interiors by vast ostentatious monuments which contributed nothing to Christian devotion. Already in 1542 the reforming Bishop Giberti of Verona was condemning burial in an elevated sarcophagus because it was contrary to the idea that dust should literally return to dust. At Milan Archbishop Carlo Borromeo (d. 1584) conducted a vigorous campaign against funerary monuments and other symbols of family pride which he said made churches look 'more like military camps than places of worship'. Denouncing the 'insolence and arrogant pomp' of tombs in which 'rotting corpses are preserved as if they were the relics of holy bodies', he ordered all offensive tombs and all arms, banners and other trophies of worldly pride to be swept from his own cathedral. But when he tried to apply the same measures to other churches he encountered opposition. At Tortona he had to call in the secular arm to get rid of some obnoxious monument, and in Milan itself he found a stubborn opponent in Gian Francesco Trivulzio.

Trivulzio was the representative of a rich and powerful family who had long been leaders of the opposition to the Sforza dukes. Early in the century his redoubtable uncle Gian Giacomo Trivulzio had contemplated commissioning an equestrian monument for which Leonardo da Vinci made some well-known sketches. But in 1512 the death of his only son made him change his mind: what he now wanted was a family chapel or mausoleum instead of a free-standing monument to himself alone. It was to be an addition to the collegiate church of S. Nazaro in Brolio, and it was to occupy the only vacant space available, a small area between the west end of the church and the street. Here the architect Bramantino designed for him a tall chapel that served also as a vestibule to the church. A domed octagon within, it was externally a square tower of two orders (Tuscan and Ionic), whose upper storey concealed the dome from sight (fig. 195). The reason for this odd and rather inelegant arrangement is not clear unless a further storey was contemplated, but of this there is no evidence. At ground level the internal facets of the octagon were marked by recesses, in some of which altars might be placed, and above each lower recess was a higher one for a sarcophagus (fig. 197). By the time St Carlo Borromeo became Archbishop of Milan, Gian Giacomo Trivulzio had long been dead, but after various vicissitudes the building had at last been completed by his nephew Francesco, and several of the recesses were occupied by the sarcophagi of the founder, his two wives and their children. Within a year of his arrival in Milan, the archbishop had demanded the removal of various banners and standards and objected to the placing of 'human corpses above the holy altars'. His vicar-general was deputed to see to it that his orders were obeyed, but, supported by two lawyers, Trivulzio maintained that the chapel (which he said had cost him and his family 15,000 *scudi*) was unconsecrated and therefore not subject to the bishop's strictures. If necessary, the altars could be removed, and the four priests whom he maintained to say masses at them could, he said, say them elsewhere in the church. The vicar-general insisted that the bodies must be reinterred, leaving the altars in place. No solution to this ecclesiastical impasse had been reached when the archbishop himself conducted a visitation in 1569 and demanded that either the tombs or the altars must be removed forthwith. When he came again in 1581 Francesco was dead, but the bodies were still entombed high above the altars and the martial prowess of the Trivulzi was still advertised by trophies, banners and other worldly insignia. The patience of a saint was at last exhausted: under threat of excommunication the banners were reluctantly taken away, and the bodies of the Trivulzi were consigned to the obscurity of a vault. The empty sarcophagi, however, remain in place high above the floor of the church (fig. 196).

If the conspicuous absence of major Sforza monuments of the fifteenth and sixteenth centuries either in the cathedral or in their own church of S. Maria delle Grazie is evidence of the success of Carlo Borromeo's campaign in his own city, the survival of similar monuments in many other Italian churches suggests that his zeal was exceptional. Nevertheless, the Council of Trent had its effect on funerary architecture. A new style of monument was encouraged whose imagery was predominantly sacred, and whose form sometimes resembled an altarpiece. All the figures were decently clothed, and even if a sarcophagus was incorporated in the design, the actual burial was below ground. Such are the Fregoso monument (by Danese Cattaneo, 1565) in Sant' Anastasia, Verona (fig. 198), and the Boncompagni monument (by Bartolomeo Ammannati, 1574) in the Campo Santo at Pisa. This type of monument, in which the commemorative element was subordinate to the religious, played a special role in the re-establishment of Catholic worship in churches in Flanders that had been devastated either by Protestant iconoclasm or by military action during the revolt of the Netherlands

195. Milan, S. Nazaro in Brolio, the exterior of the Trivulzio family chapel added at the west end of the church to the designs of Bramantino from 1512 onwards.

196. Milan, S. Nazaro in Brolio, the sarcophagi of the Trivulzi in the elevated niches inside their octagonal chapel.

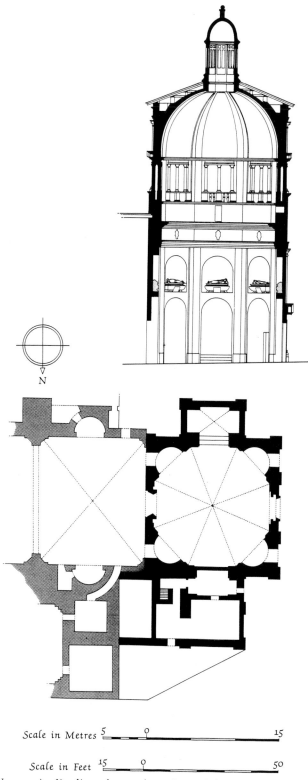

Scale in Metres 5 0 15

Scale in Feet 15 0 50

197. Milan, S. Nazaro in Brolio, plan and section of the Trivulzio chapel, showing its relationship to the church. The rooms on the north side were for the accommodation of the priests (after Baroni).

198. Verona, Sant' Anastasia, the monument to Giano Fregoso by Danese Cattaneo, 1565. In deference to Counter-Reformation ideas of religious propriety there is no sarcophagus and the central niche is occupied not by a statue of the former captain-general of the Venetian Republic, but by one of Christ (Osvaldo Böhm, Venice).

against Spanish rule from 1566 onwards. Those who in the early seventeenth century erected new monuments in Flemish churches were encouraged to make them contribute to a display of religious images that was designed to replace those that had been destroyed. Tombs became surrogates for destroyed altars, wall-tablets for lost religious statuary. Here for once the Church was able to harness the commemorative urge and to some extent to convert it into an instrument of devotion.

The Counter-Reformation not only deprecated the triumphal tombs of the

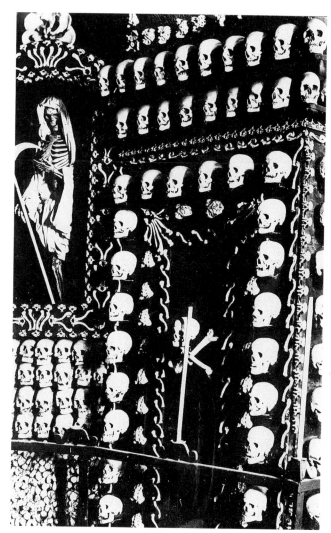

199. A baroque arrangement of human skulls and bones in an ossuary in Valletta, Malta (destroyed in the Second World War).

Renaissance, it brought with it a renewed insistence on man's mortality. Meditation on death was encouraged by the Jesuits; cardinals like Baronius and Borromeo lived ascetic lives very different from those of some of their predecessors; even popes sometimes demonstrated their piety by morbid gestures: Innocent IX (d. 1591) commissioned a painting that showed him on his death-bed, Alexander VII (d. 1667) slept like a Celtic saint with a coffin beneath his bed. The human skull became a stock instrument of piety. Saints were painted wrapped in contemplation of this symbol of mortality, and no tomb was complete without one to emphasise the transience of human life. Formalised skulls were even carved on capitals as a death's-head order (as on the monument of the first Lord Brouncker (d. 1645) in Oxford cathedral), and from Bernini onwards funerary sculpture brought whole skeletons into action as participants in the Christian drama of death. In crypts and ossuaries where human bones had been carelessly thrown in the past, they were now arranged with macabre skill as baroque tableaux of mortality (fig. 199).

In this new phase of Catholic spirituality, at once exhibitionist and introspective, there was no place either for the gracious effigies of humanist Italy, reposing

200. Rome, S. Marcello, the Frangipane family chapel (*c*.1565–70), with busts in circular recesses as if in an Ancient *columbarium*.

calmly on their elegant Renaissance tombs, or for the triumphal arches that had symbolised political and military power. But no less important for the historian of funerary architecture was a change in the character of funerary art itself that tended greatly to reduce the architectural element. For leading baroque sculptors such as Bernini or Algardi a major tomb was primarily a composition of those human figures that they carved so brilliantly: usually a group in which a dominant statue of the deceased is accompanied by personifications of religious virtues with their appropriate attributes. For lesser men a portrait bust was a favourite type of memorial, and by the middle of the seventeenth century the art of portraiture in sculpture had been brought to a high degree of excellence both in Italy and in the Low Countries. The bust, of course, required a setting, which might be architectural, but was rarely more than a frame compounded of pilasters, pediments and cartouches. Alternatively, the marble portraits might be treated as Roman busts set in circular recesses as if in an Ancient *columbarium*, as in the Frangipane chapel in the church of S. Marcello in Rome (fig. 200).

There was, however, one architectural feature that frequently played a part in the allegorical drama of the baroque monument, and that was the doorway. The combination of triumphal archway and functional doorway in some Venetian monuments has already been mentioned. Smaller tombs were often placed over doorways. Shortage of wall space and the restrictions imposed by Counter-Reformation regulation on the placing of tombs inside chancels or too near altars no doubt suggested the use of over-door spaces for the purpose, and a handsome

226

door frame often served to give greater consequence to a fairly modest mural monument. The door could, however, be an eloquent symbol, either of the separation between the living and the dead, or of the Christian belief in an after-life, expressed verbally in the Latin epigram, MORS CHRISTI IANUA VITAE ('the death of Christ is the Gate of Life'). Doors often figure on the sides of Roman sarcophagi. Sometimes they are firmly closed as if to symbolise the finality of death, but sometimes they are more poignantly shown half-open or half-closed (fig. 201). Are they slowly closing for ever on a new victim of Death, or are they opening to allow his shade a brief glimpse of the world of the living? No Ancient text authorises either interpretation, but on the monument of C. Clodius Primi-tivus (fig. 202) the two Victories are undoubtedly on the point of throwing the doors wide open, and the palm trees that rise behind them confirm that the visual image is one of triumph over Death, as it evidently is also in certain coins inscribed to the 'eternal memory' of the Emperor Maxentius and his kinsmen, in which a domed mausoleum is shown with its door ajar.

Some of these Ancient sarcophagi were known to Renaissance scholars and artists, and both the closed and the half-open door figure on the pedestal of Donatello's equestrian statue of the *condottiere* Gattamelata in Padua (1447).

201. Pisa, Campo Santo, Roman sarcophagus with the door shown ajar.

202. The monument of C. Clodius Primitivus in the Vatican Museum, Rome, with figures of Victory opening the doors of the tomb, probably second century AD.

Their message is as enigmatic as that of the Roman sarcophagi they imitate, but it may be significant that the door that is ajar is the one that faces the adjoining church of the Santo in which Gattamelata and his family are buried. In its original form, Michelangelo's design for the tomb of Pope Julius II in St Peter's envisaged a complete, free-standing mausoleum with a real door to the funerary chamber (fig. 210), but the doorway that Bernini incorporated in the tomb of Pope Alexander VII (d. 1667) was a stage-property to enable a skeletal figure of Death to play its part in the sculptural drama enacted above. Thereafter doors, real or

228

AN 1745

INNOCENTIUS XII
PIGNATTELLI

INNOCENTII XII · P·M·
INORNATUM MONUMENTUM
IN HANC ELEGANTEM FORMAM REDIGI CURAVIT
ADPRORANTE BENEDICTO XIV· P · M·
VINCENTIUS S·R·E·CARD·PETRA EP·PRÆN·
ET M PŒNITEN·
A · S · MDCCXLVI

203. Rome, St Peter's, overdoor monument of Pope Innocent XII (d. 1700), by Fuga, 1746 (from Letarouilly, *La Basilique de Saint Pierre*, Paris 1882).

The monument contains the inscription:

MARIAE·CHRISTINAE·AUSTRICICAE
ALBERTI·SAXONAE·PPINCIPIS·CONIUGI

204. Canova's monument to the Archduchess Maria Christina of Austria (d. 1798) in the Augustinian church in Vienna (from *The Works of Antonio Canova engraved in outline by Henry Moses*, London 1876).

fictive, became a standard feature of papal tombs in St Peter's and elsewhere (fig. 203). When they open to reveal a vestry or a staircase the effect is somewhat of an anti-climax, but in his pyramidal monument to the Archduchess Maria Christina of Austria (d. 1798) in the Augustinian church in Vienna (fig. 204), Canova gives the open doorway its full value as one that leads only to the grave.

205. The half-open door in a monument of 1864 in the cemetery at Bologna.

XII

THE PRINCELY BURIAL
CHURCH IN CATHOLIC EUROPE

IN THE SIXTEENTH AND SEVENTEENTH CENTURIES, as in the past, royal burial churches continued to be among the most prestigious architectural commissions in Europe. Usually they symbolised the recent achievement of power and wealth, whether by a new dynasty like the Valois of France, or by a prelate like Pope Julius II who had restored the temporal authority of the papacy in Italy. Every commission of this sort was therefore apt to be unique in its own country in its own day, and the solutions adopted by different rulers varied accordingly. Most of them, however, looked to Italy for architectural advice, and the form generally favoured by Italian architects for dynastic burial places was some variant of the geometrically regular space: round, square or polygonal, preferably with a domical roof. This was, as earlier chapters have shown, a form that carried with it both the prestige of Antiquity and the mystique of sanctity. Decorated with an appropriate programme of painting and sculpture, the structure as a whole was intended to evoke in those who could understand its message notions of personal piety, dynastic legitimacy or divinely ordained authority. If for the ruler the building was above all a symbol of sovereignty inherited or passed on, for the designer it was a problem in geometry of a kind that fascinated Renaissance architects. For him it was an opportunity to realise the dream of a centralised church that so often faded away when the practical realities of worship were taken into account. It may have been the idea of a burial church for the Sforza that sent Leonardo da Vinci covering sheet after sheet of paper with sketches on this theme. Giulio Romano had himself painted by Titian with a plan of a church of this sort in his hand, and there can have been few architects of his time whose portfolios did not contain one or two similar schemes. Not many of them were realised, for burial churches were luxuries that were peculiarly liable to interruption and non-completion. What one ruler started, another often had no interest in finishing. The examples that follow include several casualties as well as some buildings that still perpetuate the memories of those who had them built.

In 1396 Gian Galeazzo Visconti, following the example of Philip the Bold of Burgundy, began to build a great charterhouse at Pavia, the ancient capital of Lombardy. The monastery was planned on traditional lines, but as ultimately completed much of it was overlaid with a superabundance of Renaissance

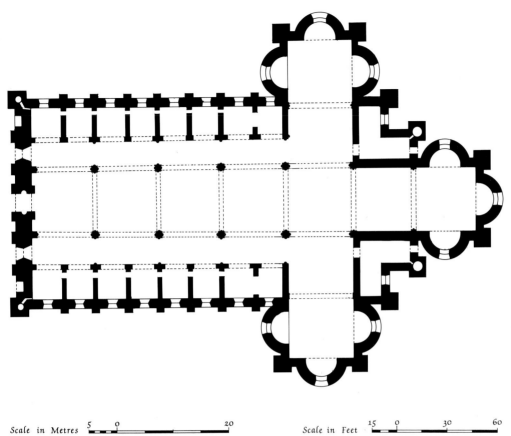

Scale in Metres 5 0 20   Scale in Feet 15 0 30 60

206. Pavia, plan of the church of the Certosa (after G. Chierici, *La Certosa*, 1942).

decoration in every medium which belied both the professed austerity of its inmates and the ideals of classical architecture as understood by men like Brunelleschi. The church was so long in building that it was completed not by the Visconti but by their successors, the Sforza. Not for the first time, a new dynasty with a dubious title endeavoured by devotion to the memory of its predecessor to strengthen the weak links between them: in this case, Francesco Sforza's marriage to the illegitimate daughter of the last Visconti. It was Francesco Sforza who in the 1470s completed the east end of the church with chancel and transepts whose triple apses (fig. 206) immediately remind an antiquarian observer of the trilobate plans of some Ancient and Early Christian mausolea (figs. 77, 98, 117), and were presumably intended to create the same image in the eyes of informed contemporaries. And in the 1490s, when Francesco's son Ludovico was converting the east end of the Dominican church of S. Maria delle Grazie in Milan into a Sforza burial place, he adopted a similar plan. Here the advice of an architect of distinction (probably Bramante) created a grand and dignified space for the Sforza tombs in which architecture speaks clearly without the superfluity of ornament which, however exquisite in detail, is at the Certosa di Pavia so otiose *en masse*.

Two Renaissance princes, Sigismondo Malatesta and Federigo da Monte-

233

207. Rimini, Italy, medal by Matteo de' Pasti representing the west front of the church of S. Francesco and the dome over the east end as envisaged in 1450 (Kress Collection, Washington, D.C.).

feltro, both patrons of art and learning as well as successful *condottieri* (mercenary generals), were much more radical in their sepulchral building schemes. At Rimini (of which his family had been the lords since the early fourteenth century) Sigismondo began in about 1450 to remodel an existing Franciscan church in which his ancestors were buried. After a false start with another architect he

208. Rimini, the south side of the church of S. Francesco, showing the sarcophagi in arcaded recesses (Alinari).

employed Alberti to give the building an authentically classical character. The west end was based on a triumphal arch, while the east end (never built) was to have been in the form of a domed rotunda. The former was no doubt meant to allude to Sigismondo's recent military exploits, while the latter was presumably intended for his place of burial. All that is known of its architectural design is the profile provided by a contemporary medal (fig. 207), which suggests an unbuttressed drum surmounted by a melon-shaped dome. The interior of the nave retained a basically medieval arrangement of chapels, decorated with an esoteric mixture of pagan and Christian iconography. It was in one of these chapels that, in default of the rotunda, Sigismondo was buried after his death in 1468. An important part of the funerary display was, however, intended to be external. The central recess in the upper part of the west front may have been intended to house the tomb of Sigismondo's saintly half-brother, Galeotto Roberto, whose humility would not allow him to be buried inside, while sarcophagi containing the bodies of members of his court were to occupy a series of recesses forming a continuous arcade on the outside of the nave walls (fig. 208).★ The practice of burial in external recesses was not new: it was to be seen in medieval churches at Bologna (S. Giacomo), Padua (Eremitani), Pistoia (S. Paolo), Prato (S. Domenico) and elsewhere, and most notably at S. Maria Novella in Florence, where Alberti himself was soon to incorporate such Gothic *avelli* into his new west front. But at Rimini he invested them with true Roman monumentality, raising them up on a podium and treating them as a continuous arcade standing free of the church walls. Against the deep and dramatic shadows created by the arcade the massive sarcophagi stand out in solemn isolation, one in each arch. The result is one of the great masterpieces of funerary architecture, without precedent in Antiquity, or parallel in the Renaissance.

At Urbino the magnificent Renaissance palace planned for Federigo da Montefeltro by Luciano Laurana in the 1460s was to have included a mausoleum standing in a courtyard. This courtyard, known as the 'Cortile del Pasquino', was still incomplete at the time of Federigo's death in 1482, and he was buried in the church of S. Bernardino. That he had intended to erect for his last rest a temple 'unsurpassed for design, beauty and noble ornament' is, however, attested by a contemporary writer, and this appears to have been the 'round temple' of which a model was still to be seen in the ducal palace at the end of the sixteenth century. So the idea of building a mausoleum, in the form apparently of a round temple, had already been conceived at Urbino before 1482. Moreover, like Diocletian's mausoleum at Split in Dalmatia, it was to stand in a palace courtyard. As Federigo's architect, Laurana, was a Dalmatian it is tempting to suggest that, at least in its siting, his mausoleum was inspired by Diocletian's. But any similarity

★ Only those on the south side actually contain sarcophagi, and of these, only three were occupied by protégés of Sigismondo Malatesta – the poets Basinio Basini (d. 1457) and Giusti di Conti (d. 1449) and the military engineer Roberto Valturio (d. 1475). The remains of a Greek philosopher called Giorgio Gemisto Platone were brought from Mistra to occupy a fourth. The other three sarcophagi were added in the sixteenth century.

may have been fortuitous, for at this time the building at Split had long been in use as a church, and was supposed to have been designed as a temple rather than as an imperial mausoleum.

The model must have been known to a young architect who was brought up at Urbino and who for a few years may actually have worked for Federigo da Montefeltro: Donato Bramante. In the absence of any drawing or description of the lost model it can be only a conjecture that it was one of the images that Bramante had in his visual memory when in about 1505 he was commissioned by King Ferdinand of Aragon to design the Tempietto at the church of S. Pietro in Montorio in Rome. Like Federigo's projected mausoleum, this is circular in plan and it stands in a courtyard (fig. 209). Although it was not a place of burial, it was intended to mark the site of St Peter's crucifixion and was, therefore, a sort of *martyrium*, for which the form of a circular temple or mausoleum was entirely appropriate. The domed tempietto followed Ancient examples then still extant in Italy and provided a model for funerary and ornamental architecture that was to be influential for over two hundred years.

Almost simultaneously Bramante was designing the great new church of St Peter in Rome for Pope Julius II. This commission began with Michelangelo's scheme for a tomb for Julius which, according to Vasari, was to 'surpass by its beauty and splendour, its richness of ornament and abundance of statues, all the imperial tombs of Antiquity'. Old St Peter's offered no satisfactory site for a grandiose free-standing monument, and the architect Giuliano da Sangallo strongly advised the pope to build a separate chapel in order to house it properly. In the event, it was decided to rebuild the basilica itself, with the tomb as a principal feature of the interior. By October 1505 the pope had accepted Bramante's plan for a church dominated by a great domed space. The focal point of the old basilica was of course the *confessio* or shrine over the tomb of St Peter, which had to be retained, and the relationship between this hallowed spot and the new tomb would have been critical. Bramante, with the pope's authority, gave precedence to the *confessio*, resulting in the abandonment of Michelangelo's first scheme for the tomb, upon which work was already well advanced. In a much reduced form it eventually found a home in the church of S. Pietro in Vincoli. As very few drawings for it survive, the form of the monument as originally conceived early in 1505 is almost as much of a puzzle for Renaissance scholars as that of the Mausoleum of Halicarnassus is for students of Ancient architecture and sculpture. It appears, however, to have been basically a rectangular structure about thirty-five feet long and twenty-three feet wide, containing a funerary chamber entered through a door in the middle of one of the ends. This chamber was described as 'oval' in plan and Michelangelo may have envisaged it either as a true oval (as supposed by Panofsky) or as a rectangle with apsidal ends (as argued by Frommel). ★

★ Had it been built as an oval it would have been the first room of this form in European architecture. The first oval space actually to be built was Vignola's S. Anna dei Palafrenieri in Rome (begun 1563). The first north of the Alps was the chapel attached to the mausoleum at Graz of the Habsburg emperor Ferdinand II (d. 1637), built in 1614–38 to the designs of an Italian architect from Lodi called Pietro de Pomis.

209. Rome, the Tempietto at S. Pietro in Montorio designed by Bramante to mark the site of St Peter's crucifixion and built during the first decade of the sixteenth century.

Externally it formed the base for a stepped composition which culminated in an effigy of the pope. Its walls were hollowed by niches housing personifications of Victory flanked by bound figures of captives or slaves, presumably symbolising the triumph of the Church over its enemies. It was these masterpieces of Michelangelo's art as a sculptor that were designed to attract attention, but for the historian of funerary architecture it is the structure as a whole that is most significant, for with its internal chamber to house the sarcophagus of the deceased

237

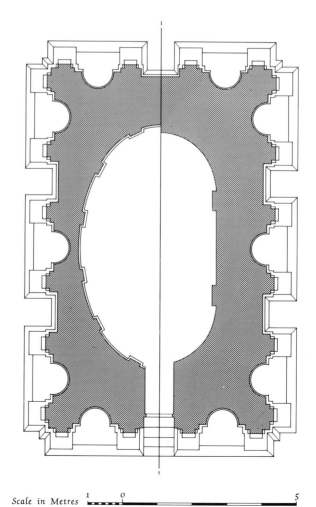

210. Michelangelo's design for the tomb of
Pope Julius II in St Peter's, Rome, as
conjecturally reconstructed by, *left*,
Panofsky and, *right*, Frommel. The
culminating figure of the pope is omitted as
its form is uncertain.

Scale in Metres   1   0   5

Scale in Feet   5   0   5   10

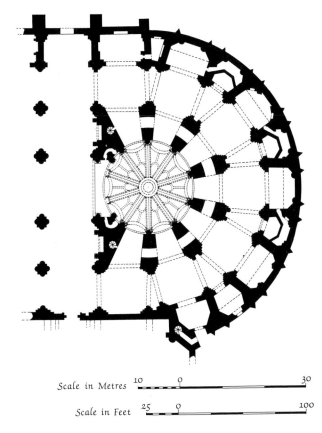

Scale in Metres 10 0 30

Scale in Feet 25 0 100

211. Granada cathedral, Spain, plan of the east end.

pope, its stepped composition and its abundance of statuary, it would immediately have been recognisable as a mausoleum in the Antique tradition (fig. 210).★ Reduced to a wall-monument in S. Pietro in Vincoli, it has retained some of its éclat as a work of sculpture, but has lost all its importance as one of architecture.

Far away in Spain, another great church was being built with a tomb in mind. But here the medieval tradition was still strong and the result was an awkward compromise between a Gothic *chevet* and a classical rotunda. In the Andalusian city of Granada the building of a new cathedral on the site of the principal mosque was an expression of Christianity triumphant over a defeated Islam. In 1505 a royal burial chapel was begun by Ferdinand the Catholic, King of Aragon and Castile. This was completed in about 1520, and in March 1523 the first stone of a new Gothic cathedral was laid with the intention of incorporating the chapel on its south side. When Ferdinand died in 1516 he was duly buried in the royal chapel, but when his grandson and successor, the Emperor Charles V, visited Granada ten years later he criticised the chapel, saying that its narrowness and

★ A wall-monument with a stepped top evidently intended to recall the Mausoleum itself was designed by Giulio Romano for the tomb of Baldassare Castiglione (d. 1529) in the church of S. Maria delle Grazie near Mantua (see M. Laskin in *Burlington Mag.* 109, 1967). Other monuments incorporating the motif of the stepped top are to be seen in the church of S. Antonio at Padua (Alessandro Contarini, *c.*1550) and the cloister of S. Zeno at Verona (Niccolò Schioppi, 1566).

darkness made it 'seem more like the chapel of a merchant than of kings'. Instead he wished to be buried in the cathedral itself. This led to a reappraisal of the design, which was taken out of the hands of the Gothic architect Enrique Egas and entrusted to Diego de Siloe as a 'master of the Roman style'. Diego had probably had Italian experience, but the cathedral that he built on the foundations laid by Egas followed the traditional Spanish five-aisled plan, and its proportions are those of the Middle Ages rather than the Renaissance. Its details are, however, consistently classical, and within the eastern *chevet* Diego contrived a domed sanctuary that has no precise precedent in European architecture. It is neither central (like the dome of St Peter's) nor semi-detached (like that of SS. Annunziata in Florence) but is integrated with the *chevet* so as to form, in plan, a complete rotunda where in a normal late Gothic church one would find a semicircle open to the nave (fig. 211). Whether or not this unusual structure was intended to recall the Holy Sepulchre (as has been claimed), it was evidently designed to serve as both sanctuary and burial place. In the event, no tomb was ever to stand before or beside the high altar, for when he died in retirement at Yuste in Estremadura in 1558, Charles V was buried in the monastery there,* and nothing came of plans to remove the tombs of the Catholic Monarchs and those of Joan of Castile and Philip the Fair from the royal burial chapel into the cathedral. Only the form of the rotunda remains to show that the east end of Granada cathedral is a mausoleum *manqué*.

Meanwhile, in Poland a funerary chapel of uncompromisingly Italianate character had been built onto the cathedral on the Wawel Hill in Cracow at the behest of King Sigismund I (1506–48). To design it Sigismund obtained the services of a little-known but very competent Italian called Bartolommeo Berecci, under whose direction it was erected between 1517 and 1533. Faced with a constricted site on the south side of the Gothic cathedral, Berecci planned a chapel consisting of a windowless cube surmounted by a tall dome and lantern which effectively assert the chapel's architectural independence from its parent church (fig. 212). Internally the four elevations are treated as richly decorated triumphal arches framing the tombs of Sigismund himself and other members of the Jagellon dynasty (fig. 213). Some minor divergences from the strictest classical harmony (e.g., the failure of the vertical ribs of the dome to align with the pilasters of the drum beneath it) scarcely distract attention from an iconographical display of tritons, nereids, putti and other mythological creatures in whose ostensibly pagan forms minds in touch with humanist circles could find hidden Christian messages appropriate to a place of burial.

The royal chapel in Cracow provided Poland with a perfect example of Renaissance architecture which was to be widely imitated. Berecci himself designed a simpler version for a bishop of Cracow in about 1530, and in 1664–70 the Vasa dynasty built a companion chapel immediately to the west of Sigismund's. In the course of the seventeenth century the domed, centrally planned funerary chapel became one of the most characteristic features of Polish architec-

*In 1574 his body was reinterred in the Escorial.

ture, and prefabricated chapels, complete with sculpture, were produced in the limestone quarry at Pinczow near Cracow and exported by water to other parts of a country in which brick and stucco were the prevailing building materials. Elsewhere simpler versions of the royal prototype were built by local craftsmen. Despite a tendency, attributable to Counter-Reformation ideals, to give greater emphasis to the religious function of such chapels and less to the display of family pride, King Sigismund's chapel remained a model for Polish architects throughout the seventeenth century, making it one of the most influential buildings of its kind in the history of European architecture.

France, like Spain, was slow to accept the logic of a Renaissance architecture uncompromised by such relics of the Gothic past as tall roofs and round turrets, but here, as elsewhere, tombs and tomb-chapels were often missionaries of the new style, and the Valois chapel at Saint-Denis was one of the most consistently classical buildings of the sixteenth century north of the Alps. It was commissioned by Catherine de Médicis, queen dowager of France, to contain a monument to herself and her husband King Henri II (d. 1559). By this time the church of Saint-Denis was so full of royal tombs, medieval and later, that a new architectural setting was needed for a prestigious monument such as Catherine envisaged. It took the form of a domed rotunda attached to the north transept of the abbey church. Work began in the 1560s, but in the 1570s it was interrupted by the civil war and when the queen died in 1589 the building was still unfinished. Although protected by a temporary roof, it was subsequently neglected and was in a ruinous state when it was finally demolished in 1719. The circular plan was obviously intended to evoke the image of an Antique mausoleum of a type often sketched by Italian architects, and the allusion was underlined in a set of tapestries in which the story of Artemisia and Mausolus was represented with complimentary reference to Catherine de Médicis and Henri II. But at Saint-Denis the complex arrangement of chapels round a central space owed more to Renaissance invention than to any authentic Ancient example and recalled church designs by Michelozzo (SS. Annunziata, Florence), Sangallo (for St Peter's), Michelangelo (for S. Giovanni dei Fiorentini, Rome) and others. Externally the pairs of columns, Doric below and Ionic above, alternated with niches and windows to form a continuous composition of the type made famous by Bramante in the Belvedere Court at the Vatican. Internally the orders were Corinthian and Composite, and tribunes at first-floor level added visual complexity to the view from the domed central chamber. In the middle stood the tomb (itself a highly architectural composition) of Catherine and her husband, adorned with statuary in marble and bronze. Round the periphery were six trefoil-shaped chapels (figs. 214–16).

When work began on the royal tomb in 1563 the Italian Primaticcio was in charge as head of the royal works, and according to Vasari (writing in 1567) he intended it to stand in the centre of a building that had six subsidiary spaces, four of which were reserved for the tombs of Catherine's sons, the fifth containing the altar and the sixth the entrance. Some materials had already been assembled before Primaticcio's death in 1570 brought the work to a standstill. In 1573 work

212. Cracow, Poland, the Vasa (*left*) and Sigismund (*right*) chapels on the south side of the Wawel cathedral (Wawel State Art Collections).

213.   Interior of the chapel of King Sigismund I at Cracow (Wawel State Art Collections).

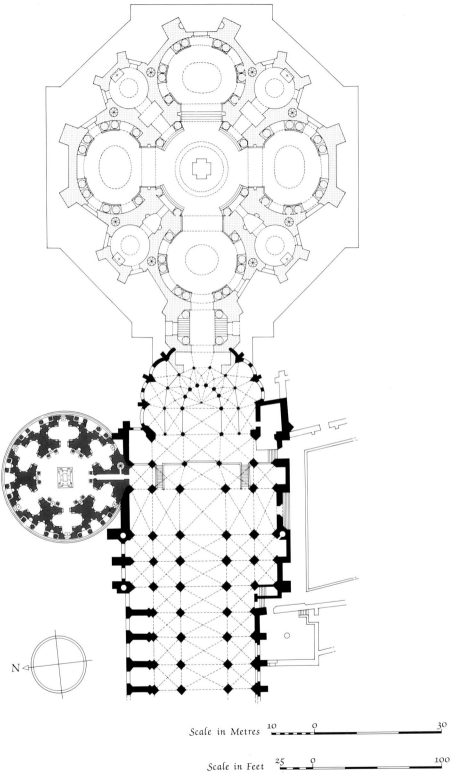

N

Scale in Metres 10 0 30

Scale in Feet 25 0 100

214. Saint-Denis, France, plan of the medieval abbey church with the sixteenth-century Valois chapel attached to the north transept and Mansart's unexecuted scheme of *c*.1662–3 for a Bourbon chapel beyond the east end.

215 (*above left*). Exterior of the Valois chapel at Saint-Denis showing the intended dome (from a seventeenth-century engraving by Marot).

216 (*above right*). Interior of the Valois chapel at Saint-Denis, with the tomb of King Henri II in the centre (from a nineteenth-century copy of an engraving in Félibien's *Histoire de l'abbaye royale de Saint-Denys en France*, Paris 1706. The original cannot be reproduced because of the way it is bound into the book).

was resumed on the basis of designs submitted to the king, Charles IX, by Primaticcio's successor, the French architect Jean Bullant, but he died in 1578 and it was Baptiste Du Cerceau who supervised the last phase of work from 1582 to 1587. How far Bullant's design followed Primaticcio's it is now impossible to say, as no original drawings for the building survive, but it is likely that he was expected to utilise the materials already assembled, which included marble columns, and his six trefoil-shaped chapels recall Vasari's reference to six subsidiary spaces, although these must have been differently disposed, as none of them now served as an entrance.

The Valois dynasty came to an end in 1589 with the death of Catherine de Médicis's last surviving son, Henri III,★ and in the 1660s Colbert, as Louis XIV's minister of works, was actively considering the idea of building a Bourbon chapel at Saint-Denis. Space for burials there was once more a problem, and a new dynastic chapel would be an obvious complement to the project for a new

★ According to an eighteenth-century French historian, Henri III had the intention of building in the Bois de Boulogne a magnificent *mausolée* to contain his heart and those of his royal successors. It was to stand at the centre of six *allées* in which each chevalier of the Order of the Saint-Esprit founded by Henri was to build a marble tomb for himself. However, contemporary evidence shows that what Henri actually began to build in the Bois de Boulogne in 1583–5 was a monastery, and if there was any truth in the story it was presumably the monastic church that was to contain the *mausolée* (see David Thomson in *Bulletin Monumental*, 148, 1990, p. 72).

Louvre. Both the Italian Gian Lorenzo Bernini, who came to Paris at the king's invitation in 1665, and the French François Mansart made designs for such a chapel. What Colbert had in mind was one big enough to contain fifteen or twenty tombs, of which the most magnificent would be that of its founder, Louis XIV. The obvious site was immediately to the east of the abbey church. Sketches by Mansart survive for a gigantic, multi-domed chapel in this position, and by Bernini for a smaller one (fig. 214). However, Colbert was opposed to the former which, as he said, would dwarf the existing abbey church, while Bernini criticised the way the Valois chapel was visually cut off from it. As a baroque architect he would naturally favour something spacially more adventurous than the closed circle of the Valois chapel, and in conversation he outlined a scheme to create a setting for the Bourbon tombs resembling the Cornaro chapel which he had designed in the church of S. Maria della Vittoria in Rome. The kneeling effigies of the kings would 'lean against a balustrade in their historical order'. As they would face the principal altar and 'be visible during all ceremonies and services', it is possible that he contemplated placing them in the *chevet*, or even in the triforium above.

The idea of building a Bourbon chapel at Saint-Denis was still in contemplation in 1675, but nothing came of it,★ and when the queen died in 1683 the Bourbon vault was so full that the body lay in state for a month while the vault was enlarged to accommodate it. However, the unfulfilled project of the 1660s had an architectural legacy. When the double church of Louis XIV's prestigious military hospital, Les Invalides, was built in 1676–1706 under the direction of Jules Hardouin-Mansart, the design for the domed portion closely resembled one of the more modest ones made by his great-uncle for the Bourbon chapel. This suggests the possibility that it was envisaged that Louis XIV would eventually be buried in the Invalides, as a warrior-king among his former soldiers. But if this idea was ever entertained, it was not implemented, and when Louis died in 1715 he joined his ancestors in the Bourbon vault at Saint-Denis. The fitness of the building for such a purpose was, nevertheless, demonstrated in the 1840s, when the space beneath the dome was adapted by the architect Visconti to receive the sarcophagus containing the body of France's most famous warrior, the Emperor Napoleon I.

In Florence the grand dukes lavished the resources of their *pietra dura* work-shops to encrust with coloured marbles and semi-precious stones the vast interior of a great new octagonal burial chapel which they erected at S. Lorenzo from 1603 onwards (fig. 173); while in Spain King Philip II began, and King Philip IV completed in 1654, a subterranean royal 'pantheon' beneath the sacristy of the Escorial. But architecturally the most important burial churches of the baroque period were those of the House of Savoy. Since the twelfth century the medieval counts of Savoy had been buried in the Cistercian abbey of Hautecombe which

---

★In 1781 there was an abortive scheme to enlarge the crypt beneath the church in order to create a subterranean Bourbon chapel. M.J. Peyre's ingenious neo-classical designs are illustrated by Andrew McLellan in *Burlington Mag.*, May 1988, pp. 340–5.

they had founded near Chambéry, and where, despite Revolutionary vandalism and other vicissitudes, some of their tombs are still to be seen. But by the end of the sixteenth century their successors were the rulers of a principality that extended far to the south of the Alps, with its capital at Turin. A new and more prestigious burial church was called for in Piedmont. The natural site for it was in or near Turin, but in the 1590s an obscure chapel at Vicoforte near the town of Mondovì, eighty kilometres to the south, attracted attention because of miracles ascribed to the Virgin Mary. Duke Carlo Emanuele I was drawn into patronising a scheme for a large pilgrimage church, served by Cistercian monks, and eventually decided to adopt it as the burial place of his dynasty. Several designs were submitted, all for centrally planned churches. The one that was preferred was an oval scheme by a military engineer, Ercole Negro di Sanfront. The oval plan was regarded by sixteenth-century churchmen as preferable to the circular, partly because the latter was considered by some to have pagan associations and partly because in an oval church the principal altar could still retain a dominant position. In Sanfront's plan the shrine, which was the object of the pilgrimage at Vicoforte, was to stand in the middle of the oval body of the church, surrounded by a continuous ring of peripheral altars.

As soon as Carlo Emanuele had decided (in 1598) to adopt the church as his family mausoleum, he employed a new architect, Ascanio Vitozzi, to adapt Sanfront's plan to its new purpose. The oval form was retained, with the shrine in the centre, but the chapels were reduced to five, one at the east end to accommodate the principal altar, and the other four to contain the tombs of the House of Savoy. Each chapel was entered through a screen of Composite columns and lit by a large semi-circular window with ingeniously designed columnar mullions. Above the central space Vitozzi planned a stupendous elliptical dome which was eventually completed by Francesco Gallo to his own designs in 1733 and decorated by Giuseppe Galli Bibiena and Mattia Bortoloni with a brilliantly theatrical rendering of the Assumption of the Virgin. Externally the huge church remained unfinished until the nineteenth century, when the main facade was at last completed (1830), and the four towers, intended by Vitozzi to terminate in spire-like finials with prominent vanes, were (after various vicissitudes) awkwardly finished off with low pyramidal roofs. From a distance the mass of the dome, rising between the towers, gives this singular building a highly individual silhouette which might almost as easily suggest a mosque as a church (figs. 217–18).

Only two of the chapels were used for their intended purpose. These were fitted up in the 1670s, one for the tomb of Carlo Emanuele, who had died in 1630, the other for that of his daughter Margherita, Duchess of Mantua, who died in 1665. The wall-monuments are effectively framed by 'Serlian' arches supported by black marble columns. The duke's monument, by the brothers Collini of Turin, was not made until 1792, by which time the 'Santuario di Vicoforte' had been superseded as the royal burial place by the church known as the Superga.

The Superga is a steep hill ten kilometres east of Turin. It was from this point of vantage that in 1706 Duke Vittorio Amedeo II, in company with his cousin Prince

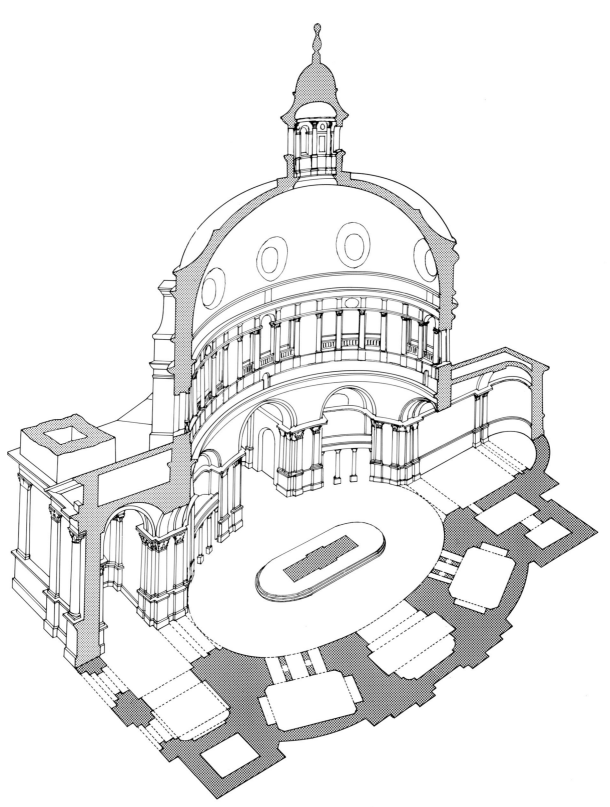

217. The pilgrimage church of the Madonna at Vicoforte in Piedmont, N. Italy, showing the central shrine and the four chapels (with columnar screens) that were designed as burial places for the House of Savoy.

218. The exterior of the church at Vicoforte from the north.

Eugene, observed the Franco–Spanish forces that were besieging his capital, and according to tradition it was to fulfil a vow made on this occasion that he subsequently founded a church and monastery of regular canons on the site. As built between 1717 and 1731 to the designs of Filippo Juvarra, the Superga is a spectacular complex comprising church, conventual buildings and royal palace (unfinished). The conventual buildings form a quadrangular block from which the domed church with its flanking towers stands out to dominate the skyline (fig. 219). Although actually octagonal in plan, with a portico projecting to the west and a chancel to the east, the church reads as a domed rotunda of a kind that in European architecture was often destined for funerary purposes. However, although Juvarra's original plans show vacant spaces beneath the church that could be used for burials, the principal ones are inaccessible, and it was not until a few years before his death in 1732 that Vittorio Amedeo II gave orders for a funerary chapel to be formed under the chancel. Work began in 1728 and in 1730 a French visitor reported that 'beneath the church is a subterranean chapel to which it is said the king intends to have the remains of his ancestors removed'. This chapel, which now contains the sarcophagi of the members of the House of Savoy from Vittorio Amedeo onwards, was not completed until the reign of Carlo Emanuele III (d. 1773). How far the Superga was intended from the first as a dynastic burial church is therefore not quite clear, but by the early nineteenth century Stendhal could rightly describe it as 'the Saint-Denis of the House of Savoy'.

By the eighteenth century nearly every ruling dynasty in Catholic Europe had its established place of burial. One of the last to be built was that of the Schönborn family who were prince-bishops of Speyer. It replaced the parish church of their residence at Bruchsal and was built in 1740–6 to the designs of Balthasar Neumann. Although his Greek-cross plan had no recent prototype, it clearly belonged to the tradition of centrally planned buildings so characteristic of

219. The Superga near Turin, 'the Saint-Denis of the House of Savoy', from the west (Alinari).

220. The west front of the abbey church of Farnborough in Hampshire, England, built by the exiled Empress Eugénie of France as a place of burial for her husband, Napoleon III, and herself.

funerary architecture in Europe, for the family vault occupied the space beneath the central crossing.

In France the Revolution of 1789 interrupted the long tradition of royal burial at Saint-Denis which went back to the beginnings of the French monarchy, and elsewhere in Europe the dynastic dislocations that ensued did not encourage the building of new royal mausolea. At Dreux King Louis Philippe (1830–48) did, it is true, remodel in Gothic style a classical rotunda built by his mother in 1816–22 for the burial of members of the cadet royal house of Orléans. But it is, paradoxically, in Protestant England that the last funerary church to commemorate a Catholic sovereign is to be found. It is at Farnborough in Hampshire, and it was built in 1883–8 by the Empress Eugénie, the Spanish widow of the Emperor Napoleon III. After the fall of the Second Empire in 1870, they had settled at Chislehurst in Kent, where Napoleon died three years later. In 1879 their only child, Louis Napoleon, the Prince Imperial, was killed fighting for Britain in the Zulu War. Desolated by these successive catastrophes, Eugénie decided to build a mausoleum for her husband and son. Difficulties with the patrons of the Catholic church at Chislehurst prevented her building it there, and in 1880 she moved to Hampshire, where she bought the house known as Farnborough Hill and secured an adjoining site for the church which she built to the designs of the French architect Hippolyte Destailleur (1822–93) (fig. 220). Destailleur was well known in France as a restorer of sixteenth- and seventeenth-century châteaux and had recently been employed by Baron Ferdinand de Rothschild to design Waddesdon Manor in Buckinghamshire in the French Renaissance style. The church at Farnborough is a scholarly essay in the latest phase of French Gothic, with an ingeniously planned east end which looks externally like a *chevet* of chapels but in fact contains a sacristy behind a three-sided apse. The detailing is predominantly *flamboyant* Gothic, with some Renaissance features, notably the dome that rises from the crossing. All of it is well studied, from the *clefs pendants* of the vaults (derived probably from the church at La Ferté-Bernard in Maine) to the long-necked gargoyles, which immediately proclaim that this is a French church on English soil. Below in a Romanesque crypt are the three tombs, of Aberdeen granite, standing on a floor of red, white and black Corsican marble. Although a detached building, as befits its purpose, the church at Farnborough is also the conventual church of the adjoining monastery founded by the empress with the express purpose of offering intercessory prayers for herself and her family. Originally a small priory of Premonstratensian canons, it is now an abbey of Benedictine monks, by whom members of the Napoleonic dynasty (including Napoleon I) are still commemorated in evening prayer every Friday, and by masses on the anniversaries of their deaths.

XIII

THE FAMILY CHAPEL
IN PROTESTANT ENGLAND
AND SWEDEN

EVERYWHERE IN EUROPE INTERCESSION FOR THE DEAD remained a characteristic feature of Christian life right up to the events of 1520–40 which left western Europe split between two rival religious ideologies, Catholic and Protestant. Piety had, of course, its regional variations, and measured by the number of new chantry foundations, Purgatory excited more apprehension in some parts of Europe than it did in others. But at a time when (as both art and literature attest) men were acutely conscious of their own mortality, it was the means of salvation rather than the need for it that was in question. A perpetual chantry of the old type could easily fall a victim either to inflation or to the mismanagement of its endowments, leaving the soul of the unfortunate founder in torment without any means of redress. Some testators spread the risk by arranging for intercession in several churches rather than in a single chantry exclusively devoted to their salvation. Others, bearing in mind that, so far as any theologian could tell, a mass today was as efficacious as one a hundred years hence, laid out their money in buying instant masses by the thousand: to give an example from Italy, a rich draper of Asti in Piedmont who died in 1420 not only left money for twelve anniversary celebrations by the Friars Minor of his native town, but also for 3,650 masses to be celebrated by various religious communities in Avignon within one year of his death. When testators demanded a plurality of masses to be said 'immediately after' or 'as soon as possible after' their death they were thinking not only of mitigating their future ordeal but of the falling value of their florins or pounds on earth and of the difficulty of managing an investment from the grave. Spiritually the result might be the same as providing for a single priest saying a daily mass in perpetuity, but architecturally it could have made the chantry chapel redundant. In practice, those who could afford it (like King Henry VII of England★) compromised by founding a conventional chantry but setting aside money for an initial burst of masses that would give their soul a favourable start in its perilous journey through Purgatory. In this way a prudent person could take steps to counter the inflation that was prevalent in early sixteenth-century Europe

★ See p. 174.

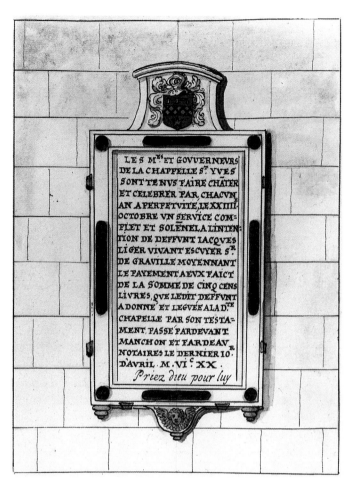

221. Paris, Saint-Yves, a tablet recording that the authorities of the chapel are bound to have a solemn service performed every year on the anniversary of the death of Jacques Liger, lord of Graville, in return for the payment of 500 livres under his will, which was proved by a named firm of notaries on 10 April 1620 (Bodleian Library, MS. Gough Gaignières 4, f. 74).

without necessarily abandoning the private chapel that would ensure the perpetuation of his or her name on earth.

To avoid the fraudulent or negligent trustee was more difficult. An obvious precaution was to have the terms of the endowment registered in some public record, such as (in England) the rolls of Chancery. Another was to have them displayed in writing in the church or chapel concerned, and in France an inscription setting out the prescribed services was a hopeful device widely adopted from the fifteenth century onwards. These tablets, often as elegantly carved as any memorial (and sometimes acting as a substitute for one), were almost invariably destroyed at the Revolution, but drawings of many of them made for the antiquary François-Roger de Gaignières (d. 1715) survive to show their character (fig. 221). Given the apprehension of purgatorial fire on the one hand and of human frailty on the other, such prudential expedients were understandable. But they were hardly to the credit of Christianity. The carefully calculated investment in masses, the no doubt often perfunctory performance of the services by stipendiary priests, and above all the associated system of indulgences whereby the Church claimed to have the power to shorten the pains of

Purgatory,[*] all contributed to the image of a mercenary and mechanistic religion sustained by theological assumptions of doubtful scriptural authority. It was the rejection of this image by Martin Luther and others that led to the withdrawal from obedience to the papacy of much of northern Europe and to the establishment of the Protestant churches of Germany, Holland, Switzerland, Sweden, England and Scotland.

Protestantism embraced many varieties of religious observance, but the abolition of masses for the dead was something upon which all the reformers were agreed. So in every Protestant country the mid-sixteenth century saw the dissolution of the chantries and the diversion of their revenues to other purposes. In Lutheran Germany the chantry endowments were merged into the common fund of the church, while in Calvinist Geneva those who had founded chantries or their heirs were allowed to resume possession of the revenues in question. In England, however, the state took all. The revenues of the chantries were confiscated by Act of Parliament (1547), and the churches or chapels of non-parochial foundations were demolished or converted to other purposes in the same way as the recently dissolved monasteries. Those churches that were used for parochial purposes as well as chantries were, however, spared and so were the numerous chantry chapels physically attached to parish churches, which could not be demolished without endangering the buildings of which they formed part. Many of them, moreover, contained family monuments and although Edward VI's government did not scruple to abandon to destruction all the tombs of the earls and dukes of Lancaster at Leicester as well as those of the dukes of York at Fotheringhay, the destruction of ancestral tombs was generally repugnant to contemporary sentiment and was expressly forbidden by royal proclamation in 1560. The accession in 1553 of a Catholic queen could not undo the expropriations and destructions of the previous reign, but several of Mary's leading subjects obtained licences to found chantries, and at least one new chantry chapel, that of Bishop Stephen Gardiner in Winchester cathedral, was actually built before the queen's death in 1558 put an end to the brief Catholic revival.

Although burial in churches was discouraged in some Protestant countries, no attempt was made by the Anglican Church to prevent it. The clergy themselves were frequently buried in the chancel, but by English ecclesiastical law patrons were responsible for the maintenance of chancels and lay patrons often used them as burial places. In extreme cases the entire chancel was appropriated for this purpose. Thus at Spilsby in Lincolnshire what was originally the chancel arch is completely blocked by one of the Willoughby family tombs, while at Warkton in Northamptonshire the chancel was rebuilt in the eighteenth century as a sort of sculpture gallery to display the magnificent tombs of the dukes of Montagu who lived at Boughton House nearby. In many other churches the monuments of the

---

[*] From 1457 onwards indulgences could be obtained by the living for the benefit of the dead. Previously they were valid only if obtained in person. The inflation in the relief they purported to confer is illustrated by the surviving brass of Roger Legh (d. 1506) in Macclesfield church, Cheshire, which encourages prayers for his soul by stating that 'The pardon for saying of 5 Paternosters and 5 Aves and a Creed is 26,000 years and 26 days of pardon.'

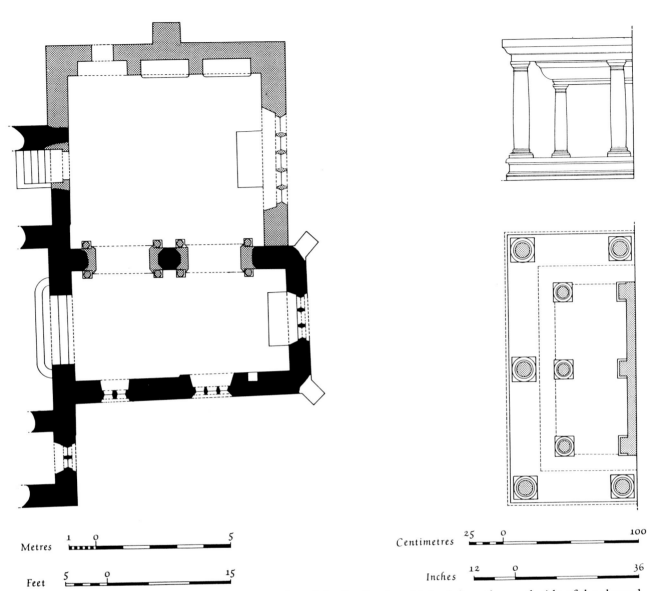

Metres
1 0 ... 5

Feet
5 0 ... 15

Centimetres
25 0 ... 100

Inches
12 0 ... 36

222. Beoley church, Worcestershire, England, plan of the family chapel (*stippled*) on the north side of the chancel, built by a Catholic gentleman named Ralph Sheldon in the reign of Queen Elizabeth and furnished with a stone altar (*right*) which still exists. The family tombs were beneath the arches on the south side of the chapel and in recesses in the north wall.

patronal family stand prominently on either side of the chancel, occupying what long tradition had made the most privileged space within the building. Sometimes they block up side windows, but they very rarely rise up in front of the east window or usurp the position of the altar, as is often the case in Holland, a country where more radically Protestant practices prevailed than in England.★ When in 1631 the powerful Earl of Cork erected a towering monument to his

★Notable examples are the tombs of William the Silent in the Nieuwe Kerk at Delft (made 1614–21), of Admiral De Ruyter (d. 1676) in the Nieuwe Kerk at Amsterdam, of Admiral Jacob van Wassenaer-Obdam (d. 1665) in the Groote Kerk at The Hague, and of Admiral William Joseph van Gendt (d. 1672) in the cathedral at Utrecht.

wife at the east end of St Patrick's cathedral in Dublin, William Laud objected to it on the grounds that it stood 'where the High Altar stood and where the Communion Table ought to stand'. Laud's ally the Earl of Strafford exerted his authority as Lord Deputy to have the monument removed to a less objectionable position, and prevailed after a trial of strength that was as much political as religious in character. At East Harptree in Somerset a similarly sited tomb, that of Sir John Newton (d. 1568), remained as a presumptuous symbol of lay proprietorship until it was removed to the porch in the nineteenth century.

Where a family owned a former chantry chapel, this normally continued to serve as a privileged place of burial. Such chapels were occasionally acquired by purchase (e.g., one at Mere in Wiltshire bought by the Chafyn family from Sir John Thynne in 1563), but they usually descended with the manorial estate to which they were attached and were maintained by their secular owners. Even the 'recusancy' (adherence to the proscribed Catholic faith) of the latter could not deprive them of their rights of burial, resulting in the curious situation, which still exists at Arundel (Sussex) and Mapledurham (Oxfordshire), of a Catholic chapel attached to an Anglican parish church.★ These two chapels were both medieval in origin, but in Worcestershire (a county 'much warped towards Popery'), one Catholic gentleman, Ralph Sheldon (d. 1613), actually built a new chapel on the north side of the parish church of Beoley and furnished it not only with splendid tombs but with an elaborate stone altar (still extant) at which masses were doubtless celebrated for the dead interred nearby (figs. 222–3).

To build what was in effect a clandestine chantry chapel in the reign of Queen Elizabeth was an altogether exceptional feat. A few chapels (e.g., that of the dukes of Norfolk at Framlingham in Suffolk and probably that of the earls of Derby at Ormskirk in Lancashire, fig. 224) were built to replace ones in abbey churches destroyed at the dissolution of the monasteries. And in Derbyshire one of the Sacheverells acquired a range of cloister windows, complete with stained glass, from the recently dissolved abbey of Dale and re-erected them to form a family aisle on the north side of Morley church. But most Elizabethan or Jacobean family chapels were erected by new landed families like the Russells and the Cecils as part of the process of establishing themselves as members of the English aristocracy. Such chapels served in addition as family pews, from which to listen in dignified privacy to the preaching of sermons. Thus in 1564 William Oxenden obtained permission from the Archbishop of Canterbury (as the diocesan bishop) to appropriate and rebuild a ruinous chapel on the north side of Wingham church in Kent, to construct seats in it for his family and to bury deceased members in it. At Adderley in Shropshire in the reign of Charles I the building of a similar pew-cum-burial place formed part of a running battle between Sir John Corbet, the patron of the church, and his neighbour Robert Needham, 2nd Viscount Kilmorey in the peerage of Ireland. In the past the two families had both been buried

★ The Fitzalan chapel at Arundel was the choir of a recently dissolved collegiate church which the 12th Earl of Arundel bought from the Crown in 1544 and used thereafter as a family chapel. Today masses are still said periodically for the repose of the souls of those buried in the chapel.

223. Beoley church, Worcestershire, exterior of the Sheldon chapel (cf. fig. 222).

in the chancel, the Needhams on the north, the Corbets on the south. In 1633 this condominium was broken by a calculated insult on the part of Sir John Corbet, who had the body of an Irish footboy buried on the Needham side. When Lord Kilmorey proceeded (with due ecclesiastical authority) to build himself a separate chapel on the north side of the nave (fig. 225), the Corbets persuaded the churchwardens to remove the screen that separated it from the church and forcibly occupied the seats themselves. The dispute was still in progress when the Civil War supervened and it was not until after the Restoration that the Needhams were once more able to occupy their pew undisturbed.

Despite their significance as symbols of social status, few of these post-Reformation chapels were buildings of great architectural pretensions. In siting and design they tended to take as their model the simpler chantry chapels of the early Tudor period. Standing usually either to the north or to the south of the chancel, they are typically lit by one east and either one or two lateral windows, and there is normally a doorway to the churchyard (fig. 226). The east window is sometimes arched and furnished with simple tracery of late Gothic character, but both it and the side windows are often of a kind with flat heads and uncusped lights which is barely distinguishable from secular windows of the same date (figs. 227–8). External heraldry is rare (at most a single shield over the doorway★), and there is, of course, no religious imagery. The hammer-beam roof with which the chapel of the Russell earls of Bedford (1556) at Chenies in Buckinghamshire was adorned was exceptional, although it had a pre-Reformation prototype in the

★ As at Spetchley, Worcs. (Berkeley chapel, 1614) or Crowcombe, Somerset (Carew chapel, 1655).

224. Ormskirk church, Lancashire, the east end of the family chapel built by the 3rd Earl of Derby in 1572.

225 (*below*). Adderley church, Shropshire, the 'Kilmorey aisle' built by the 2nd Viscount Kilmorey in 1636–7.

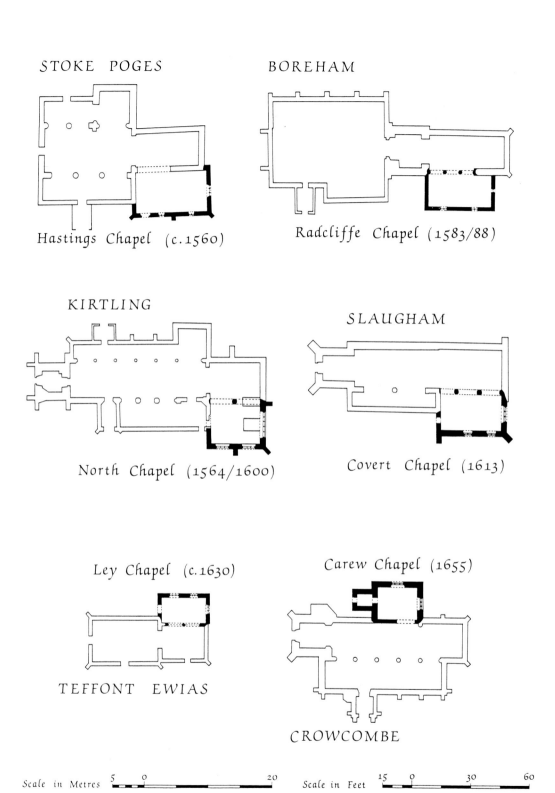

STOKE POGES

Hastings Chapel (c.1560)

BOREHAM

Radcliffe Chapel (1583/88)

KIRTLING

North Chapel (1564/1600)

SLAUGHAM

Covert Chapel (1613)

Ley Chapel (c.1630)

TEFFONT EWIAS

Carew Chapel (1655)

CROWCOMBE

Scale in Metres 5 0   20

Scale in Feet 15 0   30   60

226. English post-Reformation family chapels.

227. Stoke Poges church, Buckinghamshire, the Hastings family chapel of *c*.1560 (cf. fig. 226).

228. Hurstbourne Priors church, Hampshire, the Oxenbridge family chapel of *c*.1575.

229. St John's College, Oxford, the plaster fan-vault of the funerary chapel built in 1662 by Richard Baylie, President of the College.

Audley family chapel at Berechurch in Essex. Often the ceiling is or was plastered, and occasionally the plasterwork is ornamented – in the late sixteenth-century Kempe chapel at Pentlow in Essex with an effective pattern of Gothic tracery; in the tomb chamber added by President Baylie to the chapel of St John's College, Oxford, in 1662 with a skilfully simulated fan vault (fig. 229). If the

262

chapel itself is generally unassertive, the tombs that it houses are often large and pretentious. The typical Elizabethan or Jacobean tomb is a confection of columns, pilasters and arches framing recumbent or kneeling effigies and proclaiming the virtues of the deceased with the aid of symbol and epitaph. Two predominant types can be distinguished: one derives from the triumphal arch and is generally applied to the wall; the other is related to the elaborate catafalques used in contemporary obsequies and is often free-standing, with columns and/or arches supporting a canopy beneath which the effigies lie on a sarcophagus or table-tomb. Heraldry is conspicuous on the tomb as it was in the funeral processions of the time, and the importance of the monument as a family memorial is emphasised by attendant figures of children. Religious imagery of any kind is rare, but its place is often taken by symbolical properties such as obelisks and figures representing the Virtues. If the attitude of the effigies is generally one of piety, the monument as a whole is an unequivocal assertion of family pride and social status.

Whatever form the monument takes the contrast between the vestigially Gothic chapel and the fashionably classical tomb is striking and is a reminder that since the early sixteenth century funerary art had been one of the principal vehicles whereby the decorative vocabulary of the Italian Renaissance had been transmitted to the countries of northern Europe (another being the temporary displays at state entries and funerals). Only kings and other very great men such as Cardinal Wolsey or the Duke of Norfolk could actually import skilled Italian or Italian-trained craftsmen, but from the late sixteenth century onwards refugee Protestant craftsmen from the Low Countries had workshops in Southwark from which tombs could be ordered and sent into the country in pieces to be assembled on the spot. The family chapels, on the other hand, were built by local masons or brick-layers who had no contact with the tomb-sculptors and their repertoire of classical ornament. A Tuscan arcade (as in the Essex chapel at Watford, 1596–6, or the Salisbury chapel at Hatfield, 1618) was the most that could be expected of such artisans. It was not until 1631–2 that, at Chilham in Kent, both tomb and chapel were together designed by the same man – the English sculptor-architect Nicholas Stone, who had served his apprenticeship in Amsterdam.

Unfortunately, the chapel Stone built for Sir Dudley Digges was destroyed in 1862, but early nineteenth-century views show a rectangular structure of stuccoed brickwork attached to the south side of the chancel (fig. 231). It was lit by Venetian windows, and inside there was a vaulted ceiling rising from quarter-columns in the angles. This was, in all probability, the first classical tomb-chapel to be built in England.* The designer of the Mainwaring chapel at Over Peover in

---

*The monument that the Digges chapel contained was itself of an unusual form, consisting of a free-standing Ionic column standing on a high pedestal which also supported seated figures of the Cardinal Virtues. It commemorated Sir Dudley's wife, Mary, who had died in childbirth, and the form of the monument was evidently suggested by the pillar erected by Jacob to mark the grave of Rachel, who died in similar circumstances (*Genesis* 35:20). The biblical precedent is explicitly referred to on another pillar-tomb (Doric) at St Mary's church, Barton-on-Humber (Lincs.) to Jane, the wife of the Revd John Shipsea, who died in childbirth in 1626. This, like a third example at Winterbourne Stickland, Dorset (Rachel Sutton, d. 1653), is a half-column forming a wall-monument.

230. Over Peover church, Cheshire, the classical Mainwaring family chapel of *c.*1647–50.

Cheshire (*c.*1647–50) is not known, but its competent classical detailing suggests a mason or architect from London (fig. 230). It was doubtless a London artisan who was responsible for the less sophisticated Cambell chapel added to Barking church in Essex in 1645 and destroyed in 1842. The 1650s saw the first designs for detached (or semi-detached) mausolea, one of which was actually built at Maulden in Bedfordshire (see p. 313), and after the Restoration some simple classical family chapels were built, for example, at Lamport, Northamptonshire (1672–3) and North Leigh, Oxfordshire (1687) (fig. 232).

But the Gothic tradition persisted. Indeed, some seventeenth-century English funerary chapels were more convincingly Gothic than those of the Elizabethan period, perhaps suggesting that what in the sixteenth century had been unconscious conservatism, could in the seventeenth be a deliberate stylistic choice on the part of the patron. Certainly, it was not ignorance of any alternative that induced a man like Sir Richard Wynne to build a Gothic chapel at Llanrwst in North Wales in 1633–4 (fig. 233). For he was Treasurer to Queen Henrietta Maria and must have been familiar with the court architecture of Inigo Jones, whose name occurs frequently in his official accounts. In the Covert chapel at Slaugham, Sussex (1613), the geometry of fourteenth-century window tracery was successfully imitated, while the 'Perpendicular' windows in the Spencer chapel at Yarnton, Oxfordshire (1611), or the Ley chapel at Teffont Ewias, Wiltshire (*c.*1630) (figs. 234–5), were clearly designed and executed by masons better versed in Gothic fenestration than those responsible for the Elizabethan chapels at Stoke Poges, Buckinghamshire (*c.*1560) (fig. 227) or Turvey in Bedfordshire (soon after 1571).

231. Chilham church, Kent, the Digges chapel designed by Nicholas Stone in 1631–2 and probably the first classical family chapel in England (from an early nineteenth-century engraving in British Library, Add. MS. 32,359, f. 16).

232. North Leigh church, Oxfordshire, showing *left*, the fifteenth-century Wilcote chapel (cf. fig. 156), and *right*, the Perrot family chapel designed and built in 1687 by Christopher Kempster.

233. Llanrwst church, North Wales, the Wynne family chapel built in 1633–4 (National Monuments Record for Wales).

234. Yarnton church, Oxfordshire, the Spencer chapel built in 1611.

235. Teffont Ewias church, Wiltshire, the Ley chapel, built *c*.1630 (cf. fig. 226).

236. Ashburnham church, Sussex, the east end of the church built in 1664–5, with the Ashburnham family pew in the south chapel, the tombs in the north chapel, and a vault under the whole of the east end (Dr Maurice Howard).

At Hollingbourne in Kent the Colepeper chapel of 1638 even boasts a band of flint flushwork decoration beneath the battlements, while as late as 1675 Lord Leigh could commission a vestry-cum-family vault at Stoneleigh in Warwickshire which not only has passable curvilinear tracery in its windows, but a ribbed vault springing from angle-shafts in manner most authentically medieval.★

Few family chapels of much architectural consequence were built in England during the late seventeenth and eighteenth centuries, and it was only very occasionally that a church was completely rebuilt by its patron at his own expense, making it possible for the family pew and burial place to be symmetrically placed in transeptal projections, as at Ashburnham in Sussex (1664–5, Gothic) (fig. 236), Farley in Wiltshire (1688–9, classical) (figs. 237–8) and Shobdon in Herefordshire (1753–5, Gothick).† Most landed families continued to bury in established chapels, and most new chapels continued to be unpretentious rectangular rooms designed for the display of costly monuments with the minimum of architectural contrivance. In either case the effect of accumulated family history is often impressive, but sometimes, as at Knebworth, Hertfordshire, the close proximity of one bewigged effigy to another is ludicrous, and exhibits on a small scale the English propensity (most strikingly exemplified in Westminster Abbey) to regard a monument as a work of art in its own right to be admired quite independently of its setting.

If a professional architect was employed it was usually to design a detached mausoleum rather than to add a chapel to an old church. Even James Gibbs, the first English architect who regularly designed funerary monuments, seems never to have had a commission for a family chapel, but Hawksmoor may have designed the King chapel on the north side of Ockham church in Surrey. Nicholas Revett's revolutionary Greek temple of a church with funerary urns in flanking aedicules at Ayot St Lawrence, Hertfordshire (for Sir Lionel Lyde, 1778–9, fig. 239) found no imitators,†† and for funerary chapels attached to English parish churches either a notional Gothic or an unassertive classicism continued to be normal throughout the eighteenth century. One exception is the chapel at Ockham already mentioned. Not only does it provide an effective architectural setting for Rysbrack's monument to Lord Chancellor King (d. 1734), but its archway to the church forms an internal facade of a kind rare in England but common in Italy from the Renaissance onwards. Another is to be seen at

★ The combination of vestry and family vault is also found at Hempsted, Essex (Harvey chapel, mid-seventeenth century) and at Tottenham, Middlesex (see below p. 315).

† At Farley the family of Sir Stephen Fox sat in the south transept facing the tombs in the northern one. At Shobdon Lord Bateman's pew, rendered comfortable by a fireplace, was in the southern transept, while his servants sat opposite over the burial vault. More often it was the proprietor's pew to which the vault gave elevation, as at Melton Constable, Norfolk (Hastings pew, 1681), Hanslope, Bucks. (Watts pew, c.1800), or Chester-le-Street, Co. Durham (Lord Durham's pew by Ignatius Bonomi, c.1830). In this way the living members of the Protestant family were reunited with their deceased forbears every Sunday.

†† A somewhat similar solution was, however, adopted by the Italian architect S. Cantoni when (c.1802–6) he designed the neo-classical church at Gorgonzola near Milan with two flanking exedrae, one of which serves as the mausoleum of the Serbelloni family.

237. Farley church, Wiltshire, the view of the family monuments from the family pew.

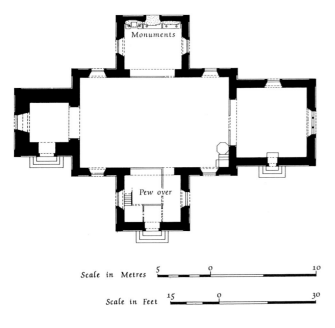

Monuments

Pew over

Scale in Metres 5   0   10

Scale in Feet 15   0   30

238. Farley church, Wiltshire, built in 1688–9, showing the Fox family pew in the south transept and their monuments in the north transept (after Royal Commission on Historical Monuments of England, *Churches of South-West Wiltshire*, 1987).

Frampton in Dorset, where paired Corinthian columns frame both the central window of the Browne family chapel and an inscription to the memory of Robert Browne (d. 1734), its founder. Funerary chambers of any architectural pretensions in the Georgian Gothic style are surprisingly rare, but the one that John Chute (d. 1776) added to the private chapel at The Vyne in Hampshire to contain the classical monument to his ancestor Chaloner Chute (d. 1659) is an elegant example by an amateur architect of ability. On the other hand, the flimsy structure at Wetheral in Cumberland, designed by unknown architect in 1791 to house a distinguished monument by Joseph Nollekens to Mrs Howard of Corby, looks more like a conservatory than a funerary chapel, while the Brocas chapel at Bramley in Hampshire (1802) serves only to demonstrate that the genius of Sir John Soane did not lie in the direction of Gothic architecture. Early in the nineteenth century some competently Gothic family chapels were designed by architects like Jeffry Wyatville or Ignatius Bonomi,* but only later would the Gothic Revival produce such architecturally convincing examples as the Vane chapel at Long Newton, Co. Durham (by P.C. Hardwick, 1859) or the Sudeley chapel at Toddington, Gloucestershire (by G.E. Street, 1873–9).† Still later are those 'Founder's Chantries', exquisitely designed by G.F. Bodley and Temple Moore, which in the church at Hoar Cross in Staffordshire and the chapel at Lancing College in Sussex respectively, so perfectly express their patrons' belief in an Anglican religion clothed in the trappings of the medieval past.

In Scandinavia, as in England, the Reformation was conservative in character. Papal jurisdiction was renounced, monasteries were dissolved, bishops were deprived of temporal jurisdiction, indulgences and prayers for the dead were abolished, but many features of the Catholic faith were retained. In Sweden it was not until 1602 that the word 'mass' was finally abandoned in favour of 'communion', and the use of Latin in the liturgy was not formally abolished until 1614. There was little iconoclasm, and when Bulstrode Whitelocke went to Sweden in 1653 as Cromwell's ambassador, he found churches still so richly furnished with crucifixes and images that he could see 'no difference' between them and the churches of the Papists. In these circumstances the Protestant family chapel or 'gravkor' succeeded the medieval chantry chapel without any break. Indeed, the word 'gravkor' is medieval in origin. 'Kor' originally meant 'choir', but in the course of the fifteenth century it came to mean any space used for liturgical singing, and in particular one devoted to the singing of masses for the dead. The larger Swedish churches like Strängnäs cathedral or the Great Church in Stock-

---

*The Bridgewater chapel at Little Gaddesden, Herts., by Wyatville (1819), the Lambton pew and vault at Chester-le-Street, Co. Durham, by Bonomi, c.1830. C.R. Cockerell designed the Gothic 'Sezincote aisle' at Longborough church, Glos., for his uncle Sir Charles Cockerell in 1822–3.

†Other examples are the octagonal Frankland chapel at Thirkleby, Yorks., by E.B. Lamb (1849–50), the Rolle chapel at Bicton, Devon, by A.W.N Pugin (1850), the de Mauley chapel at Hatherop, Glos., by Henry Clutton (1854–5), the Hotham chapel at South Dalton, Yorks., by J.L. Pearson (1858–61), the Grenville chapel at Wotton Underwood, Bucks., by G.E. Street (1867), the Milton chapel at Haselbeech, Northants., by A. Salvin (1871–2), and the Curzon aisle at Kedleston, Derbyshire, by G.F. Bodley (1907–9).

239. Ayot St Lawrence church, Hertfordshire, the church built by Sir Lionel Lyde in 1778–9 to the designs of Nicholas Revett. The funerary urn in the left-hand aedicule commemorates Lyde, another in the right-hand one, his architect.

holm had rows of chantry chapels on either side, and these were known as 'gravkoren'. The term continued to be used of the altarless funerary chapels built by the Protestant aristocracy of reformed Sweden throughout the later sixteenth and seventeenth centuries.

At Uppsala, Strängnäs and in other major churches the existing medieval chapels were taken over as burial places by leading families, but in the course of the later sixteenth and seventeenth centuries the establishment of large estates in favoured areas such as Södermanland was accompanied by the building of new family chapels as additions to medieval parish churches. These chapels were often buildings of distinction, designed by the best architects available. They reflected the importance attached to funerary rites in Sweden. The latter were among the most elaborate in Europe: 'extremely ceremonious and very expensive' in White-locke's words. As in other countries, flags and banners were carried in procession to indicate status and territorial authority, but in Sweden a prominent feature of an aristocratic funeral was the display of coats of arms elaborately carved in wood to record the ancestry of the deceased, and these heraldic scutcheons were

RIPSA

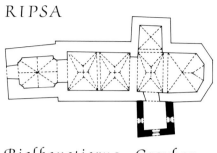

Bielkenstierna Gravkor

VADSBRO

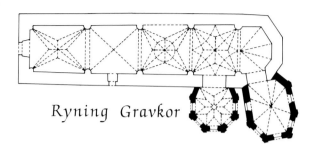

Ryning Gravkor

Falkenberg Gravkor

JÄDER

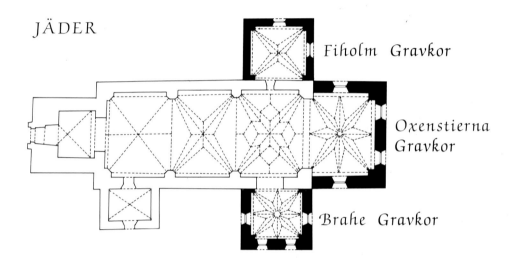

Fiholm Gravkor

Oxenstierna
Gravkor

Brahe Gravkor

VECKHOLM

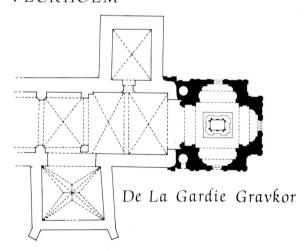

De La Gardie Gravkor

SPÅNGA

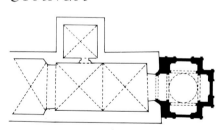

Bonde Gravkor

Scale in Metres 5 0   20   Scale in Feet 15 0   30   60

240. Swedish *gravkoren* or family chapels at the churches of Ripsa, Vadsbro and Jäder in Södermanland and Veckholm and Spånga in Uppland.

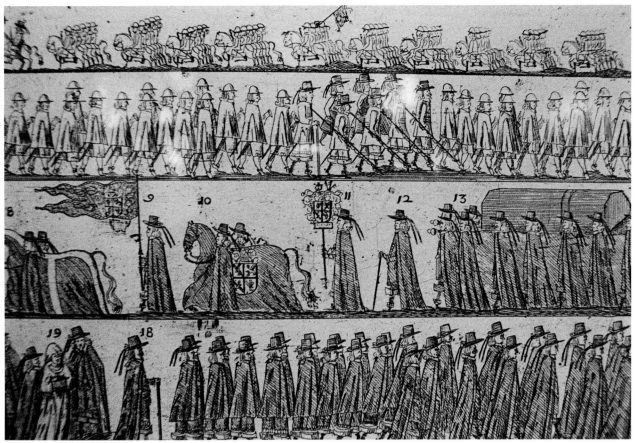

241. A seventeenth-century Swedish funeral: part of the funeral procession at Strängnäs of Admiral Karl Karlsson Gyllienhielm in February 1651, from an engraving in the Strängnäs Museum by Johan Sass. Note the carved wooden scutcheon of the dead man's arms being carried at no. 11.

afterwards hung up in the chapels like the painted hatchments in an English church (fig. 241). Many of them survive in Swedish churches, and they may be supplemented by shields of arms carved in stone or marble.

Another important element in the Swedish funerary chapel was provided by the coffins. These were often richly decorated and were intended to be seen. A gilded coffin, beautifully moulded or chased, could even be a substitute for a tomb of the kind that was normal in other European countries. Occasionally such coffins were displayed on the floor, but usually they were placed in a burial vault beneath, where glimpses of them could sometimes be obtained through a grille. Whatever form the funerary display took, heraldry was paramount, and as so much importance was attached to it, it was logical to transfer it from the interior to the exterior of the chapel. This was done, for instance, at Norrsunda in Uppland, where the gable of the transeptal chapel built by Countess Ebba Oxenstierna in 1633 was treated as an elaborate architectural composition framing an epitaph, at Jäder, another Oxenstierna church near their estate at Fiholm in Södermanland (fig. 242), and at Strängnäs cathedral, where the arms and inscriptions of the Cedercrantz family decorate the exterior of their chapel, which is almost hidden from the interior of the church by a stone wall with an iron door in the middle (fig. 244). What in England or Holland would have formed part of an internal monument is here incorporated into an external architectural feature.

By the middle of the seventeenth century the characteristic type of Swedish funerary chapel was a symmetrically planned building surmounted by a dome or spire. This might still be ornamented with external coats of arms or cartouches, but the funerary chapel associated with Sweden's age of greatness in the mid- and late seventeenth century was a classical composition in which external sculpture was subordinated to the discipline of an order. One of the earliest centrally planned chapels was at Fägre in Västergötland. It was built in 1586 by Filip Bonde, a general, and was a plain rectangular chamber surmounted by a tall shingled roof with a large cupola. It was destroyed when the church was rebuilt in 1703–5, but is recorded in a topographical drawing of 1671. At Ripsa in Södermanland another rectangular *gravkor* of the early seventeenth century is surmounted by a simple spire of the kind often found on church towers and belfries (fig. 243). At Enköpings-Näs in Uppland (1623) the plan is polygonal, but the architectural treatment is still very simple, lacking any external order.

These simple astylar chapels were the predecessors of the elaborate classical ones of the later seventeenth century. By far the most important building of this type was the royal chapel built in 1632–4 to contain the body of King Gustavus II Adolphus (1611–32), whose meteoric career had made Sweden a great European power. He chose to be buried, not in Uppsala cathedral, but in the Riddarholms-kyrkan ('nobles' church') in Stockholm, a former monastic church of royal foundation. His *gravkor* projects from the south side of the choir, and although the plan is that of an apsidal chapel, it reads externally as a semi-octagonal structure with its own cupola and lantern (fig. 245). The proportions are Gothic but the detailing is consistently classical, and the effect is much more monumental than that of any previous Swedish chapel. When Whitelocke saw it in 1654 he noted that no monument had as yet been erected to the king's memory, but no sculptured tomb appears in fact to have been contemplated: the chapel itself was the monument, and the royal arms and the proud inscriptions★ were all on the exterior. Inside there were only banners and the flags of the thirty-four terri-torial divisions of Sweden. The existing sarcophagus containing the king's remains was not added until the nineteenth century. Who designed the building is not clear, but the inscriptions were composed by John Bureus, a member of the royal council, and it is likely that he played a leading role in commissioning the chapel.

The example of the Gustavus Adolphus chapel was widely imitated in seven-teenth-century Sweden. In the course of the next twenty years the Riddarholm church itself was surrounded by satellite chapels erected by Gustavus Adolphus's

★ 'Hostes prostravit, Regnum dilatavit, Suecos exaltavit, Oppressos liberavit, Moriens triumphavit', etc.

242 (*above left*). Jäder church, Södermanland, Sweden, the Brahe *gravkor* added as a south transept in 1659 (cf. fig. 240).

243 (*above right*). Ripsa, Södermanland, Sweden, the early seventeenth-century *gravkor* of the Bielkenstierna family (cf. fig. 240).

244. Strängnäs cathedral, Sweden, the exterior of the chapel of the Cedercrantz family, built in 1695.

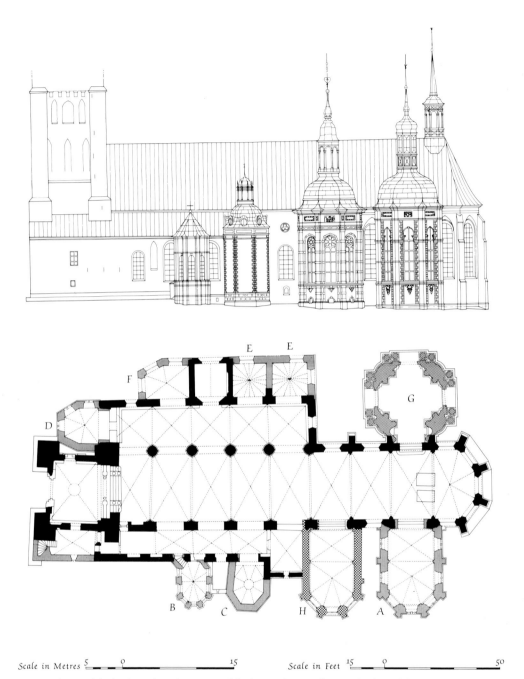

245. The Riddarholm church in Stockholm. The walls marked in black are medieval. A. The *gravkor* of King Gustavus Adolphus, 1632–4. B. The Banér *gravkor*, 1636. C. The Vasaborg *gravkor*, 1647. D. The Torstenson *gravkor*, 1651. E. The Lewenhaupt *gravkoren*, 1654. F. The Wachtmeister *gravkor*, 1654. G. The *gravkor* of King Charles X, 1675–1743. H. The Bernadotte *gravkor*, 1856–60.

generals (fig. 245). All were built of the same mixture of brick and grey sandstone with similar copper-covered cupolas and mannerist decorative details (fig. 246), while the interior of the church was filled with their banners and funeral scutcheons. In the country similar chapels were added to parish churches at places like Vadsbro and Sköldinge in Södermanland and Skokloster in

276

246. The Riddarholm church in Stockholm, from the north-west, showing the Tor-stenson and Wachtmeister *gravkoren*.

Uppland to mark the burial places of families newly risen to power (fig. 247).

Although the influence of Gustavus Adolphus's chapel persisted throughout the seventeenth century, a new, baroque, influence, was introduced by the French architect Jean de la Vallée (1620–96) and by the Pomeranian Nicodemus Tessin the elder (1615–81), who had studied in France, Holland and Italy. The Swedish tradition of the outward-looking chapel was maintained, but the design tended to conform more closely to the principles of orthodox classical architecture as understood in France and Holland, with external orders and hemispherical domes crowned by a lantern. The preferred position for the chapel was now at the east end of the church, and many of them have subsequently been adapted for use as chancels. One of the most notable of these chapels was the one at Veckholm in Uppland begun by Magnus Gabriel de la Gardie, the statesman who was intimately involved in the government of Sweden during its short-lived period as a great power. His chapel was begun in the 1650s at the east end of the church to the designs of Nicodemus Tessin the elder, but it was left unfinished because of the great resumption (*reduktion*) of crown lands in 1680, as a result of which he lost most of his estates. Only the lower storey of what was to have been a large cruciform chapel surmounted by a dome was erected (fig. 240). A similar chapel at Spånga in Uppland was, however, completed by the family of the Treasurer Gustav Bonde (d. 1667) (fig. 248). The interior, though full of the traditional armorial scutcheons, contains in addition a monument in the form of a sarcophagus surmounted by a bust of Bonde (fig. 249). The important chapel of King

247. Vadsbro, Södermanland, Sweden, the *gravkoren* of, *left*, the Ryning (1655) and *right*, the Falkenberg (1719) families (cf. fig. 240).

248. Spånga, Uppland, Sweden, the *gravkor* added to the east end of the church in 1667–73 for the burial of Lord High Treasurer Gustav Bonde and his family, and attributed to Nicodemus Tessin the elder (cf. fig. 240).

249. Spånga, the interior of the Bonde family *gravkor*. Note the heraldic scutcheons and cf. fig. 241 (Antikvarisk-topografiska arkivet, Stockholm)

Charles X (d. 1660) on the north side of the Riddarholm church was begun to Tessin's design in or about 1675, but was not completed until the eighteenth century. Although dome and decoration are both of the latter period, the subtle complexity of the plan is Tessin's and gives the building a sense both of movement and of monumentality (fig. 250). Tessin's son Nicodemus the younger (1654–1728) is best known as the architect of the royal palace in Stockholm (1687 onwards). In the architect's mind this was to have been the focus of a grand baroque scheme inspired by the Rome of Sixtus V and the Versailles of Louis XIV, a feature of which would have been a *gravkyrka*, a royal burial church, with twin west towers flanking a portico designed to face down a processional way to the palace. But the cost of Charles XII's wars ruled this out and it remained a paper scheme.

The baroque of Nicodemus Tessin the elder was restrained and mostly somewhat academic in character, and it was the Italian-trained military engineer and architect Erik Dahlberg (1625–1703) who provided Sweden with funerary chapels that most fully reflect the European architecture of their day. At Askersund (Närke) he took over a scheme for a new chapel for the Oxenstierna family from Jean de la Vallée, substituted a polygonal for a rectangular plan and completed it in 1671. Other important family chapels by or attributed to Dahlberg are those at Floda, Södermanland, for the Kagg family (*c.*1662–6), at Södertälje, Södermanland, for the Cronberg family (1673–5) (fig. 251), at the Kristine church,

279

250. The *gravkor* of King Charles X of Sweden on the north side of the Riddarholm church in Stockholm, begun *c.*1675 by Nicodemus Tessin the elder but not completed until 1743 to the designs of other architects.

251. Södertalje, Södermanland, Sweden, the Cronberg family *gravkor*, attributed to Erik Dahlberg, 1673–5.

252. Turinge, Södermanland, Sweden, the *gravkor* at the east end of the church designed by the architect Erik Dahlberg for himself and his family.

Göteborg, for the Ascheberg family (1680–2), and at Turinge, Södermanland, for his own family (1695–9) (fig. 252). All these are domed, polygonal chapels whose only singularity is the absence of the funerary effigies that elsewhere in Europe would have been the focal points of their interiors. Their vogue was, however, short-lived, for in the course of the eighteenth century the sculptor regained his place in Swedish funerary art, and the distinctive tradition which had been one of the expressions of Sweden's age of greatness was at an end.

*   *   *

In the matter of funerary architecture the contrast between England and Sweden is striking. Though both combined adherence to the Protestant faith with the retention of many traditional religious observances, the funerary chapels of their aristocratic families were markedly different in character. In England modest Gothic chapels housed ostentatious classical monuments; in Sweden grandiose classical chapels often contained no monuments at all. Why did the English funerary chapel present so conservative an image to the world while the Swedish *gravkor* offered a fashionably up-to-date one? Why did the English chapel aim to impress the visitor by what he saw inside, while the Swedish one so often concentrated its effects on the exterior?

For the frequent absence of the funerary monument from the Swedish *gravkor* it is difficult to offer an explanation, for at the same time grandiose monuments were being erected within existing chapels in cathedrals such as Uppsala and

Strängnäs, and at Skokloster the tomb of Herman Wrangel (d. 1643) is the focus of a *gravkor* filled with the trophies of his military victories. It may be that the cost both of building a chapel and of furnishing it with a tomb sometimes proved to be too great. The difference in architectural style is more easy to understand. It represented a different perception by those who commissioned these chapels of their own place in society. In England a new aristocracy anxious to be assimilated into an established order built Gothic chapels that were almost indistinguishable from those of their medieval predecessors, whereas in Sweden men newly elevated to wealth and power wanted to be seen, not as heirs to a provincial culture, but as participants in the contemporary civilisation of a Europe in which they and their country were playing a leading role for the first time in its history. In England the Reformation meant a defensive retreat into a cultural isolation mitigated in the architectural sphere chiefly by the influx of refugees from the Netherlands; in Sweden the militant Protestantism of Gustavus Adolphus carried Sweden to the front of the European stage. It is not surprising that the two countries should have had different ideas as to what was appropriate in the matter of funerary architecture.

XIV

THE RETURN OF THE MAUSOLEUM

BETWEEN THE GREAT MAUSOLEA OF ANTIQUITY and those of neo-classical Europe there is more than a merely cultural or stylistic gap. A church or a country house might assume the dress of a classical temple or villa without any fundamental change in the religious or social assumptions of those who used it. In any case, there was a long period of transition between Gothic and classical forms which in most parts of Europe made the stylistic change seem far from abrupt. But to be buried in a mausoleum that stood on its own without any provision for regular religious services was more than a gesture of aristocratic privilege or of neo-classical taste: it implied a new attitude towards the after-life which was at variance with a thousand years of Catholic belief and practice. In pre-Reformation Europe the idea of a private place of burial unconnected with a consecrated church or chapel was unthinkable, and it was in Protestant countries that the revival of the mausoleum in its most literal form was to be accomplished in the seventeenth and eighteenth centuries. In Italy by the early sixteenth century the family chapel had, however, assumed an architectural life of its own which could, in favourable circumstances, allow some of the features of the Ancient mausoleum to reappear. Indeed, the form of the mausoleum was latent in many Renaissance chapels and was waiting to be recreated at the behest of any patron sufficiently excited by the unfolding vision of the Antique World to demand it.

The fascination that Antiquity had for the artists and intellectuals of the Renaissance naturally embraced tombs and mausolea. They were among the most common and accessible of Ancient remains, and they yielded those inscriptions that, then as now, were one of the basic sources for the study of the Ancient World. Sketches and measured drawings of tombs were made by all the principal students of Roman antiquity of the fifteenth and sixteenth centuries: men such as Francesco di Giorgio Martini (1439–1501), Antonio da Sangallo the younger (1481–1546), Pirro Ligorio (1513/14–83), Giovanni Antonio Dosio (1533–1609) and Giovanni Battista Montano (1534–1621). Most of these were both architects and antiquaries. For them the study of Antiquity was not so much an academic pursuit as a source of inspiration, and what they studied as antiquaries, they longed to restore as architects. In fact, they did not always distinguish clearly between what they actually saw and what they conjecturally restored on paper.

253. Sketches by Pirro Ligorio (d. 1583) of two mausolea on the Via Labicana near
Rome, one with a pyramidal top, probably faced with stone, the other a rectangular
building of brick, with a classical entablature. (Bodleian Library, MS. Canonici Ital. 138,
f. 138).

254 (*above left*). The mausoleum of Hadrian as represented in Renaissance sculpture. The upper part of an altar-piece in the church of S. Gregorio al Celio, Rome, attributed to the sculptor-architect Andrea Bregno and commissioned in 1469. The frieze represents the success of a penitential procession organised by Pope Gregory the Great in the year 590, when Rome was afflicted by a pestilence. The archangel Michael appeared on the summit of the mausoleum, sheathing his sword as a token that the scourge was ended. The mausoleum is shown in a form closely resembling its representation in the bronze doors of St Peter's (cf. fig. 255) (Alinari).

255 (*above right*). The mausoleum of Hadrian as represented in the bronze doors of St Peter's by Filarete (1433–45). The building appears with other Roman monuments in the foreground of a scene showing the crucifixion of St Peter. By the fifteenth century the mausoleum had suffered considerably from its long use as a papal fortress, and Filarete's conjectural reconstruction shows some antiquarian erudition (cf. fig. 40).

For Montano in particular, the remains he studied were an opportunity for a series of more or less fantastic variations on the mausoleum theme which were published after his death and so entered the repertory of engraved designs upon which architects could draw for inspiration (fig. 76). The sketch-books of others remained in manuscript but were a source of ideas both to their authors and to their friends and pupils. Although these antiquarian architects of the Italian Renaissance studied tombs of every kind, it was the centrally planned domed building that particularly appealed to them, whether in the form of a temple or of a tomb. Indeed, they tended to make no clear distinction between temples and mausolea, and to employ plan-forms drawn from either when designing a chapel, a reliquary or a ciborium. When Bramante was commissioned to commemorate the traditional site of the martyrdom of St Peter within the precincts of the church of S. Pietro in Montorio in Rome, it was a rare opportunity to recreate the *martyrium* in its most classical form. The result was a free-standing temple-mausoleum which nevertheless had a legitimate Christian function (fig. 209). Another example is the bronze tabernacle given to Milan cathedral by Pope Pius IV soon after his accession in 1559. Probably designed by Pirro Ligorio for the previous pope, it is in form a miniature circular temple-mausoleum of the Doric order.

What was occasionally possible in such special circumstances as these was not, however, so easily achieved in the context of an ordinary family chapel. Both long tradition and liturgical convenience dictated that such chapels should as a rule be physically attached to churches, and in urban Italy architectural constraints

285

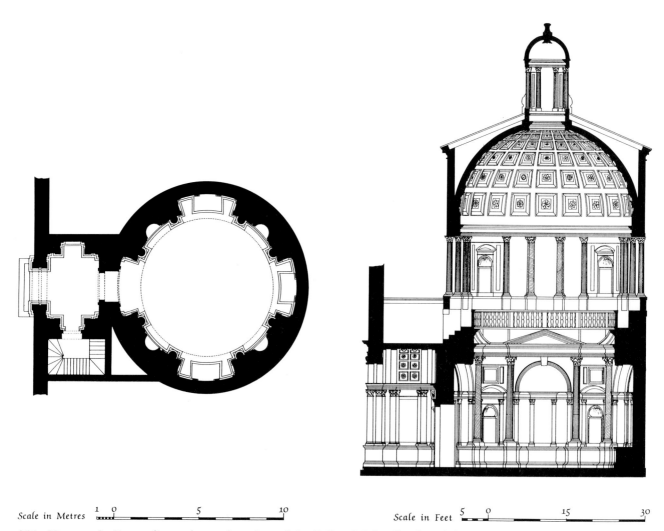

Scale in Metres 1 0   5   10

Scale in Feet 5 0   15   30

256. Verona, S. Bernardino, plan and section of the Pellegrini family chapel designed by M. Sanmicheli before 1538 and built in the 1540s (after Ronzani & Luciolli, *Le fabbriche . . . di Michele Sanmicheli*, Verona 1832).

were such that chapels thus situated were almost invariably designed to make their effect from within rather than from without. In an Ancient mausoleum, on the other hand, it was the exterior that normally counted most: the burial chamber was often small and architecturally unimportant. While some Renaissance chapels were designed with interiors whose Antique aspirations are obvious (e.g., the Trivulzian chapel at S. Nazaro in Brolio in Milan or the Pellegrini chapel at S. Bernardino in Verona, figs. 196–7, 256), chapels that gave equal or greater prominence to the exterior were rare. The outstanding exception is the Colleoni chapel at Bergamo.

The Colleoni chapel bears the name of Bartolomeo Colleoni, a *condottiere* famous both for his military services to the Venetian Republic and for their personification in the celebrated equestrian statue by Verrocchio. Born within a

257. Verona, S. Bernardino, the cupola of the Pellegrini family chapel.

few miles of Bergamo, he had a long-standing connection with the town and chose it both as the recipient of a charitable foundation and as his own place of burial. Begun in his lifetime, probably in 1470, under the direction of a young architect from Pavia called Giovanni Antonio Amadeo, the chapel was completed soon after his death in 1475. It stands against the north side of the parish church of S. Maria Maggiore, taking the place of a sacristy which was demolished to make way for it. The site was evidently chosen because it faced towards the principal piazza of the upper town of Bergamo, and the chapel was designed as an extrovert building with a highly ornamented facade which would be seen from the piazza (fig. 259). However, the view was partly blocked by the medieval town hall, and Colleoni tried unsuccessfully to persuade the townspeople to allow him to pull this down in order to make his chapel the chief ornament of the square. As it is, its facade of coloured marbles and its prominent dome distract attention from its parent church and make it the dominant architectural presence in Bergamo. The principal doorway is a virtuoso display of Renaissance sculpture, and inside, Bartolomeo's tomb, surmounted by an equestrian statue, occupies the centre of the opposite wall. A wealth of sculpture proclaims the prowess and virtues of the deceased in symbolism both pagan and Christian. Though still a chapel for the celebration of masses for the repose of its founder's soul, the building is as much a hero's tomb as any mausoleum of the Ancient World.

At Bergamo the Colleoni chapel is almost ready to break free from its architectural setting and assume the character of a free-standing mausoleum. This was, however, a step not easily taken in a Catholic country. Another *condottiere*,

287

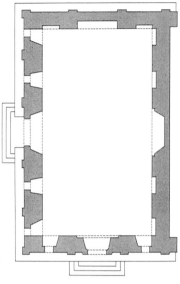

258. Naples, the Cappella Pontano, built in 1492 (after Pane).

Scale in Metres

Scale in Feet

Federigo da Montefeltro (d. 1482), had contemplated the building of a detached mausoleum within one of the courtyards of his palace at Urbino, but this came to nothing,* as did the wish of Galeazzo Maria Sforza, 5th Duke of Milan (d. 1476), for a church to be built for his burial on the model of the baptisteries of Florence or Pisa. The nearest to a detached funerary chapel that appears actually to have been built in Renaissance Italy was the Cappella Pontano in the Via dei Tribunali in Naples. This small rectangular chapel was built as a place of burial in 1492 by the humanist Giovanni Gioviano Pontano, and has been attributed to Francesco di Giorgio because its design is closely related to drawings by him of two Antique buildings in Rome (fig. 258). Although abutting on a church (S. Maria Maggiore), it has no communication with it and stands by the roadside in a manner that may have been intended to recall an Antique tomb.

* See above, p. 235.

259. Bergamo, the Colleoni chapel, c.1470–5 (Scala).

260. Design by Antonio da Sangallo for a
projected Medici chapel attached to the nave of
the abbey church of Montecassino, 1531–2
(Florence, Uffizi, Dis. Arch. 172, Gab. Fotografico, Soprintendenza Beni Artistici e Storici
di Firenze).

Evidence of anything comparable in northern Italy is hard to find,★ and although
chapels whose form was obviously intended to evoke the idea of a Roman
mausoleum were designed by Antonio da Sangallo the younger as part of his plan
for the new St Peter's in Rome (*c.*1520), and for a projected Medici chapel at
Montecassino (1531–2), the former would have been an integral part of the great
basilica and the latter an excrescence firmly attached to the nave of the existing
monastic church (fig. 260). Only in Venice does the Emiliani chapel (1527–30)
which flanks the facade of S. Michele in Isola take a advantage of its island site to
strike an architectural attitude very similar to that of the Colleoni chapel in
Bergamo (fig. 261).

★ Fifty years later Andrea Palladio was to build at Maser near Asolo a circular domed church or
chapel for the Barbaro family which was probably based as much on the mausoleum of Romulus on
the Via Appia as on the Pantheon, and which therefore has something of the form of an Ancient
mausoleum. However, the Barbaro family vault was in the church of S. Francesco della Vigna in
Venice, and there was no provision for burials in the church at Maser.

261. Venice, S. Michele in Isola, the Emiliani chapel by Bergamasco, 1527–30 (Ralph Lieberman).

It is, however, in France and eastern Europe rather than in Italy that the next stage in the slow re-emergence of the mausoleum can best be studied. Here, in the sixteenth century, several chapels were built that, although still clinging to their parent churches, were architecturally semi-autonomous structures whose exteriors were as important as their interiors, while others were actually free-standing. Among the former was King Sigismund's chapel at Cracow (1517–33), whose North Italian architect, Bartolommeo Berecci, may well have had the Colleoni

262. Vannes, Brittany, the chapel of the Holy Sepulchre built as a place of burial by Jean Danielo, canon of Vannes, and completed in 1537.

chapel in mind (fig. 212). In France the Valois chapel at Saint-Denis (1563 onwards; see p. 241) had been preceded by the Chapel of the Holy Sepulchre at Vannes in Brittany, completed in 1537 (fig. 262). The latter was built as a place of burial by Jean Danielo, a canon of Vannes who also held an office in the Roman Curia, which explains how one of the most precocious buildings of its kind in France came to be attached to a remote provincial cathedral. The tall, cylindrical chapel which Danielo added to the north side of the nave, though not based on

263. Joigny, near Auxerre, France, the sixteenth-century Ferrand chapel, from Laborde, *Les monuments de la France* 2, 1873 (Bodleian Library, Mason Z. 73).

any obvious Antique prototype, suggests a serious interest in the revival of classical architecture. Despite its attenuated proportions, the Roman pretentions of its superimposed orders and pedimented niches are obvious, and, unlike the elegantly detailed classical chapel on the south side of Toul cathedral, built by the precentor, Jean Forget, shortly before his death in 1549, it represents a complete break with the traditional type of medieval chantry chapel.

One of the first of the free-standing chapels was at Gniezno in Poland, where the primate Jan Laski chose (ostensibly out of humility) to be buried in a specially built chapel (now destroyed) in the cathedral churchyard (*c*.1520). At Salzburg in 1597–1603 Archbishop Wolf Dietrich built a circular domed chapel for himself in the centre of an arcaded burial ground attached to the church of St Sebastian. In France several private funerary chapels were built in churchyards or cemeteries in the course of the sixteenth century.★ Special circumstances rather than a mere desire for architectural display may generally be suspected in such cases. Thus, when a member of the Ferrand family (probably Etienne, Archdeacon of Sens, who died in 1569) decided to build a funerary chapel at Joigny near

---

★ Besides those mentioned in the text, reference should be made to the Chapelle de Seigne at Bléré (Indre-et-Loire), built in 1526 as the burial place of a soldier, Guillaume de Seigne, and the demolished chapel of Jean Chantereau at Ligny-le-Châtel (Yonne), of which only the classical doorway dated 1566 survives.

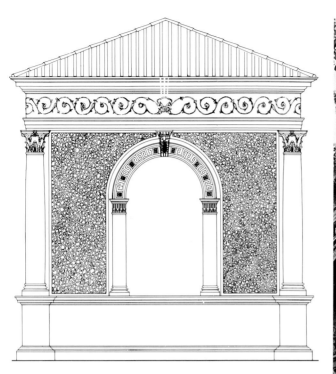

265. Valence cathedral, Drôme, France, the north-west corner of 'Le Pendentif', showing the rusticated masonry.

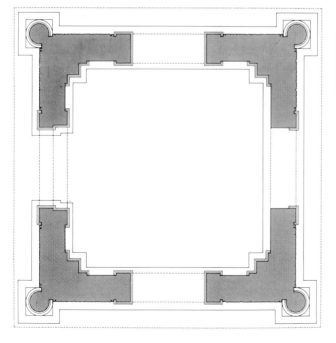

Scale in Metres

Scale in Feet

264. Valence cathedral, Drôme, France, 'Le Pendentif', the classical mausoleum built in the middle of the cloister by Nicolas Mistral, canon of Valence, in 1548: plan and north elevation.

Auxerre in the middle of the sixteenth century, his choice of site is likely to have been influenced by the fact that a large part of the town had recently been devastated by a fire in which two of its three churches had been badly damaged. Although the third (Saint-André) had survived intact, its site was so constricted that there may not have been room to add a chapel onto its nave or chancel. It did, however, have a large burial ground nearby, and it was here that Ferrand built his chapel. Vandalised at the Revolution and now almost engulfed by the Palais de Justice, the Ferrand chapel is an octagonal structure in the French Renaissance style whose most striking feature is an external frieze of scrolls and *tabulae ansatae* supported by skeletons (fig. 263). At Metz in 1547 the problem of a Protestant *seigneur* who had inherited founder's rights of burial in a Celestine church was solved by interring his body in the churchyard under a substantial classical monument whose pedimented front was recorded by Gaignières in the eighteenth century. But in the building in Valence known as 'le Pendentif' we find architectural aspirations of a different order. This elegant little classical structure was built in 1548 by Nicolas Mistral, a canon of the cathedral, as a place of burial for himself and members of his family and stands over a vault in the middle of the former cloister (fig. 264). Its celebrity as the earliest example of a building with a pendentive vault of a type for which French masons were to become celebrated has distracted attention from its resemblance to a late Roman mausoleum of the type illustrated in figure 295. Alternatively it could have been based on the first storey of a monument such as that of the Julii at Saint-Rémy in neighbouring Provence (fig. 48). The classical pretentions of its builder are evident from the inscription which (in standard Roman form) records its erection *sibi suisque heredibus*. Here then, in a region full of surviving Roman monuments, is the first literal recreation of a Roman mausoleum since Antiquity. With its four open arches it can hardly have functioned as a chantry chapel, and the commemorative masses for the founder and his family were no doubt celebrated in the adjoining cathedral.

Despite the obvious interest of such buildings as these in the history of funerary architecture, it was not in Catholic Europe but in the Protestant north that the mausoleum was eventually to separate itself completely from the parent church and even to quit consecrated ground. By the end of the eighteenth century detached mausolea were to be found in several Protestant countries, notably the British Isles, Germany and Sweden. It was, of course, the abolition of prayers for the dead that made this possible. A Catholic family chapel was designed for the celebration of regular masses in perpetuity, a Protestant one for burial services held once or twice in each generation. Without priest or altar, a Protestant chapel could easily be detached from aisle or chancel and assume the architectural character of a mausoleum. In ecclesiastically conservative countries like England and Sweden, where many of the practices of the medieval church survived the Reformation, landowning families were, however, slow to distance themselves in death from the churches in which they had worshipped in their lifetimes. In England family pew and family tomb were, indeed, sometimes combined in the same structure (above, p. 268). Often in Sweden, though less so in England, the family chapel was a centrally planned building that dominated the relatively humble church to which it was attached (figs. 248–52). But whether it was a domed *gravkor* or a Gothic 'aisle', it was still part of the church fabric. Only in Scotland did a newly reformed and radical Church effectively renew the ancient struggle against intra-mural interment and encourage the building of places of burial that were architecturally independent of a church.

The rejection of the medieval attitude to the after-life played such an important part in the Reformation that the burial of the dead was naturally one of the most sensitive areas of religious practice. There was no doubt in the minds of Protestants of all persuasions that the living could have no influence whatever on the fate of a dead man's soul. Logically, therefore, all funeral ceremonies were superfluous, and for Calvin and his followers an interment was barely a religious occasion. No prayers or singing were permitted, and even a funeral sermon was regarded as suspect, in so far as it tended to distract attention from the fundamental truth that all men were equal in the presence of God. Lutherans, however, while emphasising that any funeral ceremonial was for the edification of the living rather than for the salvation of the deceased, allowed processions with singing and regarded a funeral sermon as entirely acceptable. In this, as in other respects, the Scottish Kirk tended to follow Calvinist rather than Lutheran practice. According to the *Book of Discipline*, a detailed statement of ecclesiastical policy drawn up in 1560–1, but never fully implemented, funerals were to be carried out with the utmost simplicity, and the authors 'judged it best, that neither singing nor reading be at the burial'. As for the place of burial, both Lutherans and Calvinists were agreed that interments in churches were undesirable, and that cemeteries outside towns were to be encouraged. Enactments against burial in churches were passed at General Assemblies of the Scottish Church in 1588, 1597, 1638 and 1643, but those of sufficient rank could often obtain leave to disregard them on payment of a substantial sum to the kirk or to an associated charity. In a pamphlet published in 1606 entitled *The Blame of Kirk-Buriall*, William Birnie, the minister of Lanark, denounced the practice as a profanation. No one, he said, would think of burying a body in the Presence Chamber of a prince. How much worse, then, to do so in 'the cabinet of God'. In any case, it was 'an use that onely Papistry has hatched'. 'If thou has attained to the sepulchrall prerogative, to ly in the Kirk, why should thou want that old privilege to be prayed for in death? And if thou be to ly at the Altar, how wanst thou a Priest to say thy soule Masse?' At the best it was 'but pryde, as being a claim of exemption from [the] common case'. Pretentious monuments were particularly objectionable. Many, he wrote, 'to eternise their soon forgot memory, . . . has prepared Pyramides of pomp, others pillers of pride, some mausolies of marvel'. Anything resembling 'that sepulchrall monster that Queen Artimise made to her husband Mousolus the Carian King' was quite unacceptable. He hoped for legislation that would oblige the privileged either to build their tombs outside the church or to add 'an Ile for burial use'. In 1593 King James VI had in fact expressed himself in favour of a parliamentary enactment 'that for the avoyding of burialle in kirks, every nobleman s[h]ould bigg ane sepulture for himself and his familie'.

266. Largs, Ayrshire, Scotland, the Skelmorlie aisle. The triumphal arch forms the front of the Montgomery 'loft' or family pew. The entrance to the vault is seen below (from D. MacGibbon & T. Ross, *The Castellated & Domestic Architecture of Scotland* 5, 1892).

267. Largs, the triumphal arch in the Skelmorlie aisle as seen from the family pew.

Although no such law was passed, the moral pressure exerted by the General Assembly and by individual ministers such as Birnie did have considerable success in excluding corpses from churches and in encouraging the building of burial places that did not encroach on the area 'where the people meet for hearing of the Word, and administration of the Sacraments'. These burial places took two characteristic forms. One was the 'aisle' or annex to the church which (as in England) often served both as a place of burial and as a family 'loft' or pew. The other was the 'lair' or burial enclosure within the churchyard. The 'aisle' usually projected like a small transept from the body of the church, and external doorways both to the burial vault below and to the loft above gave it a semi-detached character which satisfied the objection to 'kirk-burial'. One of the most notable examples is the Skelmorlie aisle added to the parish church at Largs in Ayrshire by Sir Robert Montgomery of Skelmorlie in 1636. The church itself was

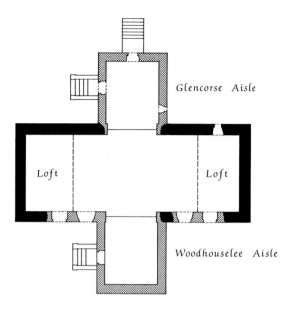

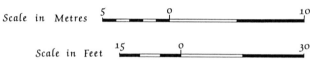

268. Glencorse, Midlothian, Scotland, plan of the church, showing the family 'aisles' added in 1699 (after Hay).

Scale in Metres

Scale in Feet

demolished in 1802, but the aisle survives complete with its painted ceiling and an exceptionally grand monument in the form of a triumphal arch (figs. 266–7). This stands over the entrance to the vault in which Sir Robert was buried when he died in 1651. Most burial aisles abutted on the church wherever convenience dictated, but at Glencorse in Midlothian the aisles of the lairds of Glencorse and Woodhouselee form symmetrical additions of 1699 to an earlier seventeenth-century church (fig. 268), while in the same year James Smith, the architect of the new church built by the 3rd Duke of Queensberry at Durisdeer in Dumfriesshire, ingeniously incorporated a ducal tomb-chamber without breaching the inhibition against burial in churches. The church follows the standard T-shaped plan favoured by the Presbyterian church, but the southern transept is matched by the burial aisle on the north in such a way as to create a regular architectural composition (figs. 269–70). Older churches, however, were apt to be divided up by local lairds in a manner very destructive of their architectural character. At Dunbar both the east end of the chancel and the north end of the north transept were cut off to form burial areas for local families, the whole of the east wall of the former being occupied by the huge monument of George Hume, Earl of Dunbar (d. 1611) (fig. 271). At Liberton near Edinburgh not only was the exterior of the church encumbered by the projecting lofts or aisles of four local lairds, but the shell of the former chancel served as a gallery for a fifth (fig. 272). When, in the late eighteenth and early nineteenth centuries, a rising population resulted in the rebuilding of many Scottish churches, the old ones were often unroofed and left to serve as burial places for the families in possession.

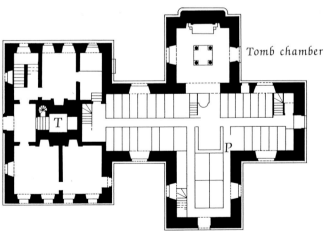

Tomb chamber

Scale in Metres

Scale in Feet

269. Durisdeer, the church as seen from the north-east, showing the tomb-chamber. Some original features now missing, including the spire and the decorative flashings of the roof-ridges, have been drawn in by Dr David Walker.

270. Durisdeer church, Dumfriesshire, Scotland, plan showing the church as built in 1699 (after Hay). P. Original position of pulpit. T. Tower. The western block contained a pew and retiring rooms for the Duke of Queensberry and his family.

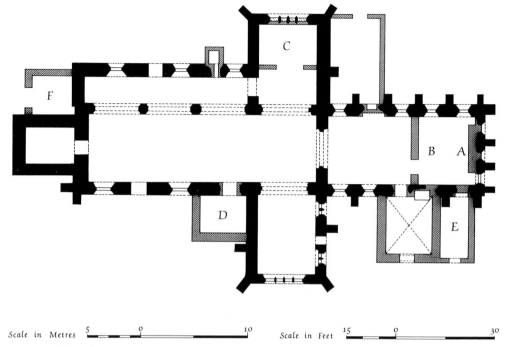

Scale in Metres 5 ___ 0 ___ 10   Scale in Feet 15 ___ 0 ___ 30

271. Dunbar church, Berwickshire, Scotland, plan of the medieval church made in 1811 before its demolition, showing the family 'aisles'. A. Monument of George Hume, Earl of Dunbar (d. 1611). B. Roxburgh aisle. C. Belton burying place. D. Warrender burying place. E. Minister's burying place. F. Hearse house. (Based on National Library of Scotland, Advocates' MS. 30. 5. 23.)

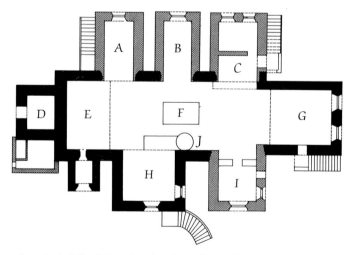

272. Liberton church, Midlothian, Scotland, in the eighteenth century. A. Somerville of Drum seat in gallery over Morton seats below. B. Craigmillar seats and family burial place. C. Family burial place of Baird of Newbyth, with seats for tenants in front and family seats with retiring-room above. D. Tower and ministers' burial place. E. Mortonhall gallery. F. Lord Somerville's burial place. G. Niddry gallery. H. Stainhouse seats on ground floor, those of Gilmerton colliers above. I. Burial-place of Gavin Nisbet of Muirhouse. J. Pulpit. (Based on a sketch-plan by the Revd John Sime in G. Good, *Liberton in Ancient and Modern Times*, 1893.)

273. Kilbirnie churchyard, Ayrshire, Scotland, the Crawfurd mausoleum, a small structure erected in 1594 and containing the effigies of Thomas Crawfurd of Jordanhill and his wife.

274 (*below*). Collessie churchyard, Fife, Scotland, two views of the mausoleum built by Sir James Melville in 1609, with an inscription condemning burial inside churches.

Meanwhile, churchyard burial had been encouraged, and the wealthier members of the congregation began to build their own places of interment round the periphery. One of the earliest structures of this sort is the Crawfurd mausoleum in the churchyard at Kilbirnie in Ayrshire. It was erected in 1594 and contains the effigies of Thomas Crawfurd of Jordanhill and his wife Janet. With its chequered corbelling and angle-shafts the building is of Scottish vernacular character (fig. 273). Another example is to be seen in the churchyard at Collessie in Fife (fig. 274). It is a small rectangular building with gable ends and a doorway in the middle of one side. On the other is an inscription (now partly illegible) which begins with the admonition: DEFYLE NOT CHRISTS KIRK WITH YOUR CARRION. Both

275. Inverness churchyard, Scotland, the Inshes mausoleum, 1660 (W.J. Durham).

276. A baroque monument with balustraded enclosure: the tomb of George Meldrum of Crombie, an episcopalian bishop (d. 1692), in the churchyard at Marnoch, Banffshire, Scotland (Mrs E. Beaton).

these early tomb-houses were roofed, but at Inverness the Inshes mausoleum of 1660 (fig. 275) was designed as an open enclosure surrounded by an elaborate classical screen with Corinthian columns supporting a frieze of skulls and cross-bones. The roofless enclosure or 'lair' was to become the characteristic family burial place in Scotland, and many examples, some with elegantly designed entrances, are to be seen in churchyards both urban and rural throughout Scotland (fig. 277). Most of them date from the eighteenth and nineteenth centuries, and many of them are still in use today.

Although these Scottish lairs, grassed and open to the sky, may remind the travelled visitor of funerary enclosures in Ancient cemeteries far away in Asia Minor, it was the roofed alternative that was eventually to be given an architectural treatment consciously based on the mausolea of Antiquity. Here the key buildings are the Clerk mausoleum in the churchyard at Penicuik in Midlothian and the Mackenzie of Rosehaugh mausoleum in the Greyfriars churchyard in Edinburgh.

Sir John Clerk of Penicuik (1649–1722) was the head of a family remarkable for its contribution to the cultural and intellectual life of Scotland. Though a strict Calvinist in religion he was in some ways a forerunner of the Scottish Enlightenment and was keenly interested in architecture. When his first wife, Elizabeth Henderson, died in 1683 he built a mausoleum outside the east end of Penicuik church which he designed himself. The vault is contained within a massive rectangular structure surmounted by a pyramid which originally supported an urn-like finial inscribed with the initials E H (fig. 278). That Clerk had the image

277. 'Lairs' or unroofed burial enclosures in the Old Calton burial ground, Edinburgh. Those illustrated are of the late eighteenth or early nineteenth centuries.

278. Penicuik, Midlothian, Scotland, the mausoleum designed and built by Sir John Clerk in 1683–4.

279. Roman mausolea with pyramidal roofs as represented in Pirro Ligorio's *Anteiquae Urbis Imago* of 1561.

280. The mausoleum of Sir George Mackenzie of Rosehaugh in the Greyfriars church-yard, Edinburgh, built in 1691 to the designs of James Smith.

of an Antique tomb in his mind is obvious, but it is less easy to point to a specific source, for he can hardly have been aware how closely his mausoleum resembled some late Roman examples in Syria (fig. 95). Tombs consisting of a rectangular base with a pyramidal top were illustrated by Pirro Ligorio in his *Anteiquae Urbis Imago* of 1561 (fig. 279), but it is doubtful whether this somewhat esoteric source

281. Derby, All Saints church, now the cathedral, the destroyed monument to the 2nd Earl of Devonshire (d. 1628), from a drawing by Smart Lethieullier in British Library, Additional MS. 27348, f. 16.

could have provided Clerk with a model for his mausoleum at Penicuik as it certainly did for some of the Roman buildings (including mausolea) in the classical paintings of Nicolas Poussin.

Sir George Mackenzie of Rosehaugh was a distinguished lawyer whose great achievement was the establishment of the Advocates' Library which laid the foundations for a national Scottish library. His mausoleum in the Greyfriars churchyard in Edinburgh was begun by himself in his lifetime and completed in 1691, the year of his death. The building accounts survive, and they show that the mausoleum was built, and doubtless designed, by James Smith, the leading Scottish architect of the day. Smith had spent some time in Italy and the building he designed was a domed tempietto of the Corinthian order. Although Bramante's tempietto in Rome inevitably suggests itself as a generic prototype, the Mackenzie mausoleum differs in several essential respects. Renouncing the logical simplicity of the Roman building, the Edinburgh one combines an octagonal body with a circular entablature carried on columns that conceal the angles, creating an ambiguity of form which is characteristically baroque. Baroque, too, is the ogee-shaped dome, a feature also of Smith's Queensberry aisle at Durisdeer (fig. 269), and of the Sinclair mausoleum (dated 1700) at Ulbster in Caithness.

By 1700, therefore, the mausoleum in two of its characteristic forms – the pyramidal rectangle and the domed drum – had been recreated in Scotland. Nothing comparable was to be seen in England, where the practice of burial within churches continued unchecked, and where memorials of the dead normally took the form of wall-monuments and occasionally of free-standing aedicules like the monument to the 2nd Earl of Devonshire (d. 1628) formerly in All Saints, Derby (fig. 281), or that of Sir Thomas Gorges and his wife (d. 1635) in

306

282. Salisbury cathedral, monument to Sir Thomas Gorges and his wife, erected in 1635 (from J. Britton, *History of Salisbury Cathedral*, 1814–15).

Salisbury cathedral (fig. 282). From time to time, however, the idea of a classical mausoleum was tried out on paper. Among the architectural drawings in the Cottonian Collection in the British Library there is a design for a gigantic funerary obelisk, with *loculi* for at least thirty-one and probably for sixty-two

283. Elizabethan design for a funerary obelisk, with *loculi* for multiple burials in the podium, redrawn from British Library, Cotton Roll XIII. 40. Assuming that each *loculus* was 6 feet long, the structure would have been similar in height to the Monument in the City of London.

bodies in the tall podium (fig. 283). The ornamental details and draughtsmanship suggest a date in the second half of the sixteenth century. As most of the Cottonian drawings originally formed part of the royal archives, it is likely that this fantastic project was connected with the Court, but no inscription betrays its authorship, exact date or proposed location.

So far as funerary architecture is concerned, the surviving drawings of Inigo Jones yield only two designs: one for a mural monument in Shropshire and another for the catafalque for the funeral of King James I in 1625. But his pupil John Webb has left a visionary design for a huge mausoleum some 300 feet square (fig. 284). In its compartmentation the rectangular base contains obvious references to the mausoleum of Hadrian, but the outer wall is battered like a fort, and above it rises a circular structure with a shallow Pantheon-like dome. Within, radiating burial chambers suggest multiple use. Like the remarkable study for an even more grandiose mausoleum often attributed to Leonardo da Vinci and sometimes to Francesco di Giorgio (fig. 285), this seems to have been an academic exercise rather than a response to any specific requirement. In 1657 Webb did, however, have a commission to add a 'depository' or burial chapel to Lamport church in Northamptonshire for Sir Justinian Isham, whose house he was then engaged in rebuilding in the classical style. His drawings show a domed building on the lines of a Late Roman mausoleum with an obelisk standing in the centre beneath an open oculus (fig. 286). From Webb's surviving letters to his patron it would seem that the combination of mausoleum and obelisk was Isham's idea, and that the latter had mentioned the church of the Ascension at Jerusalem as a model for a Christian 'depository', for Webb comments that the difference between the building he had designed and 'that of the Ascension mentioned by you wilbe . . . [that] that is round within and octangular without, yours an octagon within and circular without'.★ But for the fines to which Sir Justinian was subjected as a Royalist, the 'depository' would probably have been built in accordance with Webb's design, but in the event it was not until after the Restoration that a conventional family chapel was built on the same site.

In 1678 another domed mausoleum was projected by Sir Christopher Wren in response to a passing outburst of loyalist sentiment by the House of Commons, which would have allocated £70,000 for the reinterment of King Charles I at Windsor in 'a monument to remain to posterity'. The site was to have been in the outer ward of the castle, immediately to the east of St George's Chapel, where the 'Tomb House' (now the Albert Memorial chapel) was to be pulled down to make way for it. While obviously inspired by one of Mansart's designs for the Bourbon chapel at Saint-Denis, which Wren must have seen in Paris in 1665, his design has in its external drum of channelled masonry more of an Antique Roman character, while internally the arrangements for a Protestant *martyrium* designed to commemorate a single king were naturally simpler than those envisaged for an entire

★Isham probably derived his knowledge of this Early Christian building from the excellent engravings in B. Amico's *Trattato delle Piante & Immagini de Sacri Edifizi di Terra Santa*, published in Florence in 1620.

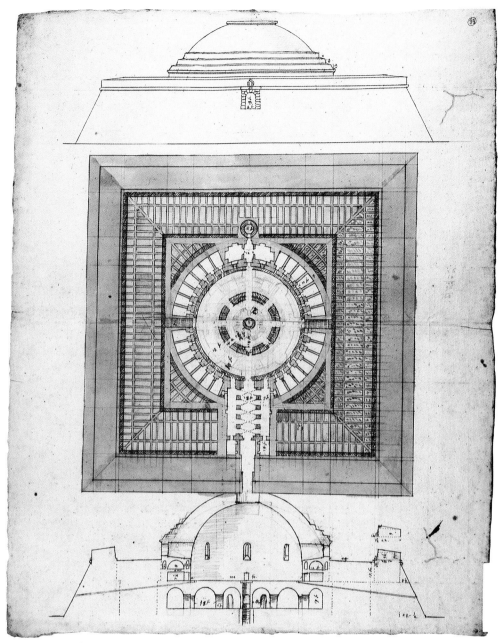

284. Design by John Webb (d. 1672) for a mausoleum recalling those of Antiquity (Worcester College, Oxford, Jones/Webb drawings, I/33).

285 (*facing page top*). Design for a mausoleum generally attributed to Leonardo da Vinci (d. 1519), but alternatively to Francesco di Giorgio Martini (d. 1502). This grandiose design envisages a huge tumulus topped by a circular tempietto with a stepped dome. Inside, radiating galleries, possibly suggested by Etruscan tombs, are lined with sarcophagi or ash-chests (Paris, Musée du Louvre).

286 (*facing page bottom*). Design by John Webb for a 'depository' or burial chapel attached to Lamport church, Northamptonshire, made for Sir Justinian Isham in 1657 but not executed (Northamptonshire Record Office, by courtesy of Lamport Hall Trust).

dynasty of Catholic rulers. Instead of the complex of subsidiary chapels and funerary recesses envisaged by Mansart, there were to be four large *exedrae* (fig. 287). For the one opposite the entrance the sculptor Grinling Gibbons designed a group showing the Royal Martyr borne aloft by figures emblematic of the 'heroick Virtues' and triumphant over the corresponding Vices of Envy, Heresy, Hypocrisy and Rebellion.

What were probably the first mausolea actually to be built in England both date from 1656. One of them was, significantly, commissioned by a Scottish noble-man who had established himself in England, the other by a Devonshire squire. Thomas Bruce, 1st Earl of Elgin, was the younger son of a Scottish baron, married two successive English heiresses and died the owner of a large estate in Bedfordshire. His second wife, Diana, daughter of William Cecil, 2nd Earl of Exeter, died in 1654, and it was to commemorate her that two years later he built

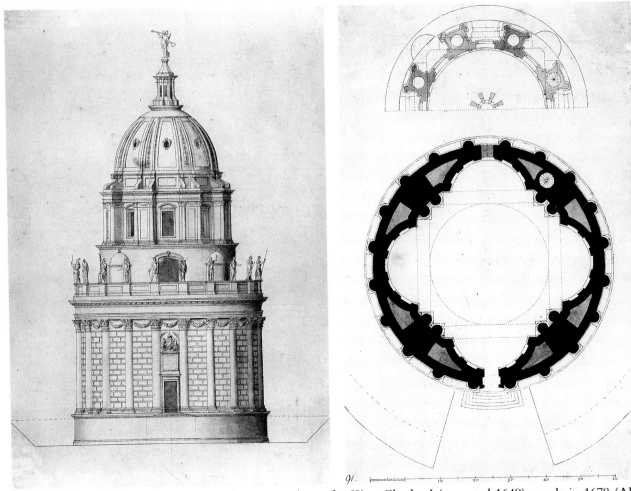

287. Design by Sir Christopher Wren for a mausoleum for King Charles I (executed 1649), made in 1678 (All Souls College, Oxford, Codrington Library, Wren Drawings, vol. II, 91–2). *Left*, elevation. *Right*, plan at two levels.

288. Maulden churchyard, Bedfordshire, the Bruce mausoleum built by the 1st Earl of Elgin in 1656, before Gothicisation in 1859 (Luton Museum and Art Gallery).

a mausoleum in the churchyard at Maulden in Bedfordshire. This is octagonal in plan, but with two sides longer than the others – an odd design for which there is no obvious prototype (fig. 288).★ Originally it was lit by oval windows (Gothicised when it was rebuilt in 1859), and inside there was what was known locally as 'the lady in the punchbowl', a marble figure of the countess in her shroud rising from an oval sarcophagus. In the churchyard at Buckfastleigh in Devon a much more modest structure commemorates members of the Cabell family of Brook Manor in that parish. Consisting of little more than a pyramidal slated roof supported by four granite pillars, it shelters a tomb inscribed with the names of Richard Cabell who died in 1655 and of his father who had died in 1613. A weathervane formerly on the roof is said to have borne the date 1656.

Despite the visionary designs of Webb and Wren and the actual examples of Edinburgh, Penicuik and Maulden, no other major classical mausoleum was to be built in Britain until the reign of George II. In Scotland the unroofed enclosure continued to be the rule, in England the family chapel. The latter might, as at

★The lower building with oval windows seen in the background in the early nineteenth-century drawing was obviously of the same date and may possibly have linked the mausoleum to the church. However, as the two buildings are thirty feet apart, it seems more likely that it was a vestry.

313

289. Tottenham church, Middlesex, the circular domed mausoleum–cum–vestry built at the east end by Lord Coleraine in 1696 (from *One Hundred Views of Churches in the Environs of London*, 1811).

290. Flitton church, Bedfordshire, eighteenth-century monuments in the north transept of the mausoleum of the earls of Kent.

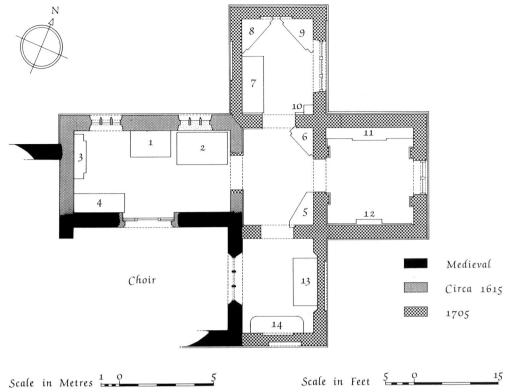

N

Choir

Scale in Metres 1 0   5   Scale in Feet 5 0   15

291. Flitton church, Bedfordshire, the 'mausoleum' of the earls of Kent, showing how it developed out of the seventeenth-century family chapel on the north side of the choir or chancel. 1. Tomb of Henry Grey, 6th Earl of Kent (d. 1615). 2. Henry Grey, 10th Earl of Kent (d. 1651, erected 1658). 3. Lady Elizabeth Talbot (d. 1651). 4. Lady Jane Hart (d. 1671). 5. Lady Amabell de Grey (d. 1727). 6. Lady Anne de Grey (d. 1730). 7. Anthony de Grey, Earl of Harold (d. 1723). 8. Lady Henrietta de Grey (d. 1716). 9. Lord Henry de Grey (d. 1717). 10. Lady Mary Gregory (d. 1761). 11. Henry de Grey, Duke of Kent (d. 1740). 12. Philip, 2nd. Earl of Hardwicke (d. 1790). 13. Earl de Grey (d. 1859). 14. Henrietta Countess de Grey (d. 1848).

Tottenham or Flitton, assume something of a character of a mausoleum, but it was still compromised architecturally by its physical attachment to a church. At Tottenham the circular domed structure built by Lord Coleraine in 1696 was designed to serve both as a vestry and as a place of burial for himself (fig. 289), and the 'mausoleum' of the de Greys at Flitton is simply a greatly extended family chapel (fig. 291). Burial outside consecrated ground was still almost unknown. In Scotland in the seventeenth century one small and unpretentious place of burial does seem to have been built in a wood on a laird's estate in Fife, while on the island of Stroma a mausoleum was economically combined with a dovecot.★ In England one or two eccentrics were buried in folly or farmyard, but with-

★ At Rossie House in north-west Fife a small rectangular building standing within a circular earthwork in Tomb Wood contains the bodies of two people who were probably Sir James Scott and his wife, the latter of whom died in 1663 and the former before 1669. Although it resembles a chapel, this tiny building (now roofless) was lit by only one narrow window, and it is doubtful whether it had any function other than as a place of burial. For the Kennedy mausoleum on Stroma, dated 1677, see Elizabeth Beaton, *The Doocots of Caithness* (Dundee, 1980), pp. 8–10.

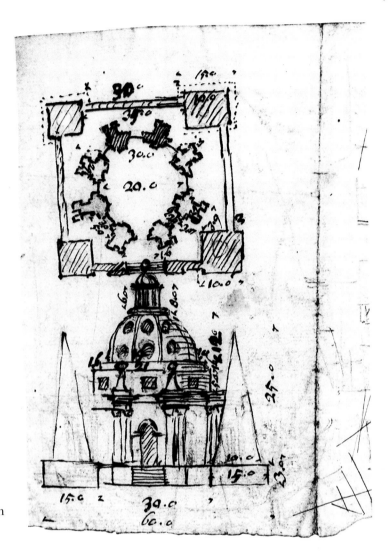

292. Sketch by Sir John Vanbrugh, probably for a mausoleum (from album at Elton Hall, Huntingdonshire, by courtesy of William Proby, Esq.)

out architectural consequences of any significance.* In 1729, however, Charles Howard, 3rd Earl of Carlisle, began to build a mausoleum at Castle Howard in Yorkshire which was not only grand in scale and Antique in inspiration, but which stands, not in a churchyard, but in the middle of a park.

Lord Carlisle's decision to build a mausoleum proceeded (as Mr Saumarez Smith has shown) from a rational and sceptical attitude towards organised religion that was in tune with contemporary deist thought. He followed Hobbes in

---

* In 1712 Sir James Tillie of Pentillie Castle in Cornwall died, leaving instructions in his will that he was to be buried 'in such place at Pentillie Castle as I have acquainted my dearest wife . . . with' (P.R.O., PROB 11/537, PCC 255 LEEDS). This 'place' was a folly-like structure which survives in a ruinous condition. In 1699 a Quaker called Thomas Nobes was buried in a simple, vaulted stone tomb which he had erected at Tomb Farm, Basildon, Berkshire (W. Money, *Stray Notes on Basildon*, 1893, pp. 20–1). The roofless walls of Nobes's Tomb, measuring about nine by eight feet, still stand just outside the entrance to the farmyard.

316

rejecting the 'useless or unneccessary ceremonies which ever have been invented by the Priests to amuse and delude man'. A church monument would have been a recognition of priestly power, and long before his death he had discussed with his friend and architect Sir John Vanbrugh the idea of building a mausoleum at Castle Howard. Vanbrugh, whose anti-clericalism is so evident in his plays, embraced the idea with enthusiasm. It was, he wrote, 'what . . . has been practis'd by the most polite peoples before Priestcraft got poor carcases into their keeping, to make a little money of'. When the Duke of Marlborough died in 1722 Vanbrugh tried to persuade his executors to build 'some plain, but magnificent and durable monument over him' in the park at Blenheim in Oxfordshire. Unfortunately, they did not feel able to disregard the duke's expressed wish to be buried in the chapel of Blenheim Palace. 'Here is a pompous funeral preparing', Vanbrugh wrote to Carlisle, 'I don't know whether it won't cost . . . ten thousand pounds. What a noble monument wou'd that have made, whereas this idle show, will be gone in half an hour, and forgot in two days.' For Carlisle, as for Vanbrugh, the purpose of such a monument would be the essentially worldly one of per-petuating the memory of the dead 'to many future ages'. For his epitaph he wanted 'no other inscription . . . than this, here lyes Charles the 3rd. Earl of Carlisle of the Family of the Howards who built this house called Castle Howard & made the plantations that belong thereunto'.

It was in this secular spirit that in 1726 (Vanbrugh being dead) Carlisle turned to Nicholas Hawksmoor for designs for his monument. He thought at first in terms of 'a Greek Temple', but when Hawksmoor pointed out that the 'polite people' of Antiquity, 'never buryed near their temples', he accepted that his tomb would take the form of a mausoleum. The design first considered was a version of the tomb of Caecilia Matella – a stone drum standing on a square base. Although Hawksmoor considered that this could not 'fail of being a Noble family Monu-ment', it was soon abandoned in favour of a domed cylinder encircled by an arcade, later transformed into a colonnade (fig. 293). The final result is so similar to published reconstructions of circular Roman buildings by Palladio and Bartoli, especially to the latter's engravings of the mausoleum on the Via Appia generally known as 'the tomb of Gallienus' (though mistakenly identified by Bartoli as 'the Temple of Domitian'), that Hawksmoor must clearly have referred to them, in particular for the profile of the dome (fig. 294). Although a dozen drawings connected with the mausoleum are preserved at Castle Howard, the 'sixty-two drawings for mausolea' sold after Hawksmoor's death might well have thrown further light on the evolution of the design. The mausoleum was finished in 1736, and in it the body of Lord Carlisle was laid to rest after his death two years later. It had cost him at least £10,000, more than enough to build a substantial country house. As an expression of patrician privilege in death it has never been surpassed. Others were commemorated incongruously wearing togas and buskins on their monuments in Gothic churches, but Lord Carlisle lay like an ancient Roman in his authentically classical mausoleum – a mausoleum that, as Horace Walpole put it, 'would tempt one to be buried alive'.

As one of the most prominent ornaments of a much visited country seat, the

293. Castle Howard, Yorkshire, the mausoleum (Barry Capper).

294. The mausoleum on the Via Appia, Rome, known as 'the tomb of Gallienus', as conjecturally restored by Bartoli for D. Rossi's *Romanae magnitudinis monumenta* (1699), where it is erroneously described as 'the Temple of Domitian'.

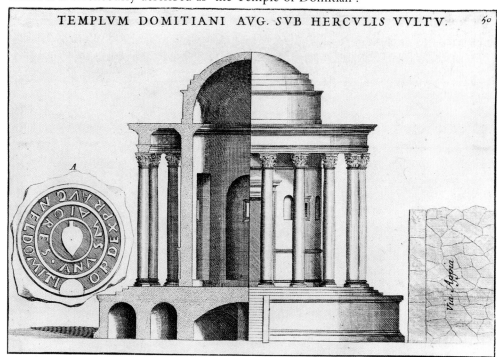

TEMPLVM DOMITIANI AVG. SVB HERCVLIS VVLTV.

Scale in Metres

Scale in Feet

295. Elmore churchyard, Gloucestershire, the Guise mausoleum built in 1733 and its source, the engraving of a Roman mausoleum at Terracina in Italy in Fréart's *Parallel of the Antient Architecture with the Modern*, 1684, 2nd ed. 1702. The Guise mausoleum collapsed early in this century, but the lower part of the four piers remains standing up to the broken line, and surviving portions of the capitals, frieze, etc. enable an accurate reconstruction to be made on paper. This was probably the first building in Europe since Antiquity to use the Roman Doric order without bases.

296. Chiddingstone churchyard, Kent, the Streatfield mausoleum of 1735.

297. Kirkleatham church, Yorkshire, the Turner mausoleum designed by James Gibbs in 1740.

298. Mellerstain, Berwickshire, Scotland, the Baillie mausoleum or burial enclosure in the grounds of the family seat, built in 1736.

The Mausoleum in the garden at Boughton.

299. Boughton Park, Northamptonshire, drawing by the antiquary William Stukeley of a mausoleum for the 2nd Duke of Montagu, made in 1742 (Bodleian Library, Oxford, MS. Top. gen. d. 14, f. 43ᵛ).

Castle Howard mausoleum must have been seen by innumerable visitors, and it no doubt helped to suggest the desirability of a family mausoleum to others. Certainly, it is from the 1730s onwards that mausolea begin to proliferate in England, Scotland and Ireland, though few of these early Georgian examples make any attempt to rival the solitary grandeur of Hawksmoor's masterpiece. One of the most notable was the pyramidally roofed mausoleum, faithfully copied from an engraving of a Roman prototype at Terracina in Italy, that was built at Elmore in Gloucestershire in accordance with the will of Sir John Guise, who died in 1732 (fig. 295). This stands in a churchyard, as do the vernacular version of the same type that forms the Streatfield monument of 1735 at Chidding-stone in Kent (fig. 296), or the rectangular mausoleum that the 1st Duke of Montrose built at Aberuthven in Perthshire in 1736–8 to the designs of William Adam. At Kilberry Castle in Argyllshire the simple pedimented mausoleum erected to the memory of Captain Dugald Campbell, R.N.(d. 1733) stands in a former churchyard (now within the castle grounds) of which it is the sole sur-viving relic. At Kirkleatham in Yorkshire the striking mausoleum designed by James Gibbs for the wealthy landowner Cholmley Turner in 1740 takes the form of a pyramidal octagon (fig. 297). It was probably derived from one of the fanciful reconstructions of Egyptian pyramids in the *Entwurff einer historischen Architectur* published in 1721 by the Austrian Fischer von Erlach, like Gibbs a pupil of Carlo Fontana. It is still attached to the chancel of the parish church and consequently retains something of the character of a family chapel. Almost contemporary with the Howard mausoleum and, like it, sited in private grounds, is one at Mellerstain in Berwickshire, built by George Baillie of Jerviswood in 1736 (fig. 298). What Baillie had envisaged here was a simple burial enclosure of the usual Scottish type,

321

300. Stockholm, a row of private mausolea in the Maria Magdalena churchyard, dating from 1709 onwards.

situated near the house 'to save the trouble of carrying him far' for burial (the parish church being over four miles distant), and it was 'with difficulty' that he was persuaded by his family 'to have it built with some ornaments'. The only early eighteenth-century English mausoleum which might have compared with Castle Howard was one which John, 2nd Duke of Montagu (d. 1749), thought of building in the grounds of his seat at Boughton in Northamptonshire. A circular domed building encircled by trees and standing on a rectangular earthwork almost surrounded by water, it figures in a drawing by the antiquary William Stukeley dated 1742 (fig. 299). Both the architecturally well-informed duke and his friend Dr Stukeley would have been well aware of the Antique precedents that this building was evidently intended to recall. Although Stukeley's drawing shows it as if it actually existed, nothing now remains on the site, and it seems never to have been built.

By 1760 there were in England and Scotland at least twenty free-standing mausolea, of which several stood in parks, fields or woods.* In Sweden too, private mausolea were to be found, notably in Stockholm, where a series of small, roofed burial places was constructed in the churchyards of the Maria Magdalena and Klara churches, evidently for the benefit of urban families who could not all

---

* In chronological order, these were at Pentillie, Cornwall (c.1712; note p. 316 above), Castle Howard, Yorks. (1729–36), Mellerstain, Berwickshire (c.1735), Dinlabyre, near Newcastleton, Roxburghshire (1749), and Felsham, Suffolk, built by an anti-clerical gentleman called John Reynolds (d. 1759).

have traditional *gravkoren* in the churches themselves. A row of twenty-six, uniform in design and dating from 1709 onwards, survives on the south side of the former churchyard, twenty-one more on the east side having been demolished (fig. 300). Two of those in the Klara churchyard are dated 1725 and 1730. In Swedish country churchyards the earliest detached mausoleum appears to be that of the Banér family at Gottröra in Uppland, which is dated 1735. It is a rectangular structure with rounded corners in front and a Vignolesque doorway under a pediment. *

Elsewhere in Europe few if any detached mausolea were built before the third quarter of the eighteenth century. From time to time some visionary scheme for a free-standing mausoleum heavily charged with dynastic symbolism would be laid before a Protestant prince,† but much of the enthusiasm for this sort of funerary display was satisfied by the immensely elaborate and expensive catafalques or *castra doloris* with which the passing of rulers both Protestant and Catholic was marked (figs. 301, 333), and such royal mausolea as were actually built in Protestant countries tended to remain firmly within the tradition of the funerary chapel attached to a major church. Such are the baroque *gravkor* of King Charles X of Sweden on the north side of the Riddarholm church in Stockholm, built in 1675–1743 (fig. 250), the neo-classical chapel of King Frederick V of Denmark at Roskilde (1774–9) and the remarkable chapel that the Italian architect Nosseni added to the east end of the church of St Martin in Stadthagen in 1609–25 for

---

* Later examples are to be found at Lenhovda, Småland (1764; very simple), Gävle, Gästrikland (1774), Ostuna, Uppland (1774; square, with ogee roof), Edebo, Uppland (1780s; a simple cube with pyramidal roof), and Valbo, Gästrikland (1800). No mausolea appear to have been built on private estates in Sweden in the eighteenth century.

† For the projects for mausolea for King Charles I of England and King Frederick the Great of Prussia, see above, p. 309 and below, p. 358. In 1649–52 the idea of removing the body of King Gustavus Adolphus of Sweden from his chapel in the Riddarholm church in Stockholm to a free-standing mausoleum was considered by his daughter Queen Christina. Nicodemus Tessin the elder submitted a scheme for a simple circular mausoleum of Roman character to stand within the precincts of the royal palace, while the French Protestant artist Sébastien Bourdon proposed to build a more elaborate one of two orders (Ionic and Corinthian) with an abundance of sculpture and tapestries illustrating the king's victories (see G. Axel-Nilsson, 'Pompa memoriae Gustavi Adolphi magni', in *Queen Christina of Sweden, Documents and Studies*, ed. M. von Platen, Stockholm, 1966).

In 1574 a remarkable project for a mausoleum was published, ostensibly in Turin, but actually in La Rochelle, then a Huguenot stronghold. It was to commemorate Margaret, daughter of Francis I, King of France, and wife of Philibert-Emanuel, Duke of Savoy, who had recently died in the Savoyard capital. Neither its author nor its intended location is known and no drawing of it survives, only an elaborate description. References to Pliny and the 'maison de Liban' (that is the description by the fourth-century writer Libanius of Diocletian's palace at Antioch) show that the author's sources were wholly Antique, and he contemptuously rejects contemporary French funerary architecture as 'barbarous and Gothic'. The result would have been an entirely secular monument, square in plan, consisting of a double peristyle of Corinthian columns, surrounding a central tomb surmounted by figures of the duchess and her husband sitting on a terrestial globe and accompanied by eight statues representing her father, King Francis, her mother, Queen Claude, her brother, King Henri II, her sister, Madeleine, Queen of Scots, and her four royal nephews. No altar was envisaged, and the elaborate imagery was derived entirely from pagan classical sources. As Margaret, though tolerant of Protestantism, had remained faithful to the Catholic faith, it is not surprising that nothing came of this unsolicited scheme, for particulars of which I am indebted to Dr David Thomson.

323

301. The catafalque designed by Jean Marot for the lying-in-state at Saint-Denis in France of Queen Henrietta Maria of England in 1669 (Nationalmuseum, Stockholm, Department of Prints & Drawings, Cronstedt Collection, Portfolio XII. 2).

302. Stadthagen, Germany, plan of the funerary chapel built at the east end of St Martin's church for the Protestant Count Ernst of Schaumberg to the designs of Nosseni in 1609–25.

Count Ernst of Schaumberg (fig. 302). Here the seven-sided plan left no space for an altar, thus giving the building its special character as a Protestant place of burial, and the central space was occupied by an outstanding sculpture of the Resurrection by Adriaen de Vries.

There was, however, one Protestant ruler whose mode and place of burial were without precedent in western Europe. This was Prince John Maurice of Nassau-Siegen (1604–79), Stadtholder or governor of the town of Cleves (now Kleve). Brought up a Calvinist, he needed no church for his burial, but as a humanist and an informed patron of architecture (the Mauritshuis at The Hague was built by

303. Cleves (Kleve), Germany, the mausoleum of Prince John Maurice of Nassau-Siegen (d. 1679) in the park he created: an eighteenth-century drawing in the Print Room of Leiden University.

him and bears his name), he conceived of his monument as a classical incident in the extensive woodland plantations that he carried out round Cleves. The tomb itself was a massive rectangular sarcophagus embellished with coats of arms and trophies in high relief and an inscription giving his rank and titles. Like some of the other ornaments in Maurice's gardens, it was made of iron cast in a foundry in his native town of Siegen. It formed the focal point of an *exedra* of rustic masonry whose compartments were occupied by Roman altars and tombstones (fig. 303). Standing near to the road between Cleves and Xanten, the whole was a romantic evocation of an Antique tomb and close in spirit to a classical landscape by Poussin. When Maurice died in 1679 he was duly buried in the sarcophagus, but his remains were subsequently removed to the family vault at Siegen. The tomb and its setting remain, much restored, at Bergental to the south-east of Cleves.

   To anyone ignorant of its origin, the tomb at Cleves might easily be supposed to date from the eighteenth rather than the seventeenth century. Indeed, it made a deep impression on that quintessentially eighteenth-century ruler, Frederick the Great of Prussia. In a will that he drew up in 1769 he stated that he wished to be buried on a terrace at his palace of Sanssouci in a manner similar to that in which Maurice, Prince of Nassau, 'a été inhumé . . . dans un bois proche de Clèves'. To be buried in a garden in the semblance of an Antique mausoleum was in fact to be

325

304. West Wycombe, Buckinghamshire, England, the mausoleum built by Francis Dashwood, Lord Le Despenser, in 1764–5. This enormous mausoleum, probably the largest built in Europe since Antiquity, originated in a legacy of £500 from George Bubb Dodington, Lord Melcombe Regis, to 'build an arch or temple' at one of Dashwood's seats. The building stands prominently on a hill close to the parish church. The hexagonal enclosure formed of linked triumphal arches has no obvious precedent either in Antiquity or later.

one of the symbols of the profound intellectual changes that in the course of the eighteenth century were to transform both architectural taste and men's attitude towards death and the after-life.

XV

FUNERARY ARCHITECTURE IN THE EIGHTEENTH AND EARLY NINETEENTH CENTURIES

IN THE COURSE OF THE EIGHTEENTH CENTURY attitudes towards death and the after-life were transformed as part of the cultural and intellectual changes known to historians as the Enlightenment. The cessation of the great plagues that had been endemic in Europe since the fourteenth century, the gradual improvement in the expectation of life, made death seem less arbitrary than it had in the past. As a result of advances in medical science its causes were better (if still very imper-fectly) understood, so that it could be seen as a natural phenomenon instead of as a manifestation of the incomprehensible workings of Divine Providence. Advanced Christian thought – both Catholic and Protestant – encouraged the idea of a benign deity incapable of ordaining eternal punishment for sinners. Sceptical thought went further and reduced the notion of God to an abstraction: 'Grand Architect' or 'Supreme Being'. Meanwhile, anti-clerical attitudes were challenging the need for an organised church at all. Enlightened man was freed at last from the terror of Purgatory and the spiritual tyranny of priests. Death could be faced, if not with equanimity, at least without those dire apprehensions that had been foisted on humanity by medieval theology. These profound changes in religious thought had their consequences in religious practice: a reduction in most Catholic countries both in the testamentary provision for masses and in funeral ceremonial; the partial toleration, in Protestant ones, of deism and dissent; and in both the occasional appearance of *esprits forts* who spurned the last offices of the Church and insisted on a wholly secular funeral.★

★ In 1729 Louis Recle of Cernon in France 'was laid to rest in his garden, bottle of wine at head and to the sound of violins' (J. McManners, *Death and the Enlightenment*, 1981, p. 280). In 1733 John Underwood was buried at Whittlesey in Cambridgeshire in a coffin painted green in the presence of six gentlemen who sang the last stanza of the 20th Ode of the second book of Horace ('Absint inani funere neniae . . . ') (*Notes & Queries*, 6th series 1 (1880), p. 210). In his will of 1808 the poet Lord Byron directed that he was to be buried at Newstead Abbey in a vault beneath the monument to his dog Boatswain, 'without any ceremony or burial service whatever'. As he sold Newstead before his death in 1824, his body was buried in the Byron family vault in Hucknall Torkard Church, and the dog is the only occupant of the vault at Newstead (Rosalys Coope, 'Lord Byron's Newstead: The Abbey . . . during the Poet's Ownership', *Thoroton Society's Trans.*, 91 (1987), pp. 151–2).

But death itself could never be conquered. Men and women still died, and most of them died and were buried with the rites of the Church. In Britain the productions of the 'graveyard poets', notably Edward Young (*Night Thoughts*, 1742–5), Robert Blair (*The Grave*, 1743) and Thomas Gray (*Elegy written in a Country Churchyard*, 1751), represented a continuation, in the conventions of a politer age, of the *memento mori*s of the past. Their message was essentially the same as that of the medieval paintings of the encounter between 'the three quick and the three dead', the cadaver or *transi* tombs of the fifteenth and early sixteenth centuries, the skulls and skeletons of seventeenth-century funerary art. It was one of Christian resignation in the face of death and emphasised the common lot of mankind rather than the boast of funeral heraldry or the pompous symbols of dynastic power. Gray's elegy had its setting in a country churchyard, not in a family chapel, still less in a mausoleum. Although they were all writing in the middle of the century, the popularity of these writers saw no diminution in its later years. Numerous editions, translations and imitations of all three poems were published up to the end of the century and beyond. Of Gray's *Elegy* alone there had been by 1800 over thirty English editions and several translations into other languages. Blair's poem achieved its greatest popularity between 1780 and 1800 and was illustrated by Blake in 1813.

So far, indeed, was death from being forgotten in the latter part of the eighteenth century that for the first time in European history funerary art and architecture ceased to be concerned exclusively with funerary occasions and infiltrated both the stage and the garden. The taste for the macabre, for which baroque funeral ceremonial had catered, still demanded to be satisfied, so that just as the latter was going out of fashion in churches, the Parisian theatre was featuring dramas in which tombs and skeletons figured prominently. In these 'sepulchral farces' (as a satirist called them) funeral vaults and graveyards provided the settings for scenes of violence or despair. Piranesi's *Carceri* were the inspiration for many of these stage-sets, in which sarcophagi were seen in perspective in a gloomy setting of prison-like vaults, drawn with all the skill of the baroque scenographers (fig. 305). The architecture, however, was neo-classical rather than baroque, and the sombre mood was far removed from the glittering elegance of a stage-set by Bibiena or Righini. In France these artificial horrors lost their appeal when they were overtaken by the all too real horrors of the Revolution. But in Italy funereal stage-sets continued to be popular and indeed became an established genre of such celebrated theatrical designers as Francesco Fontanesi (1751–95), Pietro Gonzaga (1751–1831) or Antonio Nic-colini (1772–1850).

While the appetite of eighteenth-century audiences for violence and horror was being exploited in the theatre, the gentler sentiment of melancholy was being encouraged by the introduction of tombs, real and fictitious, into gardens. Here they formed part of the apparatus of temples and artificial ruins that was carefully calculated both to please and direct the eye and to evoke an appropriate sentiment in the mind. The idea that gardens, like pictures, might convey a moral or even a political message went back to the sixteenth century, and an 'Etruscan tomb' had

305. Stage set by Pietro Gonzaga (1751–1831), featuring burial vaults and sarcophagi (Milan, Museo Teatrale della Scala).

featured in that riddle of a garden, the one created by Vicino Orsini (1532–85) at Bomarzo near Viterbo. But (with the notable exception of Cleves) tombs had no place in the great formal gardens of the seventeenth century. In eighteenth-century Europe they came in with the informal landscape that English garden designers began to develop in the 1730s. As garden features they could take three forms: one was the 'Roman' tomb that, with other architectural properties (columns, arches, temples, etc.), was intended to evoke an ideal classical land-scape of the kind painted by Claude or Poussin; the second was the ornamental building (obelisk or pyramid or urn) that was also a memorial or tribute to a real person who was buried elsewhere; and the third was the tomb or mausoleum that was the actual place of burial of an individual or a family. All three forms go back to the late 1720s, and it is hardly possible to give priority to any one of them. At Castle Howard Lord Carlisle built a pyramid in memory of his ancestor Lord William Howard (d. 1640) the year before he began his own mausoleum, while at Stowe Lord Cobham dedicated to the memory of Sir John Vanbrugh (d. 1726) a

306 (*above left*). Stowe, Buckinghamshire, England, ornamental pyramid designed by Sir John Vanbrugh (d. 1726) and later dedicated to his memory: since demolished (engraving by George Bickham, 1756).

307 (*above right*). Werrington, Devon, England, eighteenth-century park ornament based on the Roman mausoleum known as 'the Tomb of the Horatii and the Curiatii' (fig. 66).

308. Paris, fictitious tombs in the Parc du Monceau laid out by the duc de Chartres in the 1770s.

pyramid he had already built to the latter's design as a 'Roman' monument (fig. 306). At Castle Hill in Devon the half formal, half naturalistic landscape laid out by Lord Clinton in the 1730s included another pyramid, 'with an inscription on it to the memory of a gentleman who travelled with Lord Clinton and died here'. Here the commemorative function gave extra point to what would otherwise have been just an ornamental feature. But in the park at Werrington in the same county, the curious structure known locally as 'the Sugar Loaves', but correctly identified by Bishop Pococke in 1750 as a rough copy of the Roman mausoleum at Albano called 'the tomb of the Horatii and the Curiatii' (fig. 307), was purely ornamental in character, as was the similar monument seen by Pococke at Stoke Park near Bristol. In Charles Hamilton's celebrated garden at Pains Hill in Surrey a picturesque arch masquerading as a 'Mausoleum' was rightly ridiculed by Horace Walpole, but the builder of an 'Arcadian Mausoleum' in the garden of The Grove in Hertfordshire took considerable pains to give it an air of authenticity by placing urns and sarcophagi in a circular wall. Even this might not have satisfied the philosopher d'Holbach, who after visiting an English garden embellished with sepulchral urns and ancient funerary inscriptions, commented acidly that 'what I called a Roman cemetery, the owner called an Elysium'.

Nevertheless, by the end of the eighteenth century the tomb in the garden had migrated to the Continent with the 'jardin Anglais' with which it was associated. Tombs and sarcophagi formed part of the carefully contrived ambience of arcadian melancholy in gardens such as the French Clisson or the Polish Arkadia. But here, as in England, the idea was in some danger of trivialisation. There was a 'Wood of Tombs' (still in part extant, fig. 308) in the duc de Chartres's garden at Monceau on the outskirts of Paris, an 'Island of Tombs' at the duc d'Artois's Bagatelle, and a 'Valley of Tombs' at the princesse de Monaco's Betz. As the prince de Ligne complained, in places such as these the fictive tombs were apt to be degraded by serving a secondary function as kitchens, wine cellars, larders and the like. In Poland a version of the mausoleum of Caecilia Metella did duty as a water cistern in the gardens of the Lazienki villa near Warsaw. A real mausoleum was another matter, but burials in gardens were rare in Catholic countries. In France most of these were clandestine, for after the Revocation of the Edict of Nantes in 1685 non-Catholics had no legal right of burial, and it was not until 1787 that any provision was made for the interment of Protestants and others in cemeteries. Probably the first – and certainly the most famous – person to be openly buried in a garden was Jean-Jacques Rousseau (a non-Catholic), whose death took place in 1778 on the estate of his friend the marquis de Girardin at Ermenonville. Here the tomb took the form of a sarcophagus, pictures-quely sited on an island in a lake and overhung by willows. When the distin-guished Protestant linguist Court de Gebelin was buried in the comte d'Albon's garden at Franconville in 1784, the tomb was again a sarcophagus, but four ruined columns gave the impression that it had once formed part of a larger structure. It was also with a sarcophagus that in his garden at Maupertuis the marquis de Montesquieu commemorated the Huguenot admiral Gaspard de Coligny, a victim of the Massacre of St Bartholomew's Day in 1572.

331

Élevation en Perspective d'vne Chapelle Sepulcrale.

309. Design for a 'Sepulchral Chapel' by the French architect Nicolas Jardin, engraving published in Rome in 1748.

The taste for funerary architecture which made itself felt in the theatre and in the garden was also apparent wherever architectural drawings were exhibited, whether in Paris at the Académie royale d'architecture or in London at the Royal Academy from 1769 onwards. Some of the earliest architectural drawings in the neo-classical style, made by French architects such as Jardin (1720–99) and Le Geay (c.1720–c.1786) were for tombs and mausolea (fig. 309). During the latter part of the eighteenth century many of the best architects in Europe turned their minds to funerary architecture. Boullée, in particular, gave up his career as a government architect in order to devote himself to writing and to drawing visionary schemes for vast public buildings, many of which were funerary monuments and necropolises for which no commission was ever likely to be forthcoming. Strange though this obsession may seem, it is not difficult to see why funerary buildings made so strong an appeal to architects imbued with neo-classical ideals. For the tomb was one of the most authentic of Ancient building types, one, moreover, in whose design no compromise with the practical necessities of eighteenth-century life was required. The American architect Frank Lloyd Wright once admitted to 'gloating' over the beautiful buildings he could have built, 'if only it were unnecessary to cut windows in them'. Had his rich clients wanted mausolea rather than houses his wish would have been granted. For the eighteenth-century architect not only did the mausoleum need neither windows nor chimneys: it invited him to think in terms of those simple, elementary forms that appealed particularly to a neo-classical taste in revolt against the arbitrary complexity of the baroque and the frivolous décor of the rococo. The best-known mausolea of Antiquity were pyramidal (Caius Cestius) or cylindrical (Caecilia Metella) or in the form of a small rectangular temple or a circular tempietto. Of the elaborate compositions of superimposed orders only that at Saint-Rémy in Provence survived intact in Europe; all the others were reduced to battered cores whose reconstruction on paper awaited the patient work of the modern archaeologist. Montano, it is true, offered his fantastic confections, but in general these made no more appeal to eighteenth-century taste than they do to twentieth-century scholarship. Pietro Santi Bartoli's *Antichi Sepolchri* of 1697 was both a more accurate and a better presented record of such Roman funerary monuments as remained standing in a recognisable form, while Piranesi, the comte de Caylus and others added their quota of exemplars.

From these archaeological sources the neo-classical architect derived not only authority for mausolea in the form of pyramids, cylinders and temples, but also the idea of buildings half-buried in the ground which appealed so strongly to some French architects of the Revolutionary period. Theirs was, however, a visionary architecture that found few clients. For actual examples of neo-classical mausolea it was necessary to visit the rural churchyards and parks of Britain and later of Germany and Scandinavia. Even in Britain the vogue of the mausoleum as an ideal subject for architectural composition considerably exceeded the demand. Between the foundation of the Royal Academy by George III in 1768 and his death in 1820, 164 designs for mausolea and 'sepulchral chapels' were shown at its annual exhibitions, but during the same period only about 70 were actually built. The catalogue entries do not specify style, but of the executed mausolea a dozen were in the Gothic style.[*] Of the classical mausolea built in Georgian Britain from 1730 onwards, many were simple rectangular structures often of minimal architectural interest,[†] but there were several major monuments designed by leading architects. Very few of these were Palladian in style. After Hawksmoor's death his mausoleum at Castle Howard was given over-elaborate steps of a

---

[*] The earliest Gothic mausoleum seems to have been that of the earls of Waltham in the churchyard at Boreham in Essex, which bore the date 1764 and was destroyed in 1944. It was octagonal in plan, was built of white brick and had a doorway of Tudor Gothic character and small quatrefoil windows (fig. 310). In designing a Gothic mausoleum there were no ancient precedents to follow, and most of those built in the late eighteenth and early nineteenth centuries took the form of small rectangular chapels. Few of them are buildings of any distinction. It apparently did not occur to any English architect to take a chantry chapel as the model for a Gothic mausoleum, as it did to the designer of the tomb of the connoisseur Stanislas Kostka Potocki (d. 1821) and his wife in the garden of their palace at Wilanóv in Poland. The enormous castle-like mausoleum of the Trench family at Woodlawn, Co. Galway, Ireland (fig. 310), complete with central donjon and curtain-wall, has no parallel in England or Scotland. It was built by Francis Trench (d. 1797) 'for his 21 children, for each of whom there is a separate vault' (S. Lewis, *Topographical Dictionary of Ireland*, 1850, *s.v.* 'Killane').

[†] Architecturally, the most distinguished mausolea of this sort were those at Ossington, Notts. by John Carr for the Denison family (1782–3; destroyed), at Lundie, Angus, by Robert Mylne for the Duncan family (1787), and at Alva, Clackmannanshire, and Westerkirk, Dumfriesshire, by Robert Adam for the Johnstone family (1789–90) (fig. 332). In Northern Ireland the elegant Templetown mausoleum at Castle Upton near Templepatrick is also by Robert Adam (1789).

310. Gothic and castellated mausolea in Britain. *Top*: the octagonal mausoleum of the earls of Waltham in Boreham churchyard, Essex, built in 1764 and demolished in 1944. *Bottom*: the castellated mausoleum of the Trench family at Woodlawn, Co. Galway, Ireland, built by Francis Trench (d. 1797) (Dr Maurice Craig).

311. Fawley churchyard, Buckinghamshire, England, the Freeman mausoleum, designed and built by the amateur architect William Freeman in 1750 (cf. fig. 76).

Palladian character by another architect, but the Palladian movement in British architecture was over before mausoleum-building became fashionable. Designs for a mausoleum in the form of a Palladian pavilion were made by the amateur architect William Freeman in the late 1740s, but the one eventually adopted (fig. 311) derived from one of Montano's plates (fig. 279), and the only existing

335

312. *Top*, the Palladian Simeon mausoleum at Aston Hall, Staffordshire, England, dated 1757. *Bottom*, the undated Jervis mausoleum in Stone churchyard, Staffordshire.

313. Valletta, Malta, Conventual Church of St John, representation of a pyramidal mausoleum on the floorslab of Octavius Tancredi, Knight of Malta, who died in 1722. The original is in coloured marbles.

mausolea that exemplify Palladian principles of design are an almost identical pair at Stone in Staffordshire, one in the churchyard and the other in the grounds of the neighbouring Aston Hall. The latter was built by the Catholic Sir Edward Simeon in 1757, the former by the Jervis family at a date unknown but probably after 1757. Both consist of a pedimented rectangle flanked by lateral projections containing spaces for coffins (fig. 312). The identity of the architect is not known.★

Most of the major Georgian mausolea in Britain were variations on well-known Antique prototypes such as the pyramid, the rotunda and the temple. Although the triangular outline of a pyramid had been frequently used as a background for funerary monuments in churches or chapels since Raphael had introduced it into his Chigi chapel of 1513–16 (fig. 186), the first free-standing pyramids appear to date from the 1720s. As early as 1722 a pyramidal mausoleum is represented in coloured marbles on a tombstone to a Knight of Malta in the floor of the conventual church of St John in Valletta (fig. 313), and in 1724 a small 'cone pyramid' was constructed near Calais in memory of a party of English travellers murdered by highwaymen. In 1727 the French writer Titon du Tillet suggested that pyramids should be erected to the memory of the great ministers of the reign of Louis XIV, while in the same year one was introduced into the painting (by three Italian artists) of an allegorical tomb commemorating the English statesman Sidney Godolphin. The commemorative pyramids in land-

★ At Gibside, Co. Durham, the chapel that James Paine designed for George Bowes in 1760 is essentially Palladian in character, but the place of burial in the basement appears to have been an after-thought, and there is no provision for monumental display at the upper level.

337

scape gardens at Stowe (before 1726), Castle Howard (1728) and Castle Hill (*c.*1735) have already been mentioned. Early examples of tombs with pyramids as an upper feature have also been described (above, pp. 303–6). The most striking mausoleum of this kind was the one built in the park at Cobham Hall in Kent in 1783–4. This was designed by James Wyatt in accordance with the will of the 3rd Earl of Darnley (d. 1781), who left instructions that it should consist of 'four fronts supporting a pyramid in the middle high enough to be conspicuous'. Wyatt's interpretation of this posthumous brief was a clever composition based on a square with the corners cut off. Paired columns supporting sarcophagi are placed diagonally at the canted angles and provide a counterpoint to the dominant pyramid behind (fig. 314). In 1814 it was with a domed Ionic version of Wyatt's design that the English architect T.F. Hunt won a competition for a monument to the Scottish poet Robert Burns to be erected in St Michael's churchyard, Dumfries, but the sarcophagi were omitted in execution (fig. 315).

Meanwhile, two monuments in the form of small pyramids rising straight from the ground like that of Caius Cestius in Rome had been erected almost simultaneously in churchyards in England and Sweden. The English example is at Nether Wallop in Hampshire. It covers the grave of Dr Francis Douce (d. 1760), whose will indicates that he had built it in his lifetime. The Swedish one is at Järfälla in Uppland (fig. 316). It was erected in 1762 and commemorates Herr Olof Adlerberg, Chamberlain to King Frederick I, who had died in 1757. The

314. Cobham Hall, Kent, the Darnley mausoleum designed by James Wyatt, *c.*1783–4.

315. Dumfries, Scotland, the Burns mausoleum in St Michael's churchyard, built in 1815 to the designs of T.F. Hunt.

316. Järfälla churchyard, Uppland, Sweden, pyramidal monument to Olof Adlerberg, erected 1762.

first pyramids designed as mausolea with internal chambers are to be found in Germany. One, of stepped profile, in the park of Schloss Baum near Bückeburg (Lower Saxony), to the memory of a local count, bears the date 1776. A second, in the park of the Eben and Möhring families at Rosen near Kreuzberg in the Rhineland, dates from 1780, and a third, on an island in the park at Wilhelmsbad near Hanau, enshrines the heart of a prince of the electoral house of Hesse who died in 1784 (fig. 317). Yet another, erected before 1788 in the park of the Schloss at Gotha in Thuringia, contains a sarcophagus visible through a grille.

In England the first mausoleum of pyramidal form was the one designed by Joseph Bonomi for the executors of John Hobart, Earl of Buckinghamshire, a former Lord Lieutenant of Ireland. It was built in 1794 and stands in a wooded glade in the park at Blickling in Norfolk (fig. 318). Here the internal chamber is domed, as it is at Cobham, and in many designs for pyramidal mausolea by French architects. Although several small pyramidal tombs were subsequently erected in various parts of Britain,★ the major funerary pyramids of the nineteenth

★ E.g., one in the churchyard of St Mary's, Wimbledon, S. London, erected by Gerard de Visme (d. 1797); another in Brightling churchyard, Sussex, to 'mad' Jack Fuller (d. 1834); the slate pyramid in Llandegai churchyard in Gwynedd to the architect Benjamin Wyatt (d. 1818); the red granite one in the Dean Cemetery in Edinburgh designed by W.H. Playfair over the grave of his old friend Sarah Rutherford (d. 1852); and the stone one in the churchyard at Sharow in Yorkshire erected by that keen student of the Pyramids, Charles Piazzi Smyth, Astronomer Royal for Scotland, to the memory of his wife Jessie (d. 1896), described in the inscription as 'his faithful and sympathetic friend and companion through 40 years of varied scientific experiences by land and sea . . . as well as underneath and upon the GREAT PYRAMID of EGYPT.'

317. Wilhelmsbad, Hanau, Germany, pyramidal tomb of Prince Friedrich of Hesse (d. 1784) (O. Mittelstaedt).

318. Blickling Park, Norfolk, England, the Earl of Buckinghamshire's mausoleum, built in 1794 to the designs of Joseph Bonomi (Angelo Hornak).

century were to be found on the Continent and in the United States of America. At Karlsruhe the pyramidal tomb of its ruler the Margrave Karl Wilhelm of Baden-Durlach, erected in 1825 to the designs of the state architect Friedrich Weinbrenner, forms a focal point of one of the grandest urban layouts in Europe. At Novara in northern Italy a pyramid very similar to Bonomi's at Blickling contains the bones of those who fell fighting the Austrians in 1849; at Richmond in Virginia 18,000 Confederate soldiers killed in the American Civil War were commemorated in 1869 by the erection of a splendidly rugged pyramid built of blocks of undressed granite (fig. 319); and at Branitz in Brandenburg Count Pückler-Muskau, a keen student of the picturesque who died in 1871, outdid Rousseau by being buried in a large pyramid (of Egyptian rather than Roman profile) which was reflected in the waters of a lake (fig. 320).

Closely allied to the pyramid was the obelisk. Obelisks brought from Egypt were prominent among the public monuments of Ancient Rome, and when Pope Sixtus V (1585–90) transformed the town plan of the city, several of them were re-erected to mark key points in his new road system. From the end of the first century a pair of obelisks had stood on either side of the entrance to the mausoleum of Augustus, but in Antiquity the use of the obelisk as a funerary symbol was rare. Nevertheless, from the late sixteenth century onwards tombs and catafalques were frequently embellished with obelisks. These were usually subsidiary architectural features, but as early as 1561 a tomb consisting of a single obelisk was erected in Cremona cathedral to the memory of a cardinal, and another in Bordeaux cathedral contained the heart of Antoine de Noailles, who died in 1562. When Michelangelo's funeral was held in the church of S. Lorenzo in Florence in 1564, a large obelisk was the central feature of the catafalque. In England among the earliest recorded examples of free-standing obelisk-tombs are those of Lady Heydon (d. 1593) formerly in Saxlingham church, Norfolk, and of Lady Hoby (d. 1605) in Bisham church, Berkshire (fig. 321). The extraordinary Elizabethan project for a mausoleum in the plinth of a huge obelisk (fig. 283) was never carried out, nor was John Webb's for one standing under the oculus of the domed chapel that he designed for Sir Justinian Isham in 1657 (fig. 286). This would, as he said, 'be rarely new and take well', but even finer would have been the obelisk marking the 'burying place' of the Jacobite Earl of Mar in the church at Alloa which he designed in exile in 1722 (fig. 323). Diagonally placed beneath a cupola, it was to be silhouetted against a Bramantesque arch as one ascended a double flight of stairs to Lord Mar's family pew at one end of the church. On the white marble pedestal heraldry was to recall the alliances of the earl's family with those of Panmure, Kingston and Kinnoull. Recumbent lions and mourning putti guarded the base of the black marble shaft, whose sides were to be decorated with gilded trophies of Roman armour and Scottish claymores. At the apex the drawings show a heart 'with flames coming out of it of guilt brass'. In 1688 a

319. Richmond, Virginia, U.S.A., pyramidal monument to Confederate soldiers, 1869.

320. Branitz, Brandenberg, Germany, pyramidal tomb of Prince Pückler-Muskau (d. 1871) (Klaus G. Beyer).

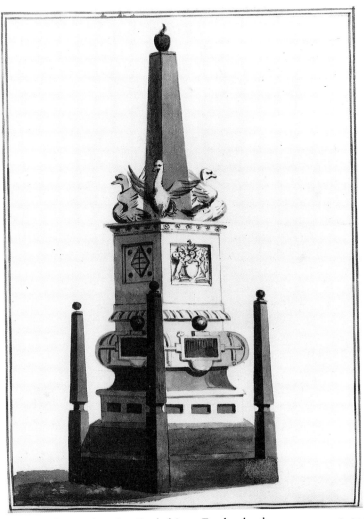

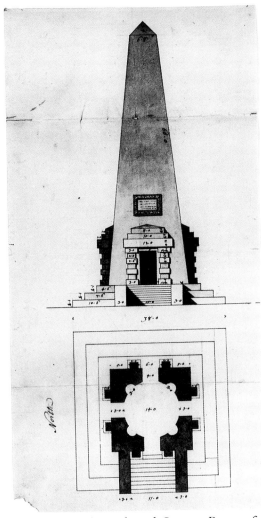

321. Bisham church, Berkshire, England, the monument to Lady Hoby (d. 1605). The four subsidiary obelisks at the base have disappeared since this drawing was made in the nineteenth century (Bodleian Library, MS. Top. Berks. c. 49, no. 84).

322. Design by Edward Lovett Pearce for an obelisk over the burial place of the Allen family at Stillorgan near Dublin, 1732, carried out in modified form (from album at Elton Hall, Huntingdonshire, by courtesy of William Proby, Esq.)

similar obelisk formed the centrepiece of a firework display held in Paris to celebrate the birth of the royal child known to history as the 'Old Pretender'. The flaming heart, in the description of this event, represented the ardour which the prince's birth aroused in his Catholic subjects. So at Alloa the obelisk was to be not just a funerary monument but a symbol of loyalty to the Stuart cause.

In later years obelisks were to become a common form of memorial, funerary or commemorative. Representative examples are: in Ireland, one in the grounds of Stillorgan House near Dublin, designed by Edward Lovett Pearce in 1732 to mark the burial chamber of the Allen family (fig. 322); in Scotland, one more than fifty feet high erected c.1714 over the vault of the earls of Cromartie in the

323. Design by John Erskine, 11th Earl of Mar, for a family pew and burial place to be added to Alloa church, Scotland, made in exile in 1722, and never carried out (Scottish Record Office, RHP 13258/41).

churchyard at Dingwall in the far north of the country, and a second to the memory of the Revd Henry Duncan (d. 1846), the founder of savings banks, which stands close to the site of the Free Church that he established near Ruthwell in Dumfriesshire; in France, the obelisk to Marshal Masséna (d. 1817), which is the focal point of the 'Champ des Braves' in the Père-Lachaise cemetery in Paris; and in Germany, one formerly in a park near Berlin which marked the tomb of Johann Georg Sulzer (d. 1779), an early exponent of landscape gardening in that country. Less conventional is the obelisk-crowned tower that in 1816–22 was built onto the church of Jonitz near Dessau as a mausoleum for Prince Leopold Franz of Anhalt-Dessau and his wife Luise.

In neo-classical eyes the rotunda was equal to the pyramid as an appropriate architectural form for funerary purposes. For the annual festival of the Chinea in Rome, whose temporary buildings were in the 1740s a vehicle for advanced neo-classicism, circular structures resembling mausolea were designed by French architects in 1746, 1747 and 1749, and the drawings made by William Chambers in 1751–2 for a mausoleum for Frederick, Prince of Wales, were similar in character (fig. 324). Of the circular domed mausoleum of the Colebrooke family, designed by Sir Robert Taylor and built on the north side of Chilham church in Kent in 1755, but demolished in 1862, there survives only a small engraving which shows the interior ringed by Ionic columns, between which were the burial compartments. The slightly later Thompson mausoleum at Little Ouseburn in Yorkshire is notable for the baseless Doric columns that encircle its drum (fig. 325), but the monument to David Hume in the Calton Hill cemetery at Edinburgh, designed by Robert Adam in 1778, achieves a greater effect by the boldness of its scale and the economy of its architectural vocabulary (fig. 326). The masterpiece of this type of mausoleum is, however, the one at Brocklesby in Lincolnshire designed by James Wyatt for the 1st Earl of Yarborough in 1787 (figs. 327–8). It was a tribute by the distraught earl to the memory of his young wife, and the delicacy of every part is entirely appropriate in a monument to a young and beautiful woman. Equally elegant is the mausoleum built by Queen Victoria on an artificial mount in the royal gardens at Frogmore near Windsor for her mother the Duchess of Kent (d. 1861) (fig. 329). Indeed, it was 'so constructed as to be capable of being used as a summer-house' if for any reason it was decided that the duchess should be buried elsewhere. Much more solemn – and much closer to an ancient prototype – is the enormous mausoleum in which the 10th Duke of Hamilton is buried at Hamilton in Lanarkshire (fig. 330). Obsessively proud of his lineage, the duke was determined to provide himself and his family with a place of burial of fitting grandeur. No mausoleum has ever been more carefully pondered by its future inmate than this, and the collection of rejected designs in the Hamilton archives is an anthology of funerary architecture by architects French, Italian, English and Scottish. Work began in the 1840s to designs by David Hamilton, but he died in 1843, and it was David Bryce under whose direction it was completed in 1853 at a cost of over £100,000. The source was the tomb of the Plautii at Ponte Lucano near Tivoli, as restored by Canina, but with a domed rather than a conical roof.

324. Design by Sir William Chambers for a mausoleum for Frederick, Prince of Wales (d. 1751) (Victoria & Albert Museum, London).

325. Little Ouseburn churchyard, Yorkshire, England, the Thompson mausoleum built by Henry Thompson (d. 1760).

327 (*above*). Brocklesby, Lincolnshire, England, the Yarborough mausoleum designed by James Wyatt in 1787 (Barry Capper).

328 (*right*). Interior of the Yarborough mausoleum at Brocklesby (*Country Life*).

326 (*left*). Edinburgh, monument to David Hume in the Calton Hill cemetery, designed by Robert Adam in 1778 (Dr David King).

329. Frogmore near Windsor, Berkshire, England, mausoleum for Queen Victoria's mother the Duchess of Kent (d. 1861), designed by Ludwig Grüner and A.J. Humbert.

330. Hamilton, Lanarkshire, Scotland, the mausoleum of the 10th Duke of Hamilton (d. 1852), completed in 1853.

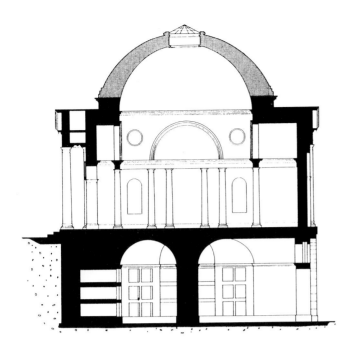

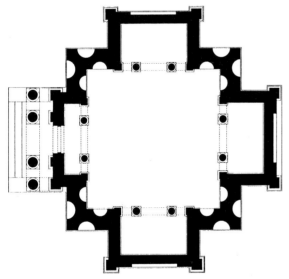

Scale in Metres
Scale in Feet

331. Bowood House, Wiltshire, England, plan and section of the Shelburne mausoleum designed by Robert Adam, 1761–4.

Mausolea with temple-fronts were rare in the eighteenth century, the most notable examples being, in England, the one that Robert Adam designed for Lord Shelburne at Bowood in Wiltshire in 1761–4, which is cruciform, with a domed interior and a Doric portico (fig. 331), and in Germany, the ducal mausoleum at

332. Westerkirk churchyard, Dumfriesshire, Scotland, the Johnston family mausoleum designed by Robert Adam, 1790.

Oldenburg, built in 1786–90 as a simplified version of the Maison Carrée at Nîmes.★ With the Greek Revival, however, the temple form came into its own. It was used for every kind of building, from town halls to churches, including mausolea. One of the earliest Greek Revival buildings in Europe was the catafalque constructed in the Spanish church in Rome to mark the death of King Charles III of Spain in 1788. This was designed by the painter Giuseppe Pannini and took the form of a reduced version of the 'Theseion' in Athens (fig. 333). The 'Theseion' itself (really the Temple of Hephaistos) had long been converted into a church, and in the early nineteenth century it was used as a place of burial for Protestant (and especially English) travellers. When the architect C.R. Cockerell fell dangerously ill in Athens in 1813, he wished to be buried in this 'mausoleum of British travellers', and when his friend, the archaeologist Haller

★ In 1576 the Maison Carrée itself had narrowly escaped being converted into a mausoleum for the 1st duc d'Uzès (d. 1573), whose widow tried to buy it from the city of Nîmes for that purpose. She intended to found two almshouses beside it, one for men, the other for women (J.C. Balty, *Etudes sur la Maison Carrée de Nîmes*, 1960, p. 33).

333. Greek Revival catafalque to mark the death of King Charles III of Spain, set up in the Spanish church in Rome in 1788 to the designs of Giuseppe Pannini (*c*.1745–*c*.1812) (Werner Oeschlin, Bonn).

von Hallerstein, died in Thessaly in 1817, it was in the Theseion that his body was interred. In Edinburgh the 'National Monument' on Calton Hill, intended to be a replica of the Parthenon, and begun under Cockerell's direction in 1824, was to have been a place of burial as well as a memorial to Scotsmen killed in the Napoleonic wars. The sale of the vaults in the podium was to help to finance the building above. In England the most ambitious Grecian mausoleum was the one Robert Smirke designed for the 4th Duke of Newcastle at Markham Clinton in Nottinghamshire in 1831–2. It was combined with a church to form a cruciform building of unrelenting severity (fig. 334). In Germany princely or aristocratic mausolea at Dyhernfurth near Breslau (F. Gilly, for Countess Maltzan, 1800–2), Ludwigslust (Joseph Ramée, for the Prince of Mecklenburg Schwerin, 1806), Charlottenburg (K.F. Schinkel, for King Frederick William II of Prussia, 1810), Kassel (Heinrich Jussow, for the Elector William II of Hesse, 1826), and Herren-hausen (by G.L. Lavès, for the King of Hanover, 1842–7) were all externally in

334. Markham Clinton church, Nottinghamshire, England, combined church and mausoleum built by the 4th Duke of Newcastle to the designs of R. Smirke in 1831–2.

the form of Greek Doric temples. In France the Revolutionary period was not conducive to the building of mausolea, but after the restoration of the Bourbon monarchy in 1815, one funerary building was erected of which the focus is a chapel with a temple-front (fig. 335). This is the 'chapelle expiatoire' authorised by the National Assembly in 1816 and built in the course of the next ten years on the site of the old cemetery where the bodies of Louis XVI and Marie Antoinette had been buried after their execution. The commission was, rather surprisingly, given to Napoleon's favourite architect, Pierre-François Fontaine. After the sublime imaginings of Boullée and Ledoux, Fontaine's elegant domed chapel comes as something of an anti-climax. Only the blind walls flanking the entrance strike an effectively funerary note. Inside the courtyard the enfilade of fictive tombs is more appropriate than evocative, and the whole building is less convincingly expressive of a nation's penitence than its promoters may have intended.

Except in Britain, the compositions of grouped or superimposed columns so popular in Antiquity as funerary monuments were rarely if ever seen in eighteenth-century Europe. Apart from the scarcity of published exemplars, this type of mausoleum was much less calculated to appeal to neo-classical taste than the simpler forms of pyramid or temple. Even in Britain mausolea of this sort were rare. In fact, if the engaging but eccentric Hopper mausoleum at Shotley Chapel in Northumberland (fig. 336) is dismissed as a provincial baroque survival, the only examples of this kind of monument are the two versions of the tomb of the Julii at Saint-Rémy in Provence, one at Downhill in Ireland (*c.*1779–83), the other at Wentworth Woodhouse in Yorkshire (1785–91) (figs. 337–9). Like their original, neither actually served as a place of burial, the former being a memorial to the 2nd Earl of Bristol (d. 1775), erected by his brother the 'Earl-Bishop', the latter a tribute to the 2nd Marquis of Rockingham (d. 1782) by his nephew and successor Lord Fitzwilliam. A third monument of this sort, departing considerably from the prototype, was designed by Joseph Bonomi for the 5th Duke of Argyll, but was never built.

The essentially archaeological approach that inspired most of the eighteenth-

335. Paris, the Chapelle Expiatoire, built 1816–26 to the designs of P.F.L. Fontaine.

336. Shotley Chapel, Northumberland, England, the Hopper family mausoleum erected in or shortly after 1752.

century mausolea so far mentioned produced some highly accomplished funerary architecture, but the most striking examples were those designed by a few architects who transcended the limitations of archaeology and gave classical architecture a new intensity of meaning by stripping it down to its essentials and eliminating the clichés of the classical vocabulary. Of this new style of geometric simplicity and often of historical archaism, the French architects Etienne-Louis Boullée and Claude-Nicolas Ledoux, the German Friedrich Gilly and the English George Dance the younger were among the pioneers. The visionary schemes of Boullée and others for gigantic tombs and vast cities of the dead are well known as essays in the sublime (figs. 340–1). Gilly's design of 1797 for a

354

337. Downhill, Co. Down, Ireland, monument to his brother the 2nd Earl of Bristol (d. 1775), Lord Lieutenant of Ireland, erected by the 4th Earl in 1779 to the designs of Michael Shanahan, and based on the monument of the Julii at Saint-Rémy (fig. 48). The upper storey was blown down in 1839 (J.A.K. Dean).

338. Reconstruction of the Downhill monument by Mr J.A.K. Dean, based on the surviving fragments and recorded dimensions. The disproportionate height of the upper storey may have contributed to its collapse in 1839.

339. Wentworth Woodhouse, Yorkshire,
England, monument to the 2nd Marquis of
Rockingham (Prime Minister 1765–6 and
1782), erected by his nephew Lord Fitzwilliam
in 1785–91 to the designs of John Carr of York
(from C.L. Stieglitz, *Plans et Desseins tirés de la
Belle Architecture*, Paris & Leipsig 1798–1800).

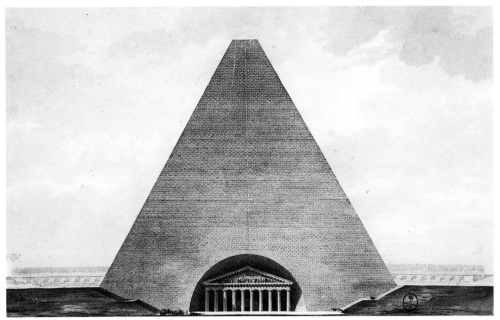

340. Design by the French architect E.L. Boullée for a vast pyramidal monument (Florence, Uffizi, Gab. Fotografico, Soprintendenza Beni Artistici e Storici di Firenze).

341. Design by P.F.L. Fontaine for 'a sepulchral monument for the sovereign of a great empire'. It won the second prize in the Académie de l'architecture in 1785 (Paris, Ecole des Beaux-Arts).

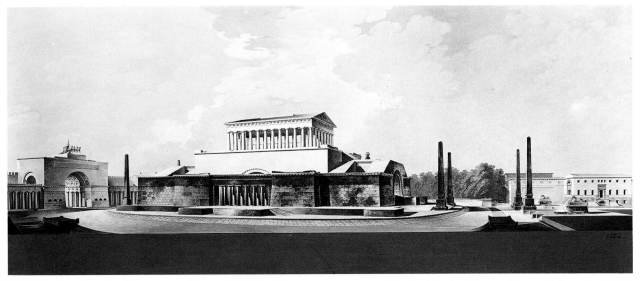

342. Design by the German architect F. Gilly for a monument to Frederick the Great, King of Prussia, 1797 (Sammlung der Zeichnungen, National-Galerie, Staatliche Museum, Berlin).

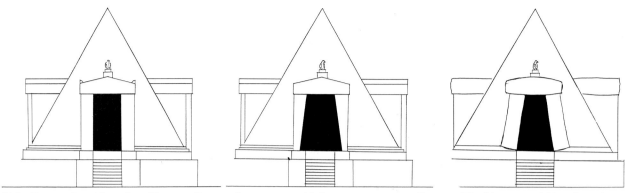

343. Successive ideas by George Dance for a pyramidal monument to George Washington, 1800 (based on sketches in Sir John Soane's Museum, London).

monument to Frederick the Great is notable for its combination of orthodox Greek Revival architecture, abstract geometrical forms and archaic cyclopeian masonry (fig. 342). Another kind of primitivism is illustrated in George Dance's sketches for a monument to George Washington, made in 1800 at the request of Benjamin West, the American-born President of the Royal Academy. The statue was to stand in the centre of a circular space carved out of a pyramid whose four entrances were defined by doorways each consisting of three colossal monoliths. In a second sketch Dance gave these entrances a more archaic character by sloping the jambs inwards, but in a third he turned them into megaliths straight from some prehistoric dolmen (fig. 343). Architecture could do no more to emphasise the rugged fortitude of one of the founders of American independence.

What was actually built was generally much less grandiose, but it could still be movingly eloquent. At Methven in Perthshire a carapace of rusticated masonry envelops the mausoleum that James Playfair designed for Thomas Graham of Lynedoch to enclose the body of his beautiful and accomplished wife who died in 1792 aged only thirty-five (fig. 344). Here is none of the feminine elegance of Brocklesby, only the impenetrable barrier that Death had set between husband and wife. At Trentham in Staffordshire the message of the fortress-like mausoleum which C.H. Tatham built for the Marquis of Stafford in 1807–8 is the same, though the expression is less subtle (fig. 345).

But in England the outstanding exponent of the sepulchral in architecture was Sir John Soane. Soane's life-long preoccupation with what Sir John Summerson has called 'the furniture of death' is well attested. One of his earliest designs was for a mausoleum to the memory of a friend who was drowned in a boating accident in 1776, and one of his last was for a 'sepulchral church and military chapel' to be erected in St James's Park as a memorial to the Duke of York who had died in 1827. In the intervening years only two mausolea and a handful of tombs were actually built to his designs, but these are among the most remarkable of their time.

The first mausoleum was designed in 1807 to contain the body of Noel Desenfans, an art collector who, whatever his religious views may have been –

344. Methven churchyard, Perthshire, Scotland, the Graham mausoleum designed by James Playfair, 1793.

345. Trentham, Staffordshire, England, mausoleum designed by C.H. Tatham for the Marquis of Stafford, 1807–8.

the indications are that they were deistic – may well have been fastidious about being buried in an overcrowded London churchyard. The site at the back of Desenfans's house in Charlotte Street, London, was cramped and awkward, but Soane, with his usual skill in exploiting confined spaces, planned what was in essence a circular temple or 'tholos' in which an inner row of Doric columns supported a low dome with an oculus. On one side a segment was cut away to reveal a smaller rectangular chamber, the mausoleum itself, illuminated from a concealed source in the roof. Against the far wall there was space for three sarcophagi. What was original was not so much the elegance of the neo-classical detailing, so appropriate in a connoisseur's tomb, as the conception of the mausoleum as a theatrical spectacle. Other mausolea were open to public inspection (at Brocklesby a visitors' book was provided), but once inside one shared the space with the dead. Here in Charlotte Street the sense of mystery was maintained by a separation akin to that between auditorium and stage. Desenfans's heir was Francis Bourgeois, who in 1811 bequeathed the paintings that he had inherited to Dulwich College, which already had a small art collection of its own. Desenfans's widow then offered sufficient funds to build a new picture gallery to house the united collection, together with a new mausoleum to replace the one in Charlotte Street. Instead of being hidden in a back yard, the mausoleum was now to be a prominent feature of the new building, a public monument to the munificence of those who had founded the gallery and the almshouses that were associated with it. Using only London stock brick for the walls and Portland stone for the architectural details, Soane treated the exterior in his most abstract manner (fig. 346). Within, the essential features of the earlier mausoleum are repeated, but all the details have been simplified, and the elementary forms are suitably solemn. Not a Christian symbol is, however, to be seen (fig. 347).

The same is true of the tomb in the former St Giles's cemetery (now a public garden near St Pancras station) which Soane designed for himself and his wife after her death in 1815 (fig. 348). This strange confection of unorthodox architectural forms consists of a rectangular marble monument bearing the inscriptions, sheltered by a primitivist canopy and standing within a balustraded enclosure. The roof of the canopy takes a shallow domical form which Soane made peculiarly his own, and it is decorated with emblems of eternity (a coiled snake and a continuous wavy line). The corners of the enclosure are marked by curiously voluted antefixes, and the coping of the balustrade extends stalactite-like fingers down the dies. How much is unexplained symbolism and how much wilful architectural perversity – a kind of neo-classical mannerism – it is difficult to say.

Although Soane did not choose, like Desenfans, actually to be buried in a domestic mausoleum, it is in his houses that his predilection for funerary themes is most strikingly apparent. At Lincoln's Inn Fields, in a crypt-like basement, the visitor was confronted first by an Egyptian sarcophagus and then by a 'Monk's Tomb'. In a building that was half dwelling, half museum, these and other relics of funerary art were, if unexpected, not wholly out of place, but in Soane's country house at Pitzhanger near Ealing the walls of the principal living rooms

346. Dulwich, South London, exterior of the mausoleum attached to the Art Gallery and designed by Sir John Soane, 1811–14 (Barry Capper).

347. Interior of the mausoleum at Dulwich.

were designed to look like *columbaria*, their recesses filled with cinerary urns and vases. Sitting at Soane's fireside, the guest could almost have had the illusion that he was inside a Roman mausoleum.

Soane's houses were an extreme example of that tendency for funerary art to spill over into other areas which has already been remarked upon (p. 328). But Soane's obsession with the symbols of mortality should not be exaggerated. Ancient funerary art was rarely morbid, and often elegant. Funerary vases and cinerary chests were among the most easily acquired relics of the ancient world, and figured largely in most collections of Antique art. For readers of Winckelmann, Greek vases were one of the touchstones of Greek civilisation. An artist like Adam Buck would introduce them into the backgrounds of his portraits, while a leader of taste like Thomas Hope would have a roomful of them in his London house. Such rare and beautiful objects demanded to be properly displayed. In his description of this house Hope explained that 'as these vases were all found in tombs, some, especially of the smaller sort, have been placed in recesses, imitative of the ancient columbaria, or receptacles of cinerary urns' (fig. 349). Another great collector, Horace Walpole, toyed with the idea of building a Gothic *columbarium* at Strawberry Hill in order to display his vases, and took the credit for suggesting that the gallery Robert Adam designed for the Duke of Northumberland at Sion House should incorporate funerary vases in appropriate

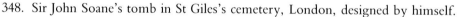

348. Sir John Soane's tomb in St Giles's cemetery, London, designed by himself.

349. One of the rooms in Thomas Hope's house in Duchess Street, London, decorated with funerary urns and features derived from Ancient *columbaria* (from Hope's *Household Furniture and Interior Decoration*, 1807).

settings. At Strawberry Hill Walpole had had several chimney-pieces copied from the canopies of Gothic tombs at Westminster Abbey and elsewhere, and another antiquarian builder, Sir Roger Newdigate, did the same at Arbury Hall in Warwickshire. At Lincoln's Inn Fields in the 1820s and 1830s the sepulchral ornaments may have been attuned to the melancholy disposition of an eccentric old man, but they were also a characteristic manifestation of English antiquarian taste in the reign of George III.

XVI

THE TRIUMPH OF THE CEMETERY

THIS BOOK HAS BEEN CONCERNED chiefly with the privileged dead: for only the rich and the powerful could normally afford to be buried in tombs that were architectural monuments. An inscribed stone, a painted board or just a mound of earth was all that marked the graves of countless ordinary people, pagan or Christian, Catholic or Protestant. In the course of the nineteenth century the public cemetery was to bring both rich and poor together in a common city or garden of the dead whose galleries and walks, crowded with tombs, constituted a new chapter in the long history of funerary architecture. In a sense, the wheel had come full circle, for in the nineteenth-century city interment within the built-up area was prohibited by law as it had been in Antiquity, though now for hygienic rather than religious reasons, and cemeteries became once more a characteristic feature of the suburban scene.

Here and there, as at Arles and Bordeaux,★ an Ancient cemetery continued in use well into the Middle Ages, and occasionally the unusually spacious burial ground of one parish came, like that of the Holy Innocents at Paris, to serve several others. But the history of the Christian cemetery (as distinct from the churchyard) begins anew in Pisa in the latter part of the thirteenth century. In the past citizens of Pisa had been buried within and around the cathedral, access to which was said to be obstructed by their tombs. These have long since been cleared away, but the names of some of those buried close to the walls of the church can still be seen cut in its marble masonry. The need for a new and better-organised place of burial exercised the minds of the civic and ecclesiastical authorities, and in 1277 the archbishop agreed to provide a site for an enclosed cemetery immediately inside the city walls to the north of the cathedral (fig. 350). An inscription records the commencement of the work in that year under the direction of Giovanni di Simone, the *capomaestro* of the cathedral works and the architect of the Ospedale di S. Chiara on the opposite side of the piazza. He planned it as an arcaded quadrangle, and he built it in the same white marble that had been used for the cathedral and its baptistery (fig. 351). The model was presumably a cloister rather than an *atrium* – both had, of course, been regularly used for burial for centuries – and the elongated plan was doubtless due to the

★ See above, p. 131.

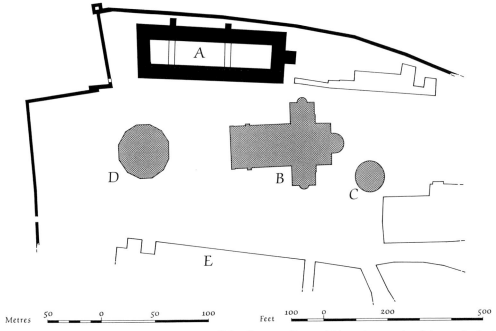

350. Pisa, plan showing the position of the Campo Santo (A) to the north of the cathedral (B), the campanile (C) and the baptistery (D). The contemporary hospital of S. Chiara is at E.

configuration of the site. A careful examination of the fabric suggests that work began at the east end and was continued westwards (with minor variations of design) after an interruption, probably caused by the defeat of the Pisans by the Genoese in 1284. Inside, the round-headed arches were originally open, and the Gothic window tracery (once glazed) was not inserted until the fifteenth century. The blank outer walls were probably intended from the first to be frescoed and had by the middle of the fourteenth century been painted with the Triumph of Death, the Last Judgement and other appropriate subjects. The regulation of burial within the Campo Santo would repay further study, but it is known that the covered walks were reserved for the families of the Pisan aristocracy, the open ground in the centre being common to all.★ Masses for the dead could no doubt be sung in the adjoining cathedral, as well as in a small chapel (since rebuilt) at the east end of the Campo Santo itself, but some private chapels were constructed

★ Social segregation of the dead is a topic that deserves further investigation. In general, the interiors of churches were reserved for those of wealth and status, the poor being relegated to the churchyard. At Geneva in 1455 the chapter divided the cathedral into three areas, each of which was reserved for the burial of a different class: bishops and canons on either side of the choir (including the transepts); barons and nobles at the eastern end of the nave; bourgeois, citizens and tradespeople in the western part of the nave. In 1483 this was modified to allow ecclesiastics and laity alike to choose any place of burial in the nave on payment of certain fees, the eastern part of the church still being reserved for the clergy. No one was to be buried in the sanctuary itself (L. Blondel, 'Autels, chapelles et cloître de Saint Pierre Ancienne Cathédrale de Genève', *Genava* 24, 1946). Such a formal agreement appears to have been exceptional, but a study of wills in conjunction with registers like the *Libellus Sepulchrorum* of S. Maria delle Grazie at Milan (*Arte Lombarda* 67, 1983) might reveal some unsuspected patterns of burial.

351. Pisa, two views of the Campo Santo.

within the roofed area by families or confraternities. They were presumably wooden enclosures of which no trace now remains.

Apart from the loss of its frescoes (now exhibited separately under museum conditions), the Campo Santo of Pisa remains essentially as it was conceived in the thirteenth century and completed in the fifteenth. The delicately traceried windows enliven the otherwise somewhat monotonous succession of arches and give a predominantly Gothic character to what is essentially a late Romanesque design. Yet despite its striking architectural beauty and its apparent success as a civic cemetery, the Pisan Campo Santo found no imitators in other Italian cities, where (as elsewhere in Europe) burial in church and churchyard continued to be the rule. Few cities, in Italy or any other country, had open space so conveniently available for a cemetery within their walls, and to establish one outside the urban area would have been too drastic a step for clergy and parishioners alike, depriving the former of their fees and the latter of long-established rights of burial in proximity to a church where masses could be said for their souls. With a stable population, most churchyards were capable of assimilating a regular intake of corpses that was balanced by the removal of displaced bones to ossuaries and charnel-houses, themselves a distinctive type of funerary building whose history has yet to be written.★ This balance – often no doubt precarious – could easily be

★ Generally demolished in Protestant countries, ossuaries persisted in Catholic Europe, especially in Brittany, Austria, southern Germany and Bohemia. In England surviving examples are the Carnary chapel (now part of the cathedral school) at Norwich and the charnel chapel beneath the north transept of All Saints, Newcastle (now the cathedral).

upset either by an increase in the local population or by an epidemic. Given the tendency in the sixteenth century for the urban population of Europe to rise and its susceptibility to plague, it is likely that crises arose in some churchyards in the course of that century. It was certainly in the sixteenth century that the old objection to burial in churches was taken up anew by Protestant reformers, with results discussed elsewhere in this book,★ and it was early in the seventeenth century that the German Protestant author of *Christianopolis* (1619) proposed as part of his scheme for a Utopian state that burial should be in a spacious cemetery outside the city, with only iron crosses as memorials to the dead and a written register of the interments.

In several countries it was the Reformation itself that provided an opportunity to solve the problem of overcrowded churchyards. At Geneva one of the first acts of the newly established Protestant republic in 1536 was to close all the parochial cemeteries within its walls and to convert the extensive graveyard of a plague hospital on the south-western outskirts into a general cemetery for the city. In the same way, at Marburg in Germany the inadequate graveyard round the parish church of the Virgin Mary was supplemented in 1530 by taking over one associated with a former pilgrimage chapel on the edge of the town, while in 1568–74 a new graveyard was created outside the town walls by the purchase of gardens with the aid of a private benefaction. In Kassel the two existing grave-yards were closed in 1526–33 and the sale of church plate financed the purchase of land outside the town walls where a cemetery was created which, as the 'Altstädte Friedhof', remained in use until 1843. In Edinburgh in 1562 the town council, anxious to discontinue burial within St Giles's church and aware that 'the kirk-yard is not of sufficient room for burying of the dead', obtained a grant of the spacious site of the former Franciscan friary from the Crown, and converted it into the Greyfriars cemetery. London was deprived by the grasping regime of King Henry VIII of any opportunity to benefit in this way from the dissolution of its numerous monastic houses, but early in the seventeenth century several new cemeteries were established by the initiative of individual parishes, and the amalgamation of parishes after the Great Fire of 1666 enabled others to provide more space for burials by building vaults on the sites of demolished churches. Despite such opportunist measures the state of the churchyards in London, Paris and many other cities was by the eighteenth century shocking both to religious sentiment and to Enlightened opinion. In London John Evelyn expressed concern about the pollution of both air and water by the city graveyards, while Sir John Vanbrugh complained of 'that inhuman custom of churches being made burial-places for the dead', and in 1721 the author of a pamphlet on 'the indecent and dangerous custom of burying in churches and church-yards' denounced the practice as 'begun through Pride, improved by Superstition, and encouraged for Lucre'.

Although burial was prohibited in the new churches built in the suburbs of

★ See above, p. 296.

London under the Act of 1711,★ no English government showed a disposition to tackle the problem by general legislation until the nineteenth century, and it was in France that Enlightened opinion first succeeded in bringing about a national revolution in burial practice. According to contemporary science it was by infecting the air that many diseases were transmitted, and there was every reason to suppose that the effluvia from overcrowded burial grounds like that of the Holy Innocents in Paris were a danger to public health. In 1765 the Parlement of Paris ordered all parochial cemeteries to be removed to new sites outside the city, and in 1776 a royal decree ordained a general review of burial grounds throughout the country. Those deemed too small were to be enlarged, and those located within built-up areas that were considered to be harmful to the salubrity of the air were to be removed to new sites.

Other countries soon followed the French example. In Sweden burial in churches was banned in 1783. In Spain the publication by a clerical professor of a treatise demonstrating that burial in churches was a medieval innovation encouraged the state to prohibit the practice by decrees of 1785–7. In 1784–8 edicts of the Emperor Joseph II made similar regulations throughout the imperial territories (which then included the Austrian Netherlands and much of northern Italy). In Bavaria burial within city boundaries was forbidden in 1803. Finally, in 1804 all interment within churches in France was prohibited by a decree of Napoleon I, and every urban community was required to establish a cemetery at a distance of at least 35–40 metres from its boundaries. The result was not only the general closure of urban burial grounds, but often the paving, and sometimes the building, over of former churchyards and the establishment of new cemeteries on the outskirts of towns. The British government showed no inclination to follow a Napoleonic example, and it was not until 1852–7 that comparable legislation was passed for the British Isles. Even then, there was no general prohibition of burial in existing churchyards, but the Home Secretary was given powers to prohibit further interment in any given place, and provision was made for the construction of new cemeteries in appropriate localities. Cemeteries had, in fact, already been established by private enterprise – sometimes philanthropic, more often commercial – in several British cities, notably Edinburgh (Calton Hill, 1718), Belfast (1774), Norwich (1819), Manchester (1821), Liverpool (1825–9), Glasgow (1831) and London (Kensal Green, 1832).

It was a characteristic feature of the new European cemeteries of the nineteenth century that they owed their existence to secular rather than to ecclesiastical initiative and were under the control of municipalities or boards rather than of the local clergy. Many of them catered for religious denominations of all kinds and the officiating clergy came and went with the undertakers. The link between patronal saint and place of burial that a thousand years earlier had influenced the topography of so many European towns had at last been broken. And so in large

★Notwithstanding the Act, the vaults beneath Christ Church, Spitalfields, were used for burials as soon as the church was consecrated, while the parishioners of two other churches, St Paul's Deptford and St Alphege's, Greenwich, subsequently obtained Acts of Parliament permitting burial within their walls.

352. Père-Lachaise cemetery, Paris, family tombs in the form of miniature chapels.

353. Père-Lachaise cemetery, Paris, a family tomb of the 1820s, based on the choragic monument of Thrasyllus (319 BC) in Athens, published in vol. 2 of Stuart & Revett's *Antiquities of Athens* (1787).

measure had the almost symbiotic relationship between the living and the dead that, however undesirable on hygienic grounds, had been for so long one of the basic expressions of Christian piety. Only in Britain could people still be buried in many cathedral closes and in those urban churchyards that remained in use. On the Continent the destruction of the old churchyards and the establishment of the new municipal cemeteries were not always accomplished without opposition. In France the interference with long-established custom met with a good deal of passive resistance, both popular and bureaucratic, and in Lille and Cambrai it led to serious riots.

Architecturally, the new cemeteries fell broadly into two types: in the north the picturesque, in the south the monumental. Of the picturesque layout the Père-Lachaise cemetery in Paris was the archetype. It was one of three new cemeteries laid out on the outskirts of the city during the first quarter of the nineteenth century. The architect Alexandre-Théodore Brongniart envisaged from the first that the layout would be partly informal, with tombs flanking winding paths amid trees and shrubs, but the whole was to be dominated by a centrally placed funerary pyramid of the kind with which French architects had been preoccupied

369

for a generation. In the event, the pyramid was never built, and without a focal point, the cemetery unfolds as a *jardin anglais* of tombs. The monuments themselves were eclectic in design – some classical (columns, obelisks, sarcophagi, etc.), some Gothic (crosses, chapels, etc.). At first they were mostly fairly modest (more than half of the 2,000 tombs erected between 1804 and 1816 were simple headstones), but as many of the plots could be held in perpetuity, a family could bid to immortalise itself in stone, and more pretentious monuments were built as the century advanced. Many of these took the form of a miniature chapel, which could be either classical or Gothic to choice (fig. 352); others of domed or pillared aedicules derived directly or indirectly from Ancient Greek or Roman exemplars (fig. 353).

In England, the original home of the landscape garden, there was no difficulty in assimilating the idea of the garden cemetery. At Liverpool a large quarry and at Glasgow a hill, provided ideal terrains for winding paths at different levels. In 1843 J.C. Loudon, a professional landscape gardener, published a systematic treatise on the laying-out of cemeteries. His approach was rational rather than romantic, and he disapproved of cemeteries that bore 'too great a resemblance to pleasure-grounds'. Nevertheless, his abundantly planted layouts were characteristic products of the English tradition of landscape gardening, and most nineteenth-century cemeteries in Britain were planned on picturesque rather than formal lines, although not always with the flair shown at Liverpool and Glasgow.

Although in layout Père-Lachaise and the major British cemeteries had so much in common, as reflections of their respective societies they differed considerably. In France burial was now effectively concentrated in the new cemeteries, and nearly all the great men of the French republic were buried in one or other of them. Père-Lachaise, in particular, became a national necropolis and an international tourist attraction. Although it was open to those of any denomination (including Jews), it contained the graves of many who rejected the rites of the Church, and in a country sharply divided between Catholic and anti-clerical the tombs of some of the latter became objects of secular pilgrimage. In Britain only the Edinburgh cemeteries enjoyed anything approaching the status of Père-Lachaise as a gallery of the illustrious dead. In England, although some celebrities were buried in the new cemeteries, the aristocracy were still normally laid beside their ancestors in family chapels or mausolea, the political leaders were still commemorated (if not always actually buried) in Westminster Abbey, the military heroes in St Paul's cathedral. In the urban cemeteries the monuments were overwhelmingly those of the middle classes – academics, actors, architects, civil servants, doctors, engineers, lawyers, librarians, merchants and soldiers. It is no accident that in Highgate cemetery the most celebrated tomb should be that of the expatriate Karl Marx, and that although royalty is represented at Kensal Green, it is only by a minor princess and by two dukes who had defied the Royal Marriage Act by illegal marriages which debarred their wives from burial at Windsor or Frogmore.

In Italy the formal usually prevailed over the picturesque, and the serried ranks of marble mausolea stand in streets rather than in groves. In the larger cemeteries

354. Lecce, southern Italy, the Greek Doric gateway to the cemetery of 1845.

355. Bologna, the interior of one of the galleries in the early nineteenth-century cemetery.

356. Père-Lachaise cemetery, Paris, neo-classical and Art Nouveau in a great nineteenth-century cemetery. In the background the Demidoff monument of 1818, in the foreground the Guet family monument of 1905.

classical order is maintained by an axial road focussed on a monumental gateway (fig. 354), and by a more or less symmetrical layout of vaulted galleries against whose walls the individual monuments could be set as in a church. Of this type of cemetery the prototype is the one at Brescia designed by Rodolfo Vantini in 1815,

357. Versions of the altar-tomb of C. Scipio Barbatus (fig. 47) in the Père-Lachaise cemetery in Paris. These two are dated 1849 and 1867.

but one of the most striking and extensive is the great complex of galleries at Bologna, where the cemetery was begun in 1801 by taking over the buildings and site of a former Carthusian monastery (fig. 355). Other notable and well-known examples are at Verona and Genoa where, as at Brescia, the dominant feature is a Greek Doric version of the Pantheon.

In the late eighteenth and early nineteenth centuries there had been little room for pretentious monuments in the crowded graveyards of Europe. Now in the new cemeteries there was space for every grave-plot to have its carved memorial or its mini-mausoleum. Architects and others began to provide printed patterns for funerary monuments in various styles, and in any large cemetery in western Europe every variety of form, from the Egyptian to the Romanesque, from the Byzantine to the Gothic, from the baroque to the neo-classical, is to be found. Pyramids stand side by side with broken columns, Roman altars with Christian crosses. Nowhere is the eclecticism of nineteenth-century architectural taste more apparent than in a cemetery (fig. 356). Although some favourite formulae – the altar-tomb of Cornelius Scipio Barbatus, for instance, versions of which can be found from Malta to Glasgow, and from Paris to Richmond, Virginia (fig. 357) – recur all over the western world, uniformity of design was rarely if ever imposed in Europe and only once (to the author's knowledge) in America, where, in the Rock Creek cemetery at Washington, deceased members of Congress are still buried from time to time beneath elegant tombs of republican simplicity first designed in about 1815 by the architect B.H. Latrobe (fig. 358). Elsewhere stylistic anarchy prevails, and with it every diversity of material from marble or granite to cast-iron or terra-cotta. A laborious typological analysis might reveal

373

358. Monuments to Congressmen in the Congressional cemetery, Washington, D.C., U.S.A., following a design provided by B.H. Latrobe in about 1815.

some social, political or religious determinants of choice, and trace the influence, by pattern-book, photograph or monumental mason's catalogue, of one cemetery on another.

In Britain the triumph of the cemetery in its nineteenth-century form has been relatively short-lived. Death is no longer an event to be celebrated by major ceremonial, the grave no longer a place to be marked by substantial architectural or sculptural monuments. Indeed, many nineteenth-century British cemeteries lie neglected, vandalised and overgrown. Only the village churchyard can still, in sympathetic hands, retain something of the romantic melancholy so perfectly captured by Gray's *Elegy*. In the Catholic south, on the other hand, above all in Italy, the *cimitero monumentale* continues to fulfil a social and religious function which has not significantly changed. Vandalism and decay are little in evidence in the well-tended streets of tombs and *columbaria*. New mausolea of concrete and glass spring up to house the twentieth-century dead as stone and marble did in the past. At Modena a vast new sepulchral complex – realising in the starkest spirit of the Modern Movement some of the elementary forms of Boullée and his contemporaries – is being built to the designs of a celebrated modern architect. Like the Pisan Campo Santo in the thirteenth century, it is a civic enterprise which represents a new episode in the continuing story of architecture in its relation to the after-life.

374

BIBLIOGRAPHY

The main purpose of this bibliography is to list the books, articles and (in a few cases) manuscript sources that have been used in writing this book. Some books and articles describing select structures not mentioned in the text are, however, included.

Thus, under Chapter V the reader will find a fairly extensive (but far from exhaustive) bibliography of Roman mausolea, many of which do not figure by name in that chapter.

GENERAL

Ariès P., *The Hour of our Death* (London 1981, trans. from French edn of 1977).

Curl, J. Stevens, *A Celebration of Death. An introduction to some of the buildings, monuments, and settings of funerary architecture in the Western European tradition* (London 1980).

Panofsky, E., *Tomb Sculpture* (New York 1964).

Vovelle, M., *La Mort et l'Occident de 1300 à nos Jours* (Paris 1983).

Whaley, J., ed., *Mirrors of Mortality: Studies in the Social History of Death* (London 1981).

I MEGALITH AND TUMULUS

Neolithic

Atkinson, R.J.C., 'Neolithic Engineering', *Antiquity* 35 (1961).

Ceschi, C., *Architettura dei Templi Megalithici di Malta* (Rome 1939).

Chapman, R., 'The emergence of formal disposal areas and the problem of megalithic tombs in prehistoric Europe', in *The Archaeology of Death*, ed. R. Chapman, I. Kinnes and K. Randsborg (Cambridge 1981).

Daniel, G., *The Prehistoric Chamber Tombs of France* (London 1960).

Eogan, G., *Knowth and the Passage-tombs of Ireland* (London 1986).

Evans, E.E. & Davies, O., 'Excavation of a . . . Cairn [at] Browndod, Co. Antrim', *Proceedings of the Belfast Natural History & Philosophical Society* 1934–5.

Evans, J.D., *Prehistoric Antiquities of the Maltese Islands* (London 1971).

Evans, J.D., Cunliffe, B.; and Renfrew, C., *Anti-*

quity and Man, Essays in Honour of Glyn Daniel (London 1981).

Fergusson, J., *Rude Stone Monuments* (London 1872).

Fleming, A., 'Vision and design: approaches to ceremonial monument typology', *Man*, N.S. 7 (1972).

Fleming, A., 'Tombs for the Living', *Man*, N.S. 8 (1973).

Giot, P.R., *Brittany* (London 1960).

Guido, M., *Sardinia* (London 1963).

Hedges, J., *Tomb of the Eagles* [Isbister, Orkney] (London 1984).

Henshall, A.H., *The Chambered Tombs of Scotland*, 2 vols. (Edinburgh 1963, 1972).

Herity, M., *Irish Passage Graves* (Dublin 1974).

Joussaume, R., 'Le dolmen à couloir dit la Ciste des Cous à Bazoges-en-Pareds (Vendée)', *Bulletin de la Société préhistorique française*, 75 (1978).

Joussaume, R., *Des Dolmens pour les Morts* (Paris 1985).

Kinnes, I., 'Monumental function in British

neolithic burial practice', *World Archaeology* 7 (1975–6).

Leisner, G. & V., *Die Megalithgräber der Iberischen Halbinsel*, 3 vols. (Berlin 1956–65).

Lynch, F., *Prehistoric Anglesey* (Anglesey Antiquarian Society 1970).

Mackie, E., *The Megalith Builders* (London 1977).

O'Kelly, M., *Newgrange* (London 1982).

Piggott, S., *Neolithic Cultures of the British Isles* (Cambridge 1954).

Piggott, S., 'Architecture and Ritual in Megalithic Monuments', *Journal of the Royal Institute of British Architects*, 3rd ser. 63 (March 1956), pp. 175–80.

Powell, T.G.E., *Megalithic Enquiries in the West of England* (Liverpool 1969).

Renfrew, C., *Before Civilisation* (London 1973).

Renfrew, C., 'Megaliths, Territories and Population', in *Acculturation and Continuity in Atlantic Europe*, ed. S.J. de Laet (Brugge 1976).

Shand, P. & Hodder, I., 'Haddenham', *Current Archaeology* 118 (1990).

Trump, D., 'Megalithic Architecture in Malta', in Evans, Cunliffe & Renfrew, *Antiquity and Man, Essays in Honour of Glyn Daniel* (London 1981).

Trump, D., 'I primi architetti: i costruttori dei Templi Maltesi', in *Miscellanea di Studi Classici in onore di Eugenio Manni* 6 (Rome 1980).

Twohig, E. Shee, *The Megalithic Art of Western Europe* (Oxford 1981).

Mycenae and the Tholos Tomb

Blegen, C.W., et al., *The Palace of Nestor at Pylos*, 3 (Princeton 1973).

Boyd, T.D., 'The Arch and the Vault in Greek Architecture', *American Journal of Archaeology* 82 (1978).

Branigan, K., *The Tombs of Mesara, a study of Funerary Architecture and Ritual in Southern Crete, 2800–1700 BC* (London 1970).

Cabré, J. & De Motos, F., 'La Necrópolis Ibérica de Tútugi', *Junta Superior de Excavaciones y Antigüedades*, 4, 1918 (Madrid 1920).

Caputo, G., 'La Montagnola di Quinto Fiorentino . . . e le Tholoi dell' Arno', *Bollettino d'Arte* 47 (1962).

Cavanagh, W.G. & Laxton, R.R., 'The Structural Mechanics of the Mycenean Tholos Tomb', *Annual of the British School at Athens* 76 (1981).

Cavanagh, W.G. & Laxton, R.R., 'Problem Solving and the Architecture of Tholos Tombs', *Problems in Greek Prehistory*, ed. French & Wardle (Bristol 1988).

Danov, H. & Ivanov, T., *Antique Tombs in Bulgaria* (Sofia 1980).

Dickinson, O.T.P.K., 'Cist graves and Chamber Tombs', *Annual of the British School at Athens* 78 (1983).

Dinsmoor, W.B., *The Architecture of Ancient Greece* (New York 1975).

Filov, B., 'Die Kuppelgräber von Mezek', *Bulletin de l'Institut archéologique bulgare* 11 (1937) and summary in *Antiquity* 11 (1937), pp. 300–5.

Frizell, B.S. & Santillo, R., 'The construction and structural behaviour of the Mycenean tholos tomb', *Opuscula Atheniensia* 15 (Stockholm 1984).

Harding, A.F., *The Myceneans and Europe* (London 1984).

Hasluck, F.W., 'A Thracian Tholos Tomb', *Annual of the British School at Athens*, 17 (1910–11).

Heurtley, W.A. & Skeat, T.C., 'The Tholos Tomb of Marmáriane', *Annual of the British School at Athens* 31 (1930–1).

Hood, M.S.F., 'Tholos Tombs of the Aegean', *Antiquity* 34 (1960).

Hooker, J.T., *Mycenean Greece* (London 1977).

Kurz, D.C. & Boardman, J., *Greek Burial Customs* (London 1971).

Minns, E.H., *Scythians and Greeks* (Cambridge 1913).

Mylonas, G., *Mycenae and the Mycenean Age* (Princeton 1966).

Pelon, O., *Tholoi, tumuli et cercles funéraires* (Athens and Paris 1976).

Persson, A.W., *The Royal Tombs at Dendra near Midea* (Lund 1931).

Piggot, S., 'The Tholos Tomb in Iberia', *Antiquity* 27 (1953).

Popham, M., et al., 'The hero of Lefkandi', *Antiquity* 56 (1982).

Roux, G., *L'Architecture de l'Argolide aux IVe et IIIe siècles avant J.C.* (Paris 1961).

Snodgrass, A.M., *The Dark Age of Greece* (Edinburgh 1971).

Talbot Rice, T., *The Scythians* (London 1957).

Taylour, Lord W., *The Myceneans* (London 1964).

Thiersch, F., 'die Tholos des Atreus zu Mykenae', *Mittheilungen des Deutschen Archäologischen Instituts in Athen* 4 (1879).

Valmin, N., 'Tholos Tombs and Tumuli', *Corolla Archaeologica Gustavo Adolpho dedicata* (Lund 1932).

Wace, A.J.B., et al., 'Excavations at Mycenae', *Annual of the British School at Athens* 24, 25 (1920–3).

Wace, A.J.B., 'The Treasury of Atreus', *Antiquity* 14 (1940).

Wace, A.J.B., *Mycenae* (Princeton 1949).

Wilkie, N.C. & McDonald, W.A., 'How the Myceneans buried their Dead', *Archaeology* 37, no. 6 (1984).

Xanthoudides, S., *The Vaulted Tombs of Mesará* (Liverpool 1924).

II · FROM TUMULUS TO MAUSOLEUM

Andronikos, M., *Vergina. The Royal Tombs and the Ancient City* (Athens 1984).

Andronikos, M., 'Some Reflections on the Macedonian Tombs', *Annual of the British School at Athens* 82 (1987).

Benndorf, O. & Niemann, G., *Das Heroön von Gjölbaschi-Trysa* (Vienna 1889).

Bérard, C., *Eretria III: L'Héroön à la porte de l'ouest* (Berne 1970).

Borchhardt, J., 'Das Heroon von Limyra', *Jahrbuch des Deutschen Archäologischen Instituts: Archäologischer Anzeiger* 85 (1970).

Borchhardt, J., *Die Bausculptur des Heroons von Limyra* (Berlin 1976).

Boyd, T.D., 'The Arch and the Vault in Greek Architecture', *American Journal of Archaeology* 82 (1978).

Cahill, N., 'Taş Kule: a Persian-Period Tomb near Phokaia', *American Journal of Archaeology* 92 (1988).

Childs, W.A.P., 'Prolegomena to a Lycian chronology: the Nereid Monument from Xanthos', *Opuscula Romana* 9 (1973).

Coarelli, F. & Thébert, Y., 'Architecture funéraire et pouvoir: réflections sur l'Héllenisme Numide', *Mélanges de l'école française de Rome: Antiquité* 100 (1988).

Collignon, M., *Les Statues funéraires dans l'art Grec* (Paris 1911).

Cormack, S., 'A Mausoleum at Ariassos, Pisidia', *Anatolian Studies* 39 (1989).

Coupel, P. & Demargne, P., *Fouilles de Xanthos*, 3 and 5 (Paris 1969–74).

Deler, P., 'Megalithic Thracian Tombs in Southeastern Bulgaria', *Anatolica* 11 (1984).

Deltour-Levie, C., *Les piliers funéraires de Lycie* (Louvain 1982).

Dyggve, E., *Das Heroön von Kalydon* (Copenhagen 1934).

Fellows, C., *The Xanthian Marbles, their acquisition and transmission to England* (London 1848).

Frazer, J.G., *Pausanias' Description of Greece*, 6 vols. (London 1898).

Garland, R., *The Greek Way of Death* (London 1985).

Hammond, N.G.L., 'Philip's Tomb in Historical Context', *Greek, Roman and Byzantine Studies* 19 (1978).

Hanfmann, G.M.A., *From Croesus to Constantine. The Cities of Western Asia Minor and their Arts in Greek and Roman Times* (Ann Arbor, Michigan 1975).

Hansen, E.V., *The Attalids of Pergamon* (Cornell 1971).

Kjeldsen, K. & Zahle, J., 'Lykische Gräber',

Jahrbuch des Deutschen Archäologischen Instituts: Archäologischer Anzeiger, 90 (1975).

Kjeldsen, K. & Zahle, J., 'A Dynastic Tomb in Central Lycia', *Acta Archaeologica* 47 (Copenhagen 1976).

Koenigs, W., Knigge, U. & Mallwitz, A., *Rundbauten im Kerameikos* (Deutsches Archäologisches Institut, *Kerameikos*, 12, Berlin 1980).

Kontoleon, N.M., *Aspects de la Grèce préclassique* (Paris 1970).

Kurtz, D.C. & Boardman, J., *Greek Burial Customs* (London 1971).

Lenormant, F., *Monographie de la voie sacrée Eleusinienne* (Paris 1864).

Macridy, T., 'Un tumulus Macédonien à Langaza', *Jahrbuch des Deutschen Archäologischen Instituts* 26 (1911).

Martin, R., 'Le Monument des Néréides et l'architecture funéraire', *Revue archéologique* N.S. 1971.

Martin, R., 'Bathyclès de Magnésie et le "trône" d'Apollon à Amkylae', *Revue archéologique* N.S. 1976(2).

Miller, S.G., 'Macedonian Tombs: their Architecture and Architectural Decoration', *Studies in the History of Art* 10 (National Gallery of Art, Washington, 1982).

Oleson, J.P., *The Sources of Innovation in Late Etruscan Tomb Design* (Rome 1982).

Paton, W.R. & Myres, J.L., 'Karian Sites and Inscriptions', *Journal of Hellenic Studies* 18 (1898).

Pedley, J.G., *Sardis in the Age of Croesus* (Oklahoma 1968).

Petsas, P.M., *O Taphos ton Lefkadion* (Athens 1966).

Robert, F., *Thymélé* (Paris 1939).

Roos, P., 'The Rock-cut Tomb Doors of the Lyco-Carian Borderland', *Opuscula Atheniensia* 10 (Stockholm 1971).

Roos, P., *The Rock-cut Tombs of Caunus* (Göteborg 1972).

Roux, G., 'Le monument des Néréides à Xanthos', *Revue des études grecques* 88 (1975).

Snell, B., *Scenes from Greek Drama* (California 1964).

Tomlinson, R.A., 'The Architectural Context of the Macedonian Royal Tombs', *Annual of the British School at Athens* 82 (1987).

Tsirivakos, E.K., 'Kallithea: Ergebnisse der Ausgrabung', *Athens Annals of Archaeology* 4 (1971), pp. 108–10.

Vollgraff, W.W., 'Le pilier tombal', *Comptes rendus de l'Académie des inscriptions et belles-lettres* 1846, pp. 281 et seq.

Waelkens, M., 'Das Totenhaus in Kleinasien', *Antike Welt* 11 (1980).

III THE MAUSOLEUM OF HALICARNASSUS

The Mausoleum and Similar Buildings in Greece and Asia Minor

Adler, F., *Das Mausoleum zu Halikarnass* (Berlin 1900).

Ashmole, B., *Architect and Sculptor in Classical Greece* (London 1972), chap. 6.

Badian, E., 'A King's Notebooks', *Harvard Studies in Classical Philology* 72 (1967) (for the diversion of Alexander's body to Alexandria).

Bean, G.E. & Cook, J.M., 'The Halicarnassus Peninsula', *Annual of the British School at Athens* 50 (1955).

Bernier, L., French 'Envoi' drawings made in 1877, reproduced in *Paris, Rome, Athens. Travels in Greece by French Architects in the Nineteenth and Twentieth Centuries* (Museum of Fine Arts, Houston, Texas 1982).

Breen, J. van, *Het Reconstructieplan voor het Mausoleum te Halikarnassos* (Amsterdam 1942).

Broneer, O., *The Lion Monument of Amphipolis* (Cambridge, Mass. 1941).

Canina, L., *Architettura Greca* (Rome 1834–41).

Caylus, Comte de, 'Dissertation sur le tombeau de Mausole', *Mémoires de l'Académie royale des inscriptions et belles-lettres* 26 (1759 for 1753–4).

Ceka, N., 'La Ville Illyrienne de la Basse-Selce', *L'Illyrie* 2 (Tirana 1972).

Dinsmoor, W.B., 'The Mausoleum at Halicarnassus', *American Journal of Archaeology* 12 (1908).

Falkener, E., *The Museum of Classical Antiquities* (London 1860), chap. 15.

Fedak, J., *Monumental Tombs of the Hellenistic Age* (Toronto 1990).

Frazer, P.M., *Ptolemaic Alexandria* (Oxford 1972).

Goodchild, D.E., *A Study of the Halicarnassian Marbles in the British Museum with reference to the Restorations of the Tomb of Mausolus by the late Prof. C.R. Cockerell* (Walthamstow 1888).

Hornblower, S., *Mausolus* (Oxford 1982).

Jeppesen, K., *Paradeigmata* (Aarhus 1958).

Jeppesen, K., *The Maussolleion at Halikarnassos*, 2 vols. (Aarhus 1981, 1986).

Jeppesen, K., 'Neue Ergebnisse zur Wiederherstellung des Mausolleions von Halikarnassos', *Istanbuler Mitteilungen* 26 (1976).

Krischen, F., 'Ionische Bauten Kleinasiens und der Aufbau des Maussoleums von Halikarnass', *Bonner Jahrbücher* 128 (1923).

Krischen, F., *Weltwunder der Baukunst in Babylonien und Ionien* (Tübingen 1956).

Krüger, E., 'Der Aufbau des Mausoleums von Halikarnass', *Bonner Jahrbücher* 127 (1922).

Law, H.W., 'The Mausoleum', *Journal of Hellenic Studies* 59 (1939).

Lethaby, W.R., *Greek Buildings represented by Fragments in the British Museum* (London 1908).

Newton, C.T., 'On the Sculptures from the Mausoleum of Halicarnassus' (with restoration by C.R. Cockerell), *Classical Museum* 16 (1847).

Newton, C.T. & Pullan, R.P., *A History of Discoveries at Halicarnassus, Cnidus and Branchidae* (London 1862).

Oldfield, E., 'The Mausoleum at Halicarnassus. A new Restoration', *Archaeologia* 54 (1895).

Pars, W., *Antiquities of Ionia published by the Society of Dilettanti* 2 (London 1797).

Picard, C., *Manuel d'Archéologie grecque* 4(2) (Paris 1963), pp. 1180–91, 1284–5.

Praschniker, C. & Theuer, M., *Das Mausoleum von Belevi* (Forschungen in Ephesos 6, Vienna 1979).

Richard, J.C., 'Mausoleum: D'Halicarnasse à Rome, puis à Alexandrie', *Latomus* 29 (1970).

Robertson, M., *A History of Greek Art* (Cambridge 1975), chap. 7.

Roger, J., 'Le Monument au Lion d'Amphipolis', *Bulletin de Correspondance Hellénique* 63 (1939).

Schazmann, P., 'Das Charmileion', *Jahrbuch des Deutschen Archäologischen Instituts* 49 (1934).

Sherwin-White, S.M., 'Inscriptions from Cos', *Zeitschrift für Papyrologie und Epigraphik* 24 (1977), pp. 205–217.

Six, J., 'Het Mausoleum', *Architectura* 23 (1904).

Stevens, G.P., 'Model of the Monument of the Lion of Amphipolis', *Mélanges Ch. Picard* 2 (Paris 1949).

Stevenson, J.J., 'A Restoration of the Mausoleum at Halicarnassus', *Builder* 29 Aug. 1896.

Thiersch, H., 'Die alexandrinische Königsnekropole', *Jahrbuch des Deutschen Archäologischen Instituts* 25 (1910).

Waywell, G.B., *The free-standing Sculptures of the Mausoleum at Halicarnassus in the British Museum* (London 1978).

Waywell, G.B., 'Mausolea in South-west Asia Minor', *Yayla, Third Report of the Northern Society for Anatolian Archaeology* (Newcastle upon Tyne 1980).

Williams, C., 'The Corinthian Temple of Zeus Olbios at Uzuncaburç', *American Journal of Archaeology* 78 (1974), pp. 408–9 (for the Belevi mausoleum).

Hellenistic Tombs in North Africa

Camps, G., *Monuments et rites funéraires protohistoriques* [de la Bérberie] (Paris 1961).

Camps, G., 'Le Médracen, mausolée royal de Numidie', *Comptes rendus de l'Académie des inscriptions et belles-lettres* 1973.

Camps, G., 'Les Numides et la civilisation punique', *Antiquités Africaines* 14 (1979).

Cassels, J., 'The Cemeteries of Cyrene', *Papers of the British School at Rome* 23 (1955).

Christofle, M., *Le Tombeau de la Chrétienne* (Paris 1951) and review by P. Romanelli in *Archaeologia Classica* 4 (1952), p. 274.

Gsell, S., *Les Monuments Antiques de l'Algérie* (Paris 1901).

Picard, C., 'La conception du mausolée chez les Puniques et chez les Numides', *Rivista di Studi Fenici* 1 (1973).

Poinssot, C. & Salomonson, J.W., 'Un monument punique inconnu: le mausolée d'Henchir Djaouf', *Oudheidkundige Mededelingen* 44 (1963).

Rakob, F., 'Architecture royale Numide', in *Architecture et Société d'archaisme grec à la fin de la République Romaine* (Collection de l'école française de Rome 66, Paris and Rome 1983).

Reygasse, M., *Monuments funéraires préislamiques de l'Afrique du Nord* (Paris 1950).

Rowe, A., 'The . . . Rock-cut Tombs at Cyrene', *Cyrenaican Expedition of the University of Manchester* (Manchester 1952).

Stucchi, S., 'L'architettura funeraria suburbana cirenaica', *Quaderni di Archeologia della Libya* 12 (1987).

Tomlinson, R.A., 'False-facade tombs at Cyrene', *Annual of the British School at Athens*, 62 (1967).

Vita, A. Di, 'Il mausoleo Punico-Ellenistico B di Sabratha', *Mitteilungen des Deutschen Archaeologischen Instituts* (Rome), 83 (1976).

IV THE MAUSOLEA OF THE ROMAN EMPERORS

Rome (Augustus, Hadrian and Maxentius)

Bartoli, A., 'L'Architettura del Mausoleo di Augusto', *Bollettino d'Arte* 7 (1927).

Boatwright, M.T., *Hadrian and the City of Rome* (Princeton 1987).

Borgatti, M., *Castel Sant' Angelo in Roma* (Rome 1931).

Bruhl, A., 'Le souvenir d'Alexandre le Grand et les Romains', *Mélanges d'archéologie et d'histoire* 47 (1930).

Buchner, E., *Die Sonnenuhr des Augustus* (Mainz 1982).

Buchner, E., 'L'Orologio solare di Augusto', *Rendiconti. Atti della Pontificia Accademia Romana di Archeologia* 53–4 for 1980–2 (1984).

Coarelli, F., *Roma Sepolta* (Rome 1984), chap. 4.

Cordingley, R.A. & Richmond, I.A., 'The Mausoleum of Augustus', *Papers of the British School at Rome* 10 (1927).

De'Spagnolis, M., 'Contributi per una nuova lettura del Mausoleo di Adriano', *Bollettino d'Arte* 61 (1976).

Eisner, M., 'Zur Typologie der Mausoleen des Augustus und des Hadrian', *Mitteilungen des Deutschen Archaeologischen Instituts* (Rome), 86 (1979).

Fiorilli, E., 'A proposito del Mausoleo di Augusto', *Bollettino d'Arte* 7 (1927).

Frazer, A., 'The Iconography of the Emperor Maxentius' Buildings in Via Appia', *Art Bulletin* 48 (1966).

Frazer, A.K., 'The pyre of Faustina Senior', *Studies in Classical Art & Archaeology: a tribute to P.H. von Blanckenhagen* (Locust Valley, New York 1979).

Giglioli, G.Q., 'Il Mausoleo d'Augusto', *Capitolium* no. 10 (1930).

Holloway, R.R., 'The Tomb of Augustus and the Princes of Troy', *American Journal of Archaeology* 70 (1966).

Horsfall, N., 'Augustus' Sundial', *Omnibus* (University Coll. London), 9 (1985).

Kienast, D., 'Augustus und Alexander', *Gymnasium* 76 (1969).

Pierce, S. Rowland, 'The Mausoleum of Hadrian and the Pons Aelius', *Journal of Roman Studies* 15 (1925).

Platner, S. & Ashby, T., *A Topographical Dictionary of Ancient Rome* (Oxford 1929), pp. 247, 332–8, 479.

Price, S., 'From noble funerals to divine cult: the consecration of Roman Emperors', in *Rituals of Royalty*, ed. Cannadine & Price (Cambridge 1987).

Rasch, J.J., *Das Maxentius-Mausoleum an der Via Appia in Rom* (Mainz 1984).

Reekmans, L., 'Le développement topographique de la région du Vatican à la fin de l'antiquité et au début du Moyen Age (300–850)', in *Mélanges d'archéologie et d'histoire de l'Art offerts au Professeur Jacques Lavalleye* (Louvain 1970).

Res Gestae Divi Augusti, ed. P.A. Brunt & J.M. Moore (London 1967).

Richard, J.C., 'Incineration et inhumation aux funérailles impériales: Histoire du rituel de l'apothéose pendant le Haut-Empire', *Latomus* 25 (1966).

Richard, J.C., 'Tombeaux des empereurs et temples des divi', *Revue de l'histoire des Religions* 170 (1966).

Richard, J.C., 'Mausoleum: D'Halicarnasse à Rome, puis à Alexandrie', *Latomus* 29 (1970).

Rodriguez-Almeida, E., 'Il Campo Marzio settentrionale: Solarium e Pomerium', *Rendiconti. Atti della Pontificia Academia Romana di Archeologia* 51–2 for 1978–80 (1982).

Syme, R., *The Roman Revolution* (Oxford 1952).

Virgili, P., 'A proposito del Mausoleo di Augusto: Baldassarre Peruzzi aveva ragione', *Archeologia Laziale* 6 (1984).

Salonica (Galerius)

Hébrard, E., 'L'arc de Galère et l'église Saint-Georges à Salonique', *Bulletin de Correspondance Hellénique*, 44 (1920).

Split (Diocletian)

Hébrard, E. & Zeiller, J., *Spalato, Le Palais de Dioclétien* (Paris 1912).

Wilkes, J.J., *Diocletian's Palace, Split* (Sheffield

1986) and review by N. Duval in *Bulletin Monumental* 144 (1986), pp. 354–6.

Williams, S., *Diocletian and the Roman Recovery* (London 1985).

Ravenna (Theodoric)

Bovini, G., *Il Mausoleo di Theodorico* (Ravenna 1959).

De Angelis d'Ossat, G., *Studi Ravennati* (Ravenna 1962).

Dyggve, E., 'Mausoleo di Teodorico, le origini della cupola', *Corso di Cultura sull'arte ravennate e bizantina* 2 (Bologna 1957).

Gaddoni, W., *Il Mausoleo di Teodorico* (Ministero per i Beni Culturali, 1987).

Heidenreich, R. & Johannes, H., *Das Grabmal Theoderichs zu Ravenna* (Deutsches Archäologisches Institut, Wiesbaden 1971), and review by R. Krautheimer in *Art Bulletin* 55 (1973).

Tabarroni, G., 'La Cupola Monolithico del Mausoleo di Teodorico', *Felix Ravenna* 105 (1973).

V THE ROMANS AND THEIR MONUMENTS

General

Alcock, J.P., 'Classical Religious Belief and Burial Practice in Roman Britain', *Archaeological Journal* 137 (1980).

Altmann, W., *Die römischen grabaltäre der Kaiserseit* (Berlin 1905).

Ampolo, C., [on burial practices in Lazio in the sixth century BC] in *Dialoghi di Archeologia* N.S. 2 (1980), pp. 185–7.

Cagnat, R. & Chapot, U., *Manuel d'archéologie romaine* 1 (Paris 1916), pp. 342–61.

Cid Priego, C., 'El sepulcro de torre mediterráneo y sus relaciones con la tipología monumental', *Ampurias* 11 (1949).

Clapham, A.W., 'Roman Mausolea of the cartwheel type', *Archaeological Journal* 79 (1922).

Colini, A.M., *Il fascio littorio* (Rome 1933).

Colonna, G., 'L'ideologia funeraria e il conflitto delle culture,' *Archaeologia Laziale* 4 (1981).

Crema, L., *L'Architettura Romana*, vol. 12 of *Enciclopedia Classica* (Turin etc. 1959), s.v. 'Architettura Sepolcrale'.

Cumont, F., *After Life in Roman Paganism* (New Haven 1922).

Cumont, F., *Recherches sur le symbolisme funéraire des Romains* (Paris 1942).

Cumont, F., *Lux Perpetua* (Paris 1949).

Daremberg, C. & Saglio, E., *Dictionnaire des antiquités grecques et romaines*, 10 vols. (Paris 1877–1919).

D'Arms, J.H., *Commerce and Social Standing in Ancient Rome* (Cambridge, Mass. 1981).

Duncan-Jones, R., *The Economy of the Roman Empire* (2nd edn Cambridge 1982).

Eck, W., 'Senatorial Self-Expression . . . in the Augustan Period', in *Caesar Augustus: Seven Aspects*, ed. Millar & Segal (Oxford 1984).

Frischer, B., '*Monumenta et Arae Honoris Virtutisque Causa*: Evidence of Memorials for Roman Civic Heroes', *Bulletino della Commissone Archeologica di Roma* 88 (1984).

Gabelmann, H., *Römische Grabbauten der frühen Kaiserzeit* (Stuttgart 1979).

Hopkins, K., *Death and Renewal . . . in Roman History* (Cambridge 1983).

Huelsen, C., 'Piante icnografiche incise in marmo', *Mittheilungen des Deutschen Archaeologischen Instituts* (Rome), 5 (1890).

Kleiner, D.E.E., 'Roman funerary art and architecture: observations on the significance of recent studies, *Journal of Roman Archaeology* 1 (1988).

Kovacsovics, W.K., *Römische Grabdenkmäler* (Waldsassen 1983).

Lachmann, K. & Rudorff, A., *Die Schriften der Römischen Feldmesser* (Berlin 1848–52).

Lawrence, M., 'Season Sarcophagi of Architectural Type', *American Journal of Archaeology* 62 (1958).

MacDonald, W.L., *The Architecture of the Roman Empire* 2 (New Haven and London 1986).

Parrot, A., *Malédictions et Violations de Tombes* (Paris 1939).

Picard, G.C., *Les Trophées Romains* (Paris 1957).

Price, S.R.F., *Rituals and Power, the Roman imperial cult in Asia Minor* (Cambridge 1984).

Purcell, N., 'Tomb and Suburb', in *Römische Gräberstrassen*, ed. von Hessberg & Zanker (Munich 1987).

Rawson, E., 'Architecture and Sculpture: the Activities of the Cossutii', *Papers of the British School at Rome* 43 (1975).

Reece, R. ed., *Burial in the Roman World* (Council for British Archaeology 1977).

Rushforth, G. McN., 'Funeral Lights in Roman Sepulchral Monuments', *Journal of Roman Studies* 5 (1915).

Sanpaolese, P., 'Strutture a cupola autoportanti', *Palladio* 21 (1971).

Shackleton-Bailey, D.R. ed., *Cicero's Letters to Atticus* 5 (Cambridge 1966).

Strong, D.E., 'The Administration of Public Works during the late Republic and Early Empire', *Bulletin of the Institute of Classical Studies* 15 (1968).

Stucchi, S., 'Fari, Campanili e Mausolei', *Aquileia Nostra* 30 (1959).

Torelli, M., 'Monumenti funerari romani con fregio dorico', *Dialoghi di Archeologia* 2 (1968).

Toynbee, J.M.C., *Death and Burial in the Roman World* (London 1971).

Visscher, F. de, *Le Droit des Tombeaux Romains* (Milan 1963).

Walker, S., *Memorials of the Roman Dead* (British Museum 1985).

Ward-Perkins, J.B., *Roman Imperial Architecture* (Penguin Books 1981).

Wightman, E.M., *Gallia Belgica* (London 1985).

Windfeld-Hansen, H., 'Les couloirs annulaires dans l'architecture funéraire antique', *Acta of the Institutum Romanum Norvegiae* 2 (Rome 1965).

Zanker, P., *The Power of Images in the Age of Augustus* (Michigan 1988).

Inscriptions on Funerary Monuments

Brelich, A., *Aspetti della morte nelle inscrizioni sepolcrali dell' Impero Romano* (Budapest 1937).

Corpus Inscriptionum Latinarum, 17 vols. (1863–1986), cited as *C.I.L.*

Huttunen, P., *The Social Strata in the Imperial City of Rome* (Oulu 1974).

Kubińska, J., *Les Monuments funéraires dans les inscriptions grecques de l'Asie Mineure* (Warsaw 1968).

Lattimore, R., *Themes in Greek and Latin Epitaphs* (Illinois 1942).

Saller, R.P. & Shaw, B.D., 'Tombstones and Roman family relations in the Principate', *Journal of Roman Studies* 74 (1984).

Pyramids

Demus-Quatember, M., *Est et alia pyramis* (Osterreiches Kulturinstitut in Rom 1974).

Dens, C. & Poils, I., 'La pyramide cinéraire de Ladeuze', *Annales de la Société d'archéologie de Bruxelles* 27 (1913).

Neuerburg, N., 'Greek and Roman Pyramids', *Archaeology* 22 (1969).

Roullet, A., *The Egyptian and Egyptianizing Monuments of Imperial Rome* (Leiden 1972).

Funerary Monuments of the Roman Empire by Regions

AFRICA

Berthier, A., *La Numidie: Rome et le Maghreb* (Paris 1981).

Caputo, G., 'Scavi Sahariani', *Monumenti Antichi* 41 (1951), pp. 252–67.

Daniels, C.M., *The Garamantes of Southern Libya* (Oleander Press, Roughton, Wisconsin and North Harrow, U.K. 1970).

Ferchiou, N., 'Le mausolée anonyme de Thuburnica', *Mélanges de l'école française de Rome: Antiquité* 98 (1986).

Gsell, S., *Les Monuments Antiques de l'Algérie* (Paris 1901).

Renier, L., 'Notice sur le Tombeau de T. Flavius Maximus', *Revue archéologique* 7 (1850–1).

ASIA MINOR

Akurgal, E., *Ancient Civilisations and Ruins of Turkey* (Istanbul 1978).

Bean, G.E., *Turkey's Southern Shore* (London 1968).

Perrot, G. & Chipiez, C., *Histoire de l'Art dans l'Antiquité* 5 (Paris 1890).

Rosenbaum, E., et al., *A Survey of Coastal Cities in Western Cilicia* (Ankara 1967).

Monumenta Asiae Minoris Antiqua, ed. Calder et al., 8 vols. (Manchester 1928–62).

Tituli Asiae Minoris, ed. Kalinka et al. (Vienna 1901–   ).

Caria

Maiuri, A., 'Viaggio di esplorazione in Caria', *Annuario della Scuola archeologica di Atene*, 4–5 (1924).

Ephesus

Keil, J., 'Vorläufiger Bericht über die Ausgrabungen in Ephesos', *Jahreshefte des Österreichischen archäologischen Institutes in Wien* 26 (1930), Beiblatt.

Hierapolis (Phrygia)

Schneider Equini, E., *Le Necropoli di Hierapolis di Frigia*, *Monumenti Antichi*, ser. Misc. I. ii (1972).

Kanytelleis

Verzone, P., 'Kanytelleis', *Palladio* 7 (1957), pp. 66–8.

Limyra (Cenotaph of Gaius Caesar)

Borchhardt, J., 'Ein Kenotaph für Gaius Caesar', *Jahrbuch des Deutschen Archäologischen Instituts* 89 (1974).

Eisner, M., et al., *Das Kenotaph für Gaius Caesar in Limyra* (Tübingen 1984).

Nemrud-Dagh (Cappadocia)

Goell, T., 'Excavation of the Hierotherion of Antiochus I of Commagene', *Bulletin of the American School of Oriental Research* 147 (Oct. 1957).

Musti, D., 'Morte e culto del sovrano in ambitu ellenistico', in *La mort, les morts dans les sociétés anciennes*, ed. Gnoli & Vernant (Cambridge 1982).

Sardis

Butler, H.C., *Sardis*, 2 vols. (Leiden 1922–5).

Side

Mansel, A.M., *Die Ruinen von Side* (Berlin 1963).

Mansel, A.M., *Side* (in Turkish, Ankara 1978).

Termessos (Pisidia)

Heberdey, R. & Wilberg, W., 'Grabbauten von Termessos in Pisidia', *Jahreshefte des Österreichischen archäologischen Institutes in Wien* 3 (1900).

Lanckoronski, K., et al., *Städte Pamphyliens und Pisidiens* (Vienna 1890–2).

BRITAIN

Dunning, G.C. & Jessup, R.F., 'Roman Barrows' *Antiquity* 10 (1936).

Fox, Sir C., *The Archaeology of the Cambridge Region* (Cambridge 1923).

Gillam, J.P. & Daniels, C.M., 'The Roman Mausoleum on Shorden Brae, Beaufront, Corbridge, Northumberland', *Archaeologia Aeliana* 4th ser. 39 (1961).

Jessup, R.F., 'Barrows and Walled Cemeteries in Roman Britain', *Journal of the British Archaeological Association* 3rd ser. 22 (1959).

Meates, G.W., *The Roman Villa at Lullingstone* (Maidstone 1979–87).

Rook, T. et al., 'A Roman Mausoleum . . . from Welwyn, Hertfordshire', *Britannia* 15 (1984).

Smith, I.F. & Simpson, D.D.A., 'Excavation of three Roman Tombs . . . on Overton Down', *Wiltshire Archaeological Magazine* 59 (1964).

Tufi, S.R., 'Le due Stele funerarie Palmirene di Arbeia (South Shields)' *Dialoghi di Archeologia* 3rd ser. 5 (1987).

Wheeler, H., 'The Racecourse Cemetery [Derby]', *Derbyshire Archaeological Journal* 105 (1985).

FRANCE, BELGIUM AND LUXEMBOURG

Barruol, G., 'Le monument funéraire de Ville-longue d'Aude', *Cahiers Ligures de préhistoire et d'archéologie* 12 (1963).

Burnard, Y., *Domitii Aquenses: une famille de chevaliers Romains de la région d'Aix-en-Provence, Mausolée et Domaine* (*Revue archéologique de Narbonnaise*, Supplément 5, Paris 1975).

Burnard, Y., 'Le monument Gallo-Romain dit la Sarrasinière à Andance (Ardèche)', *Gallia* 37 (1979).

Clerc, M., *Aquae Sextiae* (Aix-en-Provence 1916).

Espérandieu, E., *Recueil général des Bas-Reliefs de la Gaule Romaine*, 16 vols. (Paris 1907–81).

Euzennat, M., 'Le Monument à Rotonde de la Nécropole du Cirque à Arles', *Comptes rendus de l'Académie des inscriptions et belles-lettres*, 1972.

Faider-Feythmans, G., 'Le pilier funéraire du site des Castellains à Fontaine-Valmont (Hainault)', *Revue du Nord* 66 (1984).

Gérin-Richard, H. de, 'Les Pyramides de Provence', *Bulletin Archéologique* 1902.

Hatt, J.J., *La tombe gallo-romaine* (Paris 1951).

Heyart, H., 'Römischer Grabhügel mit ringmauer bei Bill', *Hémecht* 21 (1969).

Joulia, J.C., 'Ensemble monumental de Lanuéjols' (Losère), *Revue archéologique de Narbonnaise* 8 (1975).

Kleiner, F.S., 'Artists in the Roman World: an itinerant workshop in Augustan Gaul', *Mélanges de l'école française de Rome: Antiquité* 89(2) (1977).

Kleiner, F.S., 'Ugernum (Beaucaire) in Narbonensis', *Journal of Roman Archaeology* 2 (1989), pp. 191–4.

Lauzun, P., 'Inventaire général des piles gallo-romaines du sud-ouest de France', *Bulletin Monumental* 7th ser. 3 (1898).

Maurin, L. *Saintes Antique* (Saintes 1978).

Mortet, V., 'Les piles gallo-romaines et les textes antiques de bornage et d'arpentage', *Bulletin Monumental* 7th ser. 3 (1898).

Rolland, H., *Le Mausolée de Glanum* (Paris 1969).

GERMANY

Dragendorff, H. & Krüger, E., *Das Grabmal von Igel* (Trier 1924).

Kähler, H., 'Die rheinischen Pfeilergrabmäler', *Bonner Jahrbücher* 139 (1934).

Kähler, H., 'Das Grabmal des L. Poblicius in Köln', *Antike Welt* 1 (1970).

Koethe, H., 'Kaiserzeitliche Grabhügel mit Ringmauer im Trierer Land', *Germania* 19 (1935).

Koethe, H., 'La sculpture romaine au pays des Trévires', *Revue archéologique* 1937 (2).

Massow, W. von, *Die Grabmäler von Neumagen* (Berlin, Leipzig 1932).

Precht, G., *Das Grabmal des L. Poblicius* (Römisch-Germanisches Museum, Köln 1975).

Rebecchi, F., 'A proposito dei monumenti "a torre" nella regione renana', *Archaeologia Classica* 27 (1975).

Wightman, E.M., *Roman Trier and the Treveri* (London 1970).

Will, E., 'De l'Euphrate au Rhin: étude sur quelques motifs orientaux', *Syria* 31 (1954), pp. 271–85.

Will, E., 'Le problème du pilier funéraire de Belgique et de Germanie', *Actes du Colloque sur les influences helléniques en Gaule* (Dijon 1958).

ROME AND ITALY

Rome

Bartoli, P. Santi, *Gli antichi sepolchri, overo Mausolei Romani* (Rome 1697).

Boni, G., [on Trajan's Column] in *Notizie degli Scavi* ser. v, 4 (1907).

Boschung, D., *Antike Grabaltare aus den Nekropolen Roms* (Bern 1987).

Calza, G., *La Necropoli del Porto di Roma nell' Isola Sacra* (Rome 1940).

Canina, L., *La prima parte della Via Appia* 2 vols. (Rome 1853).

Castagnoli, F., 'Gli edifici rappresentati in un rilievo del sepolcro degli Haterii', *Bullettino della Commissione Archeologica di Roma* 69 (1941).

Cizek, E., *L'Epoque de Trajan* (Bucharest 1983), p. 470n for Trajan's Column.

Coarelli, F., 'Il Sepolcro degli Scipioni', *Dialoghi di Archeologia* 6 (1972).

Coarelli, F., *Roma, Guida archeologica* (Rome 1980).

Coarelli, F., *Roma Sepolta* (Rome 1984).

Coarelli, F., *Il Sepolcro degli Scipioni a Roma* (Rome 1988).

Colini, A.M., 'Via Collatina, Monumento sepolcrale del 1 sec. d.C.', *Bullettino della Commissione Archeologica di Roma* 79 (1964).

Crema, L., 'Due Monumenti sepolcrali sulla Via Nomentana', *Serta Hoffilleriana* (Zagreb 1940).

Degrassi, A., 'P. Cluvius Maximus Paullinus', *Scritti Vari di Antichità* 1 (Rome 1962), pp. 511–22.

Delbrueck, R., *Hellenistiche Bauten in Latium* 2 (Strasburg 1912), for the Tomb of Bibulus.

Eisner, M., *Zum Typologie der Grabbauten im Suburbium Roms* (Mainz 1986).

Frazer, A., 'The Porch of the Tor de' Schiavi at Rome', *American Journal of Archaeology* 73 (1969).

Gros, P., 'Les stucs du temple de Ceres et Faustine', *Mélanges de l'école française de Rome* 81 (1969), for the 'Tomb of Annia Regilla'.

Grothaus, H.K., 'Camere sepolcrali de' Liberti e Liberte de Livia Augusta ed altri Caesari', *Mélanges de l'école française de Rome: Antiquité* 91(i) (1979).

Guillaume-Coirier, G., 'Archéologie et imagination: les réprésentations du tombeau de Bibulus de Pollaiulo à Piranèse', *Gazette des Beaux-Arts* 6th ser. 81 (1973), pp. 215–26.

Lugli, G., 'Edifici Rotondi del Tardo Impero in Roma e Suburbio', *Studies presented to D.W. Robinson* 2 (St. Louis, Missouri 1953).

Le Gall, J., 'La sépulture des pauvres à Rome', *Bulletin de la Société nationale des Antiquaires de France*, 1980–1.

Magi, F., 'Un nuovo mausoleo presso il circo Neroniano', *Rivista di Archeologia Cristiana* 42 (1966).

Nash, E., *Pictorial Dictionary of Ancient Rome* 2 vols. (Rome 1961, reprinted New York 1981).

Nota, M., 'Saggi di Scavo presso il Mausoleo dei Lucilii sulla via Salaria', *Archeologia Laziale* 6 (1984).

Pietrangeli, C., *Il Monumento dei Lucili sulla Via Salaria* (Rome 1941).

Platner, S.B. & Ashby, T., *A Topographical Dictionary of Ancient Rome* (Oxford 1929).

Quilici, L., 'Per la restituzione di un monumento della Flaminia: il sepulcro a tamburi gemini di Tor di Quinto', *Bollettino d'Arte* 50 (1965).

Rakob, F., 'Die urbanisierung des nordliches Marsfelde', *L'Urbs* (Collection de l'école française de Rome 98, 1987).

Riccardi, M.L., 'Il Sepolcro Barberini sulla via Latina', *Palladio* 16 (1966).

Richard, J.C., 'Les funérailles de Trajan et le triomphe sur les Parthes', *Revue des Etudes Latines* 44 (1966).

Rossetto, P.C., *Il Sepolcro del fornaio Marco Virgilio Eurisace a Porta Maggiore* (Rome 1973).

Salvinius, A.M., *Monumentum . . . Liviae Augustae* (Florence 1727).

Sanguinetti, F., 'La Piramide di Caio Cestio e il suo restauro', *Palladio* 11 (1961).

Schneider Equini, E., *La 'Tomba de Nerone' sulla Via Cassia* (Rome 1984).

Silvestrini, F., *Sepulcrum Marci Artori Gemini: la tomba detta dei Platorini nel Museo Nazionale Romano* (Rome 1987).

Sydow, W. von, 'Die Grabexedra eines römischen Feldherren', *Jahrbuch des Deutschen Archäologischen Instituts* 89 (1974).

Sydow, W. von, 'Eine Grabrotunde an der Via Appia Antica', *Jahrbuch des Deutschen Archäologischen Instituts* 92 (1977).

Syme, R., *The Augustan Aristocracy* (Oxford 1986)

Torelli, M., 'Culto imperiali e spazio urbani in eta Flavia', *L'Urbs* (Collection de l'école française de Rome 98, 1987), for the *Templum gentis Flaviae*

Toynbee, J.M.C. & Ward-Perkins, J.B., *The Shrine of St. Peter and the Vatican Excavations* (London 1956).

Italy

Agrigento
Wilson, R.J.A., *Sicily under the Roman Empire* (Warminster 1990), pp. 130, 133.
Albano
Nibby, A., *Del monumento sepolcrale detto vulgarmente Degli Orazii e Curazii* (Rome 1834).
Amiterno
La Regina, A., 'Monumento funebre di un Triumviro Augustale al Museo di Chieti', *Studi Miscellanei* (Seminario di Archeologia dell' Università di Roma, 10 for 1963–4, 1966).
Aquileia
Brusin, G., *Nuovi monumenti sepolcrali di Aquileia* (Venice 1941).
Boretto
Aurigemma, S., 'Il monumento dei Concordii presso Boretto', *Rivista del Istituto d'Archeologia e Storia dell'Arte* 3, fasc. 3 (1931–2).
Campania
Franciscis, A. de & Pane, R., *Mausolei Romani in Campania* (Naples 1957).
Canosa
Bertocchi, F., 'Un nuovo mausoleo a Canosa', *Palladio* 11 (1961).
Chiusi
Mansuelli, G.A., 'Il monumento di Porsenna di Chiusi' in *Mélanges Huergon* (Collection de l'école française de Rome 27(ii), 1976).
Myres, J.L., 'The Tomb of Porsena at Clusium', *Annual of the British School at Athens* 46 (1951).
Civita Castellana
Götze, B., *Ein römisches Rundgrab in Falerii* (Stuttgart 1939).
Cosa
Brown, F.E., 'Cosa I', *Memoirs of the American Academy in Rome* 20 (1951).
Férento
Degrassi, A., 'Il sepolcro dei Salvii a Férento', *Rendiconti della Pontificia Accademia Romana di Archeologia* 33 (1961).
Gaëta
Fellmann, R., *Das Grab des Lucius Munatius Plancus bei Gaëta* (Basel 1957).
Grottarossa
Bruto, M.L., et al., 'Grottarossa', *Bulletino della Commissione Archeologica di Roma* 89(1) (1984).
Lucania
Bracco, V., 'Studio ricostruttivo di un mausoleo Romano in Lucania', *Archeologia Classica* 11 (1959).

Maccaretolo
Mansuelli, G.A., 'Il monumento funerario di Maccaretolo', *Archeologia Classica* 4 (1952).
Ostia
Meiggs, R., *Roman Ostia* (Oxford 1960).
Squarciapino, M.F., *Scavi di Ostia 3: Le Necropoli*, pt. 1 (1958).
Pietrabbondante
Sydow, W. von, 'Ein Rundmonument in Pietrabbondante', *Mitteilungen des Deutschen Archaeologischen Instituts* (Rome) 84 (1977).
Il Pietrolone
Gentili, G.V., *Auximum* (Istituto di Studi Romani 15, 1955), p. 131.
Po Valley
Mansuelli, G.A., 'Les monuments commemoratifs romains de la vallée du Po', *Monuments et Mémoires, Fondation F. Piot* 53 (1963).
Pompeii
Kockel, V., *Die Grabbauten vor dem Herkulaner Tor in Pompeji* (Mainz 1983).
Spano, G., 'La Tomba dell' edile C. Vestorio Prisco in Pompei', *Atti dell' Accademia dei Lincei, Memorie* 7th ser. 3 (1943).
Ponte Lucano
Lolli-Ghetti, M., 'Un documento ottocentesco sul mausoleo dei Plautii a Ponte Lucano (Tivoli)', *Archeologia Laziale* 7 (1985).
Reggio Emilia
Guida Laterza: Emilia & Venezie (1981), p. 106.
Ricina
Mercando, L., et al., 'Monumenti funerari di Ricina', *Bollettino d'Arte* 6th ser. 28 (1984).
Sabina
Reggiani, A.M., 'Monumenti funerari a Torre della Sabina', *Bollettino d'Arte* 6th ser. 5 (1980).
San Guglielmo al Goleto
Coarelli, F., 'Su un monumento funerario romano nell' abbazia di San Guglielmo al Goleto', *Dialoghi di Archeologia* 1 (1967).
Sarsina
Aurigemma, S., *I Monumenti della Necropoli Romana di Sarsina* (Rome 1963).
Finamore, N., 'Mausolei a Cuspide nella Necropoli Sarsinate', *Studi Romagnoli* 5 (1954), reprinted in *Sarsina, Studi di Antichità* (Bologna 1982).
Sestino
Verzar, M., 'Früaugusteischer Grabbau in Sestino (Toscana)', *Mélanges de l'école française de Rome: Antiquité* 86 (1974).
Syracuse
Gentili, G.V., 'Resti di un grande mausoleo ellenistico a Siracusa', *Archivio Storico Siracusana* 13–14 (1967–8).
Tusculum
McCracken, G., 'The Villa and Tomb of Lucullus at Tusculum', *American Journal of Archaeology* 44 (1942) and cf. G. Lugli, *La technica edilizia*

romana i (1957), p. 306.

Vicovaro

Daltrop, G., 'Ein rundgrab bei Vicovaro', *Rendiconti della Pontificia Accademia Romana di Archeologia* 41 (1969).

PALMYRA

Amy, R. & Seyrig, H., 'Recherches dans la Nécropole de Palmyre', *Syria* 17 (1936).

Gawlikowski, M., *Monuments funéraires de Palmyre* (Warsaw 1970).

Richmond, I., 'Palmyra under the aegis of the Romans', *Journal of Roman Studies* 53 (1963).

Sadurska, A., 'Recherches sur la sculpture funéraire de Palmyre', *Archaeologia Classica* 27 (1975).

Schmidt-Colinet, A., 'L'architecture funéraire de Palmyre' in *Archéologie et histoire de la Syrie*, ed. Dentzer & Orthmann, 2 (Saarbrücken 1989).

Will, E., 'La tour funéraire de Palmyre', *Syria* 26 (1949).

SPAIN

Cid Priego, C., 'El sepulcro de torre mediterráneo y . . . la tipología monumental', *Ampurias* 11 (1949).

Garcia Bellido, A. & Menendez Pidal, J., *El Dístylo Sepulcral Romano de Iulipa (Zalamea)* (Madrid 1963).

Garcia Merino, C., 'Un Sepulcro Romano turriforme en la Meseta Norte, el yacimiento arqueológico de Vilde (Soria)', *Boletin del Seminario de estudios de arte y arquelogia* 43 (1977).

Hauschild, T., 'Monument von Centcelles (Tarragona)', *Actas del VIII Congreso internacional de Arquelogia Cristiana*, Barcelona 1969 (Vatican 1972).

Jiménez, A., 'El grupo occidental de sepulcros turriformes Hispánicos', *XIII Congreso Nacional de Arqueologia* (Zaragosa 1975).

SYRIA

Butler, H.C., *Architecture and other Arts* [in Syria] (New York 1903).

De Vogüe, le vicomte de, *Syrie Centrale, Architecture civile et religieuse du I au VIIᵉ Siècle*, 2 vols. (Paris 1865–77).

Sartre, A., 'Tombeaux antiques de Syrie du Sud', *Syria* 60 (1983).

Sartre, A., 'Architecture funéraire de Syrie', in *Archéologie et histoire de la Syrie*, ed. Dentzer & Orthmann, 2 (Saarbrücken 1989).

Will, E., 'La tour funéraire de la Syrie', *Syria* 26 (1949).

VI FROM MAUSOLEUM TO *MARTYRIUM*
VII CHRISTIAN BURIAL AND MEDIEVAL CHURCH ARCHITECTURE

Alexander, S.S., 'Studies in Constantinian Church Architecture', *Rivista di Archeologia Cristiana* 47 (1971).

Armstrong, G.T., 'Constantine's Churches: Symbol and Structure', *Journal of the Society of Architectural Historians* 35 (1974).

Babić, G., *Les Chapelles annexes des Eglises Byzantines* (Paris 1969).

Biddle, M., 'Archaeology, architecture, and the cult of saints in Anglo-Saxon England', in *The Anglo-Saxon Church*, ed. Butler & Morris (Council for British Archaeology, 1986).

Bizot, B. & Serralongue, J., 'Un édifice funéraire du haut Moyen Age à Seyssel Albigny (Haute-Savoie)', *Archéologie du Midi Medieval* 6 (1988).

Blondel, L., 'Les premiers édifices Chrétiens de Genève', *Genava* 11 (1933).

Bonnet, C., *Les Premiers Edifices Chrétiens de la Madeleine à Genève* (Geneva 1977).

Bonnet, C., 'Les origines du groupe épiscopal de Genève', *Comptes rendus de l'Académie des inscriptions et belles-lettres*, 1981.

Bonnet, C., 'Les premiers édifices Chrétiens d'Augusta Praetoria (Aoste, Italie)', *Comptes rendus de l'Académie des inscriptions et belles-lettres,* 1986.

Brown, P.R.L., *The Cult of the Saints* (London 1981).

Bullough, D.A., 'Urban Change in Early Medieval Italy: the example of Pavia', *Papers of the British School at Rome* 34 (1966).

Bullough, D.A., 'Burial, Community and Belief in the early Medieval West', in *Ideal and Reality in Frankish and Anglo-Saxon Society*, ed. Wormald (Oxford 1983).

Cabrol, F. & Leclercq, E., *Dictionnaire d'archéologie chrétienne et de liturgie*, 15 vols. (Paris 1903–53).

Castagnoli, F., 'Il Circo di Nerone in Vaticano', *Rendiconti della Pontificia Accademia Romana di Archeologia* 32 (1960).

Clapham, A.W., *English Romanesque Architecture before the Conquest* (Oxford 1930).

Colardelle, M., *Sépulture et traditions funéraires du Vᵉ au XIIIᵉ siècle ap. J.C. dans les campagnes des Alpes françaises du Nord* (Grenoble 1983).

Colardelle, R., *Grenoble aux premiers temps chrétiens:*

Saint Laurent et ses nécropoles (Guides archéologiques de la France 1986).

Cortesi, G., 'La Chiesa di Santa Croce di Ravenna alla luce degli ultimi scavi e ricerche', *XXV Corso di Cultura sull'arte Ravennate e Bizantina* (Ravenna 1978).

Couasnon, C., *The Church of the Holy Sepulchre in Jerusalem* (London, British Academy 1974).

Crozet, R., 'Chapelles et Basiliques funéraires en France', *Actas del VIII Congreso internacional de Arqueologia Cristiana*, Barcelona 1969 (Vatican 1972).

Daras, C., 'Le Mausolée de la Boulonie et la Reliquaire d'Aubeterre', *Mémoires de la Société archéologique et historique de la Charente* (1957).

De Boüard, M., 'Le Baptistère de Port-Bail (Manche)', *Cahiers Archéologiques* 9 (1957).

Deichman, F.W. & Tschira, A., 'Das Mausoleum der Kaiserin Helena', *Jahrbuch des Deutschen Archäologischen Instituts* 72 (1957).

Delehaye, E., *Les Origines du culte des Martyrs* (Brussels 1933).

Devailly, G., 'La pastorale en Gaule au IXe siècle', *Revue d'histoire de l'église de France* 59 (1973).

D'Ossat, G. De Angelis, *Studi Ravennati* (Ravenna 1962).

Downey, G., 'The Builder of the original Church of the Apostles at Constantinople', *Dumbarton Oaks Papers* 5 (1951).

Downey, G., 'Nikolaos Mesarites' Description of the Church of the Holy Apostles at Constantinople', *Transactions of the American Philosophical Society* N.S. 47 (1957).

Dubourg-Novès, P., 'Des mausolées antiques aux cimborios romans d'Espagne', *Cahiers de Civilisation Médiévale* 23 (1980).

Duval, N. & Cintas, J., 'Le Martyrium de Cincari et les martyria triconques et tétraconques en Afrique', *Mélanges de l'école française de Rome: Antiquité* 88(ii) (1976).

Duval, N., 'Un curieux mausolée du IVe siècle en Pannonie et le mausolée de Louin dans le Poitou', *Bulletin Monumental* 148 (1990).

Duval, Y., *Loca Sanctorum Africae*, 2 vols. (Rome, Ecole française 1982).

Duval, Y. & Picard, J.C., *L'Inhumation privilégiée du IVe au VIIIe siècle en Occident* (Paris 1986).

Dyggve, E., *History of Salonitan Christianity* (Oslo, 1951).

Edwards, R.W., 'The Domed Mausoleum at Akkale in Cilicia. The Byzantine Revival of a Pagan Plan', *Byzantinoslavica* 50 (1989).

Fasola, U.M., 'Indagini nel sopraterra della catacomba di S. Callisto', *Rivista di Archeologia Cristiana* 56 (1980).

Fernie, E., 'Archaeology and Iconography: Recent Developments in the Study of English Medieval Architecture', *Architectural History* 32 (1989), for

Repton.

Ferrua, A., 'Lavori a S. Sebastiano', *Rivista di Archeologia Cristiana* 37 (1961).

Février, P.A., 'Le culte des morts dans les communautés chrétiennes durant le IIIe siècle,' *Atti del IX Congresso internazionale di archeologia cristiana*, 2 vols. (Vatican 1975).

Fletcher, Sir E. & Meates, G.W., 'The ruined church of Stone-by-Faversham', *Antiquaries' Journal* 49 (1969).

Fohlen, C., 'Connaissance et utilisation des tombes antiques pendant le haut moyen age', *Mélanges de la Société Toulousaine des études classiques* 2 (Toulouse 1946).

Forsyth, G.H., *The Church of St. Martin at Angers* (Princeton 1953).

Frantz, A., Thompson, H.A. & Travlos, J., 'The Temple of Apollo Pythios on Sikinos', *American Journal of Archaeology* 73 (1969).

Geary, P.J., *Furta Sacra: Theft of Relics in the Central Middle Ages* (Princeton 1978).

Gervers, M., 'Rotundae anglicanae', *Actes du XXIIe congrès international d'histoire de l'art*, Budapest 1969, 3 (1972).

Grabar, A., *Martyrium*, 2 vols. (Paris 1946).

Grabar, A., 'Christian Architecture, East and West', *Archaeology* 2 (1949).

Grierson, P., 'The Tombs and Obits of the Byzantine Emperors (337–1042)', *Dumbarton Oaks Papers* 16 (1962).

Grodecki, L., *L'Architecture Ottonienne* (Paris 1958).

Gsell, S., *Les Monuments Antiques de l'Algérie*, 2 vols. (Paris 1901).

Guyon, J., Strüber, L. & Manacorda, D., 'Recherches autour de la Basilique Constantinienne de Saints Pierre et Marcellin . . . à Rome', *Mélanges de l'école français à Rome* 93(2), (1981).

Guyon, J., *La Cimetière aux deux lauriers* (Rome, Ecole française, 1987).

Hauschild, T., 'Untersuchungen in der Märtyrerkirche von Marialba (Prov. Léon) und im Mausoleum von Las Vegas de Pueblanueva (Prov. Toledo)', *Actas del VIII Congreso internacional de Arqueologia Cristiana*, Barcelona 1969 (Vatican 1972).

Heighway, C. & Bryan, R., 'A reconstruction of the 10th century church of St. Oswald, Gloucester', in *The Anglo-Saxon Church*, ed. Butler & Morris (Council for British Archaeology, 1986).

Heitz, C., *Architecture et liturgie à l'époque carolingienne* (Paris 1963).

Heitz, C., 'Architecture et liturgie processionnelle à l'époque préromane', *Revue de l'Art* 24 (1974).

Hope, W.H. St. J., 'On the plan and arrangement of the first cathedral church of Canterbury', *Proceedings of the Society of Antiquaires* 30 (1917–18).

Hubert, J., 'Le Saint-Sépulchre de Neuvy', *Bulletin*

Monumental 90 (1931).

Hubert, J., *L'Art Pré-Romain* (Paris 1938).

Hubert, J., *L'Architecture Religieuse du Haut Moyen Age en France* (Paris 1952).

Hubert, J., 'Les églises à rotonde orientale', *Akten zum III Internationalen Kongress für Frühmittelalterforschung in den Alpenländern* (Lausanne 1954).

Hunt, E.D., *Holy Land Pilgrimage in the Later Roman Empire AD 312–460* (Oxford 1982).

Jurlano, R., 'I primi edifici di culto Cristiano in Brindisi', *Atti del VI Congresso internazionale di archeologia cristiana*, Ravenna 1962 (1965).

Kajanto, I., 'The Hereafter in Ancient Christian Epigraphy and Poetry', *Arctos* 12 (Helsinki 1978).

Khatchatrian, A., *Les Baptistères paleochrétiens* (Paris 1962).

Kinney, D., 'Capella Reginae: S. Aquilino in Milan', *Marsyas* 15 (New York 1970–2).

Kinney, D., 'The Evidence for the Dating of S. Lorenzo in Milan', *Journal of the Society of Architectural Historians* 31 (1972).

Koethe, H., 'Zum Mausoleum der Weströmische Dynastie bei Alt-Sankt-Peter', *Mitteilungen des Deutschen Archaeologischen Instituts* (Rome), 46 (1931).

Krautheimer, R., Frankl, W. & Corbett, S., *Corpus Basilicarum Christianarum Romae* (Rome 1937–77).

Krautheimer, R., 'Introduction to an Iconography of Mediaeval Architecture', *Journal of the Warburg & Courtauld Institutes* 5 (1942).

Krautheimer, R., *Early Christian and Byzantine Architecture* (Pelican History of Art 1965).

Krautheimer, R., *Studies in Early Christian, Medieval and Renaissance Art* (London 1971).

Krautheimer, R., *Rome, Profile of a City, 312–1308* (Princeton 1980).

Krautheimer, R., *Three Christian Capitals: Topography and Politics* (Berkeley, California, 1983).

Krogh, K.J., 'The Royal Viking-Age Monuments at Jelling in the light of recent archaeological excavations', *Acta Archaeologica* 53 (Copenhagen 1982).

Lambert, E., *L'Architecture des Templiers* (Paris 1955).

Lassus, J., *Sanctuaires Chrétiens de Syrie* (Paris 1947).

Lehner, H., 'Die Ausgrabung in der Kirche Biel-Mett BE', *Archäologie der Schweiz* 1 (1978), no. 4.

Lelong, C., 'Sépulture mérovingienne de Perrusson' (Indre et Loire), *Archéologie Médiévale* 6 (1976).

Lemerle, P., 'Aux origines de l'architecture Chrétienne. Découvertes et Théories nouvelles', *Revue Archéologique* 6th. ser. 33 (1949).

Lewis, S., 'San Lorenzo Revisited: A Theodosian Palace Church at Milan', *Journal of the Society of Architectural Historians* 32 (1973).

Lizop, R., *Les Convenae et les Consoranni (Comminges et Conserans)* (Paris and Toulouse 1931).

Louis, R., *Les églises d'Auxerre des origines au XIe siècle* (Paris 1952).

Marini, G., *I Papiri Diplomatici* (Rome 1805), p. 283 for inscription on doors of S. Vitale, Ravenna.

Matthews, J., *Western Aristocracies and the Imperial Court* (Oxford 1975).

Maurin, L., *Saintes Antique* (Saintes 1978).

Mayer, M., 'L'església de Cabeza del Griego...', *I Reunió d'Arqueologia Paleocristiana Hispànica* (Barcelona 1982).

Mertens, J., 'Quelques édifices réligieux à plan central découverts récemment en Belgique', *Genava* N.S. 11 (1963).

Morassi, A., 'La chiesa di S. Maria Formosa... in Pola', *Bollettino d'Arte* (1924–5)(1).

Morris, R., *The Church in British Archaeology* (C.B.A. Research Report 1983).

Navarre Romane (Zodiaque, La Nuit des Temps, 1967), for Eunate and Torres del Rio.

Nordenfalk, C., 'The Apostolic Canon Tables', *Gazette des Beaux-Arts* 6th ser. 62 (1963), for the Church of the Holy Apostles in Constantinople.

Osborne, J., 'The Roman Catacombs in the Middle Ages', *Papers of the British School at Rome* 53 (1985).

Palo, P. de, report on San Peretró, Mallorca, in *Actas del VIII Congreso internacional de Arqueologia Cristiana*, Barcelona 1969 (Vatican 1972), 2, pl. LII (showing burials in baptistery).

Passini, J., 'La chapelle octagonale d'Eunate', *Bulletin de la Société nationale des Antiquaires de France*, 1983.

Patitucci, S., 'La Basilica sanctae Mariae in Via Laurentina', *Rivista di Archeologia Cristiana* 45 (1969).

Perin, P., 'Des nécropoles romaines tardives aux nécropoles du Haut Moyen Age', *Cahiers Archéologiques* 35 (1987).

Perler, O., 'L'inscription du Baptistère de Sainte-Thècle à Milan', *Rivista di Archeologia Cristiana* 27 (1951).

Perogalli, C., *Architettura del altomedioevo occidentala* (Milan 1974).

Picard, G.C., 'Civitas Mactaritana', *Karthago* 8 (1957).

Picard, J.C., 'Etude sur l'emplacement de tombes des papes du IIIe au Xe siècle', *Mélanges de l'école française de Rome* 81 (1969).

Picard, J.C., 'Espace urbain et sépultures épiscopales à Auxerre', *Revue d'histoire de l'église de France* 62 (1976).

Picard, J.C., *Le Souvenir des Evêques. Sépultures, listes episcopales et culte des évêques en Italie du Nord des origines au Xe siècle* (Rome, Ecole française 1988).

Pietri, C., 'Remarques sur la topographie chrétienne des cités de la Gaule entre Loire et Rhin', *Revue d'histoire de l'église de France* 62 (1976).

Pietri, C., 'L'espace Chrétien dans la cité, le vicus Christianorum . . . de la cité Arverne (Clermont)', *Revue d'histoire de l'église de France* 66 (1980).

Pietri, L., 'Les abbés des basiliques dans la Gaule au VIe siècle', *Revue d'histoire de l'église de France* 69 (1983).

Quirk, R.N., 'Winchester Cathedral in the Tenth Century', *Archaeological Journal* 114 (1957).

Reekmans, L., 'L'implantation monumentale Chrétienne dans la zone suburbane de Rome du IVe au IXe siècle', *Rivista di Archeologia Cristiana* 44 (1968).

Reinhardt, H., 'La Cathédrale du VIe siècle à Genève et l'Eglise du Baptême de Clovis à Reims', *Genava* 11 (1963).

Reynaud, J.F. & Vicherd, G., 'St. Laurent de Choulans (Lyon)', *Comptes rendus de l'Académie des inscriptions et belles-lettres*, 1976.

Reynaud, J.F., et al., 'La Nécropole de Saint-Irénée, Saint Just (Lyon), du Ier au Ve siècle après J.C.', *Mélanges d'archéologie et d'histoire en honneur de Michel de Boüard* (Geneva 1982).

Rhein, A., 'Le temple de Lanleff', *Congrès archéologique de France* 81 (1914), pp. 542–53.

Roberti, M.M., 'La Cattedrale antica di Milano e il suo Battistero', *Arte Lombarda* 8 (1963).

Roberti, M.M., 'Il mausoleo Romano di San Vittore a Milano', *Atti del VI Congresso Nazionale di Archeologia Cristiana* 1983 (1986).

Roberti, M.M., *Milano Romana* (Milan 1984).

Rodwell, W., report of excavation of Roman mausoleum and Saxon chapel at Wells, *Medieval Archaeology* 25 (1981), pp. 176–7.

Salin, E., *La Civilisation Mérovingienne 2: Les Sépultures* (Paris 1952).

Sanderson, W., 'The Early Mediaeval Crypts of Saint Maximin at Trier', *Journal of the Society of Architectural Historians* 24 (1965).

Sapin, C., *La Bourgogne préromane* (Paris 1986).

Saxer, V., *Morts, Martyrs, Reliques en Afrique Chrétienne aux premiers siècles* (Paris 1980).

Schlunk, H. & Hauschild, T., *Hispania Antiqua. Die Denkmäler der frühchristlichen und westgotischen Zeit* (Mainz 1978).

Seston, W. & Perrat, C., 'Une Basilique funéraire païenne à Lyon', *Revue des études anciennes* 49 (1947).

Stern, H., 'Les mosaics de l'église de Sainte-Constance à Rome', *Dumbarton Oaks Papers* 12 (1958).

Strong, D.E., 'Some early examples of the Composite capital at S. Constanza', *Journal of Roman Studies* 50 (1960).

Sulser, W. & Claussen, H., *Sankt Stephan in Chur* (Zurich 1978).

Taylor, H.M. & J., *Anglo-Saxon Architecture* 3 vols. (Cambridge 1965–78).

Taylor, H.M., 'Corridor Crypts on the Continent and in England', *North Staffordshire Journal of Field Studies* 9 (1969).

Taylor, H.M., *Repton Studies* 3 vols. (1977–83).

Testini, P., *Archeologia Cristiana* (Rome 1958).

Tolotti, F., 'Le Basiliche cimiteriali con deambulatorio del suburbio Romano', *Mitteilungen des Deutschen Archaeologischen Instituts*, Rome, 89 (1982).

Tolotti, F., 'I due mausolei rotondi esistenti sul lato meridionale del vecchio S. Pietro', *Rivista di Archeologia Cristiana* 64 (1988).

Toynbee, J.M.C. & Ward-Perkins, J.B., *The Shrine of St. Peter* (London 1956).

Venanzio, O., 'Costruzioni romaniche a sistema centrale nel Bergamasco', *Arte Lombarda* Anno IV, no. 1 (1959).

Verzone, P., *L'Architettura dell' alto medio evo* (Milan 1942).

Verzone., 'Grandi Martyria dell'Oriente e problemi relativi alla loro struttura originaria', *Atti del VI Congresso internazionale di Archeologia Cristiana* 1962 (1965).

Victoria County History of Buckinghamshire 1 (1905), pp. 199–203 for the Taplow burial.

Vieillard-Troiekouroff, M., *Les Monuments religieux de la Gaule d'après les Oeuvres de Grégoire de Tours* (Paris 1976).

Vieillard-Troiekouroff, M., 'Les fouilles de la basilique funéraire d'Andernos', *Cahiers Archéologiques* 27 (1978).

Ward-Perkins, B., *From Classical Antiquity to the Middle Ages: Urban Public Building in Northern and Central Italy AD 300–850* (Oxford 1984).

Ward-Perkins, J.B., 'Constantine and the origins of the Christian Basilica', *Papers of the British School at Rome* 22 (1954).

Ward-Perkins, J.B., 'Memoria, Martyr's Tomb and Martyr's Church', *Journal of Theological Studies* N.S. 17 (1966).

Ward-Parkins, J.B., 'Imperial Mausolea and their Possible Influence on Early Christian Central-Plan Buildings', *Journal of the Society of Architectural Historians* 25 (1966).

Windfeld-Hansen, 'Un edificio sepolcrale tardo-antico sulla Via Appia e le origini dei martyria a croce con abside', *Archeologia Laziale* x(1) (1990).

Zovatto, P.L., 'Origine e significato delle Trichora-Martyrium', *Palladio* 15 (1965).

Arco, R. del, *Sepulcra de la Casa Real de Aragón* (Madrid 1945).

Aubert, M., 'Les tombeaux de l'abbaye de Longpont', *Congrès archéologique de France* 78(2) (1911).

Babelon, J.P., 'La tête de Béatrice de Provence au Musée Granet d'Aix-en-Provence', *Bulletin Monumental* 128 (1970), for the tombs of the Counts of Provence.

Boase, T.S.R., 'Fontevrault and the Plantagenets', *Journal of the British Archaeological Association* 3rd ser. 34 (1971).

Branner, R., 'The Montjoies of St. Louis', in *Essays presented to R. Wittkower*, ed. Fraser et al. (London 1967).

Cadei, A., 'Scultura e monumento sepolcrale del tardo Medioevo a Roma e in Italia', *Arte Medievale* ser. 2, Anno II, no. 2 (1988).

Claussen, P.C., *Magistri Doctissimi Romani. Die römischen Marmorkünstler des mittelalters* (Stuttgart 1987).

Curman, S. & Lundberg, E., *Sveriges Kyrkor: Östergötland* 2 (Vreta Klosters Kyrka) (Stockholm 1935).

Dawton, N., 'The Percy Tomb at Beverley Minster' in *Studies in Medieval Sculpture*, ed. F.H. Thompson (London 1983).

Deér, J., *The Dynastic Porphyry Tombs of the Roman Period in Italy* (Harvard 1959).

Edwards, M.D., 'The Tomb of Raimondino de'Lupi [at Padua], its Form and its Meaning', *Konsthistorisk Tidskrift* 52 (1983).

Erlande-Brandenburg, A., *Les Rois à Fontevrault* (Fontevrault 1979), and review in *Bulletin Monumental* 137 (1979), pp. 271–2.

Favreau, R. & Michaud, J., *Corpus des Inscriptions de la France Médiévale* 1 (Ville de Poitiers) (Poitiers 1974).

Gaignières, Robert de, Drawings of funerary monuments in French churches, made for him by Louis Boudon and others between 1670 and 1715, and now divided between the Bibliothèque Nationale in Paris (Coll. Clairambault) and the Bodleian Library, Oxford (MSS Gough Gaignières 1–16). Published by J. Adhémar and others in *Gazette des Beaux-Arts* 6th ser. 84 (1974), 88 (1976), 90 (1977) and 108 (1986).

Gardner, J., 'Arnolfo di Cambio and Roman Tomb Design', *Burlington Magazine* 115 (1973).

Gee, L.L., 'Ciborium Tombs in England 1290–1330', *Journal of the British Archaeological Association* 132 (1979).

Goldberg, P.J.P., 'The Percy Tomb in Beverley Minster', *Yorkshire Archaeological Journal* 56 (1984).

Gough, R., *Sepulchral Monuments*, 3 vols. (1786–99).

Grandi, R., *I Monumenti dei Dottori e la Scultura a Bologna 1267–1348* (Bologna 1982).

Hallam, E.M., 'Royal burial and the cult of kingship in France and England, 1066–1330', *Journal of Medieval History* 8 (1982).

Herklotz, I., *Sepulcra e Monumenta del Medioevo* (Rome 1985).

Jacob, H. s', *Idealism and Realism. A Study of Sepulchral Symbolism* (Leiden 1954).

Laban, D., *Les Evêques et la Cathédrale de Lescar* (Paris 1972), for the destroyed tombs of the Kings of Navarre.

Leask, H.G., *Irish Churches and Monastic Buildings* 3 (Dundalk 1960), pp. 167–74 on 'Tomb Niches'.

Lindley, P.G., 'The Tomb of Bishop William de Luda: an architectural model at Ely Cathedral', *Proceedings of the Cambridge Antiquarian Society* 73 (1984).

Moosbrugger-Leu, R., *Die Schweiz zur Merowingerzeit* 2 (Bern 1971), p. 73 for Einingen.

Morganstern, A., 'Quelques observations à propos de l'architecture du tombeau du cardinal Jean de la Grange', *Bulletin Monumental* 128 (1970).

Morris, R., 'Tewkesbury Abbey: the Despenser Mausoleum', *Transactions of the Bristol & Gloucestershire Archaeological Society* 93 (1974).

Morris, R., 'The remodelling of the Hereford aisles', *Journal of the British Archaeological Association* 3rd ser. 37 (1974), for the episcopal effigies.

Osborne, J., 'The Tomb of Alfanus in S. Maria in Cosmedin, Rome', *Papers of the British School at Rome* 51 (1983).

Osborne, J., 'The Roman Catacombs in the Middle Ages', *Papers of the British School at Rome* 53 (1985).

Oursel, H., 'Monuments funéraires des XIIIe, XIVe, XVe et XVIe siècles à Lille et dans ses environs immediats', *Revue du Nord* 62 (1980).

Philp, B., *Excavations at Faversham, 1965* (Bromley, 1968).

Prache, A., 'Les monuments funéraires des Carolingiens élévés à St. Rémi de Reims au XIIe siècle', *Revue de l'Art* 6 (1969).

Ramm, H.G., et al., 'The tombs of Archbishops Walter de Grey and Godfrey de Ludham in York Minster', *Archaeologia* 103 (1971).

Robinson, J. Armitage, 'Effigies of Saxon Bishops at Wells', *Archaeologia* 65 (1914).

Rogers, N.J., 'English Episcopal Monuments 1270–1350', in *The Earliest English Brasses 1270–1350*, ed. J. Coales (Monumental Brass Soc. 1987).

Santucci, E., et al., *Canosa di Puglia fra tardoantico e medioevo* (Rome, Autostrada S.P.A. 1981).

Schapiro, M., 'New Documents on St. Gilles', *Art*

Bulletin 17 (1935).

Sheingorn, P., *The Easter Sepulchre in England* (Michigan 1987).

Strygowski, J., 'Ruins of the Tombs of the Kings on the Haram in Jerusalem', *Speculum* 11 (1936).

Tummers, H.A., *Early Secular Effigies in England* (Leiden 1980).

Wright, G. Sommers, 'A royal tomb program in the reign of St. Louis', *Art Bulletin* 56 (1974).

IX   CHANTRIES AND FUNERARY CHURCHES IN MEDIEVAL EUROPE

The Obituary System

Canivez. J., ed., *Statuta Capitulorum Generalium Ordinis Cisterciensis* I–III (Louvain 1933–5).

Dykmans, M., 'Les Obituaires romains', *Studi Medioevali* (Spoleto) 3rd ser., anno XIX (1978).

Laporte, J., 'Tableau des services obituaires assurés par les abbayes de Saint-Evroul et de Jumièges (XIIᵉ et XIIIᵉ siècles)', *Revue Mabillon* 46 (1956).

Laurent, J., 'La prière pour les défunts et les obituaires dans l'ordre de Citeaux', *Mélanges St. Bernard* (Dijon 1954).

Lemaître, J., 'Les obituaires françaises', *Revue d'histoire de l'église de France* 64 (1978).

Lemaître, J., ed., *L'église et la mémoire des Morts dans la France mediévale* (Paris 1986).

Wollasch, J., 'Les obituaires, témoins de la vie Clunisienne', *Cahiers de Civilisation Médiévale* 22 (1979).

Purgatory

Burgess, C., 'A fond thing vainly imagined: an essay on Purgatory and pious motive in late medieval England', in *Parish, Church and People. Studies in lay religion 1350–1750*, ed. S.J. Wright (1988).

Le Goff, J., *The Birth of Purgatory* (London 1984).

Southern, R.W., 'Between Heaven and Hell', *Times Literary Supplement* 18 June 1982.

Chantry Foundations (institutional)

Beriou, L., 'Les chapellenies dans la province eccelésiastique de Reims au XIVᵉ siècle', *Revue d'histoire de l'église de France* 57 (1971).

Billot, C., 'Les Saintes Chapelles (XIIIᵉ–XVIᵉ siècles). Approche comparée de fondations dynastiques', *Revue d'histoire de l'église de France* 73 (1987).

Binz, L., *Vie religieuse et réforme ecclésiastique dans le diocèse de Genève pendant le grand schisme et la crise conciliare* (Mémoires et documents publiés par la société d'histoire et d'archéologie de Genève 46, 1973), pp. 414–36.

Burgess, C., 'The Anniversary in medieval Bristol', *Transactions of the Bristol & Gloucestershire Archaeological Society* 105 (1987).

Dobson, B.B., 'The Foundation of Perpetual Chantries by the Citizens of medieval York', *Studies in Church History* iv, ed. G.J. Cuming (Leiden 1967).

Edwards, K., *The English Secular Cathedrals in the Middle Ages* (Manchester 1949), pp. 291–308.

Erlande-Brandenburg, A., *Le Roi est mort. Étude sur les funérailles, les sépultures et les tombeaux des rois de France jusqu'à la fin du XIIIᵉ siècle* (Geneva 1975).

Hicks, M., 'Chantries, obits and almshouses: the Hungerford foundations, 1325–1478', in *The Church in pre-Reformation Society: Essays in honour of F.R.H. Du Boulay*, ed. Barron & Harpur-Bill (Woodbridge 1985).

Kraus, H., 'New Documents for Notre-Dame's Early Chapels', *Gazette des Beaux-Arts* 6th ser. 74 (1969).

Kraus, H., *Gold was the Mortar. The Economics of Cathedral Building* (Boston and London 1979).

Kreider, A., *English Chantries. The Road to Dissolution* (Cambridge, Mass. 1979).

Orme, N., 'The medieval chantries of Exeter Cathedral', *Devon & Cornwall Notes & Queries* 34–5 (1981–2).

Quéguiner, J., 'Recherches sur les chapellenies au moyen age', *Positions des thèses de l'Ecole des Chartes* 1950, pp. 97–100.

Rosenthal, J.T., *The Purchase of Paradise* (Toronto 1972).

Serrano, L., *El Obispobado de Burgos y Castilla Primitiva* 3 (Madrid 1936), pp. 110–12.

Thompson, A. Hamilton, *The English Clergy and their Organisation in the later Middle Ages* (Oxford 1947).

Vicaire, M.-H., ed., *La Naissance et l'essor du gothique méridional au XIIIᵉ siècle* (Cahiers de Fanjeaux no. 9, Toulouse 1974), for the financing of Mendicant churches in Toulouse.

Wood-Legh, K.L., *Perpetual Chantries in Britain* (Cambridge 1965).

The Choice of Sepulture as expressed in wills, etc.

Brentano, R., 'Burial Preferences at Rieti around 1300', in *Skulptur und Grabmal des Spätmittelalters in Rom und Italien*, ed. Garms & Romanini (Österreichischen Akademie der Wissenschaften, Vienna 1990).

Chiffoleau, J., *La comptabilité de l'au-delà. Les hommes, la mort et la religion dans le région d'Avignon à la fin du Moyen Age* (Collection de l'Ecole française de Rome, no. 47, Paris 1980).

Deregnaucort, J.P., 'L'élection de sépulture d'après les testaments douaisiens (1295–1500)', *Revue du Nord* 65 (1983).

Grevet, R., 'L'élection de sépulture d'après les testaments audomarois de la fin du XVᵉ siècle, *Revue du Nord* 65 (1983).

Lorcin, M.-Th., *Vivre et Mourir en Lyonnais a la fin du Moyen Age* (Paris 1981).

Marandet, M.-C., 'L'élection de sépulture et les croyances relatives à l'après-mort dans la région toulousaine entre 1300 et 1450, d'après les testaments', *Archéologie du Midi mediéval* 3 (1985).

Chantry Chapels, Funerary Foundations, etc. (architectural)

Aniel, J.-P., *Les Maisons de Chartreux des origines à la Chartreuse de Pavie* (Geneva 1983).

Ansar, P., 'L'église de Maignelay (Oise)', *Revue du Nord* 63 (1981).

Baux, J., *Recherches . . . sur l'église de Brou* (Paris 1844).

Binnall, P.G.B., 'Notes on the Medieval Altars and Chapels in Lincoln Cathedral', *Antiquaries' Journal* 42 (1962).

Bohrn, E., Curman, S. & Tuulse, A., *Strängnäs Domkyrka* 1 (Sveriges Kyrkor no. 100, Stockholm 1964).

Bruchet, M., *Marguerite d'Autriche* (Lille 1927), for Brou.

Chitty, H., 'Fromond's Chantry at Winchester College', *Archaeologia* 75 (1926).

Chueca Goitia, F., *Historia de la Arquitectura Espanola: edad Antigua y edad Media* (Madrid 1965).

Colvin, H.M., 'Henry VII's Chapel, Westminster', in *History of the King's Works*, ed. Colvin, 3 (1975).

Cook, G.H., *Mediaeval Chantries and Chantry Chapels* (2nd edn London 1963).

Crozet, R., *Textes et documents relatifs à l'histoire des Arts en Poitou* (Poitiers 1942).

David, H., *Claus Sluter* (Paris 1951), for Chartreuse de Champmol.

Dupasquier, L. & Didron, A.N., *Monographie de Notre-Dame de Brou* (Lyon 1842).

Erlande-Brandenburg, A., 'Le Portail de Champmol', *Gazette des Beaux-Arts* 6th ser. 80 (1972).

Garbrielli, N., *Arte nell' Antico Marchesato di Saluzzo* (Turin 1974).

Gee, E., 'The topography of altars, chantries and shrines in York Minster', *Antiquaries' Journal* 64 (1984).

Génermont, M. & Pradel, P., *Les Églises de France. Allier* (Paris 1938), for Souvigny and the tombs of the ducs de Bourbon.

Hassall, T.G., 'Excavations at Oxford 1973–4', *Oxoniensia* 39 (1974).

Laguia, C.T., 'Las Capillas de la Catedral de Teruel', *Teruel* 10 (1959).

Leedy, W.C., *Fan Vaulting* (London 1980), for Tewkesbury.

Lehmann, E. & Schubert, E., *Der Dom zu Meissen* (Berlin 1971), for the Fürstenkapelle built at the west end of the nave from 1423 onwards and vaulted in 1443–6.

Lemoine, J.B., 'Autour du tombeau de Philibert le Beau à Brou', *Revue Belge d'archéologie et d'histoire de l'art* 11 (1941).

Leoncini, G., *La Certosa di Firenze*, Analecta Cisterciensia, ed. Hogg, 71 (Salzburg 1979).

MacGibbon, D. & Ross, T., *The Ecclesiastical Architecture of Scotland* 3 (Edinburgh 1897).

Mérouville, M. Caffin de, 'A la recherche de tombeaux perdus', *Gazette des Beaux-Arts* 6th ser. 56 (1960), for Cléry.

Monumenta Henricina 3 (Coimbra 1961), pp. 131–9 for the will of King John I of Portugal.

Nodet, V., *L'église de Brou* (Paris 195-).

Orme, N., 'Sir John Speke and his Chapel in Exeter Cathedral', *Transactions of the Devonshire Association* 118 (1986).

Pradel, P., *Michel Colombe* (Paris 1953), for Brou.

Smith, J. Chipps, The Chartreuse de Champmol in 1486: the earliest visitor's account', *Gazette des Beaux-Arts* 6th ser. 106 (1985).

Stein, H., 'Jean Poncelet, architecte du duc de Bourbon et la chapelle neuve de Souvigny', *Bulletin Monumental* 79 (1920).

Victoria County History: North Riding of Yorkshire 2 (1923), pp. 554–6 for Scarborough chantries.

Vitorino, P., *Mosterio da Batalha* (Porto 1930).

Wadsworth, F.A., 'Notes on the Tombs, Chapels, Images and Lights in the Church of St. Mary the Virgin, Nottingham', *Thoroton Society's Transactions* 21 (1917).

X THE FAMILY CHAPEL IN RENAISSANCE ITALY

General

Cohn, S.K., *Death and Property in Siena 1205–1800* (Baltimore 1988).

Goffen, R., *Piety and Patronage in Renaissance Venice* (New Haven and London 1986).

Goldthwaite, R.A., *The Building of Renaissance Florence* (Baltimore and London 1980).

Gombrich, E., 'The Early Medici as Patrons of Art', in *Italian Renaissance Studies*, ed. Jacob (London 1960).

Heydenreich, L.H. & Lotz, W., *Architecture in Italy 1400 to 1600* (Pelican History of Art 1974).

Höger, A., *Studien zur Enstehung der Familierkapellen und altaren des trecento in Florentiner Kirchen* (Bonn 1976).

Kent, F.W., *Household and Lineage in Renaissance Florence* (Princeton 1977).

Kent, F.W. & Simons, P., eds., *Patronage, Art and Society in Renaissance Italy* (Oxford 1987).

Patetta, L., *L'architettura del Quattrocento a Milano* (Milan 1987).

Romanini, A.M., *L'architettura Gotica in Lombardia* 2 vols. (Milan, 1964).

Urban, G., 'Die Kirchenbaukunst des Quattrocento in Rom', *Römisches Jahrbuch für Kunstgeschichte* 9–10, 1961/2.

Wittkower, R., *Architectural Principles in the Age of Humanism* (London 1952).

Florence

(*M.K.I.F.* = *Mitteilungen des Kunsthistorischen Institutes in Florenz*)

Borsook, E., 'Notizie zu due cappelle in Santa Croce a Firenze', *Rivista d'Arte* 36 (1961–2).

Borsook, E. & Tintori, L., *Giotto. The Peruzzi Chapel* (New York 1965).

Borsook, E., 'Documents for Filippo Strozzi's Chapel in Santa Maria Novella', *Burlington Magazine* 112 (1970).

Borsook, E., *The Mural Painters of Tuscany* (Oxford 1980).

Borsook, E. & Offerhaus, J., *Francesco Sassetti and Ghirlandaio at Santa Trinità, Florence: History and Legend in a Renaissance Chapel* (Doornspijk 1981).

Botto, C., 'L'edificazione della Chiesa di S. Spirito in Firenze', *Rivista d'Arte* 13 (1931) and 14 (1932).

Botto, C., 'Note e documenti sulla chiesa di S. Trinità in Firenze', *Rivista d'Arte* 20 (1938).

Brown, B.L., 'The patronage and building history of the tribuna of SS. Annunziata in Florence', *M.K.I.F.* 25 (1981).

Brown, J. Wood., *The Dominican Church of S. Maria Novella* (Edinburgh 1902).

Burns, H., 'San Lorenzo before the building of the New Sacristy; an early plan', *M.K.I.F.* 23 (1979).

Clearfield, J., 'The Tomb of Cosimo de' Medici in San Lorenzo', *Rutgers Art Review* (Jan. 1981).

Elam, C., 'The Site and early Building History of Michelangelo's New Sacristy', *M.K.I.F.* 23 (1979).

Ettlinger, L.D., 'The Liturgical function of Michelangelo's Medici Chapel', *M.K.I.F.* 22 (1978).

Friedman, D., 'The Burial Chapel of Filippo Strozzi in S. Maria Novella in Florence', *L'arte* 9 (1970).

Gardner, J., 'The decoration of the Baroncelli Chapel in S. Croce', *Zeitschrift für Kunstgeschichte* 34 (1971).

Ginori Conti, P., *La Basilica di San Lorenzo di Firenze e la famiglia Ginori* (Florence 1940).

Hall, M., *Renovation and Counter-Reformation: Vasari and Duke Cosimo in Sta. Maria Novella and S. Croce 1565–1577* (Oxford 1979).

Hartt, F., et al., *The Chapel of the Cardinal of Portugal at San Miniato in Florence* (Philadelphia 1964).

Hatfield, R., *Botticelli's Uffizi 'Adoration'* (Princeton 1976), for the chapel of Guasparre dal Lama at S. Maria Novella.

Hueck, I., 'Stifter und Patronatsrecht. Dokumente zu zwei Kapellen der Bardi', *M.K.I.F.* 20 (1976).

Joannides, P., 'Michelangelo's Medici Chapel: Some New Suggestions', *Burlington Magazine* 114 (1972).

Jones, R., 'Palla Strozzi e la sagrestia di Santa Trinita', *Rivista d'Arte* 37 (1984).

Luchs, A., *Cestello: a Cistercian Church of the Florentine Renaissance* (Garland, New York, 1977).

Milanesi, G., *Nuovi Documenti per la storia dell'Arte Toscana dal XII al XV secolo* (Florence 1901, reprinted 1973), p. 134 for Giovanni Tornabuoni's contract with Ghirlandaio for painting his chapel in S. Maria Novella, 1485.

Paatz, W. & E., *Die Kirchen von Florenz*, 6 vols. (Frankfurt 1940–54).

Ruda, J., 'A 1434 Building Programme for San Lorenzo in Florence', *Burlington Magazine* 120 (1978).

Saalman, H., 'San Lorenzo, the 1434 Chapel Project', *Burlington Magazine* 120 (1978).

Saalman, H., 'Filippo Brunelleschi: Capital Studies', *Art Bulletin* 40 (1958).

Saalman, H., *The Church of Santa Trinità in Florence* (College Art Association 1966).

Saalman, H., 'Form and Meaning at the Barbadori-

Capponi Chapel in S. Felicità', *Burlington Magazine* 131 (1989).

Tolnay, C. de, 'Nouvelles remarques sur la chapelle Médicis', *Gazette des Beaux-Arts* 6th ser. 73 (1969).

Wilde, J., 'Michelangelo's Designs for the Medici Tombs', *Journal of the Warburg & Courtauld Institutes* 18 (1955).

Winternitz, E., 'Muses and Music in a Burial Chapel [the Strozzi Chapel at S. Maria Novella]', *M.K.I.F.* 11 (1963).

Rome

Blunt, A., *Guide to Baroque Rome* (London 1982).

Caraffa, F., 'La Cappella Corsini della Basilica Lateranense', *Carmelus* 21 (1974).

Enggass, R., *Early Eighteenth-century Sculpture in Rome* (Pennsylvania 1976), for the Corsini chapel, St John Lateran.

Ettlinger, L.D., 'Pollaiuolo's Tomb of Pope Sixtus IV', *Journal of the Warburg & Courtauld Institutes* 16 (1953).

Friedel H., 'Die Cappella Altemps in S. Maria in Trastevere', *Römisches Jahrbuch für Kunstgeschichte* 17 (1978).

Geiger, G.L., *Filippino Lippi's Carafa Chapel* (Kirksville, Missouri, 1986).

Martin, J., 'Un grand bâtisseur de la Renaissance; le Cardinal Giovanni Ricci de Montepulciano', *Mélanges de l'Ecole français de Rome: Moyen Age,* 86 (1974) for chapel in S. Pietro in Montorio.

Rossi, Giovanni Giacomo De, *Disegni de Vari Altari e Cappelle*, Rome 1713 (reprinted 1972).

Shearman, J., 'The Chigi Chapel in S. Maria del Popolo', *Journal of the Warburg & Courtauld Institutes* 24 (1961).

Spear, R.E., 'The Cappella della Strada Cupa: a forgotten Domenichino Chapel', *Burlington Magazine* 111 (1969).

Tosi, F.M., *Raccolta di Monumenti sacri e sepolcrali scolpiti in Roma nei secoli XV e XVI* (Rome 1856).

Individual Churches and Chapels

ASSISI

Brink, J., 'Sts. Martin and Francis: Sources and Meaning in Simone Martini's Montefiore Chapel', *Renaissance Studies in Honour of Craig Hugh Smith*, ed. Morrogh et al. (Florence 1985).

BERGAMO

Piel, F., *La Cappella Colleoni e il Luogo Pio della Pietà in Bergamo* (Bergamo 1975).

BOLOGNA

Brown, C.M., 'The Church of S. Cecilia and the Bentivoglio Chapel in S. Giacomo Maggiore,

Bologna', *Mitteilungen des Kunsthistorischen Institutes in Florenz* 13 (1967).

Supino, I.B., *L'Arte nelle Chiese di Bologna* (Bologna 1932–8).

ESZTERGOM (HUNGARY)

Horler, M., *The Bakócz Chapel of Esztergom Cathedral* (Budapest 1990).

GENOA

Bury, M., 'The Grimaldi Chapel of Giambologna in San Francesco di Castelletto, Genoa', *Mitteilungen des Kunsthistorischen Institutes in Florenz* 26 (1982).

Bury, M., 'The Senarega Chapel in San Lorenzo, Genoa', *Mitteilungen des Kunsthistorischen Institutes in Florenz,* 31 (1987).

MILAN

Aldeni, S., 'Il Libellus Sepulchrorum e il piano progettuale di S. Maria delle Grazie', *Arte Lombarda* 67 (1983).

Baroni, C., 'Intorno a tre disegni milanesi per sculture cinquecentesche', *Rivista d'Arte* 20 (1938).

Cipriani, R., et al., *La Cappella Portinari in Sant' Eustorgio a Milano* (Milan 1963).

Patetta, L., 'I termi nuovi dell'architettura milanese del Quattrocento e il Lazzaretto', *Arte Lombarda* 79 (1986).

MONREALE

Millunzi, C.G., 'La Cappella del Crocifisso nel Duomo di Monreale', *Archivio Storico Siciliano* N.S. 32 (1907–8).

NAPLES

Pane, R., *Architettura del Rinascimento in Napoli* (Naples 1937).

Pane, R., *Il Rinascimento nell'Italia meridionale*, 2 vols. (Milan 1975–77).

PADUA

Edwards, M.D., 'The Chapel of S. Felice in Padua as Gesamtkunstwerk', *Journal of the Society of Architectural Historians* 47 (1988).

SALUZZO

Gabrielli, N., *Arte nell'Antico Marchesato di Saluzzo* (Turin 1974).

VENICE

Howard, D., 'The dal Basso Family and their chapel in San Francesco della Vigna', *Burlington Magazine* 127 (1985), pp. 505–9.

Isermeyer, C.A., 'Le chiese de Palladio in rapporto al culto', *Bollettino del centro . . . di studi di architettura Andrea Palladio* 10 (1968).

McAndrew, J., *Venetian Architecture of the Early Renaissance* (MIT 1980), chap. 4.

WÜRZBURG
Hager, H., 'Balthasar Neumann's Schönborn Chapel at Würzburg Cathedral and its Berninesque Prototype', *Architectural History* 26 (1983).

XI TRIUMPHAL TOMBS AND THE COUNTER-REFORMATION

Abbate, F., 'La tomba di Galeazzo Caracciolo in San Giovanni a Carbonara', *Bollettino d'Arte* 64(2) (1979).

Anderson, J., 'Le roi ne meurt jamais: Charles V's obsequies in Italy', *Studia Albornotiana* 36 (Publicationes del Real Colegio de Espana en Bolonia, 1979).

Baroni, C., 'Leonardo, Bramantino ed il mausoleo di G. Giacomo Trivulzio', *Raccolta Vinciana* 15–16 (1935–9).

Baroni, C., 'Un episodio poco noto della vita di San Carlo [Borromeo] – La rimozione delle tombe dei Trivulzi nell' edicola Nazariana', *Aevum* 9 (1935).

Bernstock, J., 'Bernini's Memorials to Ippolito Merende and Alessandro Valtrini', *Art Bulletin* 63 (1981).

Bialostocki, J., 'The Door of Death', *Jahrbuch der Hamburger Kunstsammlungen* 18 (1973).

Blunt, A., *Artistic Theory in Italy 1450–1600* (London 1940), chap. 8.

Blunt, A., 'Two Drawings for Sepulchral Monuments by Bernini', in *Essays in the History of Art presented to Rudolf Wittkower* (London 1967).

Borsook, E., 'Art and Politics at the Medici Court I: the funeral of Cosimo I de' Medici', *Mitteilungen des Kunsthistorischen Institutes in Florenz* 12 (1965–6).

Chastel, A., 'Le Baroque et la Mort', in *Retorica e Barocco*, ed. E. Castelli (Atti del III Congresso Internazionale di Studi Umanistici, Rome 1955).

Clark, K., *Drawings by Leonardo da Vinci at Windsor Castle*, 2nd edn 1 (1968), pp. xxxviii–xli for designs for the Trivulzio monument.

Cohen, K., *Metamorphosis of a Death Symbol. The transi tomb in the later Middle Ages and the Renaissance* (Berkeley 1973).

Diedo, A. & Zanotti, F., *Monumenti cospicui di Venezia* (Milan 1839).

Haarlov, E., *The Half-open Door* (Odense 1977).

Hiesinger, K.B., 'The Fregoso Monument: a Study in Sixteenth-century Tomb Monuments and Catholic Reform', *Burlington Magazine* 118 (1976).

Jacquot, J., ed., *Les Fêtes de la Renaissance* 1 (Paris 1956), pp. 441–2.

Kernodle, G.R., *From Art to Theatre. Form and Convention in the Renaissance* (Chicago 1944).

Lawrence, C.H., *Flemish Baroque Commemorative Monuments 1566–1725* (Garland, New York 1981).

Mâle, E., *L'Art Réligieux de la fin du XVIe siècle, du XVIIe siècle, et du XVIIIe siècle* (Paris 1951).

Munman, R., 'The Monument to Vittore Cappello of Antonio Rizzo', *Burlington Magazine* 113 (1971).

Picone, M., *La Cappella Sansevero* [at Naples] (Naples 1959).

Pincus, D., 'The Tomb of Doge Nicolo Tron and Venetian Renaissance Ruler Imagery', in *Art the Ape of Nature*, ed. Barasch & Sandler (New York 1981).

Scotti, A., 'Architettura e riforma Cattolica nella Milano di Carlo Borromeo', *L'Arte* (1972).

Sheard, W.S., 'Asa Adorna: The Prehistory of the Vendramin Tomb', *Jahrbuch der Berliner Museen* 20 (1978).

Vanuxem, J., 'La querelle du luxe dans les églises après le Concile de Trente', *Revue de l'Art* 24 (1974).

XII THE PRINCELY BURIAL CHURCH IN CATHOLIC EUROPE

AUSTRIA

Ehrenhausen, mausoleum of Ruprecht von Eggesberg
Dehio, *Steiermark* (Die Kunstdenkmäler Österreichs 1956).

Graz, mausoleum of Emperor Ferdinand II
Dehio, *Graz* (Die Kunstdenkmäler Österreichs 1979).

ENGLAND

Farnborough, mausoleum of Emperor Napoleon III
Hughes, Dom P., *St. Michael's Benedictine Abbey* (Farnborough c.1980).

FRANCE

Hautecoeur, L., *Histoire de l'architecture classique en France* I(3) (Paris 1966), pp. 581–98.

Saint-Denis and the Church of the Invalides at Paris

Béguin, S., 'La suite d'Arthémise', *L'Oeil* Feb. 1958.

Boislisle, A. de, 'La sépulture des Valois à Saint-Denis', *Mémoires de la Société de l'histoire de Paris et de l'Ile de France* 3 (1877).

Braham, A.J., 'Bernini's Design for the Bourbon Chapel', *Burlington Magazine* 102 (1960).

Braham, A.J., 'L'église du Dôme', *Journal of the Warburg & Courtauld Institutes* 23 (1960).

Braham, A.J. & Smith, P., *François Mansart* (London 1973).

Dimier, L., *Le Primatice* (Paris 1900).

Félibien, M., *Histoire de l'abbaye royale de Saint-Denys en France* (Paris 1706).

Fréart De Chantelou, P., *Diary of the Cavaliere Bernini's Visit to France*, ed. A. Blunt (Princeton 1985).

James, F.C., 'Jean Bullant: Recherches sur l'architecture française du XVIe siècle', *Positions des thèses de l'école des Chartes*, 1968.

Jestaz, B., 'Jules Hardouin-Mansart et l'église des Invalides', *Gazette des Beaux-Arts* 66 (1965).

Monnier, G. & Johnson, W.M., 'Caron antiquaire: à propos de quelques dessins du Louvre', *Revue de l'Art* 14 (1971).

Reutersward, P., *The Two Churches of the Hôtel des Invalides* (Stockholm 1968).

Thirion, J., 'Observations sur les sculptures de la chapelle des Valois', *Zeitschrift fur Kunstgeschichte* 36 (1973).

Thomson, D., 'Baptiste Androuet du Cerceau Architecte de la Cour de Henri III', *Bulletin Monumental* 148 (1990).

GERMANY

Bruchsal

Charpentrat, P., *Du maître d'ouvrage au maître d'oeuvre: L'architecture religieuse en Allemagne du Sud de la Guerre de Trente Ans à l'Aufklärung* (Paris 1974).

Speyer

Klimm, E., *Der Kaiserdom zu Speyer* (Speyer 1953).

ITALY

Florence

Cresti, C., 'La Cappella dei Principi: un panteon foderato di Pietre Dure', in *Splendori di Pietre Dure* (catalogue of exhibition at Florence 1989).

Mantua

Signorini, R., 'Gonzaga Tombs and Catafalques', in *Splendours of the Gonzaga*, ed. Chambers & Martineau (Victoria & Albert Museum 1981),

and pp. 185–6 for Titian's portrait of Giulio Romano.

Milan

Aldeni, S., 'Il Libellus Sepulchrorum e il piano progettuale di S. Maria delle Grazie', *Arte Lombarda* 67 (1983).

Lang, S., 'Leonardo's Architectural Designs and the Sforza Mausoleum', *Journal of the Warburg & Courtauld Institutes* 31 (1968).

Pedretti, C., 'The Original Project for S. Maria delle Grazie', *Journal of the Society of Architectural Historians* 32 (1973).

Pedretti, C., 'The Sforza Sepulchre', *Gazette des Beaux-Arts* 6th ser. 89 (1977).

Schofield, R., 'Bramante and Amadeo at S. Maria delle Grazie', *Arte Lombarda* 78 (1986).

Mondovi

see SAVOY

Pavia (Certosa)

Ackerman, J.S., 'The Certosa of Pavia and the Renaissance at Milan', *Marsyas* 3 (1947–9).

Aniel, J.-P., *Les Maisons de Chartreux des origines à la Chartreuse de Pavie* (Geneva 1983).

Rimini ('Tempio Malatestiano')

Ettlinger, H.S., 'The Sepulchre on the Facade: a re-evaluation of Sigismondo Malatesta's re-building of San Francesco in Rimini', *Journal of the Warburg & Courtauld Institutes* 53 (1990).

Mitchell, C., 'Il tempio Malatestiano' in *Studi Malatestiani*, ed. P.J. Jones et al. (Rome 1978).

Ragghianti, C.L., 'Tempio Malatestiano', *Critica d'Arte* 12 (1965).

Ricci, C., *Il Tempio Malatestiano* (Milan 1925).

Rome (S. Pietro in Montorio)

Bruschi, A., *Bramante* (London 1977).

Förster, O.H., 'Bramante', in *Encyclopedia of World Art* (New York 1960).

Rosenthal, E., 'The Antecedents of Bramante's Tempietto', *Journal of the Society of Architectural Historians* 23 (1964).

Rome (Tomb of Pope Julius II)

Balas, E., 'Michelangelo's project for the tomb of Julius II', *Gazette des Beaux-Arts* 104 (1984).

Frazer, A., 'A Numismatic Source for Michelangelo's First Design for the Tomb of Julius II', *Art Bulletin* 57 (1975).

Frommel, C.L., 'Capella Iulia: Die Grabkapelle Papst Julius II in Neu-St. Peter', *Zeitschrift für Kunstgeschichte* 40 (1977).

Hirst, M., 'A Project of Michelangelo's for the tomb of Julius II', *Master Drawings* 14 (1976).

Lotz, W., 'Die Ovalen Kirchenräume des Cinquecento', *Römisches Jahrbuch für Kunstgeschichte* 7 (1955).

Panofsky, E., 'The first two projects of Michelangelo's Tomb of Julius II', *Art Bulletin* 19 (1947).

Tolnay, C. De, *The Tomb of Julius II* (Princeton 1954).

Vasari, G., *Le Vite de' piu eccellenti Architetti, Pittori, et Scultori Italiani* (first published Florence 1550), s.v. 'Michelangelo Buonarotti'.

Turin, La Superga

see SAVOY

Urbino

Rotondi, P., *Il palazzo ducale di Urbino* (Urbino 1950).

Salmi, M., *Piero della Francesca e il Palazzo Ducale di Urbino* (Florence 1945), p. 14.

POLAND

Bialostocki, J., *The Art of the Renaissance in Eastern Europe* (Phaidon, Oxford 1976).

Lozinski, J.W., 'Die Zentralen Grabkappellen in Polen (1520–1650)', *Actes du XXIIe Congrès international d'Histoire de l'Art* 1 (Budapest 1972).

SAVOY

Hautecombe

Clair, Dom R., 'L'église abbatiale d'Hautecombe', *Bulletin Monumental* 118 (1960).

Mondovi

Berra, L., 'I primordi del Santuario di Mondovi', *Bibliotheca della Società Storica Subalpina* 120 (1930).

Carboneri, N., *Ascanio Vitozzi* (Rome 1966).

Lotz, W., 'Die Ovalen Kirchenräume des Cinqecento', *Römisches Jahrbuch für Kunstgeschichte* 7 (1955), pp. 76–88.

Rossi, L.M., *The Santuario of the Madonna di Vico* (London 1907).

Turin, La Superga

Carboneri, N., *La Reale Chiesa di Superga di F. Juvarra* (Turin 1979).

Pommer, R., *Eighteenth-Century Architecture in Piedmont* (New York 1967).

SPAIN

Rosenthal, E.E., *The Cathedral of Granada* (Princeton 1961).

Tessari, C., 'Autocelebrazione e architettura: la famiglia Cobos y Molina e Andrés de Vandelvira a Ubeda', *Richerche di Storia dell' Arte* 32 (1987), for the church of El Salvador at Ubeda, built in 1536–40 on a plan resembling that of Granada cathedral.

XIII   THE FAMILY CHAPEL IN PROTESTANT ENGLAND AND SWEDEN

England

There has been no previous study or discussion of post-Reformation family chapels in England. For the dissolution of the chantries see A. Kreider, *English Chantries. The Road to Dissolution* (Cambridge, Mass., 1979), with bibliography. For licenses to found chantries in the reign of Queen Mary (1553–8) see *Calendar of Patent Rolls 1554–5*, p. 41 (Richard Lord Riche at Felsted, Essex), p. 225 (William Roper at St Dunstan's, Canterbury); *1555–7*, p. 363 (Sir Robert Rochester at Terling, Essex), p. 441 (Anthony Browne, Viscount Montague at Battle and Midhurst, Sussex), p. 542 (Sir William Petre at Ingatestone, Essex); *1557–8*, p. 92 (William Bendlowes at Great Bardfield, Essex), and *The Letters of Stephen Gardiner*, ed. J.A. Muller (Cambridge, 1933), p. 517 for Bishop Gardiner's chantry in Winchester cathedral.

For the affair of the Earl of Cork's monument at Dublin see H.F. Kearney, *Strafford in Ireland 1633–41* (Manchester 1959), p. 118. For the Chafyn chantry at Mere, see C.J. Godfrey in *Wiltshire Archaeological Magazine* 55 (1953–4). For the Sheldon chapel at Beoley see E.A.B. Barnard, *The Sheldons* (Cambridge 1936) and *Victoria County History of Worcestershire* iv, p. 16. William Oxenden's license to rebuild the chapel at Wingham is printed in *Registrum Matthei Parker Diocesis Cantuariensis*, ed. Thompson & Frere (Canterbury & York Society 1928), pp. 431–3. The dispute over the Kilmorey 'aisle' at Adderley is described at length in H.D. Harrod, *History of Shavington* (Shrewsbury 1891). The Digges chapel at Chilham is documented in *The Note-Book of Nicholas Stone*, ed. Spiers (Walpole Society 1918–19), pp. 85–6, 90. The date of the Ley chapel at Teffont Ewias, Wilts., is established by the wills of Matthew Ley (1632) and Henry Ley, 2nd Earl of Marlborough (1636) (P.C.C. 50 AUDLEY and 70 LEY). For other chapels mentioned see the *Victoria County History*, the reports of the Royal Commission on Historical Monuments, or the Buildings of England series.

Sweden

Liljegren, M., *Stormaktstidens Gravkor* (Stockholm 1947).

Lindahl, G., *Grav och Rum* (Stockholm 1969).

Paulsson, T., *Scandinavian Architecture* (London 1958).

Roberts, M., ed., *Sweden's Age of Greatness 1632–1717* (London 1973).

Sveriges Kyrkor ('The Churches of Sweden'), ed. Curman et al. (Stockholm 1912 onwards).

Wallin, S., *Kyrkoinredning för Herremän* (Stockholm 1948).

Whitelocke, Bulstrode, *A Journal of the Swedish Embassy in the years 1653 and 1654*, ed. H. Reeve (1855).

Yelverton, E.E., *The Mass in Sweden* (Henry Bradshaw Society, vol. 57, 1919).

XIV THE RETURN OF THE MAUSOLEUM

The Study of Roman mausolea by Italian architects from the fifteenth century onwards

The principal contemporary publications are Montano, G.B., *Scielta di varii tempietti antichi*, 2 vols. (Rome 1624), reissued in 1638 as *Raccolta di tempii et sepolcri disegnati dall' antico*, and Bartoli, Pietro Santi, *Gli Antichi Sepolcri overo Mausolei Romani et Etruschi* (Rome 1697).

The modern bibliography is far too extensive to be given at length, but the following are some of the more important publications:

Ashby, T., 'Sixteenth-century drawings of Roman buildings attributed to Andreas Coner', *Papers of the British School at Rome* 2 (1904) and 6 (1913).

Ashby, T., 'The Bodleian Manuscript of Pirro Ligorio', *Journal of Roman Studies* 9 (1919).

Bartoli, A., *I Monumenti antichi di Roma nei disegni degli Uffizi di Firenze*, 5 vols. (Rome 1914).

Bedon, A., 'Disegni di G.B. Montano nelle collezioni europee', *Richerche di storia dell' arte* 18 (1982).

Bedon, A., 'Architettura e archeologia nella Roma nel Cinquecento: G.B. Montano', *Arte Lombarda* 65 (1983).

Borsi, F., et al., *Roma Antica e il disegni di architettura agli Uffizi di Giovanni Antonio Dosio* (Rome 1976).

Huelsen, C., ed., *Il Libro di Giuliano da Sangallo*, 2 vols. (Leipsig 1910).

Mandowsky, E. & Mitchell, C., *Pirro Ligorio's Roman Antiquities* (London 1963).

Michailova, M., 'Mausolei romani nei disegni di un architetto del Rinascimento all' Ermitage di Leningrado', *Palladio* 19 (1969–70).

Mongeri, G., ed., *Le rovine di Roma al principio del secolo XVI* (Milan 1875).

Weiss, R., *The Renaissance Discovery of Classical Antiquity* (Oxford 1969).

Zander, G., 'Le Invenzioni architettoniche di Giovanni Battista Milanese', *Quaderni dell' Istituto di Storia dell' Architettura* 30 (1958) and 49–50 (1962).

For the failure to distinguish between temples and mausolea see Krautheimer, R., *Studies in Early Christian, Mediaeval and Renaissance Art* (London 1969).

England

Beddard, R.A., 'Wren's Mausoleum for Charles I', *Architectural History* 27 (1984).

Colvin, H., 'A Roman Mausoleum in Gloucestershire. The Guise Monument at Elmore', *Georgian Group's Journal*, 1991.

Cornforth, J., 'Kirkleatham, Cleveland', *Country Life* 6 Jan. 1977.

Djabri, S. Cabell, *The Story of the Sepulchre. The Cabells of Buckfastleigh* (Buckfastleigh *c*.1990).

Downes, K., *Hawksmoor* (London 1959) for the Castle Howard mausoleum.

Gotch, J.A., 'Some Newly found Drawings and Letters of John Webb', *Journal of the Royal Institute of British Architects* 3rd ser. 28 (1921), for Lamport.

Lysons, D. & S., *Magna Britannia* i (1806) for the Bruce mausoleum at Maulden, Beds.

Newman, J., 'An early drawing by Inigo Jones and a monument in Shropshire', *Burlington Magazine* 115 (1973).

Peacock, J., 'Inigo Jones's Catafalque for James I', *Architectural History* 25 (1982).

Saumarez Smith, C., *The Building of Castle Howard* (London 1990).

Taylor, A.C., 'Kirkleatham', *Architectural Review* (Oct. 1958).

Webb, G., ed., 'The Letters and Drawings of Nicholas Hawksmoor relating to the Building of the Mausoleum at Castle Howard 1726–1742', *Walpole Society* 19 (1930–1).

France

Hautecoeur, L., *Histoire de l'architecture classique en France* I (i–iii) (1963–67).

MacPhail, E., 'The Roman Tomb or the image of the Tomb in Du Bellay's Antiquitez', *Bibliothèque d'Humanisme et Renaissance* 48 (1986).
Palustre, L., *La Renaissance en France* 3 (1885).

AUTUN
Vuillemot, G., *La Renaissance à Autun. La Chapelle Poillot* (Autun 1974).

JOIGNY
Challe, M.A., *Histoire . . . de Joigny* (1883).

LIGNY-LE-CHÂTEL (YONNE)
Vallery-Radot, J., in *Congrès archéologique* 116 (1958), p. 161.

METZ
Gaignières drawing reproduced in *Gazette des Beaux-Arts* 6th ser. 88 (1976), p. 92, no. 1616.

NÎMES
Balty, J.C., *Études sur la Maison Carrée* (Brussels 1960), p. 33 for the proposal to convert it into a mausoleum for the duc d'Uzès (d. 1573).

TOUL
Vallery-Radot, J. in *Congrès archéologique* 96 (1933), p. 234.

VALENCE (LE PENDENTIF)
Pérouse de Montclos, J.M., *L'Architecture à la française* (Paris 1982), p. 152.
Perrot, J., *La Basilique de Saint Apollinaire (Cathédrale de Valence)* (Valence 1925).

VANNES
Mussat, A. in *Congrès archéologique* 141 (1983), pp. 304–6.

Germany

CLEVE
Boogaart, E. van den, ed., *Johan Maurits van Nassau-Siegen 1604–1679* (The Hague 1979).

STADTHAGEN
Dehio, *Niedersachsen* (Berlin 1977), pp. 881–2.

Hungary and Poland

Bialostocki, J., *The Art of the Renaissance in Eastern Europe* (Phaidon, Oxford 1976), pp. 26–34.

Italy

Sinding-Larsen, S., 'Some functional and iconographical aspects of the centralised church in the Italian Renaissance', *Acta* (of the Norwegian Institute in Rome) 2 (1965).

BERGAMO
Piel, F., *La Cappella Colleoni e il Luogo Pio della Pietà in Bergamo* (Bergamo 1975).

MASER
Marder, T.A., 'La Dedica e la Funzione del Tempietto di Palladio a Maser', *Bollettino del Centro Internazionale di Studi di Architettura Andrea Palladio* 23 (1981).
Scamozzi, B., *Le Fabbriche e i disegni di A. Palladio* (Vicenza 1776, 1786).

MILAN
Benedetti, S., 'Un' aggiunta a Pirro Ligorio: il Tabernacolo di Pio IV nel Duomo di Milano, *Palladio* 3rd ser. 25 (1978).
Eiche, S. & Lubkin, G., 'The Mausoleum Plan of Galeazzo Maria Sforza', *Mitteilungen des Kunsthistorischen Institutes in Florenz* 32 (1988).

MONTE CASSINO (MEDICI CHAPEL)
Giovannoni, G., *Antonio da Sangallo il giovane*, 2 vols. (Rome 1959).

NAPLES
Alisio, G., 'La Cappella Pontano', *Napoli Nobilissima* 3 (1963–4).
Pane, R., *Il Rinascimento nell' Italia meridionale*, 2 vols. (Milan 1975–7).

ROME
Metternich, F. Graf W., *Die Erbauung der Peterskirche zu Rom* (Vienna 1972), pl. 74.

VERONA (PELLEGRINI CHAPEL)
Langenskiöld, E., *Michele Sanmicheli* (Uppsala 1938).

Scotland

Birnie, W., *The Blame of Kirk-Buriall, Tending to perswade Cemiteriall Civilitie* (Edinburgh 1606).
Brown, I. Gordon, *The Clerks of Penicuik* (Edinburgh 1987).
Brown, J., *The Epitaphs and Monumental Inscriptions in Greyfriars Churchyard, Edinburgh* (Edinburgh 1867).
Cameron, J.K., ed., *The First Book of Discipline* (Edinburgh 1972), pp. 149–201.
Hay, G., *The Architecture of Scottish Post-Reformation Churches* (Oxford 1957).
Knox, John, *History of the Reformation in Scotland*, ed. W. Croft Dickinson 2 (1949), pp. 319–20.
MacGibbon, D. & Ross, T., *The Castellated & Domestic Architecture of Scotland* 5 (1892), pp. 130–210.
MacKechnie, A., 'Durisdeer Church', *Proceedings of the Society of Antiquaries of Scotland* 115 (1985).

Mair, W., *A Digest of Laws Ecclesiastical and Civil* [of Scotland] (Edinburgh 1912).

Murray of Stanhope, Lady, *Memoir of George Baillie of Jerviswood and Lady Grisell Baillie* (Edinburgh 1822).

Royal Commission on Ancient & Historical Monuments, *Argyllshire*, 7 (forthcoming).

Scottish Record Office, Clerk of Penicuik papers, drawings and contract for mausoleum at Penicuik, 1685 (GD 18/1752); Fothringham papers, account for building Mackenzie of Rosehaugh mausoleum, 1688–91 (GD 121/469, Box 83, Bundle 121/469; Montrose papers, account for building mausoleum at Aberuthven, 1736–8 (GD 220/6/1384/30).

XV FUNERARY ARCHITECTURE IN THE EIGHTEENTH AND EARLY NINETEENTH CENTURIES

General

Braham, A., *Funeral Decorations in Early Eighteenth-Century Rome* (Victoria & Albert Museum, London 1975).

Curl, J. Stevens, *The Egyptian Revival* (London 1982).

Diderot, *Correspondance*, ed. G. Roth 5 (Paris 1959), p. 130 for baron d'Holbach's visit to England in 1765.

Fagiolo dell'Arco, M. & Caradini, S., *L'Effemero Barocco* (Rome 1977).

Harris, J., 'Le Geay, Piranesi and international Neo-classicism in Rome 1740–1750' in *Essays in the History of Architecture presented to Rudolf Wittkower* (London 1967).

Mazza, B., 'La vicenda dei "Tombeaux des Princes": Matrici, storia e fortuna della serie Swiny tra Bologna e Venezia', *Saggi e Memorie di Storia dell' arte* 10 (1976).

McManners, J., *Death and the Enlightenment: changing attitudes to Death among Christians and Unbelievers in Eighteenth-Century France* (Oxford 1981).

Means, J.A. ed., Robert Blair, *The Grave, a poem*, 1743 (Augustan Reprints Society, California 1973).

Michea, R., 'Le plaisir des Tombeaux au XVIIIᵉ siècle', *Revue de Littérature comparée*, 18 (1938).

Northup, C.S., *A Bibliography of Thomas Gray* (New Haven 1917).

Oenslager, D., *Four Centuries of Scenic Invention* (International Exhibitions Foundation 1974).

Oechslin, W., 'Pyramide et Sphère', *Gazette des Beaux-Arts* 6th ser. 77 (1971).

Oleson, J.P., 'A Reproduction of an Etruscan Tomb . . . at Bomarzo', *Art Bulletin* 57 (1975).

Panofsky, E., '"Et in Arcadia Ego" et le tombeau parlant', *Gazette des Beaux-Arts* 1938 (1).

Panofsky, E., 'The Tomb in Arcady at the Fin de Siècle', *Wallraf-Richardtz-Jahrbuch* 30 (1968).

Pigozzi, M., et al., *Francesco Fontanesi 1751–1795* (Reggio Emilia 1988).

Tosatti, Q., 'L'Evoluzione del monumento sepulcrale nell' eta barocca: il monumento a piramide', *Bollettino d'Arte* 7 (1913), pp. 173–86.

Van Tieghem, P., *La poesie de la nuit et des tombeaux en Europe au XVIIIᵉ siècle* (Paris 1921).

Weisbach, W., 'Et in Arcadia ego', *Gazette des Beaux-Arts* 6th. ser. 18 (1937).

Wittkower, R., *Selected Lectures. The Impact of Non-European Civilisations on the Art of the West*, ed. D.M. Reynolds (Cambridge 1989), nos. 4–5 on 'The Obelisk'.

The British Isles

ENGLAND

Bangert-Laule, U., et al., *Mausoleen des 18. Jahrhunderts in England* (Berichte und Forschungen zur Kunstgeschichte 7, Freiburg 1984).

Davies, C., 'Architecture and Remembrance' [Sir John Soane's Museum], *Architectural Review*, Feb. 1984.

Du Prey, P. de la R., *Sir John Soane* (Catalogue of Drawings in the Victoria & Albert Museum, London 1985).

Harris, J., *Sir William Chambers* (London 1970).

Jenkins, I., 'Adam Buck and the vogue for Greek Vases', *Burlington Magazine* 130 (1988).

Lewis, W.S., 'The Genesis of Strawberry Hill', *Metropolitan Museum Studies* 5(i) (1934).

Mellinghof, G.T., 'Soane's Dulwich Picture Gallery', in *John Soane* (Academy Editions, London 1983).

Penny, N., *Church Monuments in Romantic England* (New Haven and London 1977).

Stillman, D., 'Death Defied and Honor Upheld: the Mausoleum in Neo-Classical England', *Art Quarterly* N.S. 1(3) (1978).

Summerson, J., 'Le tombeau de Sir John Soane', *Revue de l'Art* 30 (1975).

Summerson, J., 'Sir John Soane and the furniture of death', *Architectural Review*, March 1978.

Waterfield, G., *Soane and after: the Architecture of Dulwich Picture Gallery* (Dulwich 1987).

Watkin, D., *Thomas Hope and the Neo-Classical Idea* (London 1968).

Blickling, Norfolk
Meadows, P., *Joseph Bonomi Architect* (R.I.B.A. exhibition catalogue, London 1988).

Castle Hill, Devon
Pococke, R., in British Library, Add. MS. 14260, ff. 78–81.

Chilham, Kent
Gentleman's Magazine 1800(2), p. 825.

Cobham, Kent
Public Record Office, PROB 11/1081, f. 428, will of 3rd Earl of Darnley.

Frogmore, Berkshire
Ames, W., *Prince Albert and Victorian Taste* (London 1967).
Hobhouse, H., *Prince Albert, His Life and Work* (London 1983).

The Grove, Hertfordshire
British Library, Add. MS. 9063.

Halsham, Yorkshire
Higson, N., 'The Building of the Mausoleum at Halsham', *Transactions of the Georgian Society for E. Yorkshire* 5(ii) 1961–3.

Pains Hill, Surrey
Walpole, H., 'Visits to Country Seats', *Walpole Society* 16 (1927–8).

Saxlingham, Norfolk
Ketton-Cremer, R.W., 'The Heydon Monument at Saxlingham', *Norfolk Archaeology* 34 (1966–9).
Rye, W., *Norfolk Essays* 3 (1926).

Werrington, Devon
Pococke, R., *Travels through England*, ed. Cartwright (Camden Society 1888–9) i, p. 133.

IRELAND
Craig, M., 'Mausoleums in Ireland', *Studies: an Irish Quarterly Review*, Winter 1975.
Curl, J.S., *Mausolea in Ulster* (Ulster Architectural Heritage Society 1978).
Rankin, P., *Irish Building Ventures of the Earl Bishop of Derry* (Ulster Architectural Heritage Society 1972).

SCOTLAND

Alloa
Scottish Record Office, architectural drawings by the Earl of Mar (RHP 13256–8).
Stewart, M.C.H., 'Lord Mar's Plans, c. 1700 to 1732' (University of Glasgow, unpublished M. Litt. thesis, 1988).
Relation du Feu d'Artifice et des illuminations au College des Ecossais de Paris le 8 Juillet 1688 à l'occasion de la Naissance du Prince d'Ecosse, 1688 (copy in National Library of Scotland).

Edinburgh
Brown, I. Gordon, 'David Hume's tomb: a Roman mausoleum by Robert Adam', *Proceedings of the Society of Antiquaries of Scotland* (forthcoming).
Gow, I., 'C.R. Cockerell's Designs for the Northern Athenian Parthenon', *Journal of the Architectural Heritage Society of Scotland* 16 (1989).

Hamilton, Lanarkshire
Allan, M.J., 'Hamilton Mausoleum', unpublished thesis, Robert Gordon's College, Aberdeen, 1976.
National Monuments Record for Scotland, Edinburgh, photographs of drawings in the archives of the Duke of Hamilton at Lennoxlove.

DENMARK
Kryger, K., 'Gravkapellet i karise', *Architectura* 4 (Copenhagen 1982).
Lorensen, V., *De Gamle Danske Domkirker* (Copenhagen 1948).
Schuhl, P.M., 'Le Mémorial de Jaegerspris', *Gazette des Beaux-Arts* 6th ser. 85 (1975).

FRANCE
Adams, W.H., *The French Garden 1500–1800* (London 1979).
Biver, M.L., *Pierre Fontaine* (Paris 1964).
Bodkin, T., 'Le Tombeau de Jean-Jacques Rousseau d'après les peintures', *Gazette des Beaux-Arts* 1936(2).
Braham, A., *The Architecture of the French Enlightenment* (London 1980).
Calais, pyramidal monument near, see R. Clutterbuck, *History of Hertfordshire* 1 (1815), p. 366 and the *Minute Book of the Spalding Gentlemen's Society*, ed. Owen (Lincs. Record Society 1981), p. xi.
Caso, J. de, 'Remarques sur Boullée et l'architecture funéraire à l'âge des lumières', *Revue de l'Art* 32 (1976).
Favre, R., *La mort dans la littérature et la pensée françaises au XVIIIe siècle* (thesis published by the University of Lille 1977).
Gaignières drawing of obelisk-monument in Bordeaux cathedral reproduced in *Gazette des Beaux-Arts* 6th ser. 88 (1976), p. 105, no. 1694 (cf. p. 118, no. 1776 and p. 121, no. 1790).
Jardins de France 1760–1820 (Caisse nationale des monuments historiques 1978).
Laborde, Comte A. de, *Description des Nouveaux Jardins de la France* (Paris 1808).
Macé de Lépinay, F., 'La chapelle expiatoire du

400

duc de Berry', *Bulletin de la Société de l'histoire de l'art français 1973* (1974).

Pérouse de Montclos, J.M., *Étienne-Louis Boullée* (Paris 1969).

Pérouse de Montclos, J.M., *Les Prix de Rome. Concours de L'Académie royale d'architecture au XVIIIe siècle* (Paris 1984).

Rabreau, D., *La Chapelle expiatiore du Square Louis XVI à Paris* (Paris, c.1975).

Reutersvärd, O., 'The sinking cenotaphs of Moreau, Fontaine, Boullée and Gay', *Konsthistorisk Tidskrift* 28 (1959).

Reutersvärd, O., 'The sunken arches of Ledoux, Boullée, Cellerier and Fontaine', *Konsthistorisk Tidskrift* 29 (1960).

Titon du Tillet, E., *Description du Parnasse française* (Paris 1727).

Visionary Architects: Boullée, Ledoux, Lequeu (Houston 1968).

Wiebenson, D., *The Picturesque Garden in France* (Princeton 1978).

GERMANY

Bothe, R., et al., *Friedrich Gilly 1772–1800* (Berlin 1984).

Evers, B., *Mausoleen des 17–19 Jahrunderts, Typologische Studien zum Grab- und Memorialbau* (D. Phil. dissertation, Tübingen 1983).

Hirsch, E., *Dessau-Worlitz. Ziende und Inbegriff des XVIII Jahrunderts* (Munich 1985), pp. 107–8 for the circular domed mausoleum built at the Drehberg near Dessau in 1773 by the Duke of Anhalt-Dessau and used as the focal point of an annual popular event, part-festival, part-athletic contest, which was intended to have Antique overtones and was in every way a manifestation of Enlightened policy.

Sieb, G., 'Adels und Furstenmausoleen', in *Wie die Alten den Tod gebildet: Wandlungen der Sepulkralkultur 1750–1850* (Kassel 1981).

Watkin, D. & Mellinghof, T., *German Architecture and the Classical Ideal 1740–1840* (London 1987).

GREECE

Dinsmoor, W.B., *Observations on the Hephaisteion* (American School of Classical Studies at Athens, 1941).

Hughes, T.S., *Travels in Sicily, Greece and Albania* 1 (London 1820), pp. 251–2.

ITALY

Mezzanotte, G., *Architettura Neoclassica in Lombardia* (Naples 1966).

Vigoni, I., 'Annotazioni sulla Villa Vigoni di Loveno', *Arte Lombarda* 1980, special issue on neo-classical culture in the province of Como, p. 309 for cenotaph mausoleum in grounds of villa designed by Gaetano Besia c.1830 with sculpture by Thorwaldsen.

MALTA

Caruana, R., *Collezione di monumenti e lapidi sepolcrali dei Militi gerosolimitani nella chiesa di San Giovanni in Malta* (Malta 1838–40), no. cxciii.

Scicluna, H.P., *The Church of St. John in Valletta* (Malta 1955), pl. cclxxxix, no. 335.

POLAND

Zachwatowicz, J., *Architektura Polska* (Warsaw 1956), pl. 473 (Lazienski).

SWEDEN

Nilsson, S.A., 'A Pyramid for Gustav Adolf's Square', *Konsthistorisk Tidskrift* 33 (1964), for designs for pyramidal mausolea, etc. by Admiral Carl Augst Ehrenswärd in the 1780s.

XVI   THE TRIUMPH OF THE CEMETERY

General

Curl, J. Stevens, *A Celebration of Death* (London 1980), chaps. 5, 7, 8, 9.

Mytum, H., 'Public Health and private sentiment: the development of cemetery architecture and funeral monuments from the eighteenth century onwards', *World Archaeology* 21 (1989).

British Isles

Blair, G., *Biographical and Descriptive Sketches of Glasgow Necropolis* (Glasgow 1857).

Brooks, C., *Mortal Remains: the History and Present State of the Victorian and Edwardian Cemetery* (Exeter 1989).

Brown, J., *The Epitaphs and Monumental Inscriptions in Greyfriars Churchyard, Edinburgh* (Edinburgh 1867).

Coones, P., 'Kensal Green Cemetery', *Transactions of the Ancient Monuments Society* N.S. 31 (1987).

Curl, J., Stevens, *The Victorian Celebration of Death* (Newton Abbot 1972).

Curl, J. Stevens, 'The architecture and planning of the nineteenth-century cemetery', *Journal of Garden History* 3 (1976).

Loudon, J.C., *On the laying out, planting, and managing of Cemeteries* (London 1843, reprinted 1981).

MacCaffrey, W.J., *Exeter 1540–1640* (Cambridge,

Mass. 1958), p. 201 for new cemetery at Exeter, *c.*1600.

Meller, H., *London Cemeteries, an illustrated Guide and Gazetteer*, 2nd edn (London 1985).

Schuyler, D., ed., *Garden and Cemetery* (*Journal of Garden History* 4, no. 3, 1984).

Simo, M.L., *Loudon and the Landscape* (New Haven and London 1988).

Records of the Diocese of London in Guildhall Library, London: Register of Bishop Montague 1621–8, ff. 394, 397, 398, 400, 407 for new parochial cemeteries in London, and Vicar-General's Register 1688–1704, ff. 66, 82^v for faculties for vaults on sites of demolished churches.

France

Abgrall, Chanoine, 'Les ossuaires Bretons', *Congrès archéologique de France* 81 (1914).

Agulhon, M., 'Le Tombeau du 'Grand Homme' au XIXe siècle', *Gazette des Beaux-Arts* 6th ser. 106 (1985).

L'architecture et la mort (*Monuments Historiques*, no. 124, Dec. 1982–Jan. 1983).

Brongniart, A.T., 1739–1813 (exhibition catalogue, Musée Carnavalet, Paris 1986).

Daly, C., *Architecture Funéraire* (Paris 1871).

Etlin, R.A., *The Architecture of Death: the Transformation of the Cemetery in Eighteenth-Century Paris* (M.I.T. 1984).

Foisil, M., 'Les attitudes devant la mort au XVIIIe siècle: sépultures et suppressions de sépultures dans le cimetière des Saints-Innocents', *Revue historique* 251 (1974).

Jolimont, F.G.T. de, *Les mausolées françaises. Recueil des tombeaux les plus remarquables . . . erigées dans les nouveaux cimetières de Paris* (Paris 1821).

Ligou, D., 'L'evolution des cimetières', *Archives de Sciences Sociales des Religions* 39 (1975).

Lottin, A., 'Les morts chassés de la cité: les émeutes à Lille (1779) et à Cambrai (1780) lors du transfert des cimetières', *Revue du Nord* 60 (1978).

Mouilleseaux, J.P., 'Les charniers', *Monuments historiques* 124 (1982–3).

Sozzi, L., 'I Sepolcri e le discussioni francesi sulle tombe negli anni del Direttorio e del Consolato', *Giornale Storico della Letteratura Italiana* 144 (1967).

Suttel, R., *Catacombes et Carrières de Paris* (Paris 1986).

Thibaut-Payen, J., *Les morts, l'Eglise et l'Etat dans le ressort du parlement de Paris aux XVIIe et XVIIIe siècles* (Paris 1977).

Geneva

Histoire de Genève des origines à 1798 (Société d'histoire et d'archéologie de Genève, 1951).

Blondel, L., *Le Developpement urbain de Genève à travers les siècles* (Geneva 1946).

Germany

Hesse-Kassel, information from local archives provided by Angus Fowler, 1989.

Polley, R., 'Das Verhältnis der josephinischen Bestattungsreformen zu den französischen unter dem Ancien Regime und Napoleon I', in *Von Kirchhof zum Friedhof: Wandlungsprozesse zwischen 1750 und 1850* (Kassel *c.*1985).

Vogler, B., 'La legislation sur les sépultures dans l'Allemagne Protestante au XVIe. siècle', *Revue d'histoire moderne et contemporaire* 22 (1978).

Vogler, B., 'Attitudes devant la mort et ceremonies funéraires dans les églises protestants rhénanes vers 1600', *Archives de sciences sociales et religieuses* 39 (1975).

Wie die Alten den Tod gebildet; Wandlungen der Sepulchralkultur 1750–1850 (Kassel 1981).

Italy

Bacci, P., 'Le sculture decorative della facciata del camposanto de Pisa', *Dedalo* 1 (1920–1).

Carli, E. & Arias, P.E., *Il Camposanto di Pisa* (Rome 1937).

Cooper, R., 'The Crowning Glory of Pisa: Nineteenth-Century Reactions to the Campo Santo', *Italian Studies* 37 (1982).

Dodge, B.K., *Tradition, Innovation and Technique in Trecento Mural Painting: The Frescoes and Sinopie attributed to Francesco Traini in the Camposanto in Pisa* (unpublished D. Phil. thesis, Johns Hopkins University 1977).

Franchini, L. 'Il Cimitero Monumentale di Milano', *Arte Lombarda* 68/69 (1984).

Johnson, E.J., 'Aldo Rossi's Modena Cemetery', *Journal of the Society of Architectural Historians* 41 (1982).

Meeks, C.L.V., *Italian Architecture 1750–1914* (New Haven 1966).

Milanesi, G., *Nuovi Documenti per la Storia dell' Arte Toscana dal XII al XV Secolo* (Soest 1973), nos. 124, 129.

Settis, S., ed., *Camposanto Monumentale di Pisa. Le Antichità* (Modena 1984).

Supino, I.B., *Il Camposanto di Pisa* (Florence 1896).

United States of America

French, S., 'The Cemetery as Cultural Institution: the Establishment of Mount Auburn and the Rural Cemetery Movement', in *Death in America*, ed. D.E. Stannard (Philadelphia 1975).

INDEX